KING SIGISMUND OF POLAND
AND MARTIN LUTHER

Natalia Nowakowska is Professor of European History at the University of Oxford, and a Tutor and Fellow in History at Somerville College, Oxford. She has published widely on religion, politics, and dynasty in fifteenth- and sixteenth-century Europe, particularly in a Central European context. She has held a British Academy Mid-Career Fellowship, and was from 2013-18 Principal Investigator of the European Research Council (ERC) funded project 'Jagiellonians: Dynasty, Memory and Identity in Central Europe'. Her first book, on a Polish Renaissance cardinal, won the Kulczycki Prize in the USA. Her second monograph, *King Sigismund of Poland and Martin Luther* (2018), has won multiple book prizes in Europe and the USA.

T0355470

Further Praise for *King Sigismund of Poland and Martin Luther*

'a truly path-breaking work. It is based on a command of a large primary and secondary printed and manuscript literature. It will be a must-read for specialists in the history of the early modern Commonwealth, and, most welcome—I can't stress this enough—for important, serious scholars of the Reformation and the Counter-Reformation.'

David Frick, *Sehepunkte*

'Natalia Nowakowska's book reshapes fundamental historical paradigms about the geographic parameters of the Protestant Reformation and the chronology of the Reformation in Poland...In her marvelously vivid account of Lutheran political movements on Polish territory, Nowakowska captures the complexity of early sixteenth-century church-state relations and fluidly integrates the religious history of the Polish Republic into wider European trends, portraying it as a key example of how Protestantism dramatically ruptured worldviews across the continent.'

Comments from the judges of the 2019 Reginald Zelnik Book Prize

'This monograph by Natalia Nowakowska fills an important gap in the research on the Reformation in Poland. This excellent study will serve as a credible interpretation and a handbook not only for students, but also for the broader public.'

Maciej Ptaszynski, *Renaissance Quarterly*

'[an] excellent monograph...[it] makes important contributions to the history of religious toleration, Reformation scholarship and research on Central Europe more broadly. It introduces a new way of thinking about toleration in the first half of the sixteenth century.'

Martin Christ, *History*

'original, thoughtful and persuasive...pioneering work...fresh approach.'

Robert Frost, *Journal of Ecclesiastical History*

King Sigismund of Poland and Martin Luther

The Reformation before Confessionalization

NATALIA NOWAKOWSKA

OXFORD
UNIVERSITY PRESS

Great Clarendon Street, Oxford, OX2 6DP,
United Kingdom

Oxford University Press is a department of the University of Oxford.
It furthers the University's objective of excellence in research, scholarship,
and education by publishing worldwide. Oxford is a registered trade mark of
Oxford University Press in the UK and in certain other countries

Published in the United States of America by Oxford University Press
198 Madison Avenue, New York, NY 10016, United States of America

British Library Cataloguing in Publication Data
Data available

Library of Congress Cataloging in Publication Data
Data available

ISBN 978–0–19–881345–3 (Hbk.)
ISBN 978–0–19–888943–4 (Pbk.)

For Nick

Acknowledgements

As a doctoral student, it was hard grasp why a book might take a decade to write: today I understand better. This project has benefited from the support of a number of institutions and remarkable academic communities—University College, Oxford, which awarded me a Junior Research Fellowship to commence this work and funded the chief archival trips (2005–6); the British School at Rome, which offered a residential Rome Award in 2006; Somerville College, the History Faculty, and John Fell Fund at Oxford University which generously covered many research expenses; and above all, the British Academy which awarded a Mid-Career Fellowship in 2012–13 to complete a full draft of the manuscript and undertake further trips to Polish archives. As part of the latter Fellowship, I kept a regular blog about the process of writing this historical monograph, which can be found at historymonograph.blogspot.com.

I am grateful to the many colleagues and students who listened to parts of this book presented at conferences and seminars, offering invaluable feedback: the Late Medieval and Early Modern Europe seminars at Oxford, the Renaissance Studies Association conference in Berlin, the Reformation Studies Colloquium in Durham and again in Cambridge. Conversations and email exchanges with many colleagues, whether they realized it or not, provided sources of inspiration or forced clarifications on my part—with Andrew Gregory, Oren Margolis, Joanna Innes, Lyndal Roper, Howard Hotson, Judith Pollmann, Nicholas Davidson, Ian Forrest, Benjamin Thompson, Nicholas Davidson, Karin Friedrich, Maciej Ptaszyński, John-Paul Ghobrial, Glyn Redworth, Alex da Costa, Paul Cavill, Brian Mountfort, the Somerville medievalists' group, and, as ever, the inestimable John Watts. The anonymous project peer reviewers for the British Academy made important observations, and I am grateful in particular to the anonymous readers for Oxford University Press, who considered the manuscript so closely at a particularly busy time of the year, and whose comments were written in a spirit of scholarly generosity. The infelicities, and coarser edges to the argument, of this book remain, of course, entirely my own. My thanks also to Stephanie Ireland at OUP for her professionalism and warmth throughout.

Many people made this book possible in other ways. A number of excellent research assistants have assisted at various points along the way: Dr Christian Preusse, with a review of scholarship on Prussia; Sabrina Beck, with Simon Grunau's chronicle; Dr Madeleine Brook, with Dantiscus' German letters; Dr Duncan Hardy and Katie McKeogh, with comparative work on imperial/Austrian and English Reformation documents; and Andrew Doll, with the Bibliography. Archivists and librarians at the archdiocesan archives of Poznań and Gniezno, the diocesan archive in Włocławek, the Kraków cathedral archive, and the Jagiellonian Library Rare Books reading room were most helpful, and the Bodleian's Upper Reading Room staff have, for ten years, assisted with every enquiry, including the formidable task of taking a paperknife to several thousand uncut pages of the *Acta Tomiciana*. In particular, Dr Elżbieta Knapek at the Kraków metropolitan archive directed me to the papers of Żegota Pauli, which made a material difference to this study; and in Olsztyn, Professor Andrzej Kopiczko and his archdiocesan archival staff provided an exceptionally warm welcome. My husband Nick Kerigan, although not a historian, has spent more time hearing and discussing the arguments of this book than anybody else, applying the rigor of his strategy-director mind to them, and helping me find a breakthrough at a stage when nothing in the sources seemed to make sense. So this book, for that and so many other reasons, is for him. And, Oscar, the next one is for you.

Contents

List of Illustrations

List of Abbreviations

AAG	Archiwum Archidiecezjalne w Gnieźnie (Gniezno)
AAP	Archiwum Archidiecezjalne w Poznaniu (Poznań)
AAWa	Archiwum Archidiecezji Warmińskiej (Olsztyn)
AAWł	Archiwum Diecezjalne we Włocławku (Włocławek)
AKMK	Archiwum Kurii Metropolitalnej, Kraków
ASPK	Akta Stanów Prus Królewskich
ASV	Archivio Segreto Vaticano (Vatican City)
AT	Acta Tomiciana
BJ	Biblioteka Jagiellońska
CIP	Corpus iuris polonici
CWE	Collected Works of Erasmus
LW	Luther's Works
MWH	Monumenta Historiae Warmiensis
OiRwP	Odrodzenie i Reformacja w Polsce
PSB	Polski Słownik Biograficzny
RTA	Deutsche Reichstagsakten
RwP	Reformacja w Polsce

The Polish Monarchy and its Neighbours in the Early Reformation, *c.*1525

PART 1

HYPOTHESIS

Introduction
Beyond Toleration: The Reformation
before Confessionalization

In December 1532, Matthias Gutfor was brought before the episcopal court of Kraków. He lived on Grodzka Street, the Polish capital's chief processional thoroughfare, and was accused of eating meat on fast days, as part of a Lutheran 'conventicle' or illicit religious gathering.[1] This was a grave charge, a breach of royal and ecclesiastical law. It was over a decade since Rome had declared Martin Luther a heretic with the bull *Decet Romanum Pontificem* (1521), and two years since German Lutheran leaders at the Augsburg Diet had broken entirely with the Holy Roman Emperor and formalized their beliefs in the *Confessio Augustana* (1530). Latin Europe had witnessed the brutal upheavals of the Luther-inspired German Peasants' War (1524–5), seen towns across the Empire, Hungary, Bohemia, and Scandinavia adopt the Reformation, and hundreds executed in Austria and southern Germany for Anabaptism. In Gutfor's native kingdom too, the ageing King Sigismund I (b.1467) had faced Lutheran revolts in the Hanseatic ports of Danzig and Elbing, a peasant Reformation rising (1525), top Polish magnates embracing the Wittenberg cause, and Europe's first territorial Lutheran Reformation (1525), enacted within his monarchy by his vassal Albrecht in the newly formed Duchy of Prussia. Sigismund I's reign may be known as Poland's cultural and geopolitical Golden Age, but it was also its Lutheran moment. Yet, all this notwithstanding, the Kraków bishop's court simply issued Matthias Gutfor with a warning, and sent him on his way. Gutfor was one of at least thirty-nine Kraków inhabitants formally charged with Lutheranism in the reign of King Sigismund I of Poland. Like Gutfor, the overwhelming majority—organists, tanners, schoolmasters, banker's sons, widows—simply walked out of the bishop's courtroom without harm. If the story of Matthias Gutfor's brush with the law at Christmastide 1532 seems intrinsically strange to us, that is because it presents us with at least two problems.

The first problem with Gutfor's story is how long it has been untold. The early Reformation in the Polish monarchy in the reign of King Sigismund I (1506–48) is something of a terra incognita in English-language scholarship, meriting only

---

[1] BJ, MS 5337, vol. 9, fo. 75 (v).

passing mentions in the classic surveys.[2] Gutfor thus epitomizes a significant geographical gap in our understanding of the panorama of the European Reformation. Behind this absence lies a salutary and often alarming tale of scholarship, politics, and nationalism.[3] When professionalized historical research first emerged in the later nineteenth century, the rise of Lutheranism in the Polish monarchy was seized on enthusiastically as a subject. Books based on exhaustive archival work were published in both Polish and German—by Lutheran pastors, catholic priests, schoolmasters, and landed gentry alike, culminating in two magisterial studies by Julian Bukowski (1883) and Theodor Wotschke (1911).[4] Among Polish nationalists and patriots, the topic was popular because it demonstrated that Poland had fully participated in the great forces which had reshaped sixteenth-century Europe, and Polish-language printing by Lutherans under Sigismund I was celebrated as an early touchstone for national identity. Paradoxically, the early Reformation in the Polish monarchy simultaneously held strong appeal for German nationalism: the presence of Lutherans cited as proof that the Polish lands had always been historically German in character, and Prussian rule over annexed western Poland (1795–1918) thus justified. The popularity of the topic peaked, reaching its own golden age, in interwar Poland (1918–39), where the republic's minority Lutheran (Evangelical-Augsburg) church, led by Bishop Juliusz Bursche (d.1942), actively patronized research in this field, not least by launching a new and influential historical journal, *Reformacja w Polsce*. This Protestant church hoped to demonstrate, in the melting pot of interwar Poland, that Lutherans, whether German- or Polish-speaking, were and had been for centuries loyal citizens of the Poland state.[5] Lutheran printers, pedagogues, and heresy trials were studied by the country's leading historians in the 1920s and 1930s.[6] Even in the radically

[2] See for example: G. R. Elton, *Reformation Europe, 1517–1559* (London, 1963), pp. 137–40; Euan Cameron, *The European Reformation*, 2nd edition (Oxford, 2012), pp. 218, 280; Ulinka Rublack, *Reformation Europe* (Cambridge, 2005), p. 99; Diarmaid MacCulloch, *Reformation: Europe's House Divided, 1490–1700* (London, 2003), pp. 162, 190–2. Slightly fuller, if less well-known, surveys in Western languages include P. Fox, 'The Reformation in Poland', in W. F. Reddaway (ed.), *The Cambridge History of Poland*, vol. I (Cambridge, 1950), pp. 322–47; Ambroise Jobert, *De Luther á Mohila: la Pologne dans la crise de la chrétienté 1517–1648* (Paris, 1974); Christoph Schmidt, *Auf Felsen gesät: die Reformation in Polen und Livland* (Göttingen, 2000); and most recently Maciej Ptaszyński, 'The Polish-Lithuanian Commonwealth', in Howard Louthan and Graeme Murdock (eds), *A Companion to the Reformation in Central Europe* (Leiden, 2015), pp. 40–67.
[3] For a fuller account of the historiography of the early Reformation in Poland, see Natalia Nowakowska, 'Forgetting Lutheranism: Historians and the Early Reformation in Poland (1517–48)', *Church History and Religious Culture* 92 (2012): 281–303.
[4] Wincenty Zakrzewski, *Powstanie i wzrost Reformacyi w Polsce, 1520–1572* (Leipzig, 1870); Julian Bukowski, *Dzieje Reformacyi w Polsce od wejścia jej do Polski aż do jej upadku*, vol. I (Kraków, 1883); Theodor Wotschke, *Geschichte der Reformation in Polen* (Halle, 1911) and *Die Reformation im Lande Posen* (Lissa, 1913). Other studies published in the long nineteenth century include Georg Fischer, *Versuch einer Geschichte der Reformation in Polen*, 2 vols (Gratz, 1855–6); Otto Koniecki, *Geschichte der Reformation in Polen* (Breslau, 1872); Aleksander Brückner, *Różnowiercy polscy: szkice obyczajowe i literackie* (Warsaw, 1905); and I. Warmiński, *Andrzej Samuel i Jan Seklucjan* (Poznań, 1906).
[5] See Nowakowska, 'Forgetting Lutheranism', pp. 288–90.
[6] Key publications from the period include Jan Ptaśnik, 'Księgarze różnowiercy w Krakowie w XVI wieku', *RwP*, I (1921): 43–50; Karol Mazurkiewicz, *Początki Akademji Lubrańskiego w Poznaniu (1519–1535)* (Poznań, 1921); Władysław Pociecha, 'Walka sejmowa o przywileje kościoła w Polsce w

altered post-1945 landscape, the Stalinist regime still saw real value in study of the Reformation under Sigismund I, for its own rather different reasons: now, as an example of sixteenth-century class war, as modelled in works by Bogucka and Zins.[7] By the end of the 1950s, then, substantial primary research had been published in both German and Polish on the early Reformation in the Polish monarchy: multiple monographs, source editions, scores of articles.

Slowly, however, Matthias Gutfor, his fellow accused, and his king disappeared off the radar of wider Reformation studies. In the longer term, the study of early Lutheranism in Poland turned out to be one of the intellectual casualties of the Second World War.[8] German-speaking historians, who had made such a central contribution to this field, found from the 1950s that research into Protestant, German-speaking minorities in Central Europe had become simply too sensitive after Nazism.[9] In Communist Poland, meanwhile, state-directed, increasingly anti-German currents in scholarship turned decisively against the early Reformation. From the 1960s, attention was refocused on later aspects of the Reformation, such as the Calvinism and anti-Trinitarianism espoused in large numbers by the Polish nobility in the reign of King Sigismund's son, Sigismund Augustus (1548–72). These forms of Protestantism were celebrated as genuinely Polish, as native, enlightened and proto-Communist, in dozens upon dozens of publications.[10] In the Communist period, the Polish Reformation was in this way tacitly redefined, in ethnic instead of territorial terms—'reformacja polska' in effect came to mean Protestantism among ethnic Poles, rather than pro-Reformation activity in all the different parts of a multi-ethnic monarchy. Lutheranism, as a 'German' and thus alien phenomenon, was in this reading not necessarily part of Polish national history (even if it had occurred within the territory of the Polish monarchy). Figures like Matthias Gutfor, a Kraków citizen with a German name, thus faded into the background. Poland's leading post-war journal of Reformation studies published

latach 1520–1537', *RwP* II/7 (1922): 161–84; Henryk Barycz, *Historia uniwersytetu jagiellońskiego w epoce humanizmu* (Kraków, 1935).

[7] Henryk Zins, *Powstanie chłopskie w Prusach Książęcych 1525 roku: walki społeczne w Prusach w początkach reformacji i ich geneza* (Warsaw, 1953); Maria Bogucka, 'Walki społeczne w Gdańsku w XVI wieku', in Gerard Labuda, *Szkice z dziejów Pomorza*, vol. I (Warsaw, 1958), pp. 369–448.

[8] For a parallel intellectual casualty, see W. J. M. Levelt, *A History of Psycholinguistics: The Pre-Chomskyan Era* (Oxford, 2014).

[9] Publications in post-war Germany include Arthur Rhode, *Geschichte der evangelischen Kirche im Posener Lande* (Würzburg, 1956); Walther Hubatsch, *Albrecht von Brandenburg-Ansbach, Deutschordens-Hochmeister und Herzog in Preussen 1490–1568* (Heidelberg, 1960); Udo Arnold, 'Luther und Danzig', *Zeitschrift für Ostforschung* 21 (1972): 94–121; Gottfried Schramm, 'Danzig, Elbing und Thorn als Beispiele städtischer Reformation (1517–1558)', in Hans Fenske (ed.), *Historia Integra: Festschrift für Erich Hassinger* (Berlin, 1977), pp. 125–54.

[10] To give just a few examples of work on Calvinism and anti-Trinitarianism published in Communist Poland: Jan Dürr-Durski, *Arianie polscy w świetle własnej poezji* (Warsaw, 1948); Ludwik Chmaj, *Bracia polscy: Ludzie, idee, wpływy* (Warsaw, 1957), *Faust Socyn (1539–1604)* (Warsaw, 1963), and (ed.), *Studia nad arianizmem* (Warsaw, 1959); Lech Szczucki and Janusz Tazbir (eds), *Literatura ariańska w Polsce XVI wieku* (Warsaw, 1959); Stanisław Cynarski (ed.), *Raków: ognisko arianizmu* (Kraków, 1968); Halina Kowalska, *Działalność reformatorska Jana Łaskiego w Polsce, 1556–60* (Wrocław, 1969); Stanisław Tworek, *Działalność oświatowo kulturalna kalwinizmu małopolskiego (połowa XVI–połowa XVII w.)* (Lublin, 1970); Jerzy Misiurek, *Spory chrystologiczne w Polsce w drugiej połowie XVI wieku* (Lublin, 1984).

only five articles on the early Reformation between 1963 and 2011—fewer than it published on Shakespearean theatre in England.[11] In the Cold War, and beyond, it gradually became an orthodoxy in Polish textbooks that the Reformation had had no real impact on that country before the death of King Sigismund I, in 1548. In a short 1981 work, Marceli Kosman thus stated that Lutheranism had simply passed Poland by, because 'religious debate only erupted in Poland relatively late, in the second half of the sixteenth century'.[12] This claim has become a standard trope across a wide body of work published in Polish in learned works, textbooks, and popular histories.[13] Works printed since 2000 routinely refer to the 1520s and 1530s as a 'prelude' to the Polish Reformation.[14] Although a steady trickle of research on early Lutheranism has continued, often in regional studies or local journals, it has not eroded this dominant narrative in Polish historiography.[15] Somewhere along the line, therefore, Polish and international historians alike misplaced the rich history of the early Reformation in a major sixteenth-century European kingdom. As such, this book finds itself in the very curious (and challenging) position of being the first new research monograph considering Lutheranism right across King Sigismund's monarchy to be published since 1911.

The second problem posed by the story of Matthias Gutfor is, of course, that he walked free from that Kraków courtroom—he was not fined, imprisoned, punished, let alone executed. In this, Gutfor was typical of the overwhelming majority of subjects charged with Lutheranism in Sigismund I's reign. This book is rooted in that historical conundrum. It poses, essentially, a very simple question: why did the ruling elites of the Polish monarchy, under King Sigismund I, scarcely persecute Lutheranism in its first dramatic decades? Terror of heresy is often presented as a hallmark of medieval and early modern European society. Lee Palmer Wandel tells us that the very word 'heretic' inspired visceral terror and violence in the sixteenth century; others that it is hard for us to grasp how 'horrifying' heresy was

[11] See Nowakowska, 'Forgetting Lutheranism', p. 294. Early exceptions include Oskar Bartel, 'Filip Melanchton w Polsce', *OiRwP* 6 (1961): 73–90 and 'Marcin Luter w Polsce', *OiRwP* 7 (1962): 27–50.

[12] Marceli Kosman, *Nowinki, spory i zbory—z dziejów polskiej reformacji* (Warsaw, 1981), p. 4: 'spory religijne w Polsce wybuchły stosunkowo późno, bo dopiero w połowie XVI wieku'.

[13] See also Marian Rechowicz, *Dzieje teologii katolickiej w Polsce*, vol. II (Lublin, 1975), p. 40; Janusz Tazbir, 'Społeczny i terytorialny zasięg polskiej Reformacji', *Kwartalnik Historyczny* 82 (1975): 723–35; Wacław Urban, *Epizod reformacyjny* (Kraków, 1988), 'Prologus' (no page number); Stanisław Litak, *Od Reformacji do Oświecenia: kościół katolicki w Polsce nowożytnej* (Lublin, 1994), p. 38; Henryk Samsonowicz and Janusz Tazbir, *Tysiącletnie dzieje* (Wrocław, 2000), p. 124.

[14] See for example Marta Kacprzak, 'Z problemów Reformacji XVI wieku. "Kryptoreformacja", Erazmianism, eklezjologia. Postulaty badawcze dla historii literatury i kultury polskiej', in P. Wilczek (ed.), *Reformacja w dawnej Rzeczpospolitej i jej Europejskie konteksty* (Warsaw, 2010), pp. 15–22; Wojciech Kreigseisen, *Stosunki wyznaniowe w relacjach państwo-kościół między reformacją a oświeceniem* (Warsaw, 2010), pp. 430–53.

[15] In particular Janusz Małłek, *Prusy Książęce a Prusy Królewskie w latach 1525–1548: studium z dziejów polskiej polityki księcia Albrechta Hohenzollerna* (Warsaw, 1976) and *Dwie części Prus: studia z dziejów Prus Książęcych i Prus Królewskich w XVI i XVII wieku* (Olsztyn, 1987). See also Alojzy Szorc, *Rywalizacja katolików z luteranami o kościół Św. Mikołaja w Elblągu, 1520–1621* (Olsztyn, 2002); Marian Pawlak, *Reformacja i kontrreformacja w Elblągu w XVI i XVII wieku* (Bydgoszcz, 1994).

to medieval Europeans.[16] The presence of heretics in one's community threatened 'the ideological coherence of society', wrote the distinguished Reformation scholar Robert W. Scribner.[17]

Zealous persecution is thus what we expect premodern catholic regimes to do, yet when Luther's teachings—squarely condemned by the papacy as 'heretical'—reached the Polish monarchy of King Sigismund I, that is not what happened. King Sigismund turned a blind eye to the creation of Europe's first Lutheran polity in Ducal Prussia, and maintained highly cordial relations with its duke, his nephew and vassal Albrecht von Hohenzollern, throughout his life. He tacitly ignored, too, after 1527, the Lutheranization of Royal Prussia, the monarchy's most affluent province, even as the great port of Danzig emerged as a precocious Reformation centre. The King repeatedly declined to enforce his own heresy edicts. In his diplomacy, he formed alliances and marital ties with pro-Luther princes across northern Europe, to the scandal of many. We find very similar attitudes among leaders of the Polish church: bishops were reluctant to instigate heresy trials of Lutherans, and church courts reluctant to punish those brought before them, as we have seen, treating 'being of the Lutheran sect' as a minor offence. By the time that King Sigismund died in 1548, not a single one of his subjects had been sentenced by a church court and executed as a Lutheran heretic.[18] Throughout all this, the King and his counsellors insisted on their own, impeccable catholic piety and identity.[19] This story is especially problematic, because King Sigismund and his counsellors were not merely curious observers watching the European Reformation from the sidelines, but in the midst of the action. We might thus expect this monarchy's elites to have behaved in especially violent or vociferous ways towards Luther's supporters within their borders, but they did not.

Historians call this kind of perplexing early modern behaviour—a failure by the pious to prosecute or persecute heterodoxy—religious toleration, a topic which has generated a formidable literature of its own in recent years. Toleration is extensively debated because it has long been claimed as a special achievement of modern, Western, secular society, part of a narrative of progress.[20] Originally, toleration was studied as part of the history of ideas, as a series of intellectual breakthroughs by great individuals such as Erasmus or John Locke, leading towards

[16] Lee Palmer Wandel, *Reformation: Towards a New History* (Cambridge, 2011), p. 9; John Christian Laursen, Cary J. Nederman and Ian Hunter (eds), 'Introduction', *Heresy in Transition: Transforming Ideas of Heresy in Medieval and Early Modern Europe* (Aldershot, 2005), p. 5.

[17] Robert W. Scribner, 'Preconditions of Tolerance and Intolerance in Early Modern Europe', in Ole Peter Grell and Robert W. Scribner (eds), *Tolerance and Intolerance in the European Reformation* (Cambridge, 1996), pp. 32–47, at p. 41; see also Alexandra Walsham, *Charitable Hatred: Tolerance and Intolerance in England, 1500–1700* (Manchester, 2006), p. 2.

[18] The only formal heresy execution of the reign was for conversion to Judaism. See Chapter Six, pp. 168–9.

[19] For the piety of the Polish royal family, see Urszula Borkowska, *Dynastia Jagiellonów w Polsce* (Warsaw, 2013), pp. 390–471.

[20] See for example Perez Zagorin, *How the Idea of Religious Toleration Came to the West* (Princeton, 2003).

the Enlightenment.[21] From the 1980s, however, social historians moved into this area, investigating not just the ideal, but how coexistence worked in practice in communities. Works by Robert Scribner, Ole Peter Grell, Alexandra Walsham, and others have offered us a new history of early modern toleration, as experienced on the ground, in the village, town, or countryside, as recently seen in Kaplan's colourful micro-history, *Cunegonde's Kidnapping*.[22] This study will, however, seek to deepen further the problem posed by Matthias Gutfor's story, by suggesting that our existing models of Reformation-era toleration might be somewhat problematic.

In the (Western) scholarship on toleration, there is a high degree of consensus as to *why* sixteenth-century authorities tolerated religious dissidents—starting from the observation that toleration was never a positive moral choice because early modern Europeans simply did not have the mental tools to embrace religious pluralism as an acceptable state of affairs. As the great early historian of toleration Joseph Lecler tells us, 'the unity of the faith...became the basis of Western Christendom, a basis considered so essential that if it disappeared the breakdown would be complete'.[23] In such a context, it is pointed out that toleration was 'an invitation to apocalyptic destruction', an 'act of corporate suicide'.[24] Patschovsky concluded that it was intellectually impossible for medieval society to be 'pluralistic, or even to show tolerance'.[25] It is said that only with the Enlightenment did religious freedom/toleration become an intellectual position one could actively believe in, and that in the Reformation period only a handful of brilliant, heroic minds, such as Erasmus of Rotterdam (d.1536) or Sebastian Castellion (d.1563), had articulated anything like a genuine plea for religious freedom. Walsham explains that 'only a few isolated voices elevated respect for conscience into a universally applicable principle'.[26]

Scholarship on toleration therefore offers a clear answer as to why princes and their subjects coexisted with religious dissidents—it was a matter not of principle, but of pragmatism and politics. In this interpretation, religious toleration was a deeply painful experience which occurred when hard-headed individuals (faced with the messy complexities of the world) put aside their most deeply held beliefs, in order to secure some more pressing goal such as harmony, social order, or peace.

---

[21] For the evolution of toleration studies, see Walsham, *Charitable Hatred*, pp. 6–12; Benjamin Kaplan, *Divided by Faith: Religious Conflict and the Practice of Toleration in Early Modern Europe* (Cambridge, MA, 2007), pp. 6–8.

[22] Benjamin Kaplan, *Cunegonde's Kidnapping: A Story of Religious Conflict in the Age of Enlightenment* (New Haven, 2014).

[23] Joseph Lecler, *Toleration and the Reformation*, trans. T. L. Westow, vol. 1 (New York, 1960), p. 71.

[24] Walsham, *Charitable Hatred*, p. 2.

[25] Alexander Patschovsky, 'Heresy and Society: On the Political Functions of Heresy in the Medieval World', in Peter Biller and Caterina Bruschi (eds), *Texts and the Repression of Medieval Heresy* (Woodbridge, 2003), pp. 23–41, at p. 25.

[26] Walsham, *Charitable Hatred*, p. 4. See also Marco Turchetti, 'Religious Concord and Political Tolerance in Sixteenth- and Seventeenth-century France', *Sixteenth Century Journal* 22 (1991): 15–25; István Bejczy, 'Tolerantia: A Medieval Concept', *Journal of the History of Ideas* 58 (1997): 365–84; Randolph C. Head, 'Introduction: The Transformations of the Long Sixteenth Century', in John Christian Laursen and Carry J. Nederman (eds) *Beyond the Persecuting Society: Religious Toleration before the Enlightenment* (Philadelphia, 1998), pp. 95–106.

Katalin Peter, for example, concluded that Christian authorities tolerated dissenters due 'to political considerations'.[27] Lorna Jane Abray has written that sixteenth-century toleration was 'always...undertaken to stave off a bigger disaster', because the authorities' primary instinct was to impose religious uniformity.[28] Robert Scribner, writing on Germany, has characterized toleration by authorities as 'ad hoc', a 'working political compromise'.[29] Toleration-as-pragmatism has been reconstructed most fully by Victoria Christman, in her important study of early Reformation Antwerp. She concludes that toleration there was 'motivated by various factors, almost all of which lay outside the sphere of religion'.[30] Two varieties of pragmatic toleration can perhaps be inferred from these discussions: an involuntary type forced on authorities where religious dissidents were too strong to subdue (e.g. interim settlements with Huguenots during the French Wars of Religion), and a voluntary version where higher religious principles were opportunistically or cynically sacrificed to more worldly goals (e.g. Francis I's alliance with German Lutherans against his fellow catholic Charles V). Reformation toleration by princes has therefore become simply a variety of realpolitik, or even just of 'politics'.

There is, however, an array of problems created by this apparently sensible model, the first being that the interpretation of toleration as politics—the pursuit of rationale self-interest—does not fit the events of King Sigismund I's reign particularly well. Somewhat awkwardly, the King and his chief advisor did explicitly defend an individual's freedom to choose their own religious beliefs in accordance with their conscience, as we shall see.[31] This is no surprise to historians of Poland, who have long claimed that this kingdom was liberal, ahead of its time, and inherently tolerant, most famously in Janusz Tazbir's *State without Stakes*.[32] Moreover, King Sigismund's permitting of Lutheranism was often politically costly, and not on the face of it a sensible choice at all. The King's defence of Lutheran Ducal Prussia against the combined forces of Emperor Charles V, the pope, and Teutonic Orders of Livonia and Germany (1525+), for example, ran the very real risk of provoking an international 'crusade' against the monarchy. In such cases, the 'toleration as politics' argument fails on its own terms. In addition, tolerant attitudes towards Lutherans can be found not only at the royal court, but on the ground among diocesan clergy—here, there might be deeper cultural factors at play across the board, beyond national politics.

---

[27] Katalin Peter, 'Tolerance and Intolerance in Sixteenth-Century Hungary', in Grell and Scribner, *Tolerance and Intolerance*, pp. 249–61, at p. 250.
[28] Lorna Jane Abray, 'Confession, Conscience and Honour: The Limits of Magisterial Tolerance in Sixteenth-Century Strasbourg', in Grell and Scribner, *Tolerance and Intolerance*, pp. 94–107, at p. 96.
[29] Scribner, 'Preconditions of Tolerance', p. 39.
[30] Victoria Christman, *Pragmatic Toleration: The Politics of Religious Heterodoxy in Early Reformation Antwerp, 1515–1550* (Rochester, 2015), at p. 10.
[31] See Chapter Three, pp. 114–16.
[32] Janusz Tazbir, *Państwo bez stosów: szkice z dziejów tolerancji w Polsce XVI i XVII wieku* (Warsaw, 1967), published in English as *A State without Stakes: Polish Religious Toleration in the Sixteenth and Seventeenth Centuries* (New York, 1973).

The formula, 'toleration as politics', also presents us with challenges at a conceptual or theoretical level. It rests, firstly, on the assumption that politics is a timeless human activity, played by the same essential rules of logic, rationality, and calculation, age after age. David Onnekirk and Gijs Rommelse note that historians tend to implicitly espouse this view, which in political science is termed 'realism'.[33] In the discipline of international relations these assumptions have long come under fire. Daniel Philpott and others in the idealist or constructivist schools have argued that the very notion of what politics is, and how it is practised, is culturally specific, shaped by deep-seated contemporary ideas.[34] We should therefore be wary of projecting raw concepts of realpolitik onto early modern actors, and instead tune in more closely to period-specific ideas of what politics was and should be. In the case of King Sigismund I, this might mean disaggregating 'politics' into a series of parallel contemporary concerns, such as jurisdiction, reputation, kinship, and good kingship. We need to recover not just the politics, but the political culture of toleration.

Conceiving of toleration as politics-versus-religion requires us to treat 'religion' as an abstracted force in this period, in ways which are likewise problematic. Many scholars of religion, influenced by anthropology, argue that it is flawed to talk of 'religion' at all as a distinct category in the premodern world—because only a secular society such as the modern West can conceive of religion as a separate 'thing', rather than experiencing it as a set of beliefs and practices so fundamental that they pervade all aspects of thought, culture, and cosmology.[35] It is thus important to consider what exactly we mean, or contemporaries meant, by 'religion', if we say that religious calculations were absent or suspended. Religion too needs disaggregation: it might in this period encompass church ownership of land, objects used in worship, theological arguments, personal piety, or the very concept of church itself as a social-historic entity. Not all these things were necessarily threatened by Lutheranism in the same way, or to the same extent.

The present model of toleration, furthermore, rests not only on the presentation of 'politics' and 'religion' as identifiable abstract forces, but also on a fundamental juxtaposition of the two. This highlights a tension in our writing on early modern Europe—we take it as a truism that the 'religious' and 'political' motivations of sixteenth-century men and women cannot be separated out, because they were fundamentally entangled in the minds of premodern Europeans, yet our current explanation of toleration proposes that they did just this, knowingly and consciously. Put simply, there is a risk that our working model of 'toleration as politics trumping religion' rests on purely modern definitions of both politics and religion themselves.

---

[33] David Onnekink and Gijs Rommelse (eds), 'Introduction', in *Ideology and Foreign Policy in Early Modern Europe, 1650–1750* (Farnham, 2011), pp. 1–5. See also Kaplan, *Divided by Faith*, p. 9.

[34] Daniel Philpott, *Revolutions in Sovereignty: How Ideas Shaped Modern International Relations* (Princeton, 2001).

[35] James G. Crossley and Christian Karner (eds), *Writing History, Constructing Religion* (Aldershot, 2005); Derek Peterson and Darren Walhof, *The Invention of Religion: Rethinking Belief in Politics and History* (New Brunswick, 2002).

This book experiments with an alternative approach. Rather than focusing exclusively on the 'political' rationales for toleration, it investigates too the underlying religious-cosmological assumptions of Sigismund I and his elites, what they understood catholicism and Christian orthodoxy itself to be, and what in consequence they understood to be heterodox (or not)—i.e. their ecclesiology. Theirs was, after all, likely to be a late medieval outlook, with the decrees of the Council of Trent (1563) still fifty years away. In exploring royal and ecclesiastical forbearance towards Lutherans, this book will therefore ask not just 'what is the politics of this?', but also 'what understanding of Christian religion is revealed here?'[36] It does so not only by reconstructing individual episodes in policy, but also by looking closely at the religious language in operation across this monarchy in the 1520s and 1530s, as expressed by a wide range of actors (princes, noblemen, courtiers, diplomats, clergy, and literati), in a wide range of sources (royal edicts, political correspondence, chronicles, poetry, book dedications, parliamentary debates, and diplomatic treaties). In this way, it seeks to capture the mainstream, working ecclesiology of lay and clerical elites in early sixteenth-century Poland. The history of religious thought is traditionally written by studying formal theological writings of great thinkers of the age, in sermons and treatises. This book casts the net much more widely—it does examine Polish-Prussian anti-Reformation polemics, but places them in their local context, reading these books alongside hundreds of other documents not normally used for writing the history of belief, but in which we nonetheless find Sigismund I's subjects labelling, describing, defining, and characterizing catholic orthodoxy and its edges. Philip Haberkern has recently identified a new 'focus on ecclesiology' in Reformation studies.[37] This study, while differing in its methodology, perhaps fits within that trend.

The short answer yielded by such an investigation is that authorities and communities in Sigismund I's monarchy did not persecute Lutherans because they did not find these dissidents particularly frightening. There was one crucial exception—the 'luteranus' as an armed peasant, sailor, or urban apprentice, stirred up by radical preachers, running amok in violent insurrections such as the German Peasants' War or Danzig revolt (1525–6). Such Lutheran rebels, threatening social and political order, were not tolerated at all: they were executed (thirteen Danzig rebels in 1526), exiled, and hunted down in neighbouring territories with something bordering on paranoia. However, the loyal, peaceable subjects interested in controversial doctrines (the Duke of Prussia, the royal secretary Jan Zambocki, burghers like Matthias Gutfor) who typified Lutheranism in the monarchy after 1526, did not in fact incite real fear, but something more like bemusement or

---

[36] For a study which places language/ideas analysis alongside analysis of policy/politics, see Joanna Innes and Mark Phelp, *Re-imagining Democracy in the Age of Revolutions: America, France, Britain, Ireland, 1750–1850* (Oxford, 2013).

[37] Philip Haberkern, 'The Lands of the Bohemian Crown: Conflict, Coexistence and the Quest for the True Church', in Louthan and Murdock, *Companion to the Reformation*, pp. 11–39, at pp. 11–13; Susan Schreiner, *Are You Alone Wise? The Search for Certainty in the Early Modern Era* (Oxford, 2011); Brad S. Gregory, *The Unintended Reformation: How a Religious Revolution Secularized Society* (Cambridge, MA, 2012).

annoyance. The language of heresy was applied to them hesitantly, or not at all. Loyal, educated Lutherans were not regarded by the authorities as people who immediately threatened the social or metaphysical integrity of the sixteenth-century Latin world.

Polish-Prussian catholic elites adopted this relaxed view of the Lutherans in their midst because, bizarre though it may seem to us now, in general they did not perceive these dissidents as being outside the catholic church. In his study of the Tyrol in these same decades, M. Chisholm concluded that Lutheran and catholic were not necessarily 'distinct in the contemporary mind'.[38] That is surely a key insight. Lutheranism was not actively persecuted in Sigismund I's Poland, then, because to most catholic elites it was not yet seen as extrinsic to the church, in an already variegated catholic/Christian society, and thus did not require the urgent persecution of subjects, allies, and neighbours. R. I. Moore, in his celebrated thesis on medieval heresy, argued that there are three stages on the road to wholesale religious persecution—classification (ascribing a clear identity to a group), stigmatization, and finally violent oppression itself.[39] Those in power in King Sigismund's Polish monarchy were still firmly stuck in stage one (if that) as late as 1540. Lutherans were seen as fellow members of a universal church—as bad or unpious Christians certainly, but not, crucially, as an Other.

Such a position was possible because, as this book will argue from the Polish-Prussian sources, the concept of catholicism, or the ecclesiology, with which these elites were operating is strangely unfamiliar to us, and perhaps not the one we have routinely attributed to them. In the modern world, a church (or confession) is characterized by its distinctive set of theological positions, which are not negotiable because they are intrinsic to its identity. By contrast, for Sigismund I and very many of his subjects the *ecclesia* was defined first and foremost by its unity—both its social unity in the present, and its (alleged) historic unity down the centuries. Unity was not, as it is for ecumenical movements today, some pleasant ideal or desideratum—instead, it was the *sine qua non* of the universal church, integral to and, in a sense, constitutive of its orthodoxy. In this world view, the church's actual teaching could evolve as new doctrines were weighed up, and a consensus gradually emerged around them (or not). In this ongoing collective rumination, the coexistence of different theological-academic positions within the same church was not necessarily a problem. Expressing this ecclesiology, King Sigismund declared in 1525 that 'without consensus (general agreement) and the unity of the church, the true faith and religion cannot endure', and his primate Jan Łaski too defined catholicism as that confirmed 'by the consensus of so many centuries'.[40] To their

---

[38] M. A. Chisholm, 'The Religionspolitik of Emperor Ferdinand I (1521–64): Tyrol and the Holy Roman Empire', *European History Quarterly* 38:4 (2008): 551–77, at p. 552. See also Erasmus on the acceptability of thoughtful, non-argumentative followers of Luther, in James D. Tracy (ed.), 'General Introduction', CWE vol. 78 (Toronto, 2011), p. xx.

[39] R. I. Moore, *The Formation of a Persecuting Society: Authority and Deviance in Western Europe, 950–1250*, 2nd edition (Oxford, 2007).

[40] AT 8, p. 51: 'absque consensu et unitate Ecclesie vera Fides et Religio constare non potest'; AT 7, p. 389: 'per tot secula usus et consensus confirmavit'.

Lutheran princely or burgher interlocutors, the Polish authorities repeatedly explained that orthodoxy resided in 'the rites and institutes of the church, confirmed for so many centuries, by so many miracles, by the authority of the councils, popes, emperors, kings, kingdoms and Christian nations...'[41] Archdeacon Byliński of Przemyśl, in eastern Poland, wrote in 1535 that while it was tricky if a diversity of opinions (*sententiae*) occurred, the church could and should arrive at a unity position in a council.[42] Canon Tiedemann Giese explained to his fellow Prussians in a 1525 treatise that Saints Paul and John had themselves disagreed on the role of good works versus faith in salvation, but had nonetheless managed to fight together for the church of Christ.[43] Such a catholicism could accommodate a certain degree of internal heterogeneity. King Sigismund thus made the sanguine prediction that Lutherans would be peacefully absorbed into the one church, just as the Bohemian Utraquists had with the 1436 *Compactata*—a variant within the universal church.[44]

What we see in the Polish monarchy is therefore a pre-confessional response to the Reformation, lasting several decades, rooted in a specific ecclesiology. We think of the Reformation as a conscious conflict between different churches or confessions (catholic, Lutheran, Calvinist). Schilling and Reinhard's celebrated confessionalization thesis of the 1980s stressed how vigorously late sixteenth-century states imposed clear-cut, polarized confessional identities (catholic, Lutheran, Calvinist) on their subjects—antagonism between churches is seen as the basic fact of the Reformation.[45] Yet in Sigismund I's Polish monarchy, down to at least *c*.1540, religious policy was not predicated on outright confessional conflict. The actions of the authorities were not merely the product of the infamous religious 'confusion' often attributed to the early Reformation period, but quite the opposite— they were grounded in a coherent, internally consistent outlook. Naturally, not everyone in King Sigismund's monarchy shared this world view. Luther's own followers in this polity had rejected this church entirely, papal agents emphatically saw the church as a monarchy centred on Rome, and a handful of catholics, such as Bishop Andrzej Krzycki, anticipated the Counter/catholic Reformation by angrily starting to characterize Lutherans as entirely Other and in need of suppression. Nonetheless, by 1540 such groups and their now familiar perspective on the Reformation as a binary and bitter confessional struggle were still in a conspicuous minority within this monarchy's ruling elite.

---

[41] AT 7, p. 404: 'instituta universalis Ecclesiae, tot seculis, tot miraculis, tanta autoritate conciliorum, pontificum, imperatorum, regum, regnorumque et nationum christianarum confirmata...violasse'. See also AT 7, p. 76; AT 8, pp. 43, 50, 132.

[42] Stanisław Byliński, *Defensorium Ecclesiae adversus Laurentium Corvinum* (Kraków, 1531) fo. 48(v).

[43] Tiedemann Giese, *Flosculorum Lutheranorum de Fide et Operibus Anthelogikon* (Kraków, 1525) (unnumbered pages).

[44] AT 7, p. 357.

[45] Wolfgang Reinhard, 'Zwang zur Konfessionalisierung? Prologomena zu einer Theorie des konfessionellen Zweitalters', *Zeitschrift für Historische Forschung* 10 (1983): 257–77; Hans Schilling, 'Die Konfessionalisierung im Reich. Religiöser und gesellschaftlicher Wandel in Deutschland zwischen 1555 und 1620', *Historische Zeitschrift* 246 (1988): 1–45.

We might then question whether 'toleration' is in fact the correct paradigm to employ for the non-persecution of Luther's sympathizers in Sigismund I's Poland. Toleration, as normally defined, requires some sense of an Other, a religious community and identity separate from or opposite to one's own (as produced, for example, by confessionalization). Polish-Prussian catholic elites did not consistently see Lutherans in that way in the reign of Sigismund I. The old king was not tolerating a hated rival confession, or compromising his core ideological beliefs, but rather cleaving to his pre-confessional sense of a Latin Christian identity. We shall see later how this finding sits within wider debates on the Reformation—both those conducted across early sixteenth-century Europe by the King's contemporaries such as Erasmus, and those of modern scholarship.

The book opens with a brief introduction to the places, people, and texts which constitute our story. This study focuses principally on the years to *c.*1535, when the passing of an entire generation of counsellors born and educated in the fifteenth century marked the end of an era, and the start of Sigismund's own gradual retreat from active kingship.[46] Chapter One offers a new narrative of the early Reformation in the composite Polish monarchy, setting its often startling Reformation events squarely within their comparative European context for the first time. It shows the diverse loci of support for Luther's teaching—from Kaspar the miller leading a peasant army on Königsberg, to the top royal diplomat Johannes Dantiscus enjoying a house stay with Luther in Wittenberg—and explores the problems latent in measuring 'how Lutheran' a given polity or society was in the sixteenth century. Breaking this bigger story down into its constituent parts, the book then explores in turn key episodes which reveal the multifaceted and diverse ways in which the Polish Crown and church coexisted with Lutherans. Chapter Two examines the paradoxical and ultimately lax policy adopted by the Crown towards Lutheranism in affluent Royal Prussia, which saw such strong Reformation support in the 1525 revolts and beyond. Chapter Three explores a different kind of religious coexistence, the day-to-day political and social relations between King Sigismund I and his troublesome nephew Duke Albrecht von Hohenzollern, between the catholic Polish monarchy and its vassal, pioneering Lutheran territory. Chapter Four turns its attention to royal policy in the mainly Polish-speaking areas of the monarchy, considering the eleven anti-Lutheran edicts issued by Sigismund I, and the riddle of fierce heresy laws which went entirely unenforced by the Crown. Chapter Five considers a further perplexing area, the diplomacy of the Polish Crown in the 1520s and 1530s, which openly supported Lutheran actors on the international stage while insisting on Sigismund I's piety and protesting at the Reformation in neighbouring states. Chapter Six, by contrast, considers the actions of the Polish church in the face of the early Reformation—provincial statutes, polemic, trials, preaching endeavours, and conversion campaigns—finding among bishops and diocesan officials too a highly ambivalent, basically indulgent attitude in practice towards local Lutherans.

---

[46] See Contexts, pp. 42–5.

The second part of the book then switches tack methodologically, seeking to recover contemporary understandings of 'catholicism' and '*luteranismus*' through close linguistic analysis of the study's core corpus of sources. This analysis of *c.*500 individual documents of many genres seeks to capture, in a panoramic way, what the collective language or discourse of religion was, as employed by the Polish king, courtiers, bishops, cathedral canons, neo-Latin poets, and of course Lutherans themselves. Chapters Seven and Eight thus ask 'What is Lutheranism?' and 'What is catholicism?' They find that Lutheranism was not consistently identified as a heresy, was viewed primarily through the prism of well-established categories of religious malfaisance (such as blasphemy, sacrilege), and understood as transgressive chiefly for its schismatic impulses. Catholicism was defined with reference to history (ancestors, church Fathers, councils), consensus in the past and present, and unity, but in the Polish-Prussian sources a subtle shift towards more sectarian, confession-focused definitions is already detectable by the mid 1530s.

What implications this story might have for the wider history of Reformation and toleration depends, of course, on whether we see the Polish polity as an anomaly, and its teetotal king, tearing around hunting bears in the snow in his late sixties, as an eccentric.[47] Naturally, every polity and locality is in its own way different, and heterogeneity within a relatively small geographical space is one of the underlying characteristics of European history.

There is a long-standing historiographical and political tradition which asserts that Poland was uniquely tolerant within early modern Europe, due to its special local circumstances.[48] None of these arguments is entirely unproblematic, as no argument ever is. Many scholars have invoked individual psychological factors, painting the Polish royal family as mild by temperament, with Sigismund as an extreme case in point.[49] Kreigseisen has investigated whether an increasingly confident Polish parliament enabled Protestant nobles to carve out toleration for themselves from the Crown over the course of the century.[50] His argument focuses however on the second half of the sixteenth century, when the key parliamentary battles took place. Tazbir has argued that Polish nobles enjoyed extensive legal privileges, including immunity from arrest by royal officials, which in effect conferred religious freedom.[51] However, the trial of at least one noble for heresy in the 1530s complicates this picture.[52] It is suggested too that medieval Polish rulers had had to contend with the presence of significant religious minorities

[47] For the tradition of the King as abstemious, see Ludwig Kolankowski, *Polska Jagiellonów: dzieje polityczne*, 3rd edition (Olsztyn, 1991), p. 228; for hunts, see the report by Duke Albrecht's exasperated agent in January 1534, AT 16a, pp. 66–71.

[48] Tazbir, *Państwo bez stosów*; Marceli Kosman, *Protestanci i kontrreformacja: z dziejów tolerancji w Rzeczpospolitej XVI–XVIII wieku* (Wrocław, 1973); Janusz Tazbir, *Dzieje polskiej tolerancji* (Warsaw, 1973); Janusz Tazbir, *Reformacja, Kontrreformacja, Tolerancja* (Wrocław, 1996); Marta Małkus and Kamila Szymańska (eds), *Reformacja i tolerancja: jedność w różnoródności? Współistnienie różnych wyznań na ziemi wschowskiej i pograniczu Wielkopolsko-Śląskim* (Wschowa, 2015).

[49] Tazbir, *Państwo bez stosów*, p. 34; Włodzimierz Budka, 'Przejawy reformacji w miastach Mazowsza 1526–48', *OiRwP* XXVIII (1983): 188–94, at p. 188; Paul Fox, *The Reformation in Poland: Some Economic and Social Aspects* (Baltimore, 1924), p. 78.

[50] Kreigseisen, *Stosunki wyznaniowe*.   [51] Tazbir, *Państwo bez stosów*, pp. 27, 51.

[52] Andrzej Trzecieski, see Appendix 1.

(Jews, Orthodox Christians, Tartar Muslims), and that toleration of Protestants was thus a natural outgrowth of these earlier habits of mind.[53] The obvious counterexample to this is Castile, which graphically illustrates that a fifteenth-century experience of *convivencia* (between Christians, Jews, and Muslims) was just as likely to culminate in inquisition (1478+), purges and expulsions, as in infinitely ongoing tolerance. We cannot assume that medieval diversity inevitably endured for centuries, once planted; some further explanation is needed for its survival.

Particularly prominent, and promising, as an argument for Polish exceptionalism is the suggestion that Sigismund I's regime was tolerant because it was infused to a rare extent by the spirit of Erasmian, Renaissance Christian humanism. Jacqueline Glomski and Howard Louthan, among others, have stressed the numerous works dedicated by Erasmus to Polish dignitaries, the sale of his library to Jan Łaski the younger, and his close epistolary relationship with Bishop Piotr Tomicki of Kraków, all culminating in the Dutchman's celebrated declaration in 1535 that 'Polonia mea est'.[54] It is, however, difficult to quantify with certainty whether Erasmus was more influential in Kraków than he was in other European kingdoms in these years—in Castile, where he enjoyed a huge readership; in Hungary where the queen read his letters aloud at royal dinners; in France, where Francis I invited the wandering Dutchman to settle and run the *Collège de France*; or in England, as painstakingly reconstructed by James McConica.[55] The relationship between Erasmus and Poland was multifaceted, and not clear-cut. It is important to be clear what one means by 'Erasmianism'—it is well established that Erasmus' celebrity in Poland in the years to 1535 was primarily as a classical philologist, and only later in the century did Poles routinely invoke him as a religious authority.[56] Sigismund I himself, unlike Francis I, was no active patron of humanist scholars—the 100 gold florins he sent Erasmus in 1528 in thanks for a panegyric were sensed to be not quite enough, either by the courtiers who hurriedly sent private supplementary gifts to mollify the scholar, or by Erasmus himself who grumbled about the lack of cash from Poland.[57] If the regime's religious policy was inspired by Erasmus, it

---

[53] Tazbir, *Państwo bez stosów*, pp. 28–9, and again in 'Poland', in R. W. Scribner, Roy Porter, and Mikuláš Teich (eds), *The Reformation in National Context* (Cambridge, 1994), pp. 168–80, at p. 168.

[54] Wacława Szelińska, 'Wśród krakowskich przyjaciół książki erazmiańskiej w wieku Wielkiego Holandra', in *Erasmiana Cracoviensia*, Zeszyty Naukowe UJ, Prace Historyczne z 33 (Kraków, 1971), pp. 39–54; Henryk Zins, 'Leonard Cox i erazmiańskie koła w Polsce i Anglii', *OiRwP* 17 (1972): 27–62; Juliusz Domański, 'Der Einfluss der Erasmianismus und die Reformation in Polen', *Acta Poloniae Historica* 55 (1987): 41–56, focusing on the later Reformation; Jacqueline Glomski, 'Erasmus and Cracow, 1510–30', *Erasmus of Rotterdam Society Yearbook* 17 (1997): 1–18; Howard Louthan, 'A Model for Christendom? Erasmus, Poland and the Reformation', *Church History* 83:1 (2014): 18–37.

[55] Marcel Bataillon, *Érasme et l'Espagne: recherches sur l'histoire spirituelle du XVIe siècle* (Paris, 1937); B. J. Spruyt, '"En bruit d'estre bonne luterienne": Mary of Hungary (1505–58) and Religious Reform', *English Historical Review* CIX: 431 (1994): 275–307; Gordon Griffiths, 'Francis I', in Peter G. Bietenholz and Thomas B. Deutscher (eds), *Contemporaries of Erasmus*, vol. 2 (Toronto, 1986), pp. 50–2; James McConica, *English Humanists and Reformation Politics under Henry VIII and Edward VI* (Oxford, 1965).

[56] Claude Backvis, 'La fortune d'Erasme en Pologne', in *Collouquium Erasmianium* (Mons, 1968), pp. 173–202; Leszek Hajdukiewicz, 'Erazm z Rotterdamu w opinii polskiej XVI–XVII wieku', *Zeszyty Naukowe Uniwersytetu Jagiellońskiego* 33 (1971): 55–67; Domański, 'Der Einfluss'.

[57] Erasmus, *Opus Epistolarum Des. Erasmi Roterodami*, ed. P. S. Allen, vol. 7 (Oxford, 1928), nrs. 1952, p. 331–2; nr. 1954, p. 333; nr. 1958, pp. 337–8; nr. 2033, p. 453.

certainly did not put its money where its mouth was. There were also anti-Erasmus voices in Poland, in the university, and in the person of Primate Jan Łaski.[58] The King's chief councillor, Piotr Tomicki, was the most powerful person in the kingdom with clear Erasmian connections—yet even their correspondence amounts to twelve often generic letters in nine years, and only from 1532 did they exchange thoughts about the church.[59] Erasmus' very first epistolary contact with Bishop Tomicki occurred in December 1527, too late to have had any direct influence on the Crown's actions in the Reformation crisis years of 1518–26. To diagnose the widespread toleration of Sigismund I's reign as a uniquely triumphant royal Erasmianism is tempting (and was the original hypothesis of this book), but only part of a wider story.

All these claims of Poland's status as especially tolerant among European kingdoms have rarely been tested statistically. The figures quickly erode the image of Sigismund I as uniquely benign. It is William Monter who has most systematically tried to compare rates of heresy executions for 'Protestantism' in sixteenth-century Europe. For the 1520s, Monter has counted approximately 380 executions in the Holy Roman Empire, forty in Switzerland, thirteen in Poland (Danzig rebels), and twelve for the Netherlands, to which we can add four in France, two in Denmark, and one in Scotland.[60] In this decade, Sigismund I's lands thus look to be in the European vanguard of persecution, rather than toleration—even if we see this primarily as policing social order, with clusters of heresy executions occurring in the wake of peasant and urban revolts in Germany, Prussia, and Austria. While data for the 1530s is uneven, it is only in the reign of Sigismund I's son, Sigsimund Augustus (1548–72), that the Polish monarchy began clearly to diverge from Europe-wide patterns, becoming conspicuously 'tolerant'. Monter found that the big, sustained waves of heresy executions in Reformation Europe (after the 1520s panic) started only in the 1550s, under Mary Tudor, Philip II, and Pope Paul IV; executions of non-rebel Lutherans before this were everywhere rare.[61] It was in this second half of the sixteenth century that the Polish monarchy began to look relatively odd: in 1557 the Crown granted a toleration licence to the Lutheran cities of Royal Prussia, in 1573 the nobility drew up the celebrated Warsaw Confederation granting freedom of worship to all 'dissidents in religion', and nobody at all was executed for heresy.[62] We should therefore distinguish more

[58] Piotr Tafiłowski, *Jan Łaski (1456–1531), kanclerz koronny, prymas Polski* (Warsaw, 2007), pp. 332–6.; Janina Czerniatowicz, 'Początki grecystyki i walka o język grecki w Polsce dobie odrodzenia', in *Studia i materiały z dziejów nauki polskiej*, seria A, z. 5 (1959): 29–55.

[59] The Tomicki–Erasmus correspondence is found in Erasmus, *Opus Epistolarum*, ed. P. S. Allen, vols. 7–11 (Oxford, 1928–47).

[60] William Monter, 'Heresy Executions in Reformation Europe, 1520–65', in Grell and Scribner, *Tolerance and Intolerance*, pp. 48–64, at p. 52; Monter, *Judging the French Reformation: Heresy Trials by Sixteenth-Century Parlements* (Cambridge, MA, 1999), pp. 56–63; Ole Peter Grell, 'Scandinavia', in Andrew Pettegree (ed.), *The Early Reformation in Europe* (Cambridge, 1992), pp. 94–119, at p. 99; J. E. McGoldrick, *Luther's Scottish Connection* (Rutherford, NJ, 1989), pp. 33–52.

[61] Monter, 'Heresy Executions'.

[62] Magda Teter has stressed that this was not really a 'state without stakes' because confessional tension instead spilled over into multiple executions of Jews for sacrilege: Magda Teter, *Sinners on Trial: Sacrilege after the Reformation* (Cambridge, MA, 2011).

clearly between the Polish Crown's relatively mainstream action against heretic-rebels in the early Reformation, and its eye-catching toleration agreements of the second half of the sixteenth century.

There are further reasons for thinking that Sigismund I's diffuse understanding of catholicism was not a purely Polish phenomenon, and might therefore have wider import. The concept of a unified church with potentially flexible doctrinal boundaries, so characteristic of Polish-Prussian sources in the 1520s and 1530s, was also expressed well beyond this monarchy—not just by Erasmians, but by thinkers in the fourteenth- and fifteenth-century church, and by princes and scholars across Latin Europe in the first years of the Reformation, as we shall see. Sigismund I's 'tolerating' pre-confessional ecclesiology did not originate within, and was not confined to, the Polish monarchy. The rest of this book will look at the Polish-Prussian story in more depth; the rest of this Introduction, meanwhile, considers the wider implications of these conclusions for our understanding of the late medieval church and Reformation.

* * *

What follows is a broader hypothesis about the Reformation arising from the findings of this book: necessarily panoramic and inevitably controversial. It proposes that the sixteenth century saw a seismic shift in the very concept of religious orthodoxy in the Latin West—not just, as is perfectly obvious, in the diversifying *content* of orthodoxy (e.g. teachings on salvation, devotional practices), but also at a deep, structural, *conceptual*, and linguistic level. Content can be distinguished from concept, as software (visible to the user) can be distinguished from its underlying but invisible programming code/language. It is suggested that the Reformation affected a move from a pre-confessional concept of orthodoxy very widely held in the early sixteenth century—orthodoxy as a unified community, embodying the majority opinion of Christians across time and space—to a radically new confessionalized notion of orthodoxy as located instead in closely defined doctrines, whose absolute authority was no longer derived from the consensus they commanded. In 1985, John Bossy's *Christianity in the West*, in an anthropologically grounded reading, painted the Reformation as the transformation of Christianity in Europe from a religion of social community to one emphasizing individual belief, from 'a body of people', to 'an ism'.[63] Influenced by Foucault, Bossy argued that language was an integral part of this revolution, changing the meanings of big words such as 'religion' and 'society', and also a plethora of smaller words such as 'communion', 'charity', and 'conversation'.[64] The material presented here builds on Bossy's panoramic conclusions about three centuries of European history—tests them systematically against a body of sources from the 1520s and 1530s, seeks to pinpoint more closely where and when this radical rethinking of orthodoxy might have begun, and to identify which word lay at its heart.

---

[63] John Bossy, *Christianity in the West, 1400–1700* (Oxford, 1985), p. 171.
[64] Bossy, *Christianity in the West*, pp. 168–71 and 'Some Elementary Forms of Durkheim', *Past & Present* (1982): 3–18, at p. 12.

The hypothesis presented here has epistemological implications for historians of the late medieval and early modern churches—if the Reformation did affect a major linguistic shift, resetting the meanings of basic religious words and investing them with new meanings which have endured for centuries, there is a risk that we read our fifteenth- and sixteenth-century texts anachronistically through post-confessionalization spectacles. Arguments about language, and the deepest assumptions we bring to language, are by their nature difficult to communicate in that very language. For clarity, 'orthodoxy' is used here to mean where Christian truth was seen to reside. So let us explore why the pre-confessional ecclesiology present in the Polish monarchy might lead us to this far broader conclusion about what occurred in the sixteenth century.

We can start from the observation that historians tend to see the late medieval church as diverse and chaotic, and therefore as lacking in orthodoxy. This characterization is important because unpacking it is a first step in seeing how modern meanings are attributed to the language of premodern sources. The late medieval church is seen as distinctive for its bewildering array of devotional trends. Informed by anthropology, the study of visual culture and social history, researchers have increasingly stressed the dizzying variety of religion on the ground—the mystical piety of St Brigit (d.1373), Julian of Norwich (d.c.1416), or the *alumbrados* of Spain; a proliferation of saintly cults, miracle-working images, and lay confraternities; new movements such as the *devotio moderna* of the Low Countries or Utraquism in Bohemia; increasingly spectacular religious lay theatre in Italy; mass consumption of newly printed books of hours.[65] All this John van Engen has described as 'a carnival of religious options, multiple, competing, coexistent, contested, negotiated, overlapping'.[66] Howard Louthan has talked of it as 'a richer and more variegated world of religious life and expression', Nicolls of 'a relatively open, multivalent' church, and Robert Lutton labels its piety as 'increasingly heterogeneous'.[67]

The fifteenth century is also seen as an age of variegation in a more problematic way, in the church's actual theology. The different philosophical schools and sub-schools of scholastic theology coexisted with new humanist-philological treatments of Scripture pioneered by Lorenzo Valla (d.1457), and with a Christian Neoplatonism revived in Florence by Marsilio Ficino (d.1499), an opaque piety free of sacraments and priests.[68] Already from the nineteenth century, German scholarship had used the term '*Unklarheit*' to describe the teaching of the late

[65] John H. van Engen, *Sisters and Brothers of the Common Life: The Devotio Moderna and the World of the Later Middle Ages* (Philadelphia, 2008); John Henderson, *Piety and Charity in Late Medieval Florence* (Oxford, 1994); Nerida Newbigin, *Feste d'Oltrano: Plays in Churches in Fifteenth-Century Florence* (Florence, 1996); Eamon Duffy, *The Stripping of the Altars: Traditional Religion in England, c.1400–c.1580* (New Haven, 1992); Alistair Hamilton, *Heresy and Mysticism in Sixteenth-Century Spain: The Alumbrados* (Cambridge, 1992).
[66] John van Engen, 'Multiple Options: The World of the Fifteenth-Century Church', *Church History* 77 (2008): 257–84.
[67] Howard Louthan, 'Introduction', *Austrian History Yearbook* 41 (2010): 13–24; David Nicholls, 'France', in Pettegree, *Early Reformation*, pp. 120–41, at p. 122; Robert Lutton, *Lollardy and Orthodox Religion in Pre-Reformation England: Reconstructing Piety* (Woodbridge, 2006), pp. 4, 196.
[68] Amos Edelheit, *Ficino, Pico and Savonarola: The Evolution of Humanist Theology, 1461/2–1498* (Leiden, 2008).

medieval church—a fogginess, a cloud of doctrinal possibilities.[69] Jaroslav Pelikan too has termed the late Middle Ages 'The Age of Doctrinal Pluralism', and Alister Hamilton underscores 'the continuing dogmatic uncertainty of the Catholic church' in the 1530s.[70] Alister McGrath emphasizes the late medieval church's 'astonishing doctrinal diversity'.[71] There may have been intermittent local attempts to define catholic teaching more closely—in the campaign against Lollardy, or by the Theology Faculty of Paris—but the clear overall trend was towards diverse devotional expressions, and diverse theological positions.[72] It added up to a fissiparous church perhaps akin to cosmologists' model of an ever-expanding universe, absorbing a heady range of intellectual influences, generating new religious 'matter', holding within its ever broadening boundaries Utraquists, Erasmians, Ficino, Thomists, and Savonarolans.[73]

Many scholars have concluded, unsurprisingly, that this kaleidoscopic late medieval church suffered from a serious orthodoxy deficit—that nobody in this great confusion of voices and pieties any longer had the moral, intellectual, or institutional authority to define catholic orthodoxy. Lucy Wooding has argued that there simply was no orthodoxy in the fifteenth- and early sixteenth-century Latin church; no red lines there to be crossed.[74] David Bagchi's study of early polemics against Luther demonstrated that it was long unclear after 1517 exactly how far the content of his teaching was heterodox, because there was (embarrassingly) no definitive statement of the orthodox position to measure it against: e.g. on indulgences, on papal authority.[75] Lucien Febvre, in a celebrated turn of phrase, alluded to the absence of orthodoxy by calling the early sixteenth century a period of 'magnificent religious anarchy'.[76] Pelikan noted with puzzlement the great paradox of a late medieval church in which 'everyone went on speaking about the one true faith as in some sense still "one", despite the variety of opinions about one article of faith after another…'.[77]

Crucially, by 'orthodoxy', all these modern commentators mean doctrinal orthodoxy—i.e. an agreed set of definitive theological positions. It is here that language becomes important. Modern historical scholarship tends to treat 'doctrine' and 'orthodoxy' as largely interchangeable notions. Dictionary definitions thus offer

---

[69] The '*Unklarheit*' thesis is discussed in David Bagchi, *Luther's Earliest Opponents: Catholic Contraversialists, 1518–25* (Minneapolis, 1991), pp. 5–6.

[70] Jaroslav Pelikan, *The Christian Tradition: A History of the Development of Doctrine*, vol. 4 (Chicago, 1984); Hamilton, *Heresy and Mysticism*, p. 77.

[71] Alister McGrath, *The Intellectual Origins of the European Reformation*, 2nd edition (Oxford, 2004), p. 15; see also Berndt Hamm, trans. John M. Frymire, 'Normative Centering in the Fifteenth and Sixteenth Centuries: Observations on Religiosity, Theology and Iconology', *Journal of Early Modern History* 4 (1999): 307–54, at p. 351, on a late medieval 'state of open plurality'.

[72] James K. Farge rejects *Unklarheit*: *Orthodoxy and Reform in Early Reformation France: The Faculty of Theology of Paris, 1500–1543* (Leiden, 1985), pp. 161–2.

[73] For a sociological reading of this plurality, see Alister McGrath, *The Genesis of Doctrine: A Study in the Foundations of Doctrinal Criticism* (Oxford, 1990), pp. 42–3.

[74] Lucy Wooding, *Rethinking Catholicism in Early Modern England* (Oxford, 1990), pp. 3, 14, 20, 48.

[75] Bagchi, *Luther's Earliest Opponents*.

[76] Lucien Febvre, *Au coeur religieux du XVIe siecle* (Paris, 1968), p. 66.

[77] Pelikan, *The Christian Tradition*, vol. 4, p. 68.

us *orthodox* as: 'of, belonging to, or in accordance with the accepted theological or ecclesiastical doctrines of a particular religion'.[78] Pelikan, in his great history of Christian doctrine, defines it as 'what the church of Jesus Christ believes, teaches and confesses on the basis of the Word of God'—i.e. as professed belief.[79] Even the modern ecumenical theologian George Lindbeck, trying to define doctrine as widely as possible, offers a formulation with an emphasis on belief: 'communally authoritative teachings, readings, beliefs and practices that are considered essential to the identity and welfare of the group'.[80] Doctrine, in our modern usage, thus refers to non-negotiable, core beliefs held by Christians, which often differ between churches and typically distinguish one church from another. It is seen as logical that a church should have an articulated set of doctrinal positions, and require doctrinal uniformity.

However, in late medieval sources right across Latin Europe, the word *doctrina* had a different meaning. At the most literal level, *doctrina* simply meant 'learning' or 'teaching'—hence in 1534 the cathedral canons of the Baltic see of Kulm could congratulate their learned new bishop Johannes Dantiscus on his 'excellent *doctrina*', talent and virtue.[81] Late medieval *doctrina* in the sense of 'a teaching' was interchangeable with *opiniones*. The English anti-heresy statute of 1400 spoke consistently, for example, of 'doctrines et opiniones', seemingly presenting them as a rhetorically well-established pair of synonyms.[82] In 1530s Poland, the bishop of Kraków could complain of the 'depraved opinions' of a Lutheran conventicle in the city.[83] (Luther certainly did not regard them as mere opinions, a point we shall return to.) *Opiniones* was frequently employed in mainstream academic theology when presenting a position or hypothesis for disputation. In 1492, the printer Johannes Drach styled his edition of the theologian Duns Scotus (d.1308) as 'the opinions of the doctors and Scotus in four books'.[84] In 1497, the pope's own theologian, Silvestro Mazzolini da Prierio, issued an edition of theological texts: its title promised the reader that the book contained 'all the theological matter of the most acute doctors and all the most distinguished opinions'—'theologis materiam' and 'opiniones' equated with each other.[85] Johann Eck, denouncing Luther in 1521, referred to the Wittenberger's views merely as 'sententiae', propositions.[86] Doctrines (opinions, sentences), in the world of late medieval theological speculation, were there to be tested, debated, and weighed up: they could in that

---

[78] OED, http://www.oed.com (accessed 21 August 2015).

[79] Pelikan, *The Christian Tradition*, vol. 4, p. 2.

[80] George Lindbeck, *The Nature of Doctrine: Religion and Theology in a Postliberal Age* (London, 1984), p. 74.

[81] AT 12, p. 158.

[82] *The Statutes at Large from Magna Charta to the End of the Last Parliament*, ed. Owen Ruffhead (London, 1758), vol. 1, pp. 440–1.

[83] AT 17, p. 468.

[84] Duns Scotus, *Scotus pauperum vel abbreviatus in quo doctorum et Scoti opiniones in quattuor libris sententiarum compendiose elucidantur* (Speyer, 1492).

[85] Silvestro Mazzolini da Prierio, *Egregium vel potius diuinum opus in Iohannem Capreolum Tholosanum Sacri Predicatorum Ordinis…omnem in theologicis materiam accutissimorum doctorum pene omnium clarissimas opiniones* (Cremona, 1497).

[86] Johann Eck, *Epistola ad Carolum V de Luderi causa* (Ingoldstadt, 1521), fo. Aij.

process of intellectual scrutiny be judged to be correct, or erroneous. This is what disputation and debate were for. The great master of the Paris Schools, Simon Langton (d.1216), had praised the disputation as a situation where it was possible to pursue truth by thinking speculatively, to explore things 'believed conditionally'.[87] Medieval theology, intimately related to philosophy, was rooted in speculation, exegesis, clarification, and ongoing enquiry.[88] A *doctrina*, in the late medieval church, was therefore not necessarily an indispensable Christian belief—doctrines were auxiliary, secondary, expository, supplementary, evolving opinions, and they were naturally the preserve of doctors active in Latin Christendom's theology faculties, an academic specialism. We might therefore distinguish between the two different meanings of 'doctrine': between a modern usage (doctrine-belief) and a late medieval usage (doctrine-academic opinion). In late medieval texts, therefore, 'doctrina' was not, and could not logically be, interchangeable with Christian orthodoxy in its entirety.

In many late medieval sources, orthodoxy is instead presented as a process, rather than as a fixed set of beliefs—understood as an evolving consensus around the faith. That faith (*fides Christi, fides catholica*) had been set down in the creeds and councils of late antiquity. Medieval church councils routinely opened with a definition of this *fides catholica*. Lateran IV (1215) thus over several paragraphs defined the *fides* as belief in a creator God in three persons, the incarnation, the death, and resurrection of Christ, the existence of the universal church, and the sacraments of Eucharist and penance.[89] The Councils of Vienne (1311–12) and Florence (1431+) also defined the 'orthodox faith' as the ancient creeds and councils.[90] The oath for a new pontiff drawn up by the Council of Constance (1414–18) stated that the incumbent 'believe and uphold the catholic faith', listed as the traditions of the Apostles, the holy fathers, and the first eight church councils.[91] Faith (*fides*) and doctrine (*doctrina*) were thus not quite the same thing. Erasmus was therefore not saying anything very new when he underscored the difference between fundamental items of Christian 'faith', such as the Incarnation or Trinity, and 'doctrines' or debated 'questions' of secondary importance, such as purgatory.[92]

Orthodoxy, in this late medieval view, was 'the daughter of time'—a consensus which emerged over the years through accrued learned debate.[93] That consensus was manifested as Christian unity across time and space. In the fifth century, Vincent of Lérins (d.445) had devised the celebrated 'Vincentian canon', a formula which defined orthodoxy not by its specified theological content, but as 'that

---

[87] Alex J. Novikoff, *The Medieval Culture of Disputation: Pedagogy, Practice, and Performance* (Philadelphia, 2013), pp. 135–6.

[88] For a recent overview, see Rik van Nieuwenhove, *An Introduction to Medieval Theology* (Cambridge, 2012).

[89] *Decrees of the Ecumenical Councils*, ed. Norman Tanner (London and Washington, DC, 1990), vol. I, p. 230.

[90] *Decrees*, vol. I, pp. 587, 360–1.

[91] *Decrees*, vol. I, p. 442.

[92] CWE, vol. 76, pp. 119–20.

[93] Quote from James D. Tracy, 'Erasmus and the Arians: Remarks on the "Consensus Ecclesiae"', *The Catholic Historical Review* 67 (1981): 1–10, at p.7.

which has been believed everywhere, always and by everyone'.[94] William of Ockham (d.1347) too defined orthodoxy as a historical consensus, as that which had been accepted as 'catholic' (i.e. universally held) by all Christian and catholic peoples.[95] Nicholas of Cusa (d.1464), in his *Catholic Concordance*, defined orthodoxy as that which had been believed by the majority of the universal church.[96] Yves Congar, in his celebrated study of medieval ecclesiology, found that unity was one of its great motifs, 'le sentiment dominant'.[97] Likewise Jaroslav Pelikan, surveying fifteenth-century theology, found that it consistently placed huge emphasis on consensus and unity.[98]

In the 1520s and 1530s, across Latin Christendom orthodoxy was still routinely defined against the Reformation in this pre-confessional way as a universal consensus, well beyond the Polish monarchy. The *Assertio Septimorum Sacramentorum* (1521) and a follow-up treatise (1527–8) composed in the name of King Henry VIII explained, for example, that the church was by definition the Christian majority in agreement—it was a logical nonsense to reduce it to a minority, to 'two or three heretics whispering in a corner'.[99] Luther had abandoned the consensus of past Christians, 'were they never so many, never so wyse, never so well learned, never so holy', and inexplicably gone against 'the hole consent and agreement not only of Christes holy church from the beynnygyne therof to this day but also agaynst all common reason of all the hole worlde from the fyrste creation of the worlde hitherto…'[100] The leading German polemist Johann Fabri included in his 1528 polemic an entire chapter entitled 'De consensu et concordia'.[101] His compatriot Johannes Sichardt, writing against Luther in 1528, condemned heretics' rejection of 'the prescripts of all the Councils, against the dogmas accepted in consensus over so many centuries…'[102] Catholicism as consensus was also central to the writings and ecclesiology of Erasmus of Rotterdam in these years, as James McConica, Hilmar Pabel, and others have long stressed.[103] In his *Hyperaspistes* against Luther (1525–6), Erasmus too described the church's teaching as that 'handed down by so

[94] See Thomas G. Guarino, *Vincent of Lérins and the Development of Christian Doctrine* (Grand Rapids, 2013).

[95] Pelikan, *The Christian Tradition*, vol. 4, p. 61; see also Scott H. Hendrix, 'In Quest of the Vera Ecclesia: The Crises of Late Medieval Ecclesiology', *Viator* 7 (1976): 347–78, at pp. 361–2; Nicholas of Cusa, *The Catholic Concordance*, ed. Paul E. Sigmund (Cambridge, 1996).

[96] Pelikan, *The Christian Tradition*, vol. 4, p. 98.

[97] Yves Congar, *L'Ecclésiologie du Haut Moyen Age: de Saint Grégoire le Grand á la désunion entre Byzance et Rome* (Paris, 1968), pp. 61–5, quote at p. 94.

[98] Pelikan, *The Christian Tradition*, vol. 4, pp. 69–126.

[99] *Henry VIII Fid. Def. His Defence of the Faith and its Seven Sacraments*, ed. Richard Rex (Sevenoaks, 2008), p. 115.

[100] Henry VIII, *A copy of the letters, wherin… kyng Henry the eight… made answere vnto a certayne letter of Martyn Luther* (London, ?1527), fos. Bvii[r]–Bviiv, Dviv.

[101] Johann Fabri, *Adversus doctorem Balthasarem Pacimontanum* (Leipzig, 1528).

[102] Johannes Sichardt, *Antidotum contra diversas omium fere seculorum haereses* (Basel, 1528), fo. A3: 'tot Conciliorum praescripta, contra tam recepta omnium seculorum consensione dogmata…'.

[103] James McConica, 'Erasmus and the Grammar of Consent', in Joseph Coppens (ed.), *Scrinium Erasmianum* (Leiden, 1969), vol. II, pp. 77–99; Hilmar Pabel, 'The Peaceful People of Christ: The Irenic Ecclesiology of Erasmus of Rotterdam', in H. Pabel (ed.), *Erasmus' Vision of the Church* (Missouri, 1995), pp. 57–93; Brian Gogan, 'The Ecclesiology of Erasmus of Rotterdam: A Genetic Account', *The Heythrop Journal* 21 (1980): 393–411.

many learned and famous men and accepted by the whole Christian world with such an overwhelming consensus'.[104] This phrasing became the leitmotif of his sorties against the Reformation, as Erasmus talked insistently of orthodoxy as 'a consensus of Christian people', 'a consensus of the church', 'the consensus of very many centuries', 'an overwhelming consensus', and so forth.[105]

The wide diffusion of this understanding of orthodoxy is perhaps best captured by the recurrence, right across Latin Europe in the 1520s, of a single-sentence definition of the church. This sentence essentially articulated catholicism as a list of concurring Christian authorities, past and present: councils, princes, popes, universities, Christian nations. It was at least a century old: in 1414/18, the Council of Constance, condemning John Wyclif, invoked against him 'many most reverend fathers, cardinals of the Roman church, bishops, abbots, masters of theology, doctors in both laws and many notable persons'.[106] King Sigismund I and his royal chancellery used precisely this line as their default definition of catholicism when writing to Lutherans, as we have seen, whether to rebels, bishops, or princes: 'The rites and institutes of the church, confirmed for so many centuries, by so many miracles, by the authority of the councils, popes, emperors, kings, kingdoms and Christian nations...'[107] Piotr Rydziński, canon of Poznań, in a 1524 pamphlet stressed that Luther was against 'the universal church', the pope, emperor, Christian princes, all universities, and nations.[108] The Poznań lecturer Walenty Wróbel, in a 1535 letter, juxtaposed Luther with the 'most learned men', all the universities, the supreme pontiff, and the Emperor.[109] Johann Eck, addressing the Emperor in 1521, stressed that the Saxon doctor's teaching had been rejected by 'the holy fathers and councils' and pontiffs of the past, as well as by cardinals, universities, and top theologians of the present day.[110] In a 1521 imperial edict, Emperor Charles V too juxtaposed with Luther the collective agreement and authority of the councils, the Emperor, and the German nation.[111] In France, the Bishop of Chartres, Josse Chichtove, wrote that religious change must be agreed by the entire community of Christians, by a general council of the universal church, the pope and bishops, the *tota ecclesia*.[112] The English *Assertio* also used this phrasing, invoking the Fathers, the whole church, and 'the consent of all Christians in synods and general councils'.[113] And Erasmus, in his very first printed lines against Luther (1524), stated that the Saxon was dissenting from all 'doctors,

---

[104] CWE 76, p. 200.

[105] CWE 76, pp. 15–16, 121, 127, 144, 200; CWE 77, p. 335. Erasmus also described consensus, without using the word itself: CWE 76, pp. 88, 101, 108, 252; CWE 78, pp. 461–2.

[106] *Decrees*, vol. 1, p. 414.

[107] AT 7, p. 404: 'vos ritum et instituta ecclesie, tot seculis, tot miraculis, tanta autoritate conciliorum, pontificum, imperatorum, regum, regnorumque et nationum christianarum confirmata...violasse'. See also AT 7, p. 76; AT 8, pp. 43, 50, 132.

[108] Piotr Rydziński, *Petri Risinii in Iohannis Hessi Cachinni Sycophantias Responsio* (Kraków, 1524) (unnumbered pages).

[109] Prefatory letter in Grzegorz Szamotulski, *Vincula Hippocratis* (Kraków, 1536) (unnumbered pages).

[110] Eck, *Epistola*, fos. Aiii(v) to Bi.   [111] RTA II, pp. 531–3.

[112] Josse Clichtove, *Propugnaculum adversus Lutheranos* (Paris, 1526), fo. Ai(v).

[113] *Henry VIII Fid. Def.*, pp. 82, 88, 95, 118.

universities, all councils and all popes'.[114] Here we have a 1520s gloss on Vincent of Lerins, which is clearly not a private invention of the Polish royal chancellery. In a sign of how embedded this rhetoric of the church must have been, Luther admitted in 1520 that he too had long accepted indulgences 'seeing that they were approved by the common consent of so many'.[115] Some modern commentators have reacted with queasiness to this elusive vision of orthodoxy in Erasmus—yet these are not the voices of pseudo-Catholics, but of early sixteenth-century Catholics, speaking in a different code. In this ecclesiology, religious authority lay with the church precisely because it embodied majority opinion; the authority of the church's clerical hierarchy and pontiff derived from that consensus, and not from their office per se as a power source in itself.

There are two obvious objections to the argument that leading late medieval catholics operated with a consensus-centred concept of orthodoxy. The first (echoing on a bigger scale local Polish historiographical debate) is that such a stance is nothing more than the Erasmianism so fashionable in the early sixteenth century. Scholarship on Erasmus' religion has tended to treat him as, by definition, *sui generis*.[116] However, his passionate definition of orthodoxy as Christian consensus is not original to him, repeating as it does Vincent of Lérins, Cusa, Ockham, the Council of Constance, and a host of earlier authorities. In particular, many of the high-profile definitions of the church as consensus made in the early Reformation predate Erasmus' own initial printed pronouncement on Luther in his *De Libero Arbitrio* (September 1524). Specifically, the English *Assertio* (1521), Johann Eck's early polemic in Germany (1521), or Sigismund I's decree on Danzig (February 1524) all deploy this hallmark 'Erasmian' language of orthodoxy-as-consensus against Luther before the Dutchman himself did so. Moreover, one need not be an Erasmian to define catholicism in this way—consider Primate Jan Łaski of Poland, conservative, suspicious of humanism, grumpily anti-Erasmian, who could nonetheless in summer 1525 define orthodoxy as 'the authority of forebears, whose just life strengthened their teaching and established the unity and usage of the whole church for so many ages, and confirmed by consensus'.[117] We should consider the possibility that Erasmus was simply the most articulate exponent of a powerful late medieval pattern of thought, an ecclesiology popular because it was already widely shared.

The second objection is that the late medieval church cannot have been relaxed about doctrinal variation because it persecuted and executed heretics. Here too there is a risk that we read 'heresy' and 'orthodoxy' through a post-confessionalization lens. There is a case to be made that late medieval dissidents were persecuted primarily for threatening social and political order, a link already clearly made in Emperor Frederick II's (d.1250) heresy edicts. Henry VIII, in 1527, condemned those who 'instigate and sette out rude rebellyous people under pretext of

[114] CWE 76, p. 6.   [115] LW 36, p. 11.   [116] See Gogan, 'The Ecclesiology'.
[117] AT VII, p. 387: 'majorum autoritati, quorum doctrinam vita probata et universalis ecclesie per tot secula usus et consensus confirmavit'.

Evangelicall lyberte to ron out and fyght'.[118] Francis I's edicts (1534, 1540) spelt out that heresy was a 'disturbance of the public peace', bound up with 'sédition', stirring up rebellion.[119] In the *Epistola Apologetica* (1529), Erasmus too defined heresy as either outright blasphemy against the creeds (e.g. denying the divine nature of Christ), or as deliberate disorder: 'something that employs malicious contrivances to strive, through disturbances and revolts, after riches, power, and the ruin of human affairs'.[120] Nowhere, in Kraków or beyond, was heresy as a mass social movement remotely acceptable. The late medieval church was a violent, brutal, and murderous place when policing the boundaries of social order/unity, as the Hussites and Waldensians found. Moreover, it is not clear that late medieval dissidents or 'heretics' (unlike Luther) were in possession of (or persecuted for having) a corpus of doctrine in the modern sense, which could be consciously juxtaposed with catholic doctrine. J. Patrick Hornbeck has recently cautioned against assuming that every pre-Reformation 'heretical' group had its own doctrine—although early modern Protestant sources retrospectively insisted that was the case, he found little hard evidence of this for English Lollards.[121] Euan Cameron too, in his work on Waldensians, emphasizes that they did not 'deviate from conventional catholic doctrine', that church authorities deemed them guilty of 'disobedience, rather than wrong belief', and that they lacked 'a self-sufficient theology'.[122] Rowan Williams suggests that to grasp what exercised early Christians about heretics we should ask not 'what did they believe?', but rather 'what did they do?'—this order of priorities might also be true of the Latin church before confessionalization.[123]

J. G. A. Pocock saw the historian as an archaeologist tasked with identifying in their sources distinct 'languages' (idioms, discourses, rhetorics), such as that of civic humanism or English republicanism, and ideally able to unearth new ones.[124] What we see here, then, is a distinctive language which recurs, text after text, in the writings of kings, scholars, and clergy across early sixteenth-century Europe. It was not universal: the Roman curia, for example, had an entirely different language of catholicism centred on a forceful articulation of papal monarchy, and princes spoke back to it in its own language.[125] This language is something more than and older than 'Erasmian' ecclesiology, though clearly encompasses it. The contention here is that this is not just a new language, but an important language historically.

---

[118] Henry VIII, *The Answere*, Bvii–Bvii(v).

[119] *Recueil générale des anciennes lois francaise*, ed. A. Jourdan et al. (29 vols., 1822–33), vol. 12, pp. 407, 680; Aimé Louis Herminjard, *Correspondance des Réformateurs dans les pays de langue française* (Geneva, 1870), vol. 3, p. 407.

[120] CWE 78, p. 226.

[121] J. Patrick Hornbeck II, *What Is a Lollard? Dissent and Belief in Late Medieval England* (Oxford, 2010).

[122] Euan Cameron, *Waldenses: Rejections of Holy Church in Medieval Europe* (Oxford, 2000), pp. 2–7, 298–303.

[123] Rowan Williams, 'Defining Heresy', in Alan Kreider (ed.), *The Origins of Christendom in the West* (Edinburgh, 2001), pp. 313–35, at p. 316.

[124] J. G. A. Pocock, 'The Concept of a Language and the *métier d'historien*: Some Considerations on a Practice', in Anthony Pagden (ed.), *The Languages of Political Theory in Early Modern Europe* (Cambridge, 1987), pp. 19–38.

[125] See Chapter Eight.

So widely diffused throughout the Polish monarchy, readily detectable in a swathe of international treatises against Lutherans, detectable in the words (and policies?) of princes across Latin Christendom—this ecclesiological discourse constitutes a significant aspect of the late medieval church, and a significant context for the Reformations. It was the language, after all, of key actors and power figures in the turbulent early sixteenth century: top scholars, princes, many high clergy. What to call it is a moot point: it would be a research challenge to pin down just how far it extended in space and time. Do we diagnose this consensus-centred discourse of church as that of premodern Christianity, or pre-confessional catholicism, or of ultramontane late medieval Europe? We might ponder, in particular, what it owes to the languages of fifteenth-century conciliarism.

To recover the pre-confessional self-understanding of these many voices in the late medieval church is to make the Reformation, on the face of it, harder to account for. Commentators have for centuries suggested that the late medieval church was inevitably heading for a fall—because its flourishing pieties indicated an unmet popular desire for religious fulfilment; because its devotional and intellectual trends exhibited signs of what Berndt Hamm has termed 'normative centering', a clustering around absolute and certain principles like Scripture; because there were calls for reform everywhere (as there always had been).[126] However, if elites in the Latin church did operate with a consensus-based sense of orthodoxy, that arguably made it more, not less, robust to internal intellectual challenges. For many commentators, a certain plurality of doctrine-opinion within the church was, after all, entirely compatible with its orthodoxy. James of Viterbo, *c*.1400, had written that 'union consists in multiplicity', while Nicholas of Cusa declared the church to be like a polyphonic harmony, with no harm in a variety of opinions, so long as 'fraternal unity' was preserved in the church. The scholar Jean Gerson (d.1429) wrote with approval 'although the Christian church is one, it is distinguished by a multiple and beautiful variety'.[127] We have seen how Polish senior clergy, such as Tiedemann Giese, were similarly cheerful about the idea of different ideas of salvation coexisting peacefully in the church. Erasmus too wrote that: 'some questions...are not worthwhile to fight about so fiercely as to break asunder the harmony of Christendom', and that each should quietly hold his own opinion.[128] It was widely assumed that debate over new 'sententiae' would, in time, produce consensus and preserve unity, as it had with the 1436 Basel Compactata. It is in this spirit that we can read catholic elites' chief impulse in the face of the Reformation, which was to hold debates seeking some intellectual resolution. Calling the Speyer and Regensburg Reichstags (1526, 1532) Charles V and Ferdinand Habsburg stressed a desire to find a common 'understanding' of the Christian faith, while Francis I in his talks with the Schmaldalkic League proposed to find together 'a union of doctrines' in order to safeguard 'harmony within the

---

[126] Hamm, 'Normative Centering'; Lutton, *Lollardy and Orthodox Religion*; Hendrix, 'In Quest of the Vera Ecclesia'.
[127] Quoted in Pelikan, *The Christian Tradition*, vol. 4, p. 79.   [128] CWE 76, p. 124.

ecclesiastical polity'.[129] Johann Fabri's 1528 printed dialogue, which showcased him bringing an Anabaptist back to an orthodox position through robust but charitable debate, modelled just such approaches.[130] Such attempts at catholic-Lutheran reconciliation are often read as purely pragmatic endeavours to broker religious peace, akin to the peace conferences of modern diplomacy, but it is possible they grew instead out of a late medieval notion of Christian orthodoxy as inherently shaped by collective debate, and the pursuit of a majority consensus. Lutherans and Zwinglians knew that they had rejected this chaotic medieval church but, papal rhetoric of heresy notwithstanding, it had not yet entirely rejected or ejected them. The question, then, is precisely why Martin Luther's *doctrinae* were not simply absorbed or negotiated into the late medieval church, along with so many other rich novelties generated by the fifteenth-century church of options?

The answer most commonly given to that question is that Martin Luther's teaching had a seismic impact due to the sheer theological novelty of its contents. Berndt Hamm, Euan Cameron, Diarmaid McCullough, and Alister McGrath (and indeed Luther himself), have argued powerfully that with his doctrine of *sola fide* Luther placed an intellectual bomb beneath the late medieval church, destroying its intricate theological model of human salvation, rendering its clergy and sacraments at a stroke irrelevant.[131] Their argument runs as follows. Late medieval theologians had seen justification (the process of being made acceptable in the sight of God) as a long journey made by the individual, aided by good works and sacraments, towards salvation after death. Between 1515 and 1517 in Wittenberg, Martin Luther developed a radical alternative theology of salvation, in which the individual, realizing that they were so sinful as to be absolutely helpless in their own justification, must recognize and believe that Christ offered unconditional, unearned, and certain salvation.[132] Justification was not earned (God and people working together), but in this model granted to those who had faith (with all agency resting with God alone); it lay not in the future, but urgently in the present. *Sola fide*, in this authoritative reading, was just too new, and too big, an idea to be accommodated within the late medieval theology out of which it had emerged.

However, it will be suggested here that the impact of *sola fide* on the late medieval church went well beyond this, because it was revolutionary twice over—in content and in concept. Much has been written on *sola fide*, its antique and medieval antecedents, its emergence in Luther's writings, its long-term reception. However, one particular feature of *sola fide* has perhaps escaped the attention it deserves—it was not just a big new doctrine, but a radically new kind

---

[129] RTA V/VI, pp. 879–95 (1526); RTA X, pp. 1059–62 (1532); Herminjard, *Correspondance*, vol. III, pp. 300–1.

[130] Fabri, *Adversus doctorem Balthasarem*.

[131] Berndt Hamm, 'What Was the Reformation Doctrine of Justification?', in C. Scott Dixon, *The German Reformation: Essential Readings* (Oxford, 1999), pp. 53–90; Alister McGrath, *Iustitia Dei: A History of the Christian Doctrine of Justification* (Cambridge, 1986); Cameron, *European Reformation*, pp. 85, 150 (Figures 1 and 2).

[132] Hamm, 'What Was the Reformation Doctrine?'; McGrath, *Iustitia Dei*, pp. 208–40.

of doctrine.[133] Put simply, *sola fide* is a doctrine about doctrine. It possessed a novel intellectual structure. Earlier doctrines, or creedal positions, had been what philosophers term first-order beliefs—simple truth claims pointing to or describing some aspect of God or divine action – e.g. the Trinity, the Incarnation. *Sola fide*, by contrast, is a second-order belief, entailing two layers of belief: I believe, that if I believe I will be saved. The first belief is in *sola fide* itself as an essential Christian truth or insight, and the second belief is that faith leads to salvation. In other words, *sola fide* describes a divine action, but does so by pointing back to (and through) itself. With this double-belief layer in its intellectual structure, it is a powerfully self-referential teaching, functioning as a kind of prism, or portal, through which all Christian faith is refracted. *Sola fide* was thus a super-doctrine which, by its form and structure, claimed for itself exclusive insight, truth, and salvific agency (while attributing these to God). As such, it was not at all like the speculative doctrine-opinions of late medieval theology faculties, but a new kind of doctrine which, uniquely, claimed a quasi-creedal status (doctrine-belief). The authority of the *sola fide* doctrine was absolute and autonomous; its authority was not dependent on debate, consensus, or consent. No surprise that in Wittenberg *sola fide* was known as the 'vera theologia', termed by Luther the 'lord and prince of all forms of doctrine', given central billing in the 1530 Augsburg Confession.[134] The 110 articles penned in 1524 by one of Europe's very first Lutheran bishops, Johannes Briesemann of Ducal Prussia, made *sola fide* its centrepiece, declaring that only he who embraced this doctrine was a true Christian and 'a king in the spiritual kingdom'.[135] Calvin called it 'the main hinge on which religion turns'.[136]

With *sola fide* Luther thus dramatically moved the locus of orthodoxy. Orthodoxy no longer consisted of, and was no longer guaranteed by, the unity of the Christian community around the creeds. Instead, for Luther orthodoxy lay with true doctrine—i.e. precise and eternally correct positions in academic theology, and in particular one position. In this way, Luther took what had been separate categories in the minds of late medieval catholics—the Christian *fides*, and supplementary academic theological opinion, *doctrina*—and conflated them, as Western Christianity largely has done ever since. In the process, Luther also redefined the church. Cameron has noted that with the Reformation the church gained a different role, no longer a late medieval provider of spiritual purification, but a proclaimer of God's grace—yet more than even this, *sola fide* necessarily forced a recalibration and redefinition of 'church'.[137] In Luther's teaching, the church was no longer the universal body which encompassed all those calling themselves Christians, characterized by unity and consensus; it was not itself the

---

[133] Some of what is argued here is noted in passing by McGrath, *Iustitia Dei*, p. 223: 'Perhaps the most distinctive feature of Luther's mature doctrine of justification is the emphasis he places on its theological centrality.'

[134] Quoted by C. Scott Dixon, 'Introduction', in *The German Reformation*, pp. 1–32, at p. 8.

[135] Printed in Giese, *Flosculorum Lutheranorum*, articles 15–44, 77, 80, 100–1.

[136] Quoted in McGrath, *Iustitia Dei*, p. 254.

[137] Euan Cameron, *Enchanted Europe: Superstition, Reason, and Religion, 1250–1750* (Oxford, 2010), p. 141.

orthodoxy. Instead, *ecclesia* was that much smaller community which correctly understood the Gospel. Article VII of the Augsburg Confession, drafted by Melanchthon and signed by seven German princes, captures this, defining the 'holy, eternal church' as 'the congregation of the saints in which the Gospel is correctly taught, and in which the sacraments are correctly administered'.[138] This is a much narrower definition of church—the key word is the repeated *recte*, 'correct', meaning in keeping with the doctrine of *sola fide* (and thus beyond debate). The true church can thus be a statistical minority; exactly the conclusion which the English *Assertio* had found laughably illogical in 1521.

Dissenters from the late medieval church, such as Jan Hus or Girolamo Savonarola, had articulated searing moral critiques of it, but they had still seen orthodoxy as residing in a virtuous universal church; they imagined morally purified versions of that church, but did not replace universalism with a new doctrine, far less a new definition of doctrine.[139] *Sola fide*, an idea articulated by a doctor at a provincial German university from *c*.1517, was not thus simply a bomb which might wreak serious structural (i.e. theological) damage—it was a short circuit, the idea which broke the machine. Luther's (single) doctrine-as-faith was entirely incompatible with the late medieval idea of church as unified Christian society. *Sola fide* was an idea which, by its nature, refused to be accommodated within the system. Pocock predicted the existence of 'innovators', actors who could explosively create new language and change the rules of the game forever.[140] Pocock himself worked on early modern political, not religious, thought, but Luther fits very well his model of a rare, radical, conscious language disruptor, resetting paradigms not only in theology but also in language.

The first of the many and far-reaching implications of Luther's conceptual-linguistic shift was that it created, retrospectively, a compelling image of the medieval church as highly doctrine-focused—attributing to it the concept of orthodoxy which he himself had just developed. Luther cast that church as the perfect antithesis of his own teaching, a body wedded to a single (wrong) doctrinal position. If historians look at the late medieval church and see chaotic theological *Unklarheit* and wild devotional diversity, Martin Luther looked and, remarkably, saw a monolithic entity built by papal tyrants on a single false doctrine, a Pelagian heresy of salvation through works. McGrath has noted in passing how curiously Luther picked one of the many strands of late medieval theology on justification, and identified it as representative of the Latin church as a whole, but the implications of this are surely significant.[141] Lucas Cranach, in his vivid woodcuts, provided a visual rendition of this church, as a monstrous donkey-pope. The crowds who attended early Reformation sermons in Strassburg, Nuremberg, or Danzig were now told what the church they had belonged to all their lives 'really'

---

[138] *Confessio fidei exhibita invictiss. imp. Carolo V. Cæsari Aug. in comicijs Augustæ* (Wittenberg, 1531): 'Ecclesia congregation sanctorum in qua Evangelium recte docetur, et recte administrantur Sacramenta'.

[139] Pelikan and Schreiner stress how, in contrast to Luther, Hus was interested in virtue rather than doctrine: *The Christian Tradition*, vol. 4, p. 69 and *Are You Alone Wise?*, p. 143.

[140] Pocock, 'The Concept of a Language', pp. 32–4.

[141] McGrath, *Genesis of Doctrine*, p. 8 and *Iustitia*, p. 224.

was; Lutheranism was a collective act of imagining a theologically homogenous late medieval church, a citadel of 'Catholic' doctrine, which had possibly never existed. That church was rejected outright by the Reformation as unchristian because it had not been built around the essential Christian doctrine-belief of *sola fide*, salvation through faith alone. In 1520, Luther lambasted the 'pope and his devilish cohorts' for leading Christians into deadly error, while the *Apologia* drawn up by Lutheran Danzig in 1525 characterized the late medieval church as a darkness from which God had turned his face, a place of 'errors, deceptions and seductions', a long-lasting pharisaical age, a heresy inspired by the devil.[142] The late medieval church was defined and reconceptualized not as a community which had believed a great many things (*Unklarheit*), but as an institution which had believed one big wrong thing—the projection of a clear-cut confessional identity on a heterogenous pre-confessional church.

Luther's doctrine-focused definition of Catholicism proved self-fulfilling, because over the course of the sixteenth century that church slowly started to define itself as a Roman church built on distinctive, correct catholic doctrines, rather than as the universal Christian church of unity-consensus. Luther made the *Unklarheit* so characteristic of the late medieval church untenable, forcing it to articulate its own doctrinal position with a new clarity and certainty—as Wolgast writes, to define anew its 'dogmatic foundations'.[143] Pocock observed that where an adversary forges a new language, their respondents are inevitably forced to adopt that discourse in order to engage with it at all.[144] Under sustained doctrinal attack from the 1520s, catholic writers articulated a body of catholic doctrine— while talking loudly of consensus and unity, they were nonetheless pulled onto the doctrinal ground of conflict that Luther, in his anti-Pelagian fury, had marked out. As David Bagchi has shown, from the creatively messy theologies of the late medieval church, polemicists such as Johannes Eck or Cardinal Cajetan now had to adjudicate where the doctrinal boundaries of the 'catholic' church might lie, not least on questions which had radically divided the fifteenth-century church, such as the extent of papal authority.[145] This slippage can be seen in early printed polemics, such as Krzycki's *De Afflictione Ecclesiae* (1527) which had a foot in both worlds: it spoke of the paramount importance of a united universal church, while also starting to delineate a set of mutually incompatible catholic versus Lutheran teachings, defined against one another.[146] Erasmus spotted and noted with alarm this tendency to codify a newly narrow 'catholic', complaining that one could no longer 'toss about various questions concerning the power of the pope, indulgences…and purgatory', but was instead 'forced to believe' in a particular model of salvation.[147] In the process of defending these now more distinctively catholic doctrines (now balanced precariously between doctrine-opinion and doctrine-belief),

---

[142] LW 44, p. 132; AT 7, pp. 359, 364, 367.
[143] Eike Wolgast, 'Die deutschen territorialfürste und die Frühe Reformation', in B. Moeller and Stephen Buckwalter (eds), *Die frühe Reformation in Deutschland als Umbruch* (Heidelberg, 1998), pp. 407–34, at p. 433, 'dogmatische Grundlagen'.
[144] Pocock, 'The Concept of a Language', p. 34.   [145] Bagchi, *Luther's Earliest Opponents*.
[146] Andrzej Krzycki, *De Afflictione Ecclesiae* (Kraków, 1527).   [147] CWE 78, pp. 243–4.

these teachings—instead of historic consensus—started principally to define catholicism itself. Walenty Wróbel's 1536 anti-heresy tract, for example, systematically covered a set of questions typical of such polemics—fasting, saintly cults, sacraments, papacy, indulgences—showing how an idea of catholicism emerged in conscious juxtaposition with Protestant teachings.[148] In response to Luther, then, the late medieval church defined itself more narrowly, reaching for an identity and authority beyond unity-consensus itself. Luther thus did not just challenge the doctrinal confusion or salvation theory of the late medieval church, but its very self-understanding.

This can be traced, for example, in statements about the papacy. The medieval church had been no stranger to grand claims about the pontiff's standing. The famous 1302 bull *Unam Sanctam* stated: 'we define that it is absolutely necessary for salvation that every human creature be subject to the Roman Pontiff.' Such statements are, however, claims about jurisdiction, and not doctrinal claims about belief. Boniface VIII in 1302 was requiring catholics to obey, 'be subject', and not to believe that salvation came through the pope; far less to believe that belief in his power would bring salvation. In response to Luther's redefinition of doctrine and its status, the papacy too could became an article of faith, moving from a juridical or constitutional space into a doctrinal one; no longer a question of obedience, but of *fides*-like belief.

In the sixteenth century, the late medieval church (while vehemently rejecting Luther's content) came largely to adopt his new concept of Christian orthodoxy as a set menu of doctrine-belief. This became most apparent at the Council of Trent, and in the Tridentine reforms which followed it. The fifth session of the council (1546) expressly frowned on a plurality of doctrines-opinions, stating that it was important to the Catholic faith 'that the Christian people may not be carried away with every wind of doctrine'.[149] In 1547, in its celebrated decree on justification, the Council rejected both *sola fide* and many of the late medieval teachings on the subject, setting out a single fixed orthodox position.[150] The decrees of the Council of Trent (December 1563) were disseminated through the Tridentine Catechism (1566) and the Tridentine Creed (1564). The latter, opening with the words 'I with a firm faith believe and profess...', began with the text of the Nicene Creed before setting out doctrinal-belief positions—a rejection of *sola fide*, affirmation of the cult of saints and use of their images, the interpretation of Scripture in light of the Fathers, Mass as a sacrifice, purgatory and intercession for souls, indulgences, the power of the pontiff, and the rejection of all heresies. The Tridentine Creed presented this, then, as the 'true catholic faith, outside of which no one can be saved'—this was doctrine as faith, conflated as Luther had conflated them.[151] If anti-Reformation edicts and texts from the 1520s and 1530s had defined orthodoxy (against Luther) as unity and consensus, by 1564 the Tridentine Creed made no reference whatsoever to those ideas. Little wonder that Pelikan entitled his

---

[148] Walenty Wróbel, *Propugnaculum Ecclesiae adversus varias sectas* (Leipzig, 1536).

[149] *Decrees*, vol. II, p. 665: 'et ne populus christianus omni vento doctrinae circumferatur'. Ephesians 4:14.

[150] McGrath, *Iustitia*, pp. 308–48; *Decrees*, vol. II, pp. 671–81.

[151] Philip Schaff (ed.), *The Creeds of Christendom*, 6th edition (Grand Rapids, 1983), p. 99.

chapter on the sixteenth century 'The Doctrinal Age', the age of printed confessions, setting out precisely what each church (non-negotiably) believed.[152] The contents pages of the Tridentine catholic Creed, Catechism, or later sixteenth-century polemic are a world away from those of the *Summa Theologia* of Thomas Aquinas or Lombard's *Sentences*: the former dealing with points of doctrinal conflict with Protestants, the latter divided into books focusing on the philosophical and theological questions such as existence of God, Christology, or the process of creation. By the 1560s, the dominant, council-sanctioned concept of Catholicism was one which would not have been immediately recognizable (or palatable) to Sigismund I. Here, then, is an invitation to consider sixteenth-century Catholicism as embarking not just on a programme of self-defence or reform, but on a path of wholesale reconceptualization and doctrinalization. The shift from pre-confessional to confessionalized catholicism involved the acceptance of a new concept of orthodoxy itself.

This theory gives us a new lens for viewing sixteenth-century catholicism, and in particular some of its apparently anomalous subcurrents, such as Erasmians, irenicists, *spirituali*, and nicomedists. Erasmianism remained an influential and increasingly contested strand of catholic thought in the sixteenth century, before his entire oeuvre was placed on the Holy Office's Index of banned works. Erasmus (d.1536), like his followers, has been praised or chastised by modern scholars as a liberal, a peacemaker, a bad catholic, or a timid Protestant, the voice of a third way in polarized Reformation Europe.[153] To cast Erasmians as progressive, however, is to miss the late medieval nature of their understanding of the church—historically speaking, they are closer to being conservatives, defending the *status quo ante*, than progressive. The same can be said of the so-called *spirituali*, the group of cardinals and reformers in Italy who fought at the Council of Trent and beyond for reconciliation with the Protestants. They were opposed by a group traditionally labelled the *zelati*, led by Gian Pietro Caraffa (from 1555 Pope Paul IV), who instead wished to draw clear theological boundaries between the Roman and Protestant churches. The *spirituali* have long been portrayed as the liberal, ecumenical party and the *zelati* as arch-conservatives.[154] These labels, however, are the wrong way around, in that an energetic search for consensus and a willingness to debate or negotiate doctrine were in keeping with key late medieval traditions. It was Caraffa's triumphant party which was in historical terms revolutionary, by articulating Catholic identity in more exclusive terms. There has also been considerable scholarly interest in 'irenicists', figures such as the diplomat Lazarus von Schwendi at the court of Maximilian II (1564–76) who actively sought reconciliation between Catholic and Protestant churches.[155] Such programmes too can be seen

---

[152] Pelikan, *The Christian Tradition*, vol. 4.

[153] Lecler, *Toleration*; Pabel, 'The Peaceful People of Christ'; Brian Gogan, 'The Ecclesiology of Erasmus'.

[154] For a recent discussion of these figures and the attendant terminologies and their historiography, see Adam Patrick Robinson, *The Career of Cardinal Giovanni Morone (1509–80): Between Council and Inquisition* (Farnham, 2012).

[155] Howard Louthan, *The Quest for Compromise: Peace Makers in Counter-Reformation Vienna* (Cambridge, 1997); Howard Louthan and Randall C. Zachmann, *Conciliation and Confession: The*

either as a direct survival of late medieval instincts, or as a conscious attempt to revive them. The same can be said, finally, of those who could not or would not choose between Roman and Protestant forms of Christianity. A host of prominent sixteenth-century figures have proved difficult to classify in confessional terms— Marguerite d'Angoulême in France, Charles V's sister Mary of Hungary, or many of the German princes whom Wolgast labelled as 'neutrals'.[156] Wanegffelen's 1997 monograph stressed the many French men and women who did not see themselves as members either of the catholic or Huguenot confessions.[157] Militzer has suggested that many Teutonic Knights in the early Reformation did not have a sense of belonging to any confession.[158] Grey-area or nicodemist figures such as these might today be labelled confused and indecisive, but not to choose a confession (reforming catholic, Lutheran, Calvinist) was in effect to stay in the universalist tradition of the late medieval church. These groups were not forging a tolerant, Enlightened, ecumenical future, but facing back towards a late medieval past.

What exactly was the Reformation? The early modern answer can still be found today in Munich's central square, in the *Mariensaule* erected by the Catholic, Wittelsbach, part Polish-descended dukes of Bavaria in 1638, in thanksgiving for the city's deliverance from Swedish Lutheran armies during the Thirty Years' War. A gilded Virgin Mary stands on a column, at her feet a putto poised to decapitate a rearing serpent. The snarling, cornered serpent represents defeated heresy, and the putto the triumph of the catholic church.[159] Here, we have in bronze the Reformation as a titanic clash between two different forms of Christianity— catholic and Protestant. Modern scholarship offers a variety of readings of the Reformation. For Marxist historians, the Reformation in the 1520s and 1530s was an outright class war, with its peasant risings, urban disturbances, and social radicals.[160] For others, such as Euan Cameron and Alistair McGrath, the Reformation from 1517 onwards was primarily a theological revolution in teaching on salvation, with everything else springing from this point. For cultural historians, for R. W. Scribner, Lyndal Roper, and Susan Karant-Nunn, it was above all a massive change in the lived experience of families, women, and ordinary folk.[161] The German scholars Wolfgang Reinhard and Hans Schilling, famously, read the Reformation as a political revolution, in which rulers controlled the lives of subjects to an unprecedented extent through 'social discipline', in order to create a

Struggle for Unity in the Age of Reform (1415–1648) (Notre Dame, 2004); Suzanne Hequet, *The 1541 Colloquy of Regensburg: In Pursuit of Church Unity* (Saarbrücken, 2009).

[156] Spruyt, "En bruit d'estre bonne luterienne'; Wolgast, 'Die deutschen territorialfürste'.
[157] Thierry Wanegffelen, *Ni Rome, ni Genève: Des fidèles entre deux chaires en France au XVIe siècle* (Paris, 1997).
[158] Klaus Militzer, 'Introduction', in *The Military Orders and the Reformation: Choices, State-Building and the Weight of Tradition*, ed. Johannes A. Mol (Hilversum, 2006), pp. 5–9, at p. 9.
[159] Michael Schattenhofer, *Die Mariensäule in München* (Munich, 1971).
[160] Gerhard Brendler, *Martin Luther: Theologie und Revolution: eine marxistische Darstellung* (Köln, 1983).
[161] R. W. Scribner, *For the Sake of the Simple Folk: Popular Propaganda for the German Reformation* (Cambridge, 1981); Lyndal Roper, *The Holy Household: Women and Morals in Reformation Augsburg* (Oxford, 1989); Susan Karant-Nunn, *The Reformation of Feeling: Shaping the Religious Emotions in Early Modern Germany* (New York and Oxford, 2010).

pure confessional church (Lutheran, Calvinist, or catholic), subordinate to the nascent modern state.[162] Scott Hendrix has invited us to read the Protestant and catholic Reformations of the sixteenth century together, as at heart a common endeavour to fully 'Christianize' the European population.[163] The hypothesis outlined here would add, to all that, a story of how 'orthodoxy' itself was conceptually redefined—not just a new theology, but new definitions of theology which affected all churches in the Latin West. As such, it proposes that the Reformation was a battle which took place on two planes: the very visible, visceral struggle waged between catholic and Protestant confessions, but also their mutual rejection of a heterogenous late medieval catholicism.

Why is this latter struggle so hard to see? Arguably, it is hiding in plain sight in our sources. By the end of the sixteenth century, the bold confessional vision of orthodoxy won comprehensively in Latin Europe, squeezing older world views to the margins. If in the battle of catholic versus Protestant doctrine the two sides ultimately stalemated each other, in the battle between orthodoxy-as-unity and doctrine-as-orthodoxy, one side suffered a crushing defeat. It is an indication of the scale of that defeat that it is genuinely hard for us to hear pre-confessional voices. With the victory of the Reformations, the meaning of basic words shifted significantly. John Bossy made this case in the 1980s, but one can identity those words, the drivers, where the most important changes occurred.[164] *Doctrina* had been academic debate and opinions; it became essential Christian truth. *Ecclesia* had been Christian society; it became an exclusive group of right-thinking Christians. *Fides* had meant the defining basic parameters of Christianity as set out in the creeds; it came to be conflated with correct doctrinal positions. Therefore, when we hear late medieval voices, we think we hear perfectly well what they are saying; but perhaps we do not. The Reformations which ended the late medieval church also silenced it, and rendered some of its self-understanding invisible, precisely by appropriating its language and rhetoric for their own very different ends. As John Henderson states, 'part of the genius of neo-orthodoxy, if not its main polemical strategy, is to conceal its newness'.[165] What the Munich putto seeks to obscure is that the Reformation was not just a clash between early modern catholicism and Protestantism; it was also their mutual rejection of a different, older understanding of the nature of religious orthodoxy.

Yet perhaps to speak of the Reformation as a battle between pre-confessional and confessional understandings of Christianity, taking our lead from the armed putto, is to use the wrong metaphor. These two sides did not so much fight openly, as talk right past one another in mutual incomprehension. We find a pattern of simply not hearing one another in King Sigismund's monarchy. When the Danzig rebels delivered a lengthy speech on *sola fide* before King Sigismund at court

[162] Reinhard, 'Zwang zur Konfessionalisierung?'; Schilling, 'Die Konfessionalisierung'.
[163] Scott H. Hendrix, *Recultivating the Vineyard: The Reformation Agenda of Christianization* (Louisville, 2004).
[164] Bossy, *Christianity in the West*, 'Some Elementary Forms'.
[165] John Henderson, *The Construction of Orthodoxy and Heresy: Neo-Confucian, Islamic, Jewish and Early Christian Patterns* (Albany, 1998), p. 39.

in 1525, the Crown's reply spoke emphatically of church unity, as if replying to a different oration entirely.[166] We see it too in the correspondence of Archdeacon Stanisław Byliński and the Lutheran Laurentius Corvinus.[167] Corvinus' letters are brief and mystical in tone, talking only of salvation through faith in Christ; Byliński's replies, by contrast, for page after page stress the centrality of unity, the powerful historic consensus of councils, popes, princes, and scholars. Their letters go around and around in this same circle, eternally at cross-purposes.

Perhaps the most illuminating talking-past-each-other is the 1524–5 printed polemical exchange—*De Libro Arbitrio*, *Hyperaspistes*, and *De Servo Arbitrio*—conducted between Erasmus and Luther, the most eloquent adherents of their respective world views.[168] For the consensus-praising Erasmus, vagueness was acceptable: as Trinkaus writes, 'accommodation or adaptation was itself a religious principle'.[169] Rejecting this *Unklarheit*, Luther declared that it was intolerable for a Christian soul to live with ambiguity, 'an unforgiveable sin' to deny others doctrinal certainty.[170] This argument over certainty was an emanation of the deeper point at issue: the nature and role of doctrine. Erasmus urged Luther to distinguish between the 'fides' and secondary theological debates such as justification, and not to insist obsessively on a handful of narrow technical points. To him, Luther appeared fixated with doctrinal detail to the point of madness, sacrificing to this the obviously higher human and divine good of Christian peace. Luther denounced Erasmus as 'evasive and equivocal', an atheist and pagan—who but 'demons and the damned', he asked, 'could find doctrine and its essential Christian truth hateful?'[171] He declared 'see now, my dear Erasmus, what that most moderate and peace-loving theology of yours leads to...to despise faith'.[172] Here, the word 'doctrine' is the hinge, used in two incompatible ways—for Erasmus as a set of opinions up for debate, and for his opponent as core faith (in Luther's own words 'essential Christian truth'). Here, we have perhaps the definitive talking past each other of late medieval and early modern Latin Christianity, employing incompatible concepts of orthodoxy, using the same words to mean different things, and speaking quite different historic languages.

The story of Matthias Gutfor, with which we started, therefore opens up bigger issues than that of toleration alone. With Martin Luther, staring out in thoughtful challenge from Cranach's famous portraits, we can juxtapose not only Erasmus but also Sigismund I of Poland, painted in a gilded hat and ermine cape, possibly by Hans Suss von Kulmbach (d.*c.*1522). For Luther, the early Reformation represented a divine intervention, a revelation-like rediscovery of an authentic Christianity, a world remade by the Word; for King Sigismund, old and increasingly weary, it represented something in the Latin Christian world which he could barely begin to imagine, the end of consensus and unity. The Reformation is the gap, and the perilous journey, between these two worlds.

---

[166] AT 7, pp. 358–83, 400–4.   [167] Byliński, *Defensorium*.
[168] See, most recently, Clarence H. Miller, *Erasmus and Luther: The Battle over Free Will* (Indianapolis, 2012).
[169] CWE, vol. 76, p. xlv.   [170] LW 33, p. 34.   [171] LW 33, pp. 17, 35.
[172] LW 33, p. 43.

PART 2

CONTEXTS

Place, People, Texts

PLACE

What is Poland? If the meaning of apparently stable words such as *ecclesia* has been anything but stable historically, the same is of course true of 'Poland', a simple noun which masks multiple possible meanings and polemical intents. For the sixteenth century, Poland should be defined not as an ethnic people (a nascent nation state), but rather as a political phenomenon. As such, this study will consider all the peoples and territories under the authority of the Polish Crown in the reign of King Sigismund I, regardless of their 'ethnic' or linguistic status. Twenty years ago, John Elliott coined the phrase 'composite monarchies', pointing out that most early modern monarchies were patchworks of territories acquired at various times by different means (marriage, conquest, inheritance), held together by one monarch.[1] Sixteenth-century Poland, in its admixture of territories held by various titles, was no different. This account will thus avoid the ambiguous term 'Poland', and refer instead to 'the Polish monarchy'.

The 1521 chronicle *De Sigismundi Regis Temporibus*, composed by the royal secretary Jodocus Ludovicus Decius, opened by outlining for the reader the six separate territories which made up the Polish monarchy at that date.[2] Decius first introduced Małopolska (Lesser Poland) and Wielkopolska (Greater Poland), the heartlands of the kingdom as it had emerged in the Middle Ages under the Piast royal line. These were, respectively, the southern lands around the royal capital of Kraków on the Vistula, and the western lands centred around the trading city of Poznań on the Warta. 'Then there is the Prussian dominium', wrote Decius. The medieval kings of Poland had claimed Prussia, with its long Baltic coastline and fertile river deltas, as an integral part of their Crown. In practice, from the early thirteenth century it had been controlled by the crusading order of the Teutonic Knights, which had constructed its own theocratic state in the coastal wilderness, with German settlers, great fortifications and thriving Hanseatic towns such as Danzig. In 1454, the cities and nobles of Prussia had risen up in rebellion against the Order, asking Sigismund's formidable father, King Casimir IV (1447–92), to become their new overlord. This triggered the Thirteen Years' War—under the peace treaty finally signed at Thorn in 1466, the western half of the *Ordenstaat* passed to the Polish Crown, becoming an autonomous province within the Polish

---

[1] J. H. Elliott, 'A Europe of Composite Monarchies', *Past & Present* 137 (1992): 48–71.
[2] Jodocus Ludovicus Decius, *De Sigismundi Regis Temporibus* (Kraków, 1521).

monarchy known as 'Royal Prussia' (*Prusy Królewskie, Könglichen Preussen*).[3] This settlement partitioned Prussia into a section loyal to Kraków, and a rump Teutonic Order territory ruled from Königsberg (today's Kaliningrad). Royal Prussia, as a maritime trading hub, looked towards Lübeck, the Low Countries, Scandinavia, and England. It contained the Polish monarchy's only prince-bishopric (i.e. a theocratic enclave where the bishop was also secular ruler) in the form of Ermland (Warmia), the long-term home of Sigismund I's most famous subject, Nicholas Copernicus.[4]

Continuing with his sketch, Decius next introduced the Duke and duchy of Mazovia, 'a vassal of the kings of Poland'.[5] Mazovia, with its capital of Warsaw, lay geographically near the middle of the Polish monarchy. It was ruled by Duke Janusz III (1503–24), from a cadet branch of Poland's original royal family (Piasts). At Janusz's death, Sigismund I would oversee its legal incorporation in the *korona*.[6] Finally, Decius referred to the provinces of Ruthenia and Podolia, in the south-eastern reaches of the monarchy. These lands, populated chiefly by Orthodox Christians, had formed independent princedoms until the 1360s, when King Casimir the Great had annexed and incorporated them into the Polish Crown. These too formed part of the *korona*. Jutting out deep into present-day Ukraine, to the great fortress of Kamieniec Podolski on a cliff above a tributary of the Dniester, Rus and Podolia were the monarchy's frontier zone, dangerously exposed to raids by Tartars, Ottomans, and the princes of Moldavia. In Sigismund I's Poland, then, we have a monarchy consisting of a *korona* (Crown) with four constituent regions (Małopolska, Wielkopolska, Ruthenia, Podolia), plus a vassal duchy (Mazovia) and a semi-autonomous province (Royal Prussia). Decius did not, however, much discuss the Grand Duchy of Lithuania, the enormous polity which formed King Sigismund's family patrimony, and which had been intermittently ruled in personal union with Poland from 1386. It was only from 1569 that the Polish monarchy and grand duchy were legally fused into one commonwealth, and the Reformation in Orthodox-majority Lithuania in these years has a distinct story of its own.[7]

In common with sixteenth-century Europe's other composite monarchies, Jagiellonian Poland contained a cosmopolitan mix of peoples and languages. Royal Prussia was overwhelmingly German speaking, although many of its rural nobility had Polish names and operated in a bilingual world.[8] The mercantile elites of cities

---

[3] See Marian Biskup, *Wojny polski z zakonem krzyżackim, 1308–1521* (Gdańsk, 1993); Karin Friedrich, *The Other Prussia: Royal Prussia, Poland and Liberty, 1569–1772* (Cambridge, 2000).

[4] For the classic study, see Bogusław Leśnodorski, *Dominium Warmińskie, 1243–1569* (Poznań, 1949); also Stanisław Achremczyk, *Warmia*, 2nd edition (Olsztyn, 2011).

[5] Decius, *De Sigismundi*, fo. LVI, 'ducatus est Mazoviae, regibus Poloniae feudalis'.

[6] Piotr Węcowski, *Mazowsze w Koronie: Propaganda i legitymizacja władzy Kazimierza Jagiellończyka na Mazowszu* (Kraków, 2004).

[7] Robert Frost, *The Oxford History of Poland-Lithuania*, vol. 1 (Oxford, 2015); Antanas Musteikis, *The Reformation in Lithuania: Religious Fluctuations in the Sixteenth Century* (Boulder, 1988).

[8] For a recent study of Royal Prussian nobles, see Michał Targowski, *Na prawie polskim i niemieckim: kształtowanie się ziemskiej własności szlacheckiej na Pomorzu Gdańskim w XIII–XVI wieku* (Warsaw, 2014).

such as Kraków or Poznań often came originally from the Holy Roman Empire, and maintained links with kin in cities such as Nuremberg.[9] The Orthodox inhabitants of Podolia and Ruthenia spoke Rus, and lived alongside a significant Armenian community. There were sizeable Jewish populations in all the cities of the *korona*. Sigismund I himself was a grandson of the pagan Grand Duke of Lithuania, Jogaila (d.1434), who had come to Poland as a newly baptized bridegroom for Queen Jadwiga in 1386. If we wish to understand the events of the Reformation as they rocked this kingdom we need to see it not as modern nationalists have, as a Polish ethnic state with certain alien minorities of secondary historic importance, but as the King and his councillors saw it—as a monarchy of many parts, and many peoples—the 'regnum Poloniae'.

PEOPLE

This polity was ruled by Sigismund I (reigned 1506–48), the direct contemporary of Henry VIII (1509–47) and Francis I (1515–47), the most senior member of a successful international house which had for decades been second only to the Habsburgs in Christendom: Sigismund's brother and his descendants also ruled the kingdoms of Bohemia (from 1471) and Hungary (from 1490). Nonetheless, his reign is ill studied—minimally known in Western languages, and even in Polish Sigismund I has not yet been the subject of a research monograph/biography.[10] Subsequent chapters will make frequent reference to the actions of 'the Crown', and it is therefore worth pausing to introduce the dramatis personae who held high office during this reign. Decius' 1521 chronicle placed Sigismund I at the heart of its account, praising him as triumphant in war, 'just, pious, prudent, and virtuous'. Its frontispiece depicted him sitting in great majesty under a tasselled canopy. Sigismund Jagiellon had not been expected to wear a crown: born in January 1467, he was the fifth son of Casimir IV of Poland and his wife Elizabeth Habsburg. When Sigismund had moved with his long-term mistress, Catherin von Telnitz, to Silesia in 1501 to take up rule of the small territories of Glogau and Oppeln, granted to him by his oldest royal brother, he had seemed destined to remain a minor Central European princeling. However, the early deaths of his siblings and kings of Poland, John Albert (1492) and Alexander (1506), left that throne open. In December 1506, Sigismund was elected king by the royal council at Piotrków, and crowned early in 1507, three weeks after his fortieth birthday.[11] At the same time, he was acclaimed Grand Duke of Lithuania. He was the sixth elected king of Poland from

[9] Zdzisław Noga, *Krakowska rada miejska w XVI wieku: stadium o elicie władzy* (Kraków, 2003).
[10] The most comprehensive (but popular, and thus unfootnoted) account is by Andrzej Wyczański, *Zygmunt Stary* (Warsaw, 1985). Sigismund I's reign has instead been studied chiefly in the form of biographies of his ministers, secretaries, and queen: Anna Odrzywolska-Kidawa, *Biskup Piotr Tomicki (1464–1535): kariera polityczna i kościelna* (Warsaw, 2004) and *Podkanclerzy Piotr Tomicki (1515–35): polityk i humanista* (Warsaw, 2005); Piotr Tafiłowski, *Jan Łaski*; Andrzej Wyczański, *Między kulturą a polityką: sekretarze królewscy Zygmunta Starego (1506–48)* (Warsaw, 1990); Władysław Pociecha, *Królowa Bona (1494–1559): ludzie i czasy Odrodzenia*, 4 vols. (Poznań, 1949–58).
[11] Ludwig Finkiel, *Elekcya Zygmunta I* (Kraków, 1910).

what is now called the Jagiellonian line. It would be one of the longest reigns in Polish history, ending with his death in 1548 at the age of 81.

The image of Sigismund I which emerges in the *Acta Tomiciana*, the fullest collection of his letters, is of a serious, cautious, and in many ways conservative figure. Piety and wisdom were the leitmotifs of his self-image. In the King's prayer book, now held at the British Library, a miniature by Stanisław Samostrzelnik shows Sigismund I kneeling, receiving the Eucharist from the hands of the flagellated Christ.[12] In his funerary chapel in Kraków cathedral, sculpted by Florentine artists and with possible Neoplatonic motifs, the monarch was portrayed as King Solomon.[13] Sigismund I took counsel meticulously. In all the great crises of the reign which we will encounter—the Danzig revolt of 1525, the Kraków Treaty of 1525, the 1530 debate over Duke Albrecht's right to elect Polish kings—the royal council was consulted at length. This council, consisting of about forty men appointed for life, included all the kingdom's bishops, as well as the top lay officials appointed by the Crown—the chancellor, vice chancellor, treasurer, regional governors (*wojewoda*), and castellans.

In Sigismund I's reign, there was also a de facto inner council of the most trusted councillors, and it is their names which we will encounter most often. First among these was, without doubt, the strange double act of Krzysztof Szydłowiecki and Piotr Tomicki. Szydłowiecki, a close friend of Sigismund from the Silesian interlude, was an urbane, flamboyant figure from a minor noble family.[14] In 1515, Szydłowiecki and his clerical ally Piotr Tomicki were named Royal Chancellor and Vice Chancellor respectively. Sigismund I would rely heavily on this pair for the next twenty years. While Szydłowiecki enjoyed the prestige of his office, the Royal Chancellery was in effect run by Piotr Tomicki, the de facto first minister of the reign. Tomicki, born into a minor Wielkopolska noble family, had emerged in the first years of Sigismund I's reign as an effective envoy in foreign affairs, and was nominated by the Crown to the see of Przemyśl (1514).[15] After his breakthrough in 1515, Vice Chancellor Tomicki rose rapidly through the Polish church, promoted in 1520 to the see of Poznań and becoming bishop of Kraków in 1524. From 1514 until the early 1530s, when his influence was gradually eclipsed by Queen Bona Sforza, Piotr Tomicki was the King's factotum: advising on foreign policy, running the Chancellery, organizing the calling of sejms and local parliaments (*sejmiki*), giving counsel on nominations to royal office. He was a highly diligent Crown servant, often issuing royal papers from his sickbed during his regular bouts of illness. Tomicki also emerged as a key patron of humanist learning in Sigismund I's monarchy—the annotated Italian textbook from which he taught himself Greek can still be seen in the Jagiellonian Library, and he lured to Kraków University

---

[12] Barbara Miodońska, *Miniatury Stanisława Samostrzelnika* (Warsaw, 1983).

[13] Stanisław Mossakowski, *King Sigismund Chapel at Cracow Cathedral (1515–33)*, trans. Krystyna Malcharek (Kraków, 2012).

[14] Jerzy Kieszkowski, *Kanclerz Krzysztof Szydłowiecki: Z dziejów kultury i sztuki Zygmuntowskich czasów* (Poznań, 1912).

[15] For Tomicki's career, see Odrzywolska-Kidawa, *Biskup Piotr Tomicki* and *Podkanclerzy*.

the neo-Latin poet Rudolph Agricola Junior and a succession of Hebraists.[16] A lavish manuscript miniature painted by Samostrzelnik shows these three key figures of the reign together—Bishop Tomicki, King Sigismund I, and Krzysztof Szydłowiecki kneeling in trio before a giant figure of St Stanisław, patron saint of Poland, who holds a banner with the Polish arms and the King's 'S' monogram (Figure 0.1).[17]

Other high-profile members of the royal council in the 1520s and 1530s whom we shall encounter include Jan Łaski, archbishop of Gniezno and primate of Poland throughout the early Reformation (1510–31), uncle of the later reformer Jan Łaski the Younger. Primate Łaski had a reputation for being quarrelsome and prone to launching independent diplomatic initiatives; Sigismund I kept him politically at arm's length, and his influence lay chiefly in the ecclesiastical sphere.[18] Another key episcopal figure was Maciej Drzewicki. Born in 1467, Drzewicki had, as a royal official, been briefly imprisoned for fraud, before serving Sigismund I as Crown Chancellor from 1511 until 1515. He was nominated to the sees of Włocławek (1513–31) and, on Łaski's death, primatial Gniezno (1531–5).[19] Drzewicki is a gnomic figure, his letters sparse and cryptic, but he would emerge as a major player in Reformation policy.

There was also a younger generation of bishops who had risen to prominence under the patronage of King Sigismund I himself. The most dashing and gifted of them was Bishop Tomicki's nephew, Andrzej Krzycki (1482–1537), showered with benefices from childhood, who enjoyed a position as chief poet of the Kraków court, penning wedding poems and panegyrics, as well as satires and erotica.[20] Appointed bishop of Płock in Mazovia in 1527, Krzycki was named Primate of Poland in 1535, shortly before his death. Tomicki and Krzycki would differ sharply in their stance on Lutheranism. Other major players included the Danzig merchant's son Mauritius Ferber (1471–1537), the prince-bishop of Ermland and top cleric in Royal Prussia, and Jan Chojeński (1486–1538), bishop of Przemyśl, who emerged in the early 1530s as the old king's most trusted secretary.[21] Another heavyweight was Johannes Dantiscus (1485–1548), son of a Danzig burgher family, who enjoyed a spectacular career as King Sigismund's chief diplomat, following Charles V's court across Europe and befriending everyone from Hernan Cortes, conqueror of Mexico, to Alfonso de Valdés, Imperial Chancellor.[22] In 1533, Dantiscus switched to an ecclesiastical career, when he was offered the Prussian see of Kulm

---

[16] BJ, inc. nr. 2636; Jacqueline Glomski, *Patronage and Humanist Literature in the Age of the Jagiellons: Court and Career in the Writings of Rudolf Agricola Junior, Valentin Eck and Leonard Cox* (Toronto, 2007); Odrzywolska-Kidawa, *Podkanclerzy*, pp. 237–50.

[17] BN, COZ Cim 5 (*Vitae episcoporum Cracoviensium*); Miodońska, *Miniatury*, pp. 26–7.

[18] See Tafiłowski, *Jan Łaski* and Stanisław Grad, *Kościelna działalność arcybiskupa i prymasa Jana Łaskiego* (Warsaw, 1979).

[19] Władysław Pociecha, 'Maciej Drzewicki', *PSB* 5 (1939), pp. 409–12.

[20] Stefan Zabłocki, 'Andrzej Krzycki', *PSB* 15 (1970), pp. 544–9; Leszek Barszcz, *Andrzej Krzycki: poeta, dyplomata, prymas* (Gniezno, 2005).

[21] Henryk Zins, *Ród Ferberów i jego rola w dziejach Gdańska w XV i XVI wieku* (Lublin, 1951).

[22] Władysław Pociecha, 'Dantyszek (von Höfen, Flaschbinder)', *PSB* 4 (1938), pp. 424–30. See the *Corpus of Johannes Dantiscus' Texts*.

Figure 0.1 Saint Stanisław with Bishop Piotr Tomicki, King Sigismund I, and Chancellor Krzysztof Szydłowiecki, painted by Stanisław Samostrzelnik. In Jan Długosz, *Catalogus archi-episcoporum Gnesnensium; Vitae episcoporum Cracoviensium, 1531–35;* Biblioteka Narodowa, Rps BOZ 5.

Source: polana.pl. Reproduced with permission.

(1533–7), and later Ermland (1537–48), roles which placed him on the Reformation front line. These, then, are the principle names one will encounter in a narrative of Lutheranism in King Sigismund's monarchy.

TEXTS

As nineteenth- and early twentieth-century Polish and German scholars well knew, the sources for early Lutheranism and official responses to it in Sigismund I's Poland are rich and varied. The key source used in this study is the invaluable collection known as the *Acta Tomiciana*. When Piotr Tomicki died in autumn 1535, his secretary Stanisław Górski preserved his master's papers. This vast set of documents included the correspondence of the King and royal council, diplomatic texts, royal decrees, poems, and fragments of polemic, dating from *c.*1506 to Tomicki's death.[23] Since the 1850s, a printed *Acta Tomiciana* has been published in Poland in eighteen volumes, drawing on the surviving (and variant) manuscripts collectively.[24] Górski's *Acta Tomiciana* come to an end in 1535, at which point this rich window onto the court and reign of Sigismund I closes. The later years of Sigismund I's rule are much harder for the historian to penetrate. This study focuses on the years to *c.*1535, in large part, because that is where in the *Acta Tomiciana* our sources lie, but also because the death of Piotr Tomicki itself represented the closing of a major political chapter. The *Acta Tomiciana* end at the point where a whole 'golden generation' of men who had shaped Sigismund I's reign passed away: his Chancellor Szydłowiecki, Primates Łaski, Drzewicki, and Krzycki, as well as Piotr Tomicki himself. With the deaths of these friends and counsellors, the King seems to have retreated increasingly from public life, giving Queen Bona Sforza and her own client network space to take centre stage. As with Elizabeth I of England, therefore, we can talk of a 'second reign' of Sigismund I, from *c.*1535.[25]

Alongside the *Acta Tomiciana*, royal and episcopal policy towards the Reformation can be traced in a number of further published collections: of papal letters, instructions for papal nuncios, episcopal correspondence from Kulm and Ermland, the acts of the Prussian local diet, and letters exchanged between King Sigismund and Duke Albrecht.[26] Diocesan archives—in Kraków, Gniezno, Poznań,

---

[23] The chief study of the *Acta Tomiciana* is Ryszard Marciniak, *Acta Tomiciana w kulturze politycznej Polski okresu odrodzenia* (Warsaw, 1983).

[24] *Acta Tomiciana*, 18 vols, ed. Władysław Pociecha, Wacław Urban, Andrzej Wyczański et al. (1852–1999).

[25] J. A. Guy, *The Reign of Elizabeth I: Court and Culture in the Last Decade* (Cambridge, 1995).

[26] Augustin Theiner, *Vetera monumenta poloniae et lithuaniae gentiumque finitimarum historiam illustrantia*, 4 vols. (Rome, 1860–4); Henryk Wojtyska (ed.), *Zacharias Ferreri (1519–1521) et nuntii minores (1522–53)* (Rome, 1992); Oswald Balzer, *Corpus iuris polonici*, vols. 1–4 (Kraków, 1906–10); *Elementa ad Fontium Editiones XXX: Documenta ex archivo Regiomontano ad Poloniam spectantia*, part 1, Karolina Łanckorońska (ed.) (Rome, 1973); Paul Tschackert, *Urkundenbuch zur Reformationsgeschichte des Herzogthums Preussen*, 3 vols. (Leipzig, 1890); Ursula Benninghoven, *Die Herzöge in Preussen und das Bistum Kulm (1525–1691): Regesten aus dem Herzoglichen Briefarchiv und den Ostpreussischen Folianten* (Köln, 1993); and Stefan Hartmann, *Herzog Albrecht von Preussen und das Bistum Ermland: Regesten aus dem Herzoglichen Briefarchiv und den ostpreussischen Folianten*, 2 vols. (Köln, 1991–3).

Olsztyn (Allenstein), and Włocławek—contain a wealth of information on responses to Lutheranism and heresy trials. In all these dioceses, cathedral chapter acts, episcopal letters and the records of the bishop's court (where extant) have been examined. Although the special volume of heresy trials kept by the bishopric of Kraków in the 1520s and 1530s disappeared at an unknown point in/after the 1970s, it can be reconstructed in part from the notes and papers of the historian Żegota Pauli.[27] The Vatican Archive in Rome also sheds light on anti-Reformation activity in the kingdom. Sixteenth-century printed books are another major source: the chronicle of the Danzig Dominican Simon Grunau, synod statutes for Polish dioceses, dedicatory letters addressed to Polish dignitaries, and a substantial corpus of locally authored religious polemic.[28]

Most, but not all, of these sources were known to either the Polish or German historians who wrote on the Reformation under Sigismund I in the period *c*.1870–1940, but this corpus of evidence has not yet been pulled together and analysed collectively. Having said that, this book makes no claims to have tracked down every surviving document relating to the early Reformation in the Polish monarchy: the task of a lifetime. There are many more books which could be written on the Reformation under Sigismund I, not least on the Danzig Reformation alone. This is not a definitive and exhaustive account, but a study and an interpretation with a specific focus—on responses to, and perceptions of, Lutheranism by the Polish Crown and church from *c*.1518 to *c*.1535.

[27] The missing volume is AKMK, AE 2 (1510–82); I am very grateful to Elżbieta Knapek for pointing me in the direction of Pauli's papers. The missing volume was cited extensively by Bukowski, *Dzieje Reformacyi* and by Kazimierz Gabryel, *Działalność kościelna Piotra Tomickiego, 1464–1535* (Warsaw, 1972). Curiously, copies of Gabryel's work in certain UK libraries have missing pages, corresponding exactly to his chapter on the Kraków heresy manuscript.

[28] On polemic, see Natalia Nowakowska, 'High Clergy and Printers: Anti-Reformation Polemic in the Kingdom of Poland, 1520–36', *Historical Research* 87 (2014): 43–64 and 'Lamenting the Church? Bishop Andrzej Krzycki and Early Reformation Polemic', in Almut Suerbaum, George Southcombe, and Benjamin Thompson (eds), *Polemic: Language as Violence in Medieval and Early Modern Discourse* (Aldershot, 2015), pp. 223–36.

1

A New Narrative?
The Polish Monarchy and the Early Reformation (1517–*c*.1540)

'This Lutheran disease has spread here in this place and all around it on every side, so that it reaches my subjects, especially the Germans.'

Sigismund I to Clement VII, 1525[1]

'It was only from the middle of the sixteenth century that the Reformation developed in Poland openly and with speed.'

Janusz Tazbir, 1975.[2]

INTRODUCTION

If one characteristic of scholarship on the early Reformation in the Polish monarchy is its paucity, another is the highly fragmented nature of what has been written in the past 150 years.[3] That fragmentation denies us even a full working narrative of Lutheranism under King Sigismund I. Remarkably, the most basic facts about the early Reformation in this polity are heavily disputed. The quotes above embody two disconcertingly contradictory positions—while King Sigismund himself lamented a veritable deluge of Lutheranism within his lands in the 1520s, the leading post-war historian of the Polish Reformation, Janusz Tazbir, has repeatedly asserted that no such thing happened.[4] Here we have the early Reformation in this part of Christendom as a major event, or as non-event. We possess three book-length narratives of Lutheranism in the Polish monarchy in the 1520s and 1530s, and all are a little dusty. These authoritative accounts were penned well over a century ago, in three significant monographs produced within forty years of one another. They are Wincenty Zakrzewski's *Powstanie i wzrost Reformacji w Polsce* (Warsaw, 1870), Julian Bukowski's two-volume *Dzieje Reformacyi w Polsce* (Kraków, 1883) (a tome so old even the spelling of its title is now antiquated), and Theodor

---

[1] Theiner, *Vetera monumenta*, vol. II, p. 427: 'adeo enim hec pernicies Luterana diffusa est hic circumquaque, ut etiam ad subditos meos usque, Germanos presertim, permeet et inundet'.

[2] Tazbir, 'Społeczny i terytorialny zasięg', p. 723: 'Dopiero od połowy XVI w. ma miejsce szybki rozwój jawnego ruchu reformacyjnego.'

[3] See Introduction, pp. 3–6.

[4] Tazbir, *Reformacja*, pp. 7–9 as limited underground networks.

Wotschke's *Reformation in Polen* (1911).[5] These books—produced respectively in the Russian, Austrian, and Prussian sectors of a partitioned Poland—do not tell the same story. In other words, not only are our existing narratives of these events old, they also disagree. All three authors defined 'Poland' differently according to their personal preferences or patriotic inclinations, discussing different collections of territories under that title, a pick-and-mix approach producing quite different conclusions.[6] They also wrote from different confessional viewpoints: Bukowski was a prominent catholic priest in Kraków, and Wotschke a vocal Lutheran pastor.[7] Two of these landmark studies are in Polish, espousing a Polish national perspective; Wotschke, meanwhile, wrote as a German nationalist. Moreover, these books used different sources to tell the story/stories of the early Reformation in King Sigismund's Poland: Bukowski drew on archives and libraries in Kraków, Wotschke on materials from Poznań and Germany. Gerhard Schramm and Wojciech Kreigseisen have incorporated brief summaries of this older literature, or parts of it, in their recent wider works on the Reformation.[8] Nonetheless, we still do not have a single, joined-up master narrative of Lutheranism in this kingdom in the 1520s and 1530s.

This chapter therefore seeks to offer the reader a new integrated, updated narrative of the Reformation in the Polish monarchy from 1517 to *c*.1540. What follows is the fullest account of these events in English, and the first to cross-reference systematically the stories told by Zakrzewski, Bukowski, and Wotschke a century or more ago.[9] It augments them with recent research findings, published piecemeal and often in local history journals by Polish historians since the early twentieth century—findings which have not been integrated into a single, bigger, panoramic account of the Reformation in the 1520s and 1530s in this monarchy. This narrative also incorporates information from new source material found in the course of research for this book. After the linguistic turn, cultural turn, and visual/material turn, writing a bird's-eye narrative can feel and look wilfully old-fashioned. However, in order to deconstruct grand national Reformation narratives one needs to have narratives to deconstruct; and some European countries, due to violent clashes in their modern histories, do not have even that.

This chapter provides an outer framework for the chapters which follow, by offering a narrative in three sections—early signs (1517–24), the great Reformation year (1525), and aftershocks (1526–*c*.1540). It addresses the challenges of measuring Lutheran sentiment in the pre-confessional environment of the 1520s and 1530s, sets these Polish-Prussian events in their comparative European context, and considers what implications they might have for that bigger, familiar tale. As explained

---

[5] Bukowski, *Dzieje Reformacyi*; Zakrzewski, *Powstanie i zwrost*; Wotschke, *Reformation in Polen*.

[6] Bukowski's narrative included Silesia (once part of the Polish Crown, but by the sixteenth century in the kingdom of Bohemia), Royal Prussia, the *korona*, and Lithuania; Wotschke discussed Małopolska, Wielkopolska, Mazovia, and Lithuania, omitting Royal Prussia; Zakrzewski excluded Royal Prussia on the grounds that it was not 'Polish'. See Nowakowska, 'Forgetting Lutheranism', p. 298.

[7] Henryk Barycz, 'Udział Teodora Wotschkiego w rozwoju badań nad dziejami ruchu reformacyjnego w Polsce', *RwP* XI (1948–52): 115–22.

[8] Kriegseisen, *Stosunki wyznaniowe*, pp. 430–53; Schmidt, *Auf Felsen gesät*.

[9] For English-language summaries, see p. 4.

in the previous chapter, this account will treat Sigismund I's polity as the typical early modern composite state it was, consisting of a Polish 'Crown' of four areas (Greater Poland, Lesser Poland, Ruthenia, Podolia), the coastal province of Royal Prussia, and two vassal duchies, Mazovia and (from 1525) Ducal Prussia.[10]

'The Kingdom is a Gateway': Early Signs, 1517–24

In autumn 1517, Martin Luther issued his Ninety-Five Theses on indulgences in Wittenberg; according to tradition, just a few months later (1518) the Dominican Jakub Knade started preaching Reformation sermons in Danzig, the Polish monarchy's principal port.[11] Connections between the Polish monarchy and the jigsaw of peoples and territories which formed the Holy Roman Empire were dense in the opening decades of the sixteenth century. In building up the small university town of Wittenberg, the Elector of Saxony, Frederick the Wise (1463–1525), had hoped to lure travellers off the 'hohe Landstrasse', the great trade road connecting Poland and the Empire which lay beyond the settlement.[12] A second major trade route linked Lwów, Kraków, and Silesia with the southern Empire. Meanwhile, the chief sea ports of Sigismund I's monarchy, Danzig and Elbing, were members of the Hanseatic League, with its headquarters in Lübeck.[13] Dynastic and courtly connections were extensive too. King Sigismund's sisters, Jadwiga, Sophie, and Barbara, had been married to the major princely houses of the eastern Empire: to the Wittelsbach princes of Bavaria-Landshut, the Hohenzollern margraves of Brandenburg-Ansbach, and the Wettin lords of Saxony. Many of the princes of the Empire were Sigismund I's nephews; another nephew, Louis II, king of Hungary and Bohemia (1516–26), was, by virtue of those titles, an Elector of the Holy Roman Empire. King Sigismund's predecessor, Alexander, had once complained to Rome that 'My kingdom is transversable', its territories one great plain—he had been referring to the ease with which Ottoman or Tartar armies might pour across its eastern borders, but he could equally well have been referring to the porousness of that monarchy's western, 'German' frontier.[14]

The first years of the Luther affair (1517–21) coincided with a particularly fraught moment in the Polish Crown's relationship with the Empire. As Luther disputed, published and hid, not far to the east King Sigismund of Poland was preparing for

---

[10] The precise legal vassal relationship between the Crown and its vassal duchies was examined by Adam Vetulani, *Lenno pruskie: od traktatu krakowskiego do śmierci księcia Albrechta, 1525–68: studium historyczno-prawne* (Kraków, 1930).

[11] Zbigniew Nowak and Janina Urban, 'Pankracy Klemme: Gdański działacz reformacyjny i jego księgozbiór', *Rocznik Biblioteki Narodowej* IV (1968): 107–40, at p. 109. See also Paul Simson, 'Wann hat der Danziger Priester Jakob Knothe geheiratet?', *Mitteilungen des Westpreussischen Geschichtsvereins* 14 (1915): 2–3.

[12] Rublack, *Reformation Europe*, p. 19.

[13] For trade routes, see Jerzy Topolski, 'Wielkopolska na europejskich szlakach handlowych', in Jerzy Topolski (ed.), *Dzieje Wielkopolski do roku 1793* (Poznań, 1969), pp. 476–9.

[14] *Akta Aleksandra*, ed. Fryderyk Papée (Kraków, 1927), p. 445: 'Regnum nostrum pervium est, non portuosum, nec ullis montibus ac vallibus impeditum, sed ubique planum…' (1504).

war.[15] His opponent was his own nephew, Albrecht of Brandenburg-Ansbach, scion of an important German princely family and, from 1510, Grand Master of the Teutonic Knights in Prussia. Between 1519 and 1521, in the biggest military effort of Sigismund's forty-year reign, the Polish Crown engaged the Teutonic Knights on land and sea.[16] In summer 1520, Albrecht besieged and bombarded Danzig itself, and the Order's campaign was much strengthened by forces successfully recruited from Germany.[17]

It was German-speaking Royal Prussia, its towns besieged and its countryside devastated in the vicious conflict of 1519–21, where Luther's ideas first aroused interest. Zbigniew Nowak and Janina Urban have demonstrated that no fewer than twenty-seven editions of Luther's works were circulating in Danzig by 1520.[18] In 1521, the parish priest of Saint Barbara's church in Danzig was staying in Wittenberg, enthusiastically sending chests of Lutheran books back to the port, while within the city walls Hans Weinreich started to print Luther's work on the Ten Commandments, as well as satires against monks and the pope.[19] In Danzig and Elbing, in the 'strange carnival-tide' of 1522, the Luther affair was mockingly staged, with the monk and pontiff shooting fireworks at one another, while books were burnt by the excited, anti-clerical crowds.[20] The Dominican Knade was certainly not the only man preaching Reformation sermons in an increasingly raucous Danzig. Johannes Böschenstein, a professor of Hebrew from Ingolstadt who had spent time with Luther in Wittenberg, was reported to be preaching in the port *c.*1520.[21] Also active were a new class of local alumnae of Wittenberg. Enrollments of Danzigers at the Saxon university had risen three-fold with the start of the Luther Affair (overtaking Kraków University as a destination of choice), and upon returning home many of these graduates agitated for the Reformation.[22] Among them was Jakub Hegge, who in July 1522 delivered an inflammatory sermon against the clerical hierarchy on a hill outside Danzig. By autumn, his unofficial outdoor sermons were attracting such crowds that merchants petitioned the city council for these Wittenberg preachers to be given their own church.[23] In Marienburg, the monumental fortress-town built by the Teutonic Knights, Jakub Knade came to preach, and the local council installed another 'Lutheran' priest in its parish church.[24] In the countryside, Cistercians in Oliwa and Peplin

[15] For the road to war, see Władysław Pociecha, *Geneza hołdu pruskiego (1467–1525)* (Warsaw, 1937), pp. 30–88.

[16] Marian Biskup, *'Wojna Pruska' czyli walka Polski z zakonem krzyżackim z lat 1519–21* (Olsztyn, 1991); Hubatsch, *Albrecht von Brandenburg-Ansbach.*

[17] Edmund Cieślak, *Historia Gdańska*, vol. II (Danzig, 1982), pp. 279–80.

[18] Nowak and Urban, 'Pankracy Klemme', p. 109.

[19] Nowak and Urban, 'Pankracy Klemme', p. 109; Arnold, 'Luther und Danzig', p. 101.

[20] Simon Grunau, *Simon Grunau's Preussische Chronik*, ed. Max Perlbach, 3 vols. (Leipzig, 1875–96), vol. II, pp. 646–7; Paul Simson, *Geschichte der Stadt Danzig* (Danzig, 1918), vol. II, p. 50.

[21] Bukowski, *Dzieje Reformacyi*, p. 94; Urban and Nowak, 'Pankracy Klemme', p. 110.

[22] Arnold, 'Luther und Danzig', pp. 102–3; Marian Biskup, 'O początkach reformacji luterańskiej w Prusach Królewskich', *Kwartalnik Historyczny* 4 (1993): 101–12, at p. 103.

[23] Bogucka, 'Walki społeczne', pp. 382–3.   [24] Biskup, 'O początkach', p. 105.

were told by local nobles to leave their monastery and go beg for alms in the streets of Danzig.[25]

After a four-year truce was agreed between King Sigismund and Grand Master Albrecht in 1521, Danzig fast slid towards political disorder, with the Reformation preachers as key players in this drama. The city was ruled by a closed caste of merchant families who inherited their places on the Rat (council), and by 1521 Danzig had been involved in a long series of Baltic wars, was heavily indebted, levying punitive taxes and facing growing popular unrest.[26] In 1522, the city's flamboyant, litigious, Crown-appointed mayor Eberhard Ferber (1464–1529) was expelled in a coup by fellow councillors. In approval, angry crowds smashed up his family's grand tombs in St Mary's parish church.[27] The new council, with its mayor Matthias Lang, now aligned itself with the religious reforms coming out of Wittenberg. It appointed the Wittenberg graduate and Franciscan, Alexander Svenichen, as the city's reformer, and in February 1524 confirmed that only the pure Word of God, without any human adulteration, be preached in Danzig.[28] This is what historians often term a 'preaching mandate'. However, this did not satisfy the more radical activists such as Knade, Hegge, or Ambrose Hitfelt. They formed their own alternative Rat, headed by a blacksmith, which met in a cemetery.[29] They incited their followers to perform acts of iconoclasm, and requisition treasure from Danzig convents as communal property. In the archives of the Ermland diocese, there is preserved a small sheet of paper from this time—a plea for help, in tiny handwriting, sent to the bishop by the clergy of Saint Mary's in Danzig. 'The ferment of the common people against us grows bigger and bigger and we are afraid', they wrote, talking insistently of 'the pleb', 'this Lutheran infection', and 'the disturbance of all things'.[30]

Sympathy for Martin Luther within the Polish monarchy was not, however, confined to Royal Prussia alone in the early 1520s. In Poznań, in western Poland, the bookseller Dominic Munner was apprehended in 1522 for importing a cargo of Melanchthon's works from Breslau.[31] Vice-Chancellor Tomicki wrote to the royal governor of western Poland, Łukasz Górka, that 'I hear that in the city of Poznań, where you are, every day the Lutheran sect is growing more and more, and does so with complete impunity.'[32] In Gniezno, the church authorities apprehended a German named Pancratius in 1524, who was preaching Lutheranism in

---

[25] Biskup, 'O początkach', p. 110.

[26] For a fuller discussion, see Bogucka, 'Walki społeczne'.   [27] Zins, *Ród Ferberów*, pp. 67–73.

[28] Bogucka, 'Walki społeczne', pp. 384–5; Teresa Borawska and Henryk Reitz, 'Alexander Svenichen: ein Preussischer Franziskaner in den Wirren des Reformationzeitalters', in Udo Arnold et al. (eds), *Preussische Landesgeschichte: Festschrift für Bernhart Jähnig* (Marburg, 2001), pp. 175–86.

[29] Arnold, 'Luther und Danzig'; Bogucka, 'Walki społeczne', pp. 384–6. For a list of lapsed monks banished from the city by Bishop Drzewicki in 1526, which includes radical preachers, see *Urkundenbuch*, vol. II, pp. 171–2.

[30] AAWa, D66, fo. 74 (March 1523): 'Verum cum indito magis ac magis fermentijs in nos plebuis imprimus crescat temeritasque...', 'hec Lutherana contagione', 'omnium rerum peturbationem'.

[31] Maria Wojciechowska, *Z dziejów książki w Poznaniu w XVI wieku* (Poznań, 1927), p. 96.

[32] AT 6, p. 87 (*c.*1522): 'audio pullulare istic in civitate posnaniensi indies magis sectam luteranam et omnia impune geri'.

Wielkopolska.[33] The Crown received reports of Lutheran agitation, rioting, and the deposition of local officials in a string of towns on the Polish-Silesian/Bohemian border, and sent special commissioners to Kościan, Wschowa, and Międzyrzecz.[34] In Kraków, the humanist Andrzej Frycz Modrewski later claimed, recalling his undergraduate days, that the university and town had been awash with Lutheran books in the 1520s, openly sold and openly read.[35] The kingdom saw its first hearings for Lutheranism in 1522, when the rector of Kraków University summoned before his court the student Joachim of Loewenburg, and the episcopal court of Kraków tried a priest called Marcin Bayer, originally from the Carpathian mountain town of Biecz.[36] In the royal court itself, complaints were made that King Sigismund's talented, polished gaggle of royal secretaries freely discussed Luther and joked about the church over their dinners.[37] King Sigismund's Alsatian secretary, Jodos Ludovicus Decius, was denounced as a Lutheran heretic by the bishop of Kamieniec. Decius professed his innocence, but nonetheless visited Martin Luther in Wittenberg the following year, in 1522.[38] This same pilgrimage was made by Johannes Dantiscus, the Crown's top diplomat; upon reaching Spain, his household was investigated for Lutheran heresy by the Spanish Inquisition, and Dantiscus himself subjected to highly uncomfortable questioning by Charles V.[39]

Faced with these geographically disparate bubblings of pro-Luther interest, the Crown and church took steps against them. While holding court in Thorn, surrounded by his military commanders, the King became aware of the presence of Lutheran books in Danzig. In May 1520, Sigismund I issued an edict addressed to 'the mayor, councillors and entire community of our city of Danzig', banning Luther's works outright.[40] Also present in Thorn was the dynamic papal nuncio Zachariah Ferreri who, in spring 1521, read the papal bull against Luther, *Decet Romanum Pontificem*, in the town's main square, before burning Lutheran books, along with an effigy of the Saxon friar himself in the form of a devil.[41] Jan Konarski, the mild and enigmatic bishop of Kraków, had the anti-Lutheran papal bull *Exsurge domine* printed for his diocese, with a foreword urging people to shun the new 'errors'.[42] The busy clerks of the royal chancellery, meanwhile, promulgated six royal anti-Luther edicts for the monarchy between 1520 and 1525.[43] Anti-Reformation polemics began to roll off the printing presses of Kraków, authored by senior

---

[33] AAG, A. Cons. A84, fo. 39v.

[34] CIP, III, pp. 114–17; Gabryel, *Działalność kościelna*, p. 315; on Wschowa, see Jolanta Dworzaczkowa, *Reformacja i kontrreformacja w Wielkopolsce* (Poznań, 1995), p. 58.

[35] Barycz, *Historia uniwersytetu*, p. 98.

[36] Barycz, *Historia uniwersytetu*, p. 99; Wacław Urban, 'Reformacja mieszczańska na dawnym powiecie bieckim', *OiRwP* VI (1961): 139–74, at p. 149.

[37] Pociecha, *Królowa Bona*, II, pp. 26–7.

[38] The documents relating to this incident were published by Zakrzewski, *Powstanie i wzrost*, pp. 226–7; Maria Cytowska, 'Justus Ludovicus Decius', in Peter G. Bietenholz and Thomas B. Deutscher (eds), *Contemporaries of Erasmus: A Biographical Register of the Renaissance and Reformation*, vol. 1 (Toronto, 1985), pp. 380–2.

[39] AT 8, pp. 362–3; Pociecha, 'Dantyszek', p. 426.   [40] CIP, III, nr. 234, p. 579.

[41] Wojtyska, *Zacharias Ferreri*, pp. 118–19.

[42] Jan Konarski, *Bulla contra errores Martini Luterij* (Kraków, 1520).   [43] See Chapter Five.

clergy—an oration by Nuncio Ferreri, vituperative pamphlets by Canon Piotr Rydziński, and the satire *Encomia Luteri* by Bishop Andrzej Krzycki, which was soon reprinted across the Holy Roman Empire.[44] All these early signs of *luteranismus* in the Polish monarchy were, however, simply the start. Sigismund I's Poland was set for its great Reformation year of 1525.

1525: The Year of Revolutions

1525 was, famously, the most dramatic year of the early European Reformation— the year in which the ex-monk Martin Luther (to the scandal of many) took the ex-nun Katharina von Bora as his wife, and a peasant rising unprecedented in its scale and violence threatened to shatter the social order of the Holy Roman Empire. In just nine months, from January to September 1525, the Reformation would also shake and transform Sigismund I's Polish monarchy.

Danzig

On Sunday 22 January 1525, a full-scale, popular Reformation revolt exploded in Danzig. That morning, as Dr Svenichen mounted the pulpit of St Mary's to preach, he was physically assaulted by an artisan who insisted that friars had no right to speak. Jakub Hegge preached in the same church that afternoon: one of his listeners brandished a sword and called on followers of the Word to defend it, whereupon the armed congregation flooded onto the streets and headed for the *Rathaus*.[45] The council locked the city's internal gates and strung chains across major streets, but by Monday morning they had been forced to capitulate to Hegge's massed followers. The rebels presented Twelve Articles setting out their demands: their own council of twelve was to enjoy co-rule of the city (with cooperating remnants of the previous council), free fishing rights for all, preaching of the pure Word, the round- ing up of all Danzig's monks and friars into one house, the election of parish clergy, and the punishment of adulterers and prostitutes.[46] The ringleaders later identified by the Crown included sailors, goldsmiths, tavern workers, and bag-makers.[47] Throughout the long year of 1525, the Reformation in Danzig continued apace, chiefly in the hands of the storm-preachers. At the new council's request, Luther himself sent from Wittenberg two preachers, Michael Meurer and Arnold Warwick.[48] Contemporaries claimed that the rebels instituted a reign of terror in the city, erecting a gibbet and wheel in the town square to intimidate opponents.[49]

---

[44] Zaccaria Ferreri, *Oratio Legati Apostolici Habita Thorunij in Prussia ad Serenissimum Poloniae Regem contra Errores Fratris Martini Lutheri* (Kraków, 1521), also published in Wojtyska, *Zacharias Ferreri*, pp. 108–16; Piotr Rydziński, *Petri Risinii in Iohannis Hessi* and *In Axiomata Ioannis Hessi Wratislaviae edita* (Kraków, 1524); Andrzej Krzycki, *Encomia Luteri* (Kraków, 1524).

[45] Zins, *Ród Ferberów*, p. 81; Bogucka, 'Walki społeczne', p. 389.

[46] For the Twelve Articles, see AT 7, pp. 392–3; Tadeusz Cieślak, 'Postulaty rewolty pospólstwa gdańskiego w r. 1525', *Czasopismo Prawno-Historyczne* VI (1954): 123–52; Bogucka, 'Walki społeczne', pp. 389–90.

[47] *Elementa*, pp. 18–19.   [48] Bogucka, 'Walki społeczne', p. 395.

[49] AT 8, pp. 102–3.

Danzig was not the only town in Royal Prussia to experience a full Reformation-inspired revolt in early 1525.[50] In the Hanseatic town of Elbing, on 6 February, the preacher Matthias Bienwald led a crowd which successfully overthrew the council, closed the Dominican convent and confiscated its silver.[51] In Braunsberg (Braniewo), the chief town of the Ermland prince-bishopric, the council was ejected by Reformation-inspired rebels in May.[52] The Dominican chronicler, Simon Grunau, claimed that Lutherans desecrated the parish church, pouring urine into communion goblets, smearing dog faeces on the altar, and sitting around eating sausages and radishes.[53] At Christmas Mass 1525, Braunsberg's mayor Georg Rabe allegedly disrupted the service by running around the parish church dressed as a bear.[54] We shall see below just how precocious all these events were, in a European context. The Danzig rebels, reflecting on them, declared that the Word of God had descended to Prussia from Heaven 'like a precious pearl'; for Sigismund I, it must have seemed as if a wild spirit had blown from Wittenberg and gripped the cities of his most affluent territory.[55]

Kraków

A revolution of quite a different sort took place in Kraków's market square in April 1525. In one of the most heavily mythologized scenes in Polish history, Grand Master Albrecht of Brandenburg and King Sigismund participated in a ceremony to mark the eleventh-hour peace treaty they had hastily concluded, just before the expiry of their 1521 truce. This 'concord and perpetual peace', known as the Treaty of Kraków, was audacious.[56] Both parties agreed to dissolve unilaterally the monastic order of the Teutonic Knights in Prussia, converting its lands into a secular duchy. The new duchy would be ruled by Albrecht as its hereditary prince, but as a vassal state of King Sigismund of Poland. In the square, Albrecht von Hohenzollern knelt before his royal uncle, swore fealty, and was invested as duke in Prussia. Albrecht was given a new coat of arms, a black eagle stamped with the letter S

---

[50] Thorn city council had been overthrown by an angry crowd in 1523. It is still debated whether this was a Reformation event, although the rebels demanded that parish priests fulfil their pastoral duties and that the 'Word of God' be respected. See Marian Biskup, *U schyłku średniowiecza i w początkach odrodzenia: (1454–1548)*, Historia Torunia (Toruń, 1992), pp. 214–17.

[51] See Stanisław Waldoch, 'Początki reformacji w Elblągu i jego regionie', *Rocznik Elbląski* IV (1969): 9–43 and Pawlak, *Reformacja*, pp. 5–19.

[52] For the Reformation in Braunsberg, see Stanisław Achremczyk and Alojzy Szorc, *Braniewo* (Olsztyn, 1995), pp. 57–9. Braunsberg was occupied by Grand Master Albrecht during the 1521–5 truce, and as such was subject to the Lutheran reforms he rolled out in his territories (see the section 'Königsberg').

[53] Grunau, *Preussische Chronik*, vol. III, pp. 214–17. On Grunau, see Chapter Seven, p. 174.

[54] Achremczyk and Szorc, *Braniewo*, p. 59. In 1525, Sigismund I threatened Braunsberg with a 3,000 mark fine unless local councillors returned land seized from the Ermland cathedral chapter: AAWa, Doc Kap Z4.

[55] AT 7, p. 367, 'hoc preciosum margaritum in regiam urbem gedanensem advectum est'.

[56] 'Concordia et pax perpetua': AT 7, pp. 227–34. See also Pociecha, *Geneza hołdu*; Marian Biskup, 'Geneza i znaczenie hołdu pruskiego 1525', *Komunikaty Mazursko-Warmińskie* 4 (1975): 407–24 and Maria Bogucka and Klaus Zernack, *Um die säkularisation des Deutschens Ordens in Preussen* (Hannover, 1996).

(for 'Sigismundus'). A *Te Deum* was sung, and all parties attended Mass in Kraków cathedral.[57] Every community in the new duchy would be required to swear an oath of loyalty to King Sigismund I.[58]

This ceremony, much agonized over by the Polish royal council, had radical implications for a number of reasons. It marked, firstly, a major diplomatic reconfiguration in northern Europe. For two hundred years, major wars had been fought between the Polish Crown and the Teutonic Knights for control of the Baltic littoral (e.g. 1410, 1454–66, 1519–21).[59] With the Treaty, however, the Teutonic Order in Prussia and the threat it had long represented vanished as if into thin air, and Central European geopolitics was realigned. It was also a religious revolution. This treaty shocked the pope and emperor, not just because it unapologetically secularized church land and appropriated it for the Polish monarchy, but also because it legitimized Albrecht of Brandenburg himself, a prominent early supporter of Luther. Albrecht would later claim that he had been converted to Luther's teaching when hearing a sermon in Nuremberg by Andreas Osiander in 1522. The Grand Master spent time in Wittenberg itself, locked in discussion with Luther, while clergy appointed by Albrecht from 1523 preached evangelical sermons in Königsberg cathedral.[60] The Polish Crown had thus elevated, and embraced as its vassal, one of Europe's first Lutheran princes.

Königsberg

After spring 1525, emboldened by his new title and the protection of his uncle, Duke Albrecht embarked on an outright Lutheran reform of the Duchy of Prussia. In December 1525—as the mayor of Braunsberg made mischief at Christmas worship—the diet of Ducal Prussia met for the first time, approved a new Lutheran liturgy, and issued a Luther-inspired Ecclesiastical Ordinance.[61] Visitations were ordered throughout the former *Ordenstaat*, introducing the Reformation parish by parish, handing out copies of the duchy's new ecclesiastical Ordinances and Luther's works.[62] The Wittenberg graduate Michael Meurer, for example, was sent to proselytize Duke Albrecht's Polish-speaking subjects in the parishes of Mazuria (Mazury).[63] The celebrated, international pilgrimage shrine of Saint Dorothea at Marienwerder (Knyszyn) was secularized.[64] Königsberg attracted religious exiles not just from the Polish *korona* and Royal Prussia, but from the whole of the

[57] A description of the ceremony is given in AT 7, pp. 226–7, and in Andrzej Krzycki's apologia for the treaty, pp. 254–5. See also Marian Biskup, 'Wawrzyniec Międzyleski, autor opisu hołdu pruskiego 1525', in Stanisław Bylina (ed.), *Kultura staropolska—kultura europejska: Prace ofiarowane Januszowi Tazbirowi* (Warsaw, 1997), pp. 211–20.
[58] AT 7, p. 230.   [59] Biskup, *Wojny polski.*
[60] Małłek, *Dwie części Prus*, p. 172; Robert Stupperich, *Die Reformation im Ordensland Preussen 1523/4: Predigten, Traktate und Kirchenordnungen* (Ulm, 1966).
[61] Małłek, *Dwie części Prus*, pp. 163–9.
[62] For overviews in Polish, German, and English, see Małłek, *Dwie części Prus*, pp. 165–7; Hubatsch, *Albrecht von Brandenburg-Ansbach*, pp. 139–67; Walther Hubatsch, 'Albrecht of Brandenburg-Ansbach', in Henry J. Cohn (ed.), *Government in Reformation Europe, 1520–60* (London, 1971), pp. 169–202.
[63] Małłek, *Dwie części Prus*, pp. 166–7.   [64] See Chapter Three, pp. 107–8.

Empire. Ducal Prussia, from 1524/5, boasted the continent's first Lutheran bishops, none of them a native Prussian: the Brandenburger Erhard Quiess (d.1529), the Saxon Georg von Polentz (d.1550), and the Swabian Paulus Speratus (d.1551). Hans Weinreich set up a printing press at the foot of Duke Albrecht's castle hill, where for decades he produced a stream of Lutheran material: liturgical books, sermons, and catechisms in both Polish and German.[65] In June 1525, Duke Albrecht tried to persuade Martin Luther to travel to Königsberg to advise on the creation of this reformed church.[66] The Prussian lands of the Teutonic Knights, for so long the embodiment of the papal will in the Baltic world, were now in the very vanguard of Lutheran reform. This too, as we shall see, was well outside the mainstream of European events in the 1520s.

Kaymen Village

September 1525 saw a final Reformation upheaval in the newly extended lands of the Polish monarchy. In the village of Kaymen, in Ducal Prussia, the miller Kaspar addressed a crowd of his fellow villagers, quoting the Gospel. He told the peasants that they owed Biblical obedience to the good Duke Albrecht, but not to his nobility, from whom they would secure their liberty.[67] Thus inspired, the peasants stormed Kaymen castle and advanced on Königsberg. The capital of Ducal Prussia soon found itself besieged by a force of several thousand rebels from across the Sambia region.[68] In letters addressed to the citizenry of Königsberg, the rebels— 'We the peasants, professing the Holy Gospel'—demanded free preaching of the Scriptures and an end to the noble caste.[69] In the Natangia district, to the south of Königsberg, a new branch of the revolt sprang up, with landowners fleeing for their lives.[70] Word of the peasant rising spread across the border to Ermland in Royal Prussia, where preachers praised it.[71] It was anticipated that the peasant revolt would quickly spread beyond Ducal Prussia, right across the Polish monarchy.

Albrecht and his councillors demanded urgent military support from King Sigismund I. In October 1525, the monarch ordered officials in Royal Prussia to prepare themselves for military action against the wicked peasants, and the dangerous teaching of Christian liberty which they had espoused.[72] Mauritius Ferber, prince-bishop of Ermland, and Duke Janusz of Mazovia also raised troops at speed.[73]

---

[65] For example, Georg von Polentz, *Ein Sermon am Ostertage geprediget* (Königsberg, 1524); Vanessa Bock, 'Die Anfänge des polnischen Buchdrucks in Königsberg. Mit einem Verzeichnis der polnischen Drucke von Hans Weinreich und Alexander Augezdecki', in Axel Walter (ed.), *Königsberger Buch- und Bibliotheksgeschichte* (Köln, 2004), pp. 127–55.

[66] Małłek, *Dwie części Prus*, p. 163.

[67] This is the story of the rebellion as recounted in Richau's contemporary *Historie von dem Auffuhr*, published in Henryk Zins, *Powstanie*, pp. 102–5.

[68] See Zins, *Powstanie*, pp. 102–13.　　[69] Zins, *Powstanie*, p. 113.

[70] Zins, *Powstanie*, pp. 128–9.　　[71] Zins, *Powstanie*, p. 125.

[72] Zins, *Powstanie*, p. 133; for the King's letters to Albrecht on the uprising, see *Elementa*, pp. 3–5.

[73] Zins, *Powstanie*, p. 125; on the role of Mazovia, Stanisław Russocki, 'Nieznany mandat księcia Janusza mazowieckiego w sprawie powstania chłopskiego w Prusach Książęcych w 1525 roku', *Przegląd Historyczny* 46 (1955): 608–9.

On an autumn day, in the village of Leuthen, the peasant forces met an army hurriedly raised from across the northern territories of the Polish monarchy. The peasants, including Kaspar the miller, laid down their weapons, three ringleaders were executed in the field, and everybody went home.[74] For eighteen months, the ruling elites of Poland and Prussia had watched aghast as the Peasants' War had unfolded across the Holy Roman Empire, building to its terrible denouement at the Battle of Frankenhausen in May 1525. Now they had witnessed this same spectacle, of armed peasants quoting the Gospel and sacking castles, in their own lands.

As the heady and bloody year of 1525 drew to a close, therefore, King Sigismund I found himself as sovereign of two Hanseatic city-states controlled by radical pro-Wittenberg groups, overlord of a new duchy enacting a full-scale territorial Reformation, and he had helped to put down the most easterly manifestation of the Peasants' War. He would spend the rest of his life dealing with the consequences of these events.

Aftershocks: 1526 to *c*.1540

In 1526, in the one large-scale anti-Reformation act of the reign, the Crown responded to the tumult of the previous year by moving in force against the radicals who had seized control of its Royal Prussia towns.[75] That spring, King Sigismund marched north from Kraków. The nobility of Royal Prussia were told to make ready for war, and to meet the monarch at the fortress of Marienburg. On 17 April the King of Poland marched on Danzig, accompanied by the Polish episcopate, his royal council, and 6,000 Royal Prussian knights. He was joined by his vassals, the Dukes of Pomerania and Prussia, with their own armed contingents. The city gates were opened to admit him; the radical preachers, such as Hegge, had long since fled abroad.[76] Installed in the *Rathaus*—where, according to some rumours, radicals had planned to blow him up—Sigismund remained in Danzig for three months, restoring things to 'their former way'.[77] Thirteen citizens were executed as rebels, the divisive ex-mayor Eberhard Ferber pensioned off, and a new council sworn in. On 20 July 1526, King Sigismund issued the Danzig Statutes, a religious settlement which gave those unwilling to participate in traditional worship four days to leave the city, stressed that all preachers must be licensed by the bishop, and made the reporting of heretical activity compulsory.[78] From Danzig, the King sent anti-heresy commissions fanning out across the province. Elbing, Braunsberg, and Thorn all saw their former councils reinstated, and anti-heresy statutes were promulgated for each town.[79] The pacification of Danzig might have

---

[74] Zins, *Powstanie*, pp. 139–41. Further executions followed in subsequent weeks.
[75] A fuller account of the royal mission to Royal Prussia in 1526 is found in Chapter Two.
[76] The fullest account is Antoni Lorkiewicz, *Bunt Gdańska 1525 r. Przyczynek do historyi Reformacyi w Polsce* (Lwów, 1881). A description of the scene is given by Tomicki's secretary, Stanisław Górski, AT 8, pp. 40–1.
[77] For the alleged bomb plot, see AT 8, p. 103.
[78] Bukowski, *Dzieje Reformacyi*, vol 1, pp. 128–31; AT 8, pp. 74–83, 93–4.
[79] Pawlak, *Reformacja*, pp. 19–20; Biskup, *U schyłku średniowiecza*, pp. 217–18; Achremczyk and Szorc, *Braniewo*, pp. 60–2.

looked impressive—the first armed, princely reversal of an urban Reformation in sixteenth-century Europe—but it was a one-off event. From 1526, open support for Lutheranism grew right across Royal Prussia, embedded itself in Königsberg, and became obvious too in Kraków, Poznań, among Polish nobles, and in parliamentary sessions, gaining momentum and encountering very limited royal resistance indeed.

With the 'storm-preachers' chased off the scene by the King, the cities of Royal Prussia nonetheless proceeded apace with urban Reformations from 1526, now led by pro-Luther social elites. In Danzig, the new council in 1529 appointed as its preacher Pancratius Klemme—a man included in a list of banished apostates issued by Bishop Drzewicki just four years earlier—as preacher of Saint Mary's.[80] Polish bishops were increasingly worried by reports that Klemme was openly preaching Lutheranism and distributing communion in two kinds (utraquism). Yet when King Sigismund sent a delegation to Danzig in 1535, to secure an oath of loyalty to the Roman church, the city council demurred. The burghers protested that they were good Christians, but could pledge allegiance only to 'the Christian church'; Sigismund I did not press the issue.[81] Emboldened, Danzig council went on to create three city preaching posts on its own authority and appoint the Wittenberg graduate Andreas Aurifaber as rector of the city school, where he composed the evangelical textbook *Schola Dantiscana* (1539).[82] Klemme himself began to preach without vestments, and remove images from St Mary's, seeing off an episcopal attempt to arrest him in the 1540s.[83] This kind of unofficial, but de facto, urban Reformation was also seen in Thorn. There, Georg Zimmerman, a Wittenberg graduate and veteran of Danzig's rebel council, enjoyed a fruitful career as city secretary—the Primate of Poland accused him of converting the entire city council (bar one) to Lutheranism.[84] By 1536, Thorn's citizens had simply ceased leaving money to the church in their wills.[85] In Elbing, meanwhile, Bartholomeus Vogt for years preached Lutheranism, protected by the Rat, while the Elbingers continued to stage anti-clerical performances.[86] At the 1531 carnival, there were parodies of the pope, and a local blacked-up as an 'Ethiopian' paraded through the town in mockery of Bishop Ferber.[87] Graudenz, an important town in Kulm diocese, was claimed by its bishop Johannes Dantiscus to be 'entirely

---

[80] Nowak and Urban, 'Pankracy Klemme', p. 112.

[81] Nowak and Urban, 'Pankracy Klemme'; Zbigniew Nowak, 'Antyreformacyjna elegia Dantyszka o zagładzie Gdańska', *OiRwP* XVI (1971): 5–35.

[82] Nowak and Urban, 'Pankracy Klemme', p. 116; Zbigniew Nowak, 'Kultura, nauka i sztuka w Gdańsku na przełomie dwóch epok', in Cieślak (ed.) *Historia Gdańska*, pp. 352–402, at p. 364; Andreas Aurifaber, *Schola Dantiscana* (Danzig, 1539).

[83] Nowak and Urban, 'Pankracy Klemme', pp. 117–20; for Luther advising Klemme on Danzig reform, see Martin Luther, *D. Martin Luthers bisher grossentheils ungedruckte Briefe* (Leipzig, 1784), pp. 145–6.

[84] AT 16b, p. 308 (October 1534).   [85] Biskup, *U schyłku średniowiecza*, pp. 218–19.

[86] For the Vogt affair, see Chapter Two, p. 82.

[87] Contemporary reports of the carnival survive in: AAWa, AB A1, fos. 286–286v, 289. This was a pun, as the bishop explained, on his name 'Mauritius', meaning black/brown.

infected with Lutheranism'—the parish priest had taken a wife and preached 'Lutheran' sermons.[88]

The involvement of the local nobility ensured that Lutheranism in Royal Prussia after 1526 was not a purely urban affair, in a sea of undisturbed rural catholicism. Even in a remote spot like the marshlands of the Vistula delta, the Żuławy Malborskie, there were repeated reports that the peasants refused to pay tithes and listened to heretical sermons.[89] Both discreetly and overtly, their noble overlords supported the Reformation cause. Bishop Dantiscus, complaining about heterodoxy in Graudenz, blamed everything on the local landowner, Jan Sokołowski, who 'was and still is concerned, as some people declare, with this disease'.[90] Sokołowski permitted the Lutheran Bishop Queis to hold a service in Graudenz parish church, which he himself had attended.[91] Mikołaj Działyński, castellan of Kulm, was greatly affronted when a bishop accused him of having sex with the servant Ursula in his private bathhouse (under guise of herbal medical treatment), demanding respect because he was the only noble in the region not to support the Reformation, his neighbours having reformed, or encroached on, the churches 'of every last little town in Prussia'.[92] The nobility of Royal Prussia also crossed swords with church authorities more openly, by refusing to pay any tithes to local bishops from 1525, on theological grounds.[93] Piotr Tomicki could wearily report to Rome, in the 1530s, that the Royal Prussians, following the example of Lutheran areas, had stopped paying the Saint Peter's pence tax to the pope.[94] Top royal office holders in the province actively defended Lutheranism. The palatines of Marienburg and Pomerania, complained Bishop Ferber in 1528, openly handed the King letters 'attacking at the same time religion and the sacerdotal and pontifical offices'.[95] Particularly telling was the report of the royal delegates who led the failed mission to Danzig council in 1535. Gloomily, it recounted that Lutheran preachers such as Klemme were untouchable because they were protected by the most powerful men in the province, naming them as Johann von Werden, a senior royal official in Danzig; Philip Bischof, the mayor of Danzig, who had been instrumental in assisting the King in 1526; Achaz von Zehmen (Achacy Czema), a leading noble and castellan of Danzig; and Georg Baisen himself, palatine of Marienburg and the Crown's highest representative in Royal Prussia.[96] In the eye of the storm, in his castle at Heilsberg, Bishop Ferber of Ermland was haunted by the story of the expelled Bishop of Lübeck, convinced that he too would be violently ejected from

---

[88] AT 15, p. 120, 'totum est luteranismo infectum' (Dantiscus to Piotr Tomicki); see also *Corpus of Johannes Dantiscus' Texts*, nr. 937.

[89] AT 17, p. 202.

[90] AT 15, p. 120, 'culpa capitanei Ioannis Sokolowski, qui etiam, sicut quidam asserunt, ea lue laboravit vel laborat'.

[91] Biskup, 'O początkach reformacji', p. 105.

[92] AT 16a, pp. 362–3, 'aby szya szadna rzecz w kosczyele w brodniczkim nyenaruszyla, jako yus w kalsdim miasteczku pruskim yest naruszona'.

[93] See Chapter Two, p. 82.

[94] AT 16b, pp. 264–5. They could be induced to pay only if the sums went on border defence, Tomicki wrote.

[95] AT 10, p. 201: 'religionem ac ordinem sacerdotii simul et pontificii suggillantes'.

[96] Nowak, 'Antryreformacyjna elegia', p. 13; AT 17, pp. 214, 457.

his see by Reformation supporters, and that none of the local nobility would lift a finger to save him.[97]

A little further east, after his initial Reformation mandates, Duke Albrecht from 1526 successfully turned his Baltic duchy into a Lutheran beacon, both within the Polish monarchy and internationally. At his Königsberg court, Albrecht received nobles from across Sigismund I's polity into his service, including kinsmen of the Royal Chancellor Krzysztof Szydłowiecki, building a large clientage network.[98] He enjoyed a close alliance with the Luther-leaning Górka magnates of western Poland—Andrzej Górka (1500–51) spent time at Königsberg, entertained Albrecht in his own Wielkopolska residences in 1533 and 1536, and the family even offered him troops.[99] The printing presses of Albrecht's capital produced ever more Lutheran texts in the Polish vernacular, targeted at audiences further south.[100] Albrecht also involved himself actively in the wider politics of the Reformation. In 1526 he married Princess Dorothea of Denmark, in what was possibly Europe's first Lutheran princely match, and later intervened militarily in the Danish civil war to help her pro-Reformation brother, King Christian III (1534–59), to the throne. [101] Albrecht eagerly joined various leagues of pro-Reformation princes formed within the Empire, including the Schmalkaldic League itself.[102] By 1530, Charles V had been sufficiently antagonized to install Walter von Cronberg, at the Augsburg Diet, as Grand Master and rightful ruler of all Prussia.[103] Undeterred, Albrecht's chancellery produced prolix Apologias, which defended Lutheran teaching in polemical terms, and were printed across the Reich.[104]

In the lands of the Polish Crown too, a ripple of pro-Reformation activity continued steadily after the dramatic year of 1525, as suggested, for example, in heresy trials. When church authorities looked for those 'of the Lutheran sect' in the *korona*, they found them. Some sixty individuals in the Polish monarchy had to answer charges of heresy before church courts before the end of 1535 (see Appendix 1), the vast majority of these in the *korona*. Of the accused, only eight hearings involved members of the clergy. The great majority of those charged with Lutheran activity were men, the four exceptions being (in Kraków) the widow Dorothea domiciled near the castle (1525), the merchant's wife Barbara (1529), Barbara, wife of the royal builder Bartholomew (1532) and, in Poznań, Anna Wochowa (1535). The occupations of the accused ranged from tailor, manuscript illuminator, and church organist, to schoolmaster. Social elites were charged with Lutheran heresy too—city consuls in Kraków and Poznań, the Poznań merchant Johannes Werner, the son

[97] AT 16a, pp. 687–9.   [98] See Chapter Three, pp. 108–9.

[99] Włodzimierz Dworzaczek, 'Andrzej Górka', *PSB* VIII (1959–60), pp. 401–5 and 'Łukasz Górka', *PSB* VIII (1959–60), pp. 409–12.

[100] Warmiński, *Andrzej Samuel.*

[101] Iselin Gundermann, *Herzogin Dorothea von Preussen, 1504–47* (Köln, 1965); see also Chapter Five, pp. 137–8.

[102] See Hubatsch, *Albrecht von Brandenburg-Ansbach*, pp. 237–41.

[103] Jacek Wijaczka, *Stosunki dyplomatyczne Polski z Rzeszą Niemiecką, 1519–1556* (Kielce, 1998), pp. 58–61. For Dantiscus' account of the ceremony, see AT 12, p. 202.

[104] See Almut Bues, *Die Apologien Herzog Albrechts* (Weissbaden, 2009).

of the mayor of Warsaw, and Andrzej Salomon, scion of Kraków's top banking family.[105] As the table in Appendix 1 shows, there was a steady trickle of trials in all Polish dioceses, but with big spikes in Kraków in 1525 and Poznań exactly a decade later, when alleged Lutherans such as Matthias Gutfor were brought in clusters before clerical judges, following local panics. The most high-profile official investigation for heresy involved Jakub of Iłża, a lecturer at Kraków University. He had reportedly preached Lutheran sermons in public for years before finally being investigated by Bishop Tomicki in 1534–5. There was, however, no trial: having penned a defence of Lutheran teaching, Iłża fled to Silesia, and was found guilty of heresy in absentia.[106]

There was in fact a shadowy hinterland of apparently pro-Luther activity in Kraków. Bishop Tomicki complained that traders brazenly sold meat in the capital on church fast days (an action associated with Lutherans), that the city council supported heretics, and that heterodox groups held conventicles in the royal capital.[107] Certainly, a Kraków diarist, writing in 1530, could casually mention that he had attended a meeting 'cum luteranis' at an apothecary's shop.[108] When city councillors from Bartva in Slovakia wrote to the Kraków preacher Joannes Perger, requesting that he send them a man from Poland to preach the true 'Word of God', he was able to oblige.[109] Kraków also became a city where Lutheran works could openly be printed—albeit in translation. Hieronymus Wietor, for example, printed Reformation texts for a Magyar audience, such as Benedict Komjáthey's Hungarian paraphrase of the Pauline Epistles (1533), Imre Ozorai's Lutheran tract *De Christo et eius ecclesia* (1535), Hungarian vernacular hymnbooks and a catechism (1536–8).[110] In 1541, a book quite unabashedly entitled in Polish, *The New Testament from the German Translation by Martin Luther*, was printed in Yiddish in Sigismund I's capital.[111]

In Poznań, on the *Hohe Landestrasse*, the growing heterogeneity of Polish religion in the 1530s was a stormier experience than in the capital. In 1527, King Sigismund ordered the city council—headed by Mayor Jan Grodzicki—to remove Johannes Bomberg, the Lutheran it had installed as German-language preacher in the parish church of St Mary Magdalen, or face a 10,000 florin fine.[112] Grodzicki

[105] For the family's history, see Waldemar Bukowski, 'Salomonowie herbu Łabędź—ze studiów nad patrycjatem krakowskim wieków średnich', in *Cracovia-Polonia-Europa* (Kraków, 1995), pp. 113–45.
[106] Wacław Urban, 'Jakub z Iłży i jego uczniowie', *OiRwP* 36 (1991): 209–12. See also Chapter Six, p. 160.
[107] AT 16b, pp. 433–4; AT 17, pp. 258–9, 468–9.
[108] Barycz, *Historia uniwersytetu*, p. 106.   [109] AT 17, p. 357.
[110] Benedict Komjáthey, *Epistolae Pauli lingua hungarica donatae* (Kraków, 1533); Alodia Kawecka-Grzycowa, 'Hieronym Wietor', in *Drukarze dawnej Polski od XV do XVIII wieku*, vol.1 (Wrocław, 1983), pp. 325–52, at pp. 340–1.
[111] *Testamentum Novum. Z niemieckiego przekładu M. Lutra. Przełożył na jidisz Jan Herzuge* (Kraków, 1540/41).
[112] AT 8, p. 151, wrongly labelled as a letter to Danzig. See also Gabryel, *Działalność kościelna*, p. 314 and Maria Danuta Łabędzka-Topolska, 'Wpływy Reformacji w Poznaniu', in Jerzy Topolski (ed.), *Dzieje Poznania*, vol. 1 (Wrocław-Poznań, 1968), pp. 492–503. Some accounts talk of a Reformation riot in Poznań in 1533.

was still mayor in 1538, when the council appointed the openly pro-Reformation Stanisław of Przybysławek to preach in the same church.[113] At the end of that decade, Elizabeth Fenig, head of an established pro-Reformation printing workshop, coolly returned a batch of anti-Luther polemics to her Leipzig suppliers, telling them that such books were 'useless, inept and prohibited' in Poznań.[114] The centre of Reformation controversy in Poznań was an academic institution run by the diocese, the humanist *Academia* (f. 1519). In 1529, the Academy recruited as one of its chief lecturers the Saxon humanist Christoph Hegendorff, a Wittenberg graduate with a number of Lutheran theological works to his name, and a big readership.[115] Fellow pro-Lutheran humanists such as Stefan Reich followed Hegendorff to Poznań, with Melanchthon's encouragement.[116] Hegendorff's productive sojourn in the city began with an inaugural lecture in which he defended the doctrine of *sola fide*. It was curtailed, however, when the city's archdeacon, Grzegorz Szamotulski, accused him from the pulpit of spreading heresy through his pedagogic activities. Their quarrel sparked a printed polemical exchange, public disputations, and finally an armed confrontation inside Poznań cathedral, ending with Hegendorff's flight with his family from Poland in 1535.[117] This debacle did not prevent the city council from making its most audacious appointment yet in 1540, when the Polish pro-Lutheran friar, Andrzej Samuel, was named as city preacher.[118]

As in Danzig, Lutheranism in Poznań enjoyed the protection of a mighty nobleman. That man was Łukasz Górka, head of one of the kingdom's most powerful aristocratic families and Crown governor of Wielkopolska, who by virtue of those roles controlled the major castles on the Polish-imperial frontier.[119] The Górka magnates had long played a dominant role in Poznań's religious life: they held cathedral canonries, and Uriel Górka had been bishop of Poznań from 1479 to 1498. It was from Łukasz Górka that Hegendorff received the armed bodyguard which defended him during the skirmish at the cathedral, and in Górka's palace— today Poznań's Egyptology Museum—that pro-Luther scholars gathered in the 1520s and 1530s. They included Eustacy Trepka, a pupil of Melanchthon's and a later translator of Luther's works into Polish; Jan of Koźmin, also subsequently a Reformation translator; Górka's secretary, Bartłomiej Stawiski, and his orator, Jan Stracjusz, who ended his career as a Lutheran pastor in Antwerp.[120] Górka did not just patronize Lutheran scholars behind closed doors—in 1533, he gave to a city church of St Mary Magdalene a painted chest, in which funds could be centrally

---

[113] Łabędzka-Topolska, 'Wpływy Reformacji', p. 494; Witold Maisel, *Sądownictwo miasta poznania do końca XVI wieku* (Poznań, 1961), p. 22.

[114] Quoted by Wojciechowska, *Z dziejów książki*, p. 13: 'huius regionis ineptos, inutiliesque et prohibitos'.

[115] See Mazurkiewicz, *Początki Akademji*, pp. 27–37; Franz Bierlaire, 'Christoph Hegendorff', in *Contemporaries of Erasmus*, vol. 2 (Toronto, 1986), pp. 171–2.

[116] Mazurkiewicz, *Początki Akademji*, p. 117.

[117] The story is told most fully by Mazurkiewicz, *Początki Akademji*. The inaugural lecture was entitled *Oratio in artium liberalium laudem* (Kraków, 1531). It was later placed on a papal index.

[118] Warmiński, *Andrzej Samuel*, pp. 4–8.

[119] For a sketch of Górka's career, albeit shorn of any references to the Reformation, see Dworzaczek, 'Łukasz Górka'.

[120] Mazurkiewicz, *Początki Akademji*, p. 56.

collected for the city's poor. Such a secularization of poor relief was strongly associated with Lutheran town councils. Certainly, the priest of St Mary Magdalene's found this act so suspect that he unceremoniously ejected Górka's chest from the building.[121] In three key sites in Poznań—the cathedral, governor's mansion, and town churches—Górka thus made his religious sympathies and influence clear.

The Górka family were not an isolated example of Polish noble Reformation enthusiasm in the 1530s, as the educational choices of nobles across the *korona* made clear. Christoph Hegendorff, for example, was appointed to tutor the sons of leading Wielkopolska nobles such as Mikołaj Kościelecki, wojewoda of Kalisz, and Jan Leszczyński, castellan of Brześć.[122] To the latter's children, Hegendorff dedicated a devotional work, *Rudimenta pietatis christianae* (1533).[123] Polish nobles also sought out a Lutheran education abroad. As Wotschke demonstrated in the 1920s, the initial trickle of merchants' and goldsmiths' sons from Kraków and Poznań who enrolled at Wittenberg University in the 1520s was soon swelled by the sons of both high-ranking noble families, such as Albert Pampowski (1534) or Piotr Górka (1536), and minor nobles, such as Jan Lesniowski from Lwów. In the winter term of 1537 alone, some thirteen of Sigismund I's subjects arrived to study in Wittenberg, a town where the Mass had not been heard for years.[124] Other Lutheran institutions also attracted Polish nobles—Rafał Leszczyński, after finishing his studies with Hegendorff, was for example sent to the Goldberg grammar school in Silesia.[125] A royal decree of 1535, banning study at Wittenberg, had a limited effect on such enrolments.[126]

It is perhaps little surprise, then, that in these years the kingdom's parliament, the *sejm*, became the scene of ever more raucous protests against the existing church. At the Kraków *sejm* of 1532, by far the longest of the thirty-nine articles/petitions *(constitutiones)* submitted to the King was an attack on priests appointed to Polish benefices by the pope.[127] In 1534, the Środa sejmik complained that priests stifled vernacular printing, demanded an end to all legal appeals to Rome, and called for the Bible to be made available in Polish. In 1535, another Wielkopolska sejmik, led by Hegendorff's one-time pupil Rafał Leszczyński, called for the privileges of all convents and monasteries in Poland to be scrutinized by a future *sejm* and reconsidered by the King. More boldly, in 1536 the *sejm* asked the Crown to secularize all lands granted to the church since 1382, abolish the payment of annate taxes to the pope, and end all appeals to Rome. A horrified Bishop Chojeński claimed that anti-clerical nobles were inspired by heretical texts imported from Germany.[128] Polish scholarship has read these tempestuous parliamentary meetings as growing self-assertion by a lower nobility bent on a programme of constitutional reform

[121] AAP, CP 37, fos. 23–23(v).
[122] Mazurkiewicz, *Początki Akademji*, pp. 57–8. He also tutored Bishop Latalski's nephew.
[123] Ignacy Zarębski, 'Hegendorfer, Krzysztof', in *PSB* 9 (1960–1), pp. 337–9.
[124] Theodor Wotschke, 'Polnische studenten in Wittenberg', in *Jahrbücher für Kultur und Geschichte der Slaven* 2:2 (1926): 169–200.
[125] Mazurkiewicz, *Początki Akademji*, p. 57.
[126] Wotschke, 'Polnische studenten', pp. 172–3. For the edict, see also Chapter Four, p. 122.
[127] AT 14, pp. 53–5.
[128] These sejms have been studied most fully by Pociecha, 'Walka sejmowa'.

('egzekucja', or movement for execution of the laws).[129] However, it can be useful to weigh them as evidence of noble sympathy for (or interest in) the Reformation per se, and not *just* as slogans deployed to political ends.

Although anti-Reformation gestures remained forthcoming from the Crown and church leaders, question marks began to emerge about the orthodoxy of the royal family itself. Sigismund I issued further anti-Reformation decrees in 1527, 1535, and 1540, Primate Łaski drew up anti-heresy plans at synods, and high clergy continued to compose passionate, persuasive, or sarcastic anti-Lutheran polemics.[130] These ranged from the elegant *Anthelogikon* written by Copernicus' close friend Canon Tiedemann Giese of Ermland (1525), to the *Propugnaculum Ecclesiae* (1536), a 300-page long theological treatise by the Poznań lecturer Walenty Wróbel.[131] In 1533–4, King Sigismund quarrelled very seriously with Pope Clement VII. For several years the King had considered Rome to be blocking his ecclesiastical appointments unreasonably, and in a furious exchange implicitly threatened a full jurisdictional break (just as Henry VIII of England was taking such a step). Sigismund and his counsellors informed the pontiff that they had traditionally done him the 'honour' of sending the kingdom's ecclesiastical business to Rome, but implied they might not feel bound to do so in future.[132] In 1537, the King backed the sejm's demand that no more ecclesiastical annate taxes be sent from Poland to Rome, but instead spent locally. Sigismund I sent the Wittenberg graduate, Tomasz Sobocki, to Rome to make this request in his name.[133] Bona, Sigismund's queen, retained as her own confessor the controversial friar Francesco Lismanino, who would later emerge as a leading Reformation figure in Poland.[134] The royal couple's heir, Sigismund Augustus (b.1520), was also known to lend a sympathetic ear to reformers. Bishop Tomicki worried that the future king, who remained in his mother's household, was being exposed to dubious influences.[135] These rumours also reached Rome, and beyond. Part of Nuncio Rorario's brief in 1539 was to stress to the royal court that the junior king must be kept away from heretics.[136] Martin Luther hopefully dedicated a Bible translation to Sigismund August, John Calvin a work on prayer.[137]

In these circumstances, the royal succession became an early Reformation flashpoint. The Treaty of Kraków had made Duke Albrecht one of the most senior figures in the kingdom: duke and first senator. As son of Princess Sophia of Poland he was a high-ranking 'local' member of the royal family in his own right. The ink on that treaty was barely dry when, in 1525, Albrecht asked for the hand of Sigismund's oldest daughter Jadwiga, and to be named guardian of Sigismund

[129] For the executionist movement, see Anna Sucheni-Grabowska, *Monarchia dwu ostatnich Jagiellonów a ruch egzekucyjny* (Wrocław, 1974).

[130] For edicts, see Chapter Four; Grad, *Kościelna działalność*, pp. 270–2.

[131] Giese, *Flosculorum Lutheranorum*; Wróbel, *Propugnaculum ecclesiae*. See Chapter Six, pp. 155–7.

[132] AT 15, pp. 304, 342–3, 727–8 (1533); AT 16b, pp. 251–63 (1534).

[133] Pociecha, 'Walka sejmowa', pp. 183–4.   [134] Pociecha, *Królowa Bona*, II, pp. 68–9.

[135] AT 17, p. 290.   [136] Wojtyska, *Zacharias Ferreri*, pp. 321–2.

[137] Tazbir, *Państwo bez stosów*, p. 50. John Calvin, *Ioannis Calvini Commentarii in Epistolam ad Hebraeos* (Geneva, 1549).

Augustus in the event of his father's death.[138] As a senator he had a vote in any future royal election. When Sigismund I fell seriously ill in 1529, Albrecht corresponded with Lutheran princely allies abroad, in order to coordinate action around the succession if the King were to die.[139] It was no secret, then, that Albrecht stood very close to the throne, with a realistic prospect of a regency, or even of succeeding his uncle—the Hungarian-Bohemian line of the dynasty had been extinguished in 1526, and whereas King Casimir IV (d.1492) had been blessed with six sons, Sigismund I had only a single son born to him late in life. That heir, when the Treaty of Kraków was signed, was a mere and fragile 5 years old. In 1529, having recovered from his illness, King Sigismund presided over a hurried and semi-legal election of prince Sigismund Augustus *vivente rege*, with Queen Bona confirmed as future regent. Historians have long interpreted this as a coup by a power-hungry Italian queen, but it is at least as plausible to see this as ploy to push Albrecht away from the throne.[140] At the coronation ceremonies for 10-year-old Sigismund Augustus in 1530, it was nonetheless his uncle Albrecht who accompanied the young king and his parents as they processed around Kraków.[141] For Reformation supporters in the Polish monarchy, Albrecht's Lutheran duchy was a promise of what might yet come to pass in the *korona*: the nobles might yet chose a bellicose adult male of the royal blood, repudiating an unpopular Italian queen mother and her reputedly feminized child.[142]

The manoeuvres of 1529/30 did not successfully dispel the prospect of Albrecht as a Lutheran king of Poland. In the 1530s, there was a widespread sense throughout the Polish monarchy that the old religious order would die with Sigismund I. In Ermland, Bishop Ferber declared that the aged king was the saviour of the church, its only source of support—so long as he lived.[143] He tried to procure men, gunpowder, and firearms from Danzig with which to defend his prince-bishopric in the event of a Lutheran attack during an interregnum.[144] The castellan of Kulm, Mikołaj Działyński, promised to aid Ferber with his own forces; bishops in Royal Prussia drew up a list of those nobles whom they believed would fight for them during the succession conflict to come.[145] In the court of Ferdinand Habsburg, it was reported that the greatest magnate houses of Poland, the Szydłowiecki, Tęczyński, Tarnowski, and Górka, all supported Albrecht, rendering him king-maker.[146] In winter 1538, the 74-year-old king of Poland—a prince born before Florence's Medicean Golden Age under Lorenzo the Magnificent, during the pontificate of the ex-conciliarist Pius II—was again taken seriously ill. In Poland, evidence was reportedly found, in the form of an intercepted courier, of a Lutheran conspiracy,

---

[138] Wiktor Szymaniak, *Rola dworu polskiego w polityce zagranicznej Prus Książęcych: studium z dziejów dyplomacji Prus Książęcych w Polsce w latach 1525–1548* (Bygdoszcz, 1993), p. 79 and *Organizacja dyplomacji Prus Książęcych na dworze Zygmunta Starego, 1525–48* (Bydgoszcz, 1992), p. 43.

[139] Szymaniak, *Rola dworu*, p. 80.

[140] See Chapter Three, pp. 101–2.   [141] AT 12, pp. 56–8.

[142] For concerns about the heir, see Antoni Danysz, *O wychowaniu Zygmunta Augusta* (Kraków, 1915).

[143] AAWa, AB A1, fo. 159.   [144] AT 16a, p. 678.   [145] AT 16a, p. 675; AT 16b, pp. 5–6.

[146] The Pernstein memorandum was found by Pociecha, *Królowa Bona*, vol. II, pp. 357–8.

a confederacy of 700 Wielkopolska nobles who had sworn to ensure that the new king secularized church lands.[147]

In the event, it was other deaths which brought this first, Lutheran phase of the Reformation in the Polish monarchy to a close—those of Primate Łaski (d.1531), Chancellor Krzysztof Szydłowiecki (d.1532), Primate Drzewicki (d.1535), Bishop Tomicki (d.1535), and Primate Krzycki (d.1537). It was Denmark which instead became the first European monarchy to officially embrace Lutheranism, in 1537.[148] In the 1540s, as the longest reign in Polish history neared its end, the patterns of the 1530s continued unchecked. Lutheranism unofficially flourished across Royal Prussia, and a new Lutheran university in Königsberg (f. 1544) began to train Polish- and German-speaking ministers.[149] In Kraków, pro-Reformation groups met more openly, with increasingly high-profile attendees, bringing together courtiers, senior clergy, and burghers in the houses of men such as Trzycieski.[150] In Wielkopolska, the canons of Poznań complained that local noblemen were reforming the parishes on their estates en masse, 'usurping' benefices by seizing their incomes and appointing 'apostate' ministers.[151] In 1540, one of the brightest stars among Poland's high clergy, Jan Łaski junior—a man once offered the metropolitan see of Gniezno by Queen Bona—travelled west, married, and shortly afterwards resigned his Polish benefices, openly embracing the Reformation cause as a Protestant minister.[152] By the time that Sigismund I died on Easter Sunday 1548, the Reformation within his kingdoms was acquiring clearer form: Prussia and Wielkopolska were covered in de facto Lutheran parishes, while in southern Poland a new strand of dissent was appearing, which looked to Geneva rather than to Wittenberg. A handful of Calvinist ministers were active in parishes such as Niedźwiedź by 1546.[153] By the end of the century there would be at least 141 Lutheran congregations in the *korona* and Royal Prussia, albeit outnumbered by then by Calvinist and Arian communities.[154] By 1548, the Polish monarchy—ruled by a king whose piety was lavishly praised by Erasmus of Rotterdam and successive pontiffs—had come a very long way since Jakub Knade had thrown off his habit and began to preach a Wittenberg Gospel in Danzig in 1518. The dynamic young Sigismund Augustus, who ascended to the throne aged twenty-eight, was inheriting a different world.[155]

---

[147] The report about this courier was recorded in the royal registers, and published in Zakrzewski, *Powstanie i wrost*, pp. 237–9. See also Pociecha, 'Walka sejmowa', p. 175.

[148] Grell, 'Scandinavia', p. 111.

[149] Małłek, *Dwie części Prus*, p. 168; Warmiński, *Andrzej Samuel*.

[150] Bukowski, *Dzieje Reformacyi*, pp. 190–9.   [151] AAP, CP 37, fo. 120v (1537).

[152] AT 17, pp. 578–9; Kowalska, *Działalność reformatorska*.

[153] See Zakrzewski, *Powstanie i wrost*, pp. 50–3 and J. Miller, 'The Origins of Polish Arianism', *Sixteenth Century Journal* 16 (1985): 229–56.

[154] The number of Calvinist and Arian churches is estimated at 339. Calculated by Marek Wajsblum, using Merczyng's data: Marek Wajsblum, 'Wyznaniowe oblicze protestantyzmu polskiego i jego podstawy społeczne', in *Pamiętnik zjazdu narodowego im. Jana Kochanowskiego* (Kraków, 1931), pp. 77–97, at p. 86; Henryk Merczyng, *Zbory i senatorowie protestanccy w dawnej Rzeczpospolicie* (Warsaw, 1904).

[155] For Sigismund Augustus' reign, see Anna Sucheni-Grabowska, *Zygmunt August: Król polski i wielki książę litewski, 1520–62* (Warsaw, 1996).

The Reformation in the Polish monarchy did not, therefore, start in the middle of the sixteenth century, as often asserted in modern textbooks; by then, it was already at least a generation old.

To foreign contemporaries it was perfectly clear that Sigismund I's Polish monarchy had been, from the outset, exposed to strong Lutheran influences. In 1526, the alarmed papal nuncio, Nicolaus Fabro, warned Rome that 'really, if it were not for the great kindness of this king, Poland would already be entirely Lutheran'.[156] The Saxon polemicist, Johann Cochlaeus, in the 1530s informed the Polish king and high clergy that Poles were a visible presence in Wittenberg.[157] And even in distant England it was felt that Poland was, alongside Germany, a major centre of Lutheranism. In 1525, the Bishop of Bath and Wells informed Cardinal Wolsey that 'the King of Poland...approve[s] some of Luther's damnable opinions'.[158] In 1530, Edward Lee, Archbishop of York, summarizing for Henry VIII the problems facing Christendom, could point in particular to Luther's 'dampnable heresies', which had 'spred bothe thorough germany and also in the Realme of polyne'.[159] Historians have forgotten something that many early sixteenth-century observers, in describing the landscape of the European Reformation, knew all too well.

Analysis: The Polish Monarchy in Context

How Lutheran, then, was the Polish monarchy by *c*.1540? That question presents methodological problems, not least the issue of what threshold or definition we adopt before concluding that a society 'had' a Reformation. Historians have long struggled to classify the kind of tale told above, of diffuse, fragmentary, multifaceted manifestations of sympathy for the early Reformation—less than an organized or mass movement, but rather more than straws in the wind. This is particularly true of countries where Protestantism was not ultimately triumphant, and where catholicism instead became integral to narratives of national history. All the bits and pieces of pro-Luther sentiment in the 1520s and 1530s perplex because they are, historically speaking, seemingly going nowhere. Thus Redondo, writing about Castile and Aragon in the 1520s and 1530s, has concluded that the Spanish kingdoms experienced 'breaths of Lutheranism'.[160] Nicholls has talked about a 'formless' early Protestant movement in France, which opened up 'a cultural space for heretical thoughts'.[161] On Poland itself, Marta Kacprzak has written of a

---

[156] Wojtyska, *Zacharias Ferreri*, p. 238, 'e veramente, se non fusse la tanta bontà de questo re, la Pollonia sarai già tutta Luterana'.

[157] Johann Cochlaeus, *Adversus impia et seditiosa scripta Martini Lutheri* (Leipzig, 1534), dedicatory letter.

[158] British Library, Cotton Vitellius B/VII, fo. 126(v).

[159] Cambridge, MS Ee.4.27, fo. 2(v).

[160] Augustin Redondo, 'Luther et l'Espagne en 1520 à 1536', *Mélanges de la Casa Velazquez* 1 (1965): 109–65, at p. 164, 'souffles lutheriéns'.

[161] David J. Nicholls, 'The Nature of Popular Heresy in France, 1520–42', *Historical Journal* 26 (1983): 261–75, at p. 175.

'crypto-Reformation' under Sigismund I.[162] Euan Cameron has noted that 'there were Italian Protestants, but there was not an Italian Reformation'.[163]

The second challenge in quantifying how 'reformed' the Polish monarchy was lies in the often elusive nature of early Lutheranism itself, inconsistently defined by modern scholars and sixteenth-century sources alike. This problem forms the subject of Chapter Seven, but here we can briefly note how ambiguous and deniable allegedly 'Lutheran' incidents could be. Danticus suspected Lutheranism when the priests of Kulm sang a vernacular German hymn in 1534, yet their noble patron indignantly protested that this song had been learnt from their own mothers thirty years ago.[164] Łukasz Górka surrounded himself with Lutheran scholars, yet paid thousands of florins for Masses for his own soul and that of his wife in Poznań cathedral: canons condemned him as a protector of heretics, while thanking him effusively for his pious gifts.[165] Hanus Szniczer explained to a Kraków church court that he did keep illegal Lutheran books in his house, but that he had never read the words, his purpose being simply to enjoy the lovely pictures by Albrecht Dürer.[166] In Prussia, a puzzled Tiedemann Giese consulted his fellow canon Nicholas Copernicus about the case of a monk in the diocese, Radike, who had absconded from his monastery but was 'neither a Lutheran nor a papist'.[167] Contemporaries could not agree on how to define Lutheranism, and accused Lutherans routinely denied they were anything of the sort. To pronounce on how Lutheran Sigismund I's monarchy, or individual subjects were, is thus fraught with difficulty because, in a sense, Lutheranism is a moving, shifting target.

While keeping these problems in mind, it is possible to analyse events in the Polish monarchy comparatively, placing them in their wider European context to gauge how unusual, or not, they might be. Here, we can consider in turn the key categories of books, preachers, urban Reformation, princely-led reform, and overall Reformation typologies. In the years immediately around 1517, then, the initial influx of Lutheran books into Sigismund I's monarchy was entirely typical of a phenomenon seen right across Latin Christendom. It is estimated that 390 editions of Luther's works were printed in the Holy Roman Empire alone in 1523.[168] In the Netherlands, some twenty pro-Luther texts had been printed in the Dutch vernacular by 1524.[169] In 1519, the celebrated printer Froben could boast that he had shipped 600 copies of Luther to France and Spain.[170] In distant Castile, the Spanish Inquisition seized shipments of Lutheran texts from the holds of ships throughout the early 1520s, and worried about book smuggling through the Basque country.[171]

[162] Kacprzak, 'Z problemów Reformacji XVI wieku'.
[163] Euan Cameron, 'Italy', in Pettegree, *The Early Reformation*, pp. 188–214, at p.189.
[164] AT 16b, pp. 35–6.   [165] AAP, AE VII, fos. 113, 119(v); AAP, CP 37 fos. 23–23(v).
[166] Jan Ptaśnik (ed.), *Cracovia impressorum XV et XVI saeculorum* (Kraków, 1922), pp. 210–11.
[167] AAWa, D29, fo. 4: 'iam quasi in proverbium venerit illum neque papistam esse, neque Lutheranum, et apud neutros fidem inhaberi'.
[168] Andrew Pettegree, 'The Early Reformation in Europe: A German Affair or an International Movement?', in *The Early Reformation in Europe* (Cambridge, 1992), pp. 1–22, at p. 10.
[169] Alistair Duke, *Reformation and Revolt in the Low Countries*, 2nd edition (London, 2003), p. 16.
[170] Pettegree, 'The Early Reformation', p. 1.
[171] Hamilton, *Heresy and Mysticism*, pp. 72–3, 80; Redondo, 'Luther et l'Espagne'.

If we turn to preaching, however, we can see that the Polish monarchy was slightly more unusual—one of only a handful of states which saw public sermons in support of Luther in the early 1520s. Sustained Lutheran preaching was principally a feature of the Holy Roman Empire and the territories directly bordering it—that is the Netherlands, Scandinavia, Austria, Hungary, Bohemia, and Poland. Paulus Speratus in Vienna (1522), Conrad Cordatus in Buda (1522), or Olaus Petrus in Stockholm (1524) were thus giving their Lutheran sermons at the same time as Jakub Knade in Danzig (from 1518, reportedly) and Pancratius in Gniezno (1524), not to mention the army of itinerant preachers found the length and breadth of the Reich.[172]

It is the Reformations seen in Danzig and Elbing in the 1520s which are particularly arresting, however. Urban Reformation is often considered a hallmark of early Protestant reform, in the Holy Roman Empire in particular.[173] There has been little systematic comparisons of urban Reformations in the Reich with those found beyond it in Central Europe—and the strikingly precocious nature of what occurred in Sigismund I's Royal Prussia has thus been missed.[174] The Reformation preaching mandate, which Danzig city council issued in February 1524, was already early by European standards. According to Euan Cameron's calculations, only a handful of other urban centres had openly sanctioned Reformation preaching in this way at that date: Nuremberg (1522), Erfurt (1522), Basel (1523), Constance (1523), and Strassburg (December 1523).[175] Within this list, Danzig is notable for being a particularly large city (up to 40,000 people), and the only one which lay outside the Holy Roman Empire and Switzerland.

Yet it is the Danzig Reformation revolt of January 1525 which is truly striking when considered comparatively—early, rapid, violent, and radical. When Hegge and his fellow 'storm-preachers' took control of the port, no major city in the Holy Roman Empire had yet officially fully embraced the Reformation. Nuremberg, traditionally seen as the first pro-Luther city in the Reich, held its landmark Reformation disputation two months later, in March 1525.[176] Ozment has stressed that where Reformations did occur in the Reich, they were typically slow, negotiated, and piecemeal, unfolding over several years—'rare indeed is the example of a rapid

---

[172] Duke, *Reformation and Revolt*; Grell, 'Scandinavia'; David P. Daniel, 'Hungary', in Pettegree, *The Early Reformation*, pp. 49–69; Winfried Eberhard, 'Bohemia, Moravia and Austria', in Pettegree, *The Early Reformation*, pp. 23–48; Robert Scribner, *Popular Culture and Popular Movements in Reformation Germany* (London, 1987), pp. 123–43.

[173] See the classic Steven Ozment, *The Reformation in the Cities: The Appeal of Protestantism to Sixteenth-Century Germany and Switzerland* (New Haven, 1975) and more recently Christopher Close, *The Negotiated Reformation: Imperial Cities and the Politics of Urban Reform, 1525–1550* (Cambridge, 2009).

[174] For comparison in passing, see Schramm, 'Danzig, Elbing und Thorn'. See also Maria Bogucka, *Baltic Commerce and Urban Society, 1500–1700* (Aldershot, 2003), pp. 55–74. Danzig, Elbing, and Thorn are omitted from Heinz Schilling's 'The Reformation in the Hanseatic Cities', *Sixteenth Century Journal* 14:4 (1983): 443–56.

[175] Cameron, *European Reformation*, pp. 217–19, 238.

[176] For an overview see Brigit Heal, *The Cult of the Virgin Mary in Early Modern Germany* (Cambridge, 2014), pp. 12–13.

and unqualified institutional change'.[177] Nuremberg's own Reformation typifies this pattern: the journey from preaching mandate, to German liturgy, to Reformation disputation, and finally a local doctrinal formula took seven years (1522–8).[178] By contrast, Danzig (along with Elbing) embarked on an immediate, wholesale, far-reaching reform. In just a few weeks, citizens saw the closing of local monasteries, iconoclasm, changes to worship, and civic appointment of official Reformation preachers. These instant urban Reformations in Royal Prussia had no parallel in Christendom in the 1520s. Their speed was of a piece with their violence and radicalism. Across the Reich, urban patriciate elites maintained political control of their towns—while some Reformation violence occurred in summer 1524 in Augsburg, Strassburg, and smaller south German towns, it was successfully suppressed by the local authorities.[179] Danzig was the only city in Europe where an urban government was actually toppled in the 1520s and replaced with a popular Reformation regime. Schilling, studying urban Reformations in northern Germany's Hanseatic towns in the 1530s, found these to be usually disorderly, but because his study omitted Danzig and Elbing it did not spot that they were obvious precursors to the later phenomenon he described.[180] Arguably the closet parallel to the eighteen-month rule of Hegge and his followers in Danzig (and Hitfeld's in Elbing) is a notorious later event in the Reich. In Münster, Anabaptists took control of the city, to the scandal of Europe, and their social experiment ended only with a successful siege by its bishop, Franz von Waldeck, in 1535.[181] John of Leiden, self-appointed king of Münster, might even usefully be compared with Jakub Hegge: these were the only iconoclast, monastery-looting, popular preachers in Europe to successfully overthrow and eject a patrician *Rat* in a major city in the early Reformation. Danzig, a city which minted coins with the Polish king's image, deserves a more prominent place in narratives of sixteenth-century urban religious reform.

Also striking within a European context was Duke Albrecht's princely Reformation. Albrecht was by no means the only prince to have personally embraced Luther's teachings in the early 1520s—in this, Henry V, Duke of Mecklenburg (ruled 1520–52), the Elector of Saxony Frederick III (ruled 1483–1525), Sigismund I's nephew Georg von Hohenzollern (1484–1543, heir to the Margravate of Brandenburg-Ansbach), and Barmin XI, Duke of Pomerania (ruled 1523–73) and Wittenberg graduate, kept him company.[182] He was, however, the first prince in Christendom to impose a Lutheran Reformation on his territory, with the Ecclesiastical Ordinance of December 1525.[183] Put starkly, the very first legal,

---

[177] Ozment, *Reformation in the Cities*, p. 127.

[178] Cameron, *European Reformation*, pp. 217–18.

[179] See Thomas A. Brady, 'The Reformation of the Common Man, 1521–4', in Dixon, *The German Reformation*, pp. 94–132, at pp. 104, 112.

[180] Schilling, 'Reformation in the Hanseatic Cities'.

[181] See Sigrun Haude, *In the Shadow of 'Savage Wolves': Anabaptist Münster and the German Reformation during the 1530s* (Boston, 2000).

[182] Wolgast, 'Die deutschen territorialfürste'; Joachim Whaley, *Germany and the Holy Roman Empire*, I (Oxford, 2012), pp. 255–64.

[183] Hubatsch stressed the originality of this text, *Albrecht von Brandenburg*, pp. 153–5.

territorial Lutheran Reformation in Christendom occurred not in the Empire, but within Poland's composite monarchy. Duke Albrecht's Reformation Ordinance predated the *Reformatio Ecclesiarum Hessiae* produced for Philip of Hesse in autumn 1526, the Brunswick *Kirchenordnung* (1528) written by Heinrich Bugenhagen, and, outside the Reich, the Lutheran church ordinance for the Danish duchy of Schleswig-Holstein approved by Duke Christian Oldenburg (1528).[184] It was only in 1528 that Melanchthon penned a Reformation Ordinance for Saxony itself. Ducal Prussia is often dismissed as being, by definition, an anomaly—a sort of exotic satellite to the German Reformation because it was outside the Reich.[185] However, if one possible definition of the Reformation is the creation in law of state churches embracing Protestant theology, then the Reformation, strictly speaking, began outside the Reich. Whereas no Lutheran prince in the Holy Roman Empire—not even Philip of Hesse—had dared to roll out a territorial Reformation before the 1526 interim of Speyer created a legal opening to do so, Albrecht found that the King of Poland permitted such radical steps slightly earlier in the day.[186]

Taken as a whole, then, the Polish monarchy's experience of the Reformation in its first two decades emerges as extensive and, briefly, conspicuously precocious within Latin Europe. In the 1520s, Sigismund I's monarchy was, along with the Holy Roman Empire, the only European polity to experience the full range of early Reformation types, or models—urban Reformation, princely Reformation, and a Luther-inspired peasant rising (urban, magisterial, communal). From 1525, within eight years of Luther's Ninety-Five Theses, this was the first de facto bi-confessional monarchy of the Protestant Reformation: a catholic Crown with a Lutheran vassal territory, and a Lutheran princely elector. In the 1530s, it looked set to continue this path-breaking trajectory, as one of the most likely candidates in Europe to embark on an all-out royal Reformation. The Polish monarchy's prominent position within the early Reformation was, however, eclipsed by later shifts, at home and abroad. By 1540, Sigismund I's monarchy looked to be in a second tier of Reformation-impacted polities—three Latin kingdoms had officially embraced the Reformation (Denmark, Sweden, England). Poland, by then, looked more akin to a group of highly religiously fractured, or split, polities. About half the territory of the Holy Roman Empire was ruled by pro-Reformation princes (Brandenburg, Saxony, Hesse, Wurtenburg), Switzerland was in a similar position, while two of the Polish monarchy's six constituent parts (Ducal Prussia and Royal Prussia) were respectively de iure and de facto Lutheran, accounting for some 20 per cent of its landmass. Towards the end of his reign, Sigismund I's monarchy had retreated somewhat from the Reformation front line it had once occupied—at least until the arrival of anti-Trinitarians such as Faustus Socinus in the 1550s.

---

[184] Grell, 'Scandinavia', p. 101; Whaley, *Holy Roman Empire*, I, pp. 260, 264.
[185] Whaley, *Holy Roman Empire*, I, p. 257.
[186] Alton Hancock, 'Philip of Hesse's Views of the Relationship between Prince and Church', *Church History* 35:2 (1966): 157–69.

How might better inclusion of the Polish monarchy nuance our narratives of the early European Reformation? The story told in this chapter, in crude geographical terms, make Luther's initial impact appear bigger and deeper, stretching it eastwards. It can also, although this conclusion would have distressed Theodor Wotschke, make the early Reformation appear less uniquely German, because events in Poland-Prussia in the 1520s and 1530s highlight the international, multilingual nature of early Lutheranism.[187] Lutheranism, not least in early modern Poland, has long been celebrated as a quintessentially German cultural and historical phenomenon. On this one point Bukowski, Wotschke, and Tazbir all agreed that it was the 'Germans' in the Polish monarchy who embraced Luther's message, finding it in 'confirmation of their status as a separate ethnic group'.[188] The evidence presented here can complicate that picture. Some of the very first villages in Europe to experience a state-imposed Lutheran reform (1526–7) were the Polish-speaking communities of the Mazuria region in Ducal Prussia, who heard Luther's message from ministers such as Stanislaw of Kraków, preaching in sixteenth-century Polish.[189] When Kaspar the miller spoke of Christian liberty in the peasant rising of 1525, his audience included speakers of the now extinct language of Old Prussian.[190] The kingdom's two recorded book burnings of the reign, the presiding clergy noted, destroyed Lutheran books in Latin, German, and Polish.[191] The only individual convicted of Lutheran heresy in Sigismund I's reign was Jakub of Iłża, a Polish academic born in deep rural Małopolska. In Wielkopolska, Lutheran reformers were protected by Polish noble families, such as the Górka and Leszczyński. As Appendix 1 shows, of the *circa* sixty individuals tried for Lutheranism in Polish church courts by 1535 whose surnames are recorded, 60 per cent had identifiably German surnames (seventeen), and 40 per cent identifiably Slavonic ones (twelve). In the lakeside villages of Mazuria, in the *korona*'s bustling cities, in Baltic deltas, in seats of learning and the privacy of the noble households, Luther's ideas were encountered and disseminated across Sigismund I's monarchy in Latin, Polish, and Old Prussian, as well as, of course, in German. The advent of Lutheranism saw an extraordinary explosion in German vernacular printing and religious debate; but that does not preclude it from also having been a highly multilingual, variegated phenomenon outside the Reich.

When Matthias Gutfor walked free from the bishop's court in Kraków in 1532, he was therefore a subject of a Crown which had been rocked, as few other kingdoms had been at that date, by the impact of Luther's teaching. Nonetheless, as we know, Gutfor's alleged Lutheran activity in the heart of the royal capital, in

---

[187] Some of these comparative points were initially and briefly made in Nowakowska, 'Forgetting Lutheranism', pp. 301–3.

[188] Bukowski, *Dzieje Reformacyi*, p. 59; Wotschke, *Geschichte der Reformation*, pp. ix, 1; Samsonowicz and Tazbir, *Tysiącletnie dzieje*, p. 123; Tazbir, *Reformacja, Kontrreformacja*, p. 7: 'Dopiero w luteranizmie znaleźli oni potwierdzenie własnej odrębności etnicznej'.

[189] Małłek, *Dwie części Prus*, p. 168.   [190] Zins, *Powstanie*, p. 104.

[191] See Chapter Six, p. 153.

a diocese ruled by Sigismund I's right-hand man, resulted in no punishment. Given the profound impact of the Wittenberg Reformation on the Polish monarchy, the basically non-persecutory stance of King Sigismund's regime is particularly puzzling and the more urgently in need of explanation. So let us now zoom in on some of the component parts of this story, to investigate this 'Polish toleration' more closely.

PART 3
EPISODES

2

Drama in Danzig

The Crown and Reformation in Royal Prussia

In an oration for King Sigismund I, delivered at his funeral in Kraków cathedral by Bishop Marcin Kromer (1548), the Reformation events which had occurred in Royal Prussia twenty years earlier still resonated: Kromer praised the late king for his decisive action against the Danzig rebels back in 1526, whose ringleaders he had 'partly executed, partly exiled'.[1] King Sigismund's responses to Lutheranism in this Baltic province were, in reality, far more ambiguous than Kromer's polite episcopal speech conveyed. Urbanized, wealthy, and occupying a strategic coastal position, Royal Prussia and its Hanseatic towns formed one of the most important parts of the Polish composite monarchy. Royal Prussia was also, as we have seen, precocious in Europe for the speed with which it took up the new teachings from Wittenberg from 1518 onwards.[2] Policy here thus provides us with a fine microcosm (and good opening example) of this regime's wider, puzzlingly 'tolerant' stance towards 'the new evangelicals'. From 1518 to c.1540, royal policy towards Lutheranism zigzagged between passivity and intervention, tending overall towards a pronounced laxity. King Sigismund's dramatic 1526 march on Danzig has broader significance too, as the first armed royal intervention against an urban Reformation seen in sixteenth-century Europe—and the original precursor to what would later happen in Münster in 1535, or in Prague in 1621.[3]

This chapter opens with a brief narrative of royal policy, zooming in more closely on the Royal Prussian events broadly outlined in Chapter One. Three phases of royal responses to the Reformation in this province are identified—passivity during the turbulent initial Lutheran takeover (1518–25), a brief but concerted active

---

[1] Marcin Kromer in Kromer and Samuel Maciejowski, *De Sigismundo Primo rege Poloniae etc duo Panegyrici funebres* (Mainz, 1550), fo. 145v: 'Authores modo seditionis paucos invitus partim interfecit, partim exilio multavit.'

[2] See Chapter One, pp. 50, 53–4, 57–60.

[3] The only monographic study of Sigismund I's policy towards Reformation Danzig to date is Lorkiewicz, *Bunt Gdańska*. See also Simson, *Geschichte*, vol. 2; Jolanta Dworzaczkowa, 'O genezie i skutkach rewolty gdańskiej 1525/6', *Roczniki Historyczne* 28 (1962): 97–109; Cieślak, 'Postulaty rewolty'; Julia Możdżen, 'Miasto pod panowaniem diabelskim. Gdański dominikanin w obliczu następstw rewolty społecznej z lat 1525–6', in Cezary Kardasz, Julia Możdżen, and Magdalena Spychaj (eds), *Miasto jako fenomen społeczny i kulturalny* (Toruń, 2012), pp. 169–85. See also a number of works by Maria Bogucka: 'Walki społeczne', 'Reformation, Kirche und der Danziger Aufstand in den Jahren 1517–26', in Evamaria Engel et al. (eds), *Hansische Stadtgeschichte—Brandenburgische Landesgeschichte* (Weimar, 1989), pp. 217–24, and 'Die Wirkungen der Reformation in Danzig', *Zeitschrift für Ostforschung* 42 (1993): 195–206.

phase involving the King's march on Danzig (1526), followed by a longer-term reversion to passivity (1527–40s). We will then analyse this story through two different lenses. The first is an updated version of traditional 'political' readings which attribute princely toleration of heresy to pure realpolitik. We shall see that it is perfectly possible to read the Polish Crown's policies through a narrow (but compelling) geopolitical lens, accounting for them with reference to timing and domestic context. To then read these events through a 'religious' lens, however, reveals a less familiar picture, of a Crown responding to Reformation events on the ground without much obvious interest in either catholic or Lutheran doctrine. King Sigismund's policies towards Royal Prussia amount—in stark contrast to Habsburg-conquered Prague in the 1620s—to a pre-confessional response where violent heretics were vanquished, but private theological dissent by peaceful burghers was permissible.[4] In that sense, Polish royal policy did not involve conscious realpolitik 'toleration', because the Crown's worldly and spiritual goals, from its late medieval perspective, were not necessarily in conflict: the King pursued harmony in the body politic, and social unity in the body of Christ.

LOCAL NARRATIVE: THE POLISH CROWN AND LUTHERANISM IN ROYAL PRUSSIA (1518–c.1540)

Royal Prussia was one of the jewels of Sigismund I's Polish monarchy. The territory included the sizeable delta of the Vistula river, and a large stretch of Baltic coastline. Its principal landmarks were the Hanseatic cities, or virtual city-states, of Danzig, Elbing, and Thorn. Danzig, economically the most important city in the monarchy, was a port of up to 40,000 people, the size of Munich or Nuremberg, called by some contemporaries the wealthy star of the Baltic.[5] The eastern part of Royal Prussia, Ermland, was governed by its own prince-bishop. The province was the most urbanized part of the monarchy, with an estimated 30 per cent of the population living in at least thirty-six towns.[6] This jewel had been recently acquired (1466). It was legally guaranteed a degree of self-rule, but Danzig had one resident official representing the King's interests, and the Polish King's face on its coinage.[7]

In its first phase (1518 to May 1525), royal policy towards the rapid influx of Luther-inspired reform in Royal Prussia was cautious and essentially passive. As Danzig was flooded with Luther's books and animated by Wittenberg-graduated preachers, in 1520 King Sigismund issued a single anti-Luther edict for the city,

---

[4] For the re-Catholicization of Prague, see Howard Louthan, *Converting Bohemia: Force and Persuasion in the Catholic Reformation* (Cambridge, 2009).

[5] Ernst Eckman, 'Albrecht of Prussia and the Count's War, 1533–1536', *Archiv für Reformationsgeschichte* 51 (1960): 19–36, at p. 30.

[6] Biskup, 'O początkach', p. 102.

[7] For Royal Prussia in this period, see pp. 39–40, and also Henryk Samsonowicz, 'Rola Gdańska w życiu stanowym Prus Królewskich i w życiu politycznym Rzeczpospolitej', in Edmund Cieślak (ed.), *Historia Gdańska*, vol. II (Gdańsk, 1982), pp. 260–88; Karin Friedrich, *The Other Prussia*; Leśnodorski, *Dominium Warmińskie*.

but took no concrete steps to enforce it.[8] Primate Jan Łaski and Bishop Drzewicki were sent to the increasingly restive city in 1524 in order to attend a diplomatic summit, and part of their Instruction dealt with Danzig Lutheranism, albeit gingerly. The prelates were told to find a fluent German speaker who might explain to the city council precisely why Luther's teaching was a danger to them. The tone of the suggested speech was one of paternal encouragement to change course.[9] If this friendly chat ever took place, it fell on deaf ears. Łaski and Drzewicki had to flee Danzig for their lives after their lodgings were attacked by a mob armed with knives and stones—the Crown let this pass in silence.[10] When the King summoned a national *sejm* in winter 1524, he grumbled to other parts of the monarchy about the disorder in Royal Prussian cities, 'infected with Lutheranerror'.[11] To the Prussian diet itself, however, the Crown envoy at the end of his agenda delicately repeated warnings of the perils Lutheranism posed to civil order.[12] When crowds of fishwives, brewers, and blacksmiths deposed the patrician councils of Danzig and Elbing in the name of the Gospel in the first weeks of 1525, there was quite simply no response from the royal court for six months. The Crown had, in effect, chosen not to interpose itself between its Hanseatic towns and Luther-inspired movements in these first crucial years.

The second distinct phase of policy, lasting just over fifteen months in 1525–6, was one of sudden, aggressive, and above all brief royal anti-Reformation action. The turning point came in May 1525 when, having signed a peace treaty in Kraków with Albrecht, Grand Master of the Teutonic Order, King Sigismund I directed a blast of kingly fury at rebellious Danzig. Finally ending his long silence, the monarch wrote an epic letter to the citizens of Danzig, listing their rumoured crimes—blasphemy, looting of churches, religious novelties, rebellion, violation of royal law and rights, and on it went—demanding an immediate explanation.[13] The rebel council sent a delegation to the royal court in August 1525, which duly presented Sigismund I with two Apologias, expositions of Lutheran doctrine in fine humanist Latin.[14] The behaviour of the Danzig envoys scandalized the court, and provoked agonized debate within the Polish royal council: Primate Łaski urged Sigismund I to crush the rebels in person, while some senators argued that Danzig's Reformation was a pastoral problem for Poland's bishops, not its Crown. The Poznań nobility, meanwhile, expressed disbelief that the King had not yet used force against the perfidious rebel Prussians.[15]

When the Polish *sejm* met at Piotrków at New Year 1526, it became clear that Sigismund I had settled on the path of a direct intervention.[16] From Piotrków, Sigismund I marched north to the castle of Marienburg, where the royal party took

8 CIP, vol. III, p. 579.   9 AT 7, pp. 11–13.
10 Bogucka, 'Walki społeczne', p. 386; Grunau, *Preussische Chronik*, vol. II, pp. 756–7.
11 AT 7, p. 155: 'civitatesque Prussie luteranis erroribus infectas'.
12 AT 7, p. 160. For the diet's non-committal response, see *Akta Stanów Prus Królewskich*, vol. 8, ed. Marian Biskup and Irena Janosz-Biskupowa (Warsaw, 1993), p. 375.
13 AT 7, pp. 356–8.   14 AT 7, pp. 358–83.
15 AT 7, pp. 384–9; AT 8, p. 12.
16 AT 8, pp. 7–9; Lorkiewicz, *Bunt Gdańska*, pp. 122–3.

Lutheran preachers into custody and summoned a Royal Prussian diet.[17] Danzig chronicles describe the panic which now gripped the city.[18] From Marienburg, in April 1526, a year and a half after the Danzig revolt, an advance party composed of top senators, including Chancellor Krzysztof Szydłowiecki and Łukasz Górka, was dispatched to the city, accompanied by a force variously reported as amounting to 200 or 600 cavalry.[19] Danzig's gates were opened to them, and this group was soon reinforced by the arrival of the King's nephew, Duke George of Pomerania (1523–31), with 200 of his own knights.[20] The path was now clear for the King himself. On 17 April, Sigismund I of Poland marched into the royal port, with several thousand men at arms raised from the Royal Prussian nobility.[21] An estimated total of 6,000 armed men in a single city was a massive show of force—the previous year, for example, Duke Albrecht had faced down the Sambian Peasants' Revolt on the battlefield with an ample (reported) 600 knights.[22] Andrzej Krzycki reported, with his usual humanist wit, that during the royal entry one merchant had been heard to say that with an army this large the King could compel Danzig to worship an ass, if he so wished.[23] Zygmunt rode directly to a packed St Mary's church where relics were kissed and, in his presence, the antiphon of Easter triumph sung, *Advenisti desiderabilis*.[24]

King Sigismund I spent almost four months in Danzig restoring order, from April until late July 1526. The chronicles report that his first action was to summon both the new (i.e. rebel) and deposed city councillors, a scene which degenerated into hysterical mutual denunciations, before the monarch swore in a new *Rat*.[25] The senator Mikołaj Szydłowiecki reported, in a letter to the queen, that many men were arrested after this confrontation, and were undergoing lengthy examinations 'which kept His Majesty occupied from dawn until evening'.[26] Over the course of the summer, thirteen men were executed for their role in the Lutheran revolt, chiefly in Danzig's town square, but one at Marienburg, where he was buried in a field near a crucifix statute. They were not brought before any ecclesiastical court, but executed as 'heretics and rebels' on royal orders.[27] One July day, the entire citizenry were required to swear a mass oath of loyalty to Sigismund I, as he sat on a makeshift throne before the *Arturhaus* merchants' hall.[28] Polish bishops, meanwhile, were busy overseeing a series of solemn processions, in which the

[17] AT 8, p. 32. Lorkiewicz, *Bunt Gdańska*, p. 126. Sigismund I founded a new parish church while at Marienburg: AAWa, Doc. Varia I.
[18] Lorkiewicz, *Bunt Gdańska*, pp. 120, 124.
[19] AT 8, p. 40; Grunau, *Preussische Chronik*, III, p. 163; Lorkiewicz, *Bunt Gdańska*, p. 127.
[20] AT 8, p. 40.
[21] AT 8, p. 40; Grunau, *Preussische Chronik*, vol. III, p. 163; Lorkiewicz, *Bunt Gdańska*, p. 129.
[22] Małłek, *Prusy Książęce*, p. 35.   [23] AT 8, p. 42.
[24] AT 8, p. 40.   [25] AT 8, pp. 41, 56; Lorkiewicz, *Bunt*, p. 139.
[26] AT 8, p. 56: 'Mtas. regia ejusmodi examinationibus a mane ad vesperam quotidie occupata fuit'. For other senators' letters from Danzig, see AT 8, pp. 66–8, 69–70.
[27] AT 8, pp. 74–5; Grunau, *Preussische Chronik*, vol. III, pp. 184–7; Lorkiewicz, *Bunt*, pp. 135–8.
[28] *Eyn statlicher unnd feyerlicher Actus der holdigund sso… Sigmundt… yn seiner Künglicher Stadt Dantzigk… enthpfangen hat* (Kraków, 1526).

expelled monks and nuns of Danzig were led back into their religious houses.[29] The King promulgated a swathe of royal edicts for the city during his stay. Danzigers were ordered to surrender all Lutheran books, pictures, and ballads to Piotr Kmita, marshal of the royal court.[30] On 20 July, the Crown issued the centrepiece of its Danzig intervention, the *Statuta Sigismundi*.[31] The *Statuta* decreed that any citizen unwilling to accept the old church must leave within two weeks; priests, monks, and nuns who had married were expelled immediately; preaching was regulated, the authority of the Rat confirmed. In a final flurry of activity, Sigismund I confirmed the city's cherished privileges, and conferred pensions on key members of the new council such as Philip Bischof.[32] As that long July drew to a close, King Sigismund left Danzig and rode out of Royal Prussia, leaving a contingent of armed men in the port.[33]

What had been achieved in Danzig was to act as a blueprint for the pacification of other towns in the territory. The Crown appointed an anti-heresy commission, consisting of bishops and senior royal officials, which travelled to both Elbing and Braunsberg in August 1526, installing new councils, apprehending rebels, taking mass oaths of loyalty on behalf of the King, hearing abjurations, and issuing anti-heresy statutes, each modelled directly on those promulgated for Danzig.[34] The King himself, from afar, engaged in a mopping-up operation, hunting down absconded fugitives from Danzig—just as the ringleaders of the German Peasants' War (1524–5) were being hunted down, at the same time, in the Holy Roman Empire. Throughout 1526 and 1527, King Sigismund dispatched persistent letters to neighbouring princes, in Pomerania and Ducal Prussia, insisting on the extradition or punishment of Danzig ringleaders such as Jakub Hegge, who had fled to Stolp (Słupsk).[35] The King took a hard line too with those Danzigers imprisoned on his orders in 1526, but not executed. In 1527, the Crown ordered the resettlement of a dozen key Danzig prisoners, such as Johann Ostendorp and the city secretary Georg Zimmerman, in Elbing and Thorn—they were allowed to live and trade freely in their new homes, on condition they never set foot in Danzig again.[36] Key prisoners, such as Johann Niempcz, a secretary to the 1525 rebel council, King Sigismund was very reluctant to release at all, doing so in September 1527 only after a sustained campaign of petitioning on Niempcz's behalf, spearheaded by Bishop Tomicki.[37] The King, Tomicki noted with disappointment, was grimly determined that the guilty must be punished.[38]

By autumn 1526, King Sigismund I was basically content, as he repeatedly announced in his letters, that as a result of his armed intervention the rebellious Lutheran city of Danzig had been 'restored to its original state', and Royal Prussia's

[29] Lorkiewicz, *Bunt*, pp. 132–5.   [30] AT 8, pp. 75–6.
[31] AT 8, pp. 76–83.   [32] AT 8, pp. 90–6.   [33] Lorkiewicz, *Bunt*, pp. 147–8.
[34] AT 8, pp. 110–19; Grunau, *Preussische Chronik*, vol. III, pp. 220–2; Achremczyk and Szorc, *Braniewo*, pp. 60–2. The King also appointed an anti-heresy commissioner for Marienburg but the dating of the letter is unclear: AT 7, p. 341.
[35] AT 8, pp. 63, 141. In 1533, there is a reference to Knade as a parish minister in Ducal Prussia, *Urkundenbuch* II, p. 295.
[36] AT 8, pp. 138–41, 153–6.   [37] AT 8, pp. 148–52.   [38] AT 8, p. 150.

beacon of revolt and Reformation successfully pacified.[39] His first minister agreed: Piotr Tomicki confidently wrote to the diplomat Johannes Danticus that in the latter's home town 'Lutheranism has been driven out through our severe measures, and the city restored to its former good state and order.'[40] Heresy and sedition in Royal Prussia had, by late 1527, dropped off the official royal agenda of the Polish parliament, case closed.[41]

The third phase of royal policy, from summer 1526 to the end of the reign, saw a return to Crown passivity, even in the face of ongoing Royal Prussian Lutheran reform. The dispersal of the royal heresy commissions, in August 1526, their work done, the King gone, marked the second major turning point in Crown policy towards the Royal Prussian Reformation. Thereafter, Sigismund I simply turned a blind eye (again) to Lutheran reform in this key territory, even as evidence of pro-Reformation activity mounted, and the complaints of local bishops grew more insistent. In the decade after 1526, in contrast to its earlier, briefly draconian stance, the Crown's religious interventions were sporadic, piecemeal, and reactive, amounting to no more than about a dozen royal letters to the province.

The King's new disengaged stance towards the Reformation in Royal Prussia first became apparent in a dispute over the non-payment of tithes to the Bishop of Włocławek. Bishop Maciej Drzewicki was denied payments by the Royal Prussian nobility, who openly cited Lutheran arguments in their defence. In spring 1526, King Sigismund had issued a decree ordering these nobles to pay up, or face prosecution as heretics.[42] This command was, however, simply disregarded, with opposition to it led by the Crown's own most senior officials in the province, the palatines of Pomerania and Marienburg.[43] In the face of Bishop Drzewicki's insistent complaints, King Sigismund demanded enforcement of his decree by the 'councillors and officials of Royal Prussia', writing to the palatine of Kulm in spring 1528 and Palatine Konopacki of Pomerania that autumn.[44] King Sigismund took no more action than that, however. Bishop Drzewicki grew increasingly disappointed, and was still waiting for a full settlement on tithes in 1530.[45]

A similar lack of royal will to act was evident in the case of Bartholomeus Vogt, a layman who preached Lutheranism in Elbing from at least 1528. Bishop Ferber of Ermland, stonewalled by Elbing council in all his attempts to silence Vogt, appealed to King Sigismund for assistance, recommending that the Crown 'make an example of him to everyone'.[46] Sigismund I banished Vogt from Elbing, but when this command was ignored, took no further action for almost a decade.[47] In 1532, Bishop Ferber appealed to the King again, asking that Elbing council be

---

[39] AT 8, p. 76: 'in primum statum restituere ...'

[40] AT 9, p. 30: 'qua severitate Luteranismus illinc sit explosus ac civitas in pristinum bonum statum et ordinem resituta'.

[41] AT 9, p. 9.

[42] AT 8, pp. 15–16, 35–6. See also Biskup in 'O początkach reformacji', p. 110.

[43] As claimed by Bishop Drzewicki, AT 10, pp. 201–2.

[44] AT 10, pp. 41–2, 200–1, 385–6.   [45] AT 12, p. 325.

[46] AT 10, pp. 159–60, 409–10; also AAWa, A1, fos. 66(v)–67, 75.

[47] By May 1535, the Crown was planning to create a commission to hear the case of Vogt, who by then was associated with Duke Albrecht and under his protection. Hartmann, *Herzog Albrecht*, p. 218.

forced to end its settlement of Dutch and German exiles, 'Lutherans and Zwinglians', in the town.[48] Sigismund's two letters to Elbing council had seemingly no effect.[49] The King warned the burghers of Elbing not to use Lutheran formulae in their wills, and created a new post for anti-heretical preaching, but took no further recorded action against the city's Reformation.[50] After 1526, it came as an unpleasant surprise to Bishops Ferber and Drzewicki, the top prelates in Royal Prussia, that they could not rely upon the Crown to support their anti-Reformation actions on the ground; that Sigismund I could be looked to only for brief and symbolic gestures.

Even in Danzig, the crucible of Lutheranism in Royal Prussia, Sigismund I's regime adopted an apparently indifferent stance after 1526. From the late 1520s, Polish and Prussian bishops embarked on a vociferous campaign against Pancratius Klemme, the pro-Luther preacher of St Mary's, the port's parish church.[51] Bishop Karnkowski sent an envoy to Danzig in 1532 to demand Klemme's removal, and in 1534 the Piotrków *sejm* itself complained about 'that most pernicious preacher'.[52] In January 1535, King Sigismund finally instructed Bishop Dantiscus and Georg Baisen, palatine of Marienburg, to travel to Danzig and take from all city officials an oath of loyalty to the Polish Crown and the old church.[53] The idea of this trip, and the oath, had originally been suggested by Dantiscus himself; this was an episcopal initiative. In a brief royal letter to Danzig council, Sigismund I asked that they put an end to the preaching of Klemme, whom he labelled a wolf in sheep's clothing.[54] When the envoys arrived in Danzig in April 1535, the contrasts with King Sigismund's 1526 intervention were, however, stark.[55] The city council politely refused to accept the stipulated oath, substituting the phrase 'the holy Roman church' with 'the holy Christian church'.[56] King Sigismund I was relatively nonchalant, simply informing Dantiscus that 'we are not pleased' at the Rat's behaviour.[57] His secretary, Jan Chojeński, reported cheerfully that the King was hopeful that time would improve the situation, and see a return to good order in the port.[58] Piotr Tomicki stressed only his personal sadness at the oath fiasco.[59] The patrician councillors of Danzig had publicly rejected the Roman church before the Crown's envoys, and no ill consequences, no threats, followed. Other bishops would continue to pursue Klemme, but to no effect; the *Statuta Sigismundi* went unenforced in Danzig.[60] King Sigismund I's willingness to defend the old church in Royal Prussia had, it seemed, finally dried up.

This story of royal policy towards Lutheran reform in its prized Baltic province, on many levels, does not make sense. Were King Sigismund and his council frightened of Lutheran influence in their lands, or not? In what way was the King

---

[48] AT 14, pp. 228–30.   [49] AT 14, pp. 264–5, 272–4.
[50] AT 14, pp. 666–7.   [51] AT 14, pp. 706–7, 803–4.
[52] Nowak and Urban, 'Pankracy Klemme'; AT 16b, p. 525, 'concionatore perniciosissimo'.
[53] AT 17, pp. 17–19.   [54] AT 17, p. 201.
[55] The key account of this mission is given by Nowak, 'Antryreformacyjna elegia'.
[56] For Dantiscus' account, see AT 17, pp. 456–8.
[57] AT 17, p. 441, 'Illud non satis placet'.   [58] AT 17, p. 437.
[59] AT 17, p. 476.   [60] Nowak and Urban, 'Pankracy Klemme', pp. 118–19.

defending the old church in Danzig, when he removed Lutheran rebels and replaced them with patricians of suspected Lutheran sympathies, such as Bischof? Why was royal rhetoric so insistent that heresy had been extirpated from Danzig in 1526, mission accomplished, when that was evidently not the case? Why did the Polish monarchy at certain times empower bishops as its anti-heresy agents, and at other times entirely ignore their anti-heresy pleas? We can now try to account for the inconsistency of Sigismund I's responses by offering two readings of them, centred respectively on (what we shall term for now) political interest and religious beliefs. These readings may differ from one another, but they are not necessarily in conflict.

ANALYSIS I—THE POLITICS OF THE BALTIC

Kriegseisen has described the King's entire Reformation policy as sheer realpolitik: 'he was directed by his own sense of *raison d'état*, and not the interests of a then still dominant catholicism'.[61] If we wish to read princely toleration as simply a product of princely politics, it is certainly possible to construct such a case in this Polish-Prussian episode, and it might run as follows:

King Sigismund and his Polish royal council had a single overriding aim in the Baltic in the 1520s and 1530s—to prevent any secession or loss of Royal Prussia. It would be hard to overstate the importance of this territory to Sigismund I. For his royal line, Royal Prussia embodied one of the Lithuanian dynasty's great achievements as kings of Poland, a source of prestige and considerable income— from the handsome taxes paid by the Hanseatic cities and the royal landed estates which made up some 50 per cent of the province.[62] In royal letters, Danzig was referred to as the 'exalted city', 'exceptionally dear to the king'.[63] Little wonder that Bishop Tomicki noted anxiously, in the wake of the 1525 revolt, that the Danzig affair was 'indeed burdensome and upsetting to His Majesty'.[64]

The rise of Lutheranism, from 1518 to 1525, provoked a very real fear that Royal Prussia was about to slip from the Polish monarchy's grasp, and this anxiety led initially to a paralysed silence. Since its absorption into the Polish monarchy in 1454, Royal Prussia's patriciate mercantile elites had been firmly wedded to their new masters. Families such as the Ferbers enjoyed hereditary places on Danzig council, held top ecclesiastical benefices across the province, and saw the 1454 pact with the Polish Crown as a touchstone for their own identity and liberties.[65]

---

[61] Kriegseisen, *Stosunki wyznaniowe*, p. 45: 'kierował się on własnym rozumieniem racji stanu, a nie interesami panującego jeszcze katolicyzmu'.

[62] Friedrich, *The Other Prussia*, p. 25.

[63] AT 7, p. 384, 'civitatis sue gedanensis, quam semper ejus Mtas. singulari gratia est prosequuta', 'tam insigni civitate'.

[64] AT 7, p. 342: 'Res Gedanensium confusas et peturbatas regia Mtas. tametsi etiam aliunde jam dudum intellexerit...'

[65] Friedrich, *The Other Prussia*; Zins, *Ród Ferberów*, p. 88.

They enjoyed a close client relationship with Poland's ruling house: visiting Danzig in 1504, King Aleksander had knighted members of the Zimmerman and Ferber houses.[66] It was these people whom the wholescale urban, Lutheran revolt of January 1525 swept away, putting new groups in power. Although the Danzig rebels professed passionate loyalty to King Sigismund, their agendas were very different to those of the Ferbers.[67] The entire raison d'être of Royal Prussia rested on its inhabitants' historic rejection, in the long war of 1454–66, of the rule of the Teutonic Order—they had cast off the Grand Master, and chosen the King in Kraków instead, as a partner against a common enemy. Luther fatefully changed that calculation. For those in the province determined to see a Wittenberg-inspired Reformation, the religiously conservative Sigismund I was not an appealing master— whereas, just to the east, Grand Master Albrecht of Brandenburg had emerged as a leading early patron of the Reformation. The Polish Crown thus feared that, for its subjects in Royal Prussia, Luther's new theology had led King and Grand Master to switch roles; the Jagiellonian liberators of 1454 were now oppressors, and the Lutheran Grand Master was reborn as a potential saviour of Danzig and its Reformation. Lutheran reform, in other words, had the potential to prompt the full-scale secession of Royal Prussia, to reunite it with the *Ordenstaat* to which it had belonged for centuries. The new theology might yet trigger a geopolitical earthquake in the Baltic, to the serious detriment of the Polish Crown, which had been in the ascendant in this region since 1410.[68]

Fears of the imminent secession of Royal Prussia to Albrecht were openly expressed. Bishop Piotr Tomicki noted anxiously in spring 1525 that there were Lutherans in both the Teutonic Order and in Royal Prussia, and that it was possible both these parts would unite.[69] Bishop Ferber of Ermland wrote that the King was extremely worried that 'the larger Prussian towns and especially Danzig [would] . . . go over to the side of the Grand Master, who is the chief supporter of this sect'; the *Heilsberger Chronik* that Royal Prussian Lutherans were prepared for military action against the King.[70] Defending its controversial 1525 peace with Grand Master Albrecht, the Crown explained that the main rationale for signing the treaty had been to prevent the defection and loss of Danzig and neighbouring cities.[71] There is evidence that the Polish Crown did have reason to be afraid. As Antoni Lorkiewicz pointed out, in 1523 the rebel leader Ambrose Sturm boasted to the King that certain Danzig citizens already had an agreement with his enemy, the Grand Master, to back the latter's claims on Prussia.[72] If we believe Simon Grunau's vehemently anti-Lutheran chronicle, the 'storm-preachers' began to

[66] Zins, *Ród Ferberów*, p. 13. In the 1530s, Queen Bona was still animated by the fear of a secession of Royal Prussia: *Corpus of Johannes Danticus' Texts*, nr. 1199.

[67] AT 7, p. 382.

[68] This argument was first mooted by Lorkiewicz, *Bunt Gdańska*, p. 102. See also Henryk Zins, 'The Political and Social Background of the Early Reformation in Ermeland', *English Historical Review* 75 (1960): 589–600, at p. 598 and Biskup, 'Geneza', p. 417. This account builds on, and extends, those analyses.

[69] AT 7, p. 210.

[70] As translated by Zins, 'Early Reformation in Ermeland', p. 599. See also Biskup, 'Geneza', p. 417.

[71] ASPK, vol. 8, p. 390.   [72] Lorkiewicz, *Bunt Gdańska*, p. 102.

declare Sigismund I a 'godless tyrant' who did not want any Gospel in his lands, a lord of Babylon. Grunau describes a 1525 reformist sermon on the Passion, which presented Hegge's followers as the persecuted Christ, Danzig's mercantile dynasties as Judas, Chancellor Szydłowiecki as Pontius Pilate, and 'the godless king of Poland' as Herod himself.[73]

The defection of Danzig would have been a mighty economic and political blow to the Polish Crown at the best of times, but the timing of the 1525 Danzig and Elbing Lutheran revolts made them even more dangerous. During the Prussian War waged between King Sigismund and Grand Master Albrecht in 1519–21, Danzig had made a major contribution to the Polish campaign—supplying 600 armed men, revamping its extensive fortifications at the city's own expense, providing a fleet to blockade Königsberg, and withstanding several days of bombardment.[74] That conflict had ended with an uneasy four-year truce, which was due to expire in April 1525, just weeks after the January 1525 revolt. In any renewed bout of hostilities, a strategic defection by Danzig to Grand Master Albrecht could easily cost Sigismund I the whole of Royal Prussia.

These 'political'—constitutional, historic, geopolitical, diplomatic, military—reasons can thus help us account for the Crown's extreme caution in dealing with Lutherans in its Hanse towns in the opening years of the Reformation. The silences, the lack of open censure, can be read as an attempt to avoid alienating the powerful Lutheran groups which controlled Danzig in particular, at a tense juncture. The Crown could not risk antagonizing local Lutherans while they enjoyed significant political power in the province; it could not give them—through strong anti-Reformation action or rhetoric—a compelling reason to return to the Grand Master's rule.

Sticking with our political lens, the interventionist phase of Polish royal policy (1525–6) occurred only once an opportunity to act arose. The impasse between the King and his Baltic cities ended when, unexpectedly, the Teutonic Order was suddenly removed as a military threat. The Treaty of Kraków of April 1525, a perpetual peace deal between Albrecht and King Sigismund, at a stroke neutralized the Grand Master and isolated Lutheran Danzig. This radical peace ended the war, dissolved the Teutonic Order itself by turning its lands into a secular fief of the Polish Crown, and named Albrecht as its hereditary duke. With this move, Albrecht in 1525 instantly made enemies of all the Grand Master's historic allies—the papacy, the Holy Roman Emperor Charles V, the Teutonic Order in the Empire, and the Knights' surviving theocratic state of Livonia. Highly vulnerable, Albrecht was, from 1525, thus totally dependent on King Sigismund I's protection for his political survival, and that of his fledgling state. In effect, the price he paid for this protection was the abandonment of his co-religionists in Lutheran Danzig and Elbing to the wrath of the King. In other words, the Treaty of Kraków placed a safe

---

[73] Grunau, *Preussische Chronik*, III, p. 79 'der herr konigk ein gottloser tirann istt', p. 153 'der gottlose konigk von Polen istt Herodes', and p. 171.
[74] Samsonowicz, 'Rola Gdańska', pp. 279–80.

wedge between the Reformations in Ducal Prussia and Royal Prussia, leaving the latter's Lutheran councils with nowhere to turn for aid.

With his hands thus freed, Sigismund I could set about pacifying the rebel-held cities of Royal Prussia, and restoring the royal family's ousted patrician allies.[75] One of the King's first acts upon entering the port was to depose the 1525 rebel council, with its brewers, tailors, and middling merchants, and create a new Rat drawn from the mercantile oligarchy, from families such as the Ferbers and Bishoffs. The final decrees issued by the King in Danzig showered pensions, cash gifts, and concessions on loyal patricians such as Philipp Bischof, without any enquiry into their religious beliefs.[76] These men represented a social stratum which identified the Polish monarchy closely with their own hegemony and splendid Hanse wealth, and who would defend Sigismund I's control of Royal Prussia. The strength of this political alliance can be glimpsed in the chronicle of Berndt Stegmann, a Lutheran patrician, whose description of the events of 1525–6 was emphatically pro-royal, referring to Sigismund I as 'his royal majesty, their gracious overlord'.[77]

In political-constitutional terms, the armed anti-Reformation intervention of 1526 also gave Sigismund I's regime a welcome opportunity to bind Danzig even more intimately to the Crown.[78] The paragraph-long oath required of city officials from 1526 pledged 'eternal obedience and honour to His Majesty and the laudable Kingdom of Poland' and his officials and diets, making a passing reference to religion only in the last line.[79] Sigismund I commanded that Danzig would no longer mint its own coinage, a right promised under the original 1454 Privilege, and that a new royal mint in Thorn would instead serve the whole of Royal Prussia—a move long recognized by Polish historians as a blatant attempt at centralization, and bitterly resisted by the city.[80] Shortly after the King's visit, Primate Łaski informed Bishop Ferber that, due to the spread of heresy, the time was ripe to remove the Royal Prussian see of Ermland from the jurisdiction of Riga, and instead incorporate it directly into the Polish church and see of Gniezno.[81] Here was yet another way of capitalizing on the Reformation crisis, to curb the territory's autonomous status in the ecclesiastical sphere too.

The 1526 royal visit to Danzig was used to celebrate Polish royal rule over the city symbolically, in various performances of kingly authority. The Crown presented Sigismund I's visit to the port not as an act of retribution, but of justice—the

---

[75] With the exception of the discredited Mayor Ferber, who was given a pension and withdrew from political life, retiring to his country estates: AT 8, pp. 93–4. See also Zins, *Ród Ferberów*, pp. 90–2.

[76] AT 8, pp. 92–6.

[77] Published in Theodor Hirsch (ed.), 'Forsetzung der Danziger Chroniken', in *Scriptores Rerum Prussicarum*, vol. V (Leipzig, 1974), pp. 440–591. Quote at p. 583: 'kgl. maj. zu Polen, ihren gnedigesten erbhern'.

[78] A point made also by Dworzaczkowa, 'O genezie i skutkach', p. 105.

[79] Published in Lorkiewicz, *Bunt Gdańska*, Appendix IX, p. 222: 'obedientiam semper exhibiturum et Regie Majestatis honorem et laudabilis Regni Polonie...'.

[80] Samsonowicz, 'Rola Gdańska', p. 281. For Danzig minting, see Michael North, 'Danziger Münzen in Geldumlauf Königlichen Preussens und des Herzogtums Preussen der Frühen Neuzeit', in B. Jähnig and P. Letkemann (eds), *Danzig in Acht Jahrhunderten* (Münster, 1985), pp. 241–50.

[81] AAWa, D66, fo. 146.

King as one who hears grievances, dispenses justice, and restores order. This was the message when Sigismund I summoned the Ferbers, the old council and the rebel council to his presence in the Rathaus, and heard out their mutual denunciations, and when he sat in ceremonial splendour on a makeshift throne before the massed citizenry.[82] This message is also present in the frontispiece of the pamphlet commemorating this event, printed in Kraków by Wietor in 1526, which shows King Sigismund I enthroned in majesty with the arms of Poland and Lithuania, holding not an orb and sceptre (the normal attributes of kingship in medieval iconography), but a raised sword, a symbol of justice.[83] The King's titles—'King of Poland, Grand Duke of Lithuania and Russia, and lord of all the lands of Prussia'— are printed above his image, with a statement that he came to Danzig where he sat in majesty. On the front page of this, one of the core 'anti-heresy' texts of the reign, there is no religious imagery whatsoever. The court also performed the historic nature of Polish royal overlordship in Royal Prussia in other ways. According to Simon Grunau, one of the court's last acts in Danzig was to celebrate the Feast of the Division of the Apostles on 15 July 1526. Sigismund I himself appeared in state, says Grunau, his knights bearing halberds, the scene decorated with cloth of gold.[84] The date 15 July was loaded with significance: it was the anniversary of the Battle of Grunwald/Tannenburg, where King Władysław Jagiełło (1386–1434) had, in 1410, dealt a terrible military blow to the Teutonic Knights.[85] In Bishop Tomicki's illuminated lectionary, the most splendid image of all was a depiction of this battle, accompanying the liturgy for the Feast of the Division of the Apostles.[86] If Grunau's report is accurate, this Danzig pageantry was little more than a public celebration of the Polish Crown's seven decades of ascendancy in Prussia.

The Crown's subsequent passivity towards Lutheranism in the monarchy's northern territories (1526–40) can be explained by the fact that, in political terms, all was well in Royal Prussia after 1526. The regime's worldly interests had already been satisfactorily secured during the King's visit and so, thereafter, Sigismund I saw little compelling political reason to intervene against heterodoxy. With the secessionist, seditious, populist elements of the Danzig Reformation defeated, and loyal burghers happily installed in power, local Lutheranism no longer presented a serious political threat to the Crown. So long as public life in Danzig was orderly, piety alone, it seems, was not enough to provoke Sigismund I into further anti-heretical action, even as evidence of Lutheran belief and worship in Royal Prussia proliferated after 1526. It is at this point that royal and episcopal approaches to Reformation in the province diverged, and came into conflict. From 1526 onwards, Bischof and his council gambled correctly that if they could convincingly maintain social order in the city, and demonstrate their

---

[82] AT 8, p. 41; Lorkiewicz, *Bunt Gdańska*, p. 132.   [83] *Eyn statlicher*, frontispiece.

[84] Grunau, *Preussische Chronik*, vol. III, pp. 203–4.

[85] For the royal family's traditional pieties on this feast day, see Tadeusz Lalik, 'Kaplica królewska i publiczne praktyki religijne rodziny Kazimierza Jagiellończyka', *Kwartalnik Historyczny* 88 (1981): 391–415.

[86] Leszek Hajdukiewicz, *Księgozbiór i zainteresowania bibliofilskie Piotra Tomickiego* (Wrocław, 1961), p. 103.

loyalty to the Crown, Sigismund I would not come to Danzig again in order to remove cherished Lutheran preachers such as Klemme. When defending their choice of Klemme to the King in 1535, for example, the Rat emphatically protested its loyalty to Sigismund I: they were his very devoted subjects, promising 'to observe rules of subjugation and fealty towards His Majesty', 'in war and in peace'.[87] It is telling that where Sigismund I did continue to send grumpy, threatening letters to Danzig after 1526, these addressed the Rat's non-compliance with his minting decree, rather than any religious matter.[88]

If Sigismund I's responses to Reformation in Royal Prussia were basically predicated on a defence of the Crown's geopolitical and fiscal interests, his insouciance in the face of the Danzig patricians' increasingly open patronage of Lutheran preaching and reform, from 1526 to 1540, becomes less of a mystery. This, then, is a possible political reading of the fate of the Royal Prussian Reformation in these crucial formative decades: the King—for all his celebrated piety—wanted his Prussian subjects' money and allegiance more than he desired their loyalty to Rome.[89] Writing on Reformation Esslingen, Rublack reached a similarly cynical conclusion, claiming that the council cared 'more for the security of public order and civic unity than for loyalty to the church'.[90]

ANALYSIS II—RELIGION: LOVE OF THE OLD CHURCH?

A political reading of Sigismund I's relationship with Lutherans in Royal Prussia might be satisfying, but it is also problematic. As we saw in the Introduction, there are real problems with attempting to separate out the 'religious' and 'political' motivations of sixteenth-century men and women, because they were fundamentally entangled in the minds of premodern Europeans. This was particularly true in the case of heresy, ever since Emperor Frederick II had issued thirteenth-century decrees stating that heresy was, by its very nature (as rebellion against God), also an act of lèse-majesté, or treason, against earthly kings.[91] Offering a purely 'religious' reading of Sigismund I's actions towards Royal Prussia is thus problematic on the face of it. This second reading of the Polish Crown's responses to Reformation in Royal Prussia will therefore break 'religion' down into some of its constituent categories, distinguishing between faith, piety, worship, doctrine, and church. By paying close attention to the regime's 'religious' pronouncements in the context of Lutheranism in Royal Prussia (1518–40), Crown action in this episode can be read in a different light. This, however, is a disconcerting story, in which religion appears to diminish ever more from these events before we finally see its underlying shape.

---

[87] AT 17, p. 347: 'devotissimos animos nostros', 'erga illius Mtem eadem subiectionis et fidei norma observere', 'pace aeque ac bello'.

[88] AT 13, pp. 70–1, 99–100.

[89] This is a reading which Lorkiewicz was reluctant to contemplate, claiming that Sigismund had simply been tricked by the crafty Danzigers into inadvertently permitting heresy, *Bunt Gdańska*, p. 156.

[90] Quoted in Brady, 'Reformation of the Common Man', p. 106.

[91] Discussed in Patschovsky, 'Heresy and Society'.

There are four aspects of the Crown's religious actions in Royal Prussia in the years 1518–*c*.1540 which invite comment, and the first is the royal regime's clear tendency to talk about Lutheranism in what we would today call avowedly socio-political terms, rather than obviously theological ones. In the initial years of Crown silence, a number of texts were addressed to Danzig demonstrating precisely this. The paternal warning which the King's envoys were to deliver to the Danzigers in 1524 offered entirely pragmatic arguments against religious innovation. The envoys were to stress the dangerously divisive political and social consequences of the city's adherence to new teachings:

> religion be the only thing which binds together human affairs, which contains all laws and decrees of the Respublica and if this bond is dissolved so are all things with it…and this bond is threatened by seditious and heretical men.[92]

Heresy within their community, the Danzigers were warned, would bring insolence and tumults. Informing the Polish *sejm* in 1524 that Royal Prussian cities were 'infected with Lutheranism', King Sigismund made no reference to the content of heterodox belief, but only to its practical consequences, 'those who govern them cannot resist the fury of the multitude'.[93] Heresy was thus juxtaposed, not with orthodoxy per se, but with 'concord and a tranquil state of affairs'.[94] This pattern continued during the King's 1525–6 move against rebel Danzig: in the royal texts issued during his armed visit, Lutheranism was never condemned for its heterodox beliefs *alone*, but instead chiefly for its terrible social consequences of disorder and disobedience. In the King's first, angry letter to Danzig (May 1525), the religious crimes committed by the port's citizens are followed by a symmetrical list of six crimes against the Crown and good order:

> [You have done] much against the dignity of God, the blessed Virgin his mother and all the saints, blasphemed the most holy sacrament, taken and wickedly broken pictures, images, and liturgical apparatus from the churches, looted chalices, crosses, patens and other jewels, despoiled monks and nuns and thrown them out of their houses, brought in new sects and a new religion, treated our royal envoys shamefully and offensively, licentiously deposed the officials of your city,…wrongfully deposed the mayor against our authority, violated our laws, erected a fork and wheel in the market in violation of the citizens' privileges…and installed priests in royal benefices without our consent.[95]

---

[92] AT 7, nr. p. 11: 'licet religio vero unicum sit vinculum in rebus humanis, quo leges ac instituta omnium rerumpublicarum continentur, quo dissoluto, dissolvi necesse est universa, cumque non novum sit, hoc vinculum a seditiosis ac hereticis hominibus impeti'.

[93] AT 7, p. 156: 'civitates Prussie heresi luterana infectas ad tantam licentiam devenisse, ut hi, qui presunt, furorem multitudinis coercere non possint'.

[94] AT 7, p. 157, 'concordia et tranquillo statu'.

[95] AT 7, pp. 356–7: 'ut plurima contra deum et beatissimam virginem, matrem ejus, ac omnes sanctos indigmissima committerentur in divinissimum sacramentum blasphemaretur, ciboria, altaria, imagines, picturas in ecclesiis esse confracta et contumeliose ejecta, calices, patenas, cruces et alia clenodia de ecclesiis accepta et asportata, monachos et moniales spoliatos et de monasteriis ejectos, novas sectas et novam religionem invectam, oratores nostros infamatos et contumeliis affectos, pro-consules, consules et alios officiales civitatis licentissime depositis et opprobriis licentissime affectos aliosque in locum ipsorum indebite suffectos, burgrabium contra auctoritatem nostram exauctoratum et novas de illis constitutiones in derogationem potestatis nostre factas, judicia nostra regia violata,

Describing this fusion of religious irreverence, disorder, and affront to the Polish Crown, the Royal Chancellery, in 1525–6, developed a catchphrase, 'crimes against the divine and royal majesty', or the pithier phrase, 'tumults and errors'.[96] The *Statuta Sigismundi*, the great 'anti-heretical' body of rules issued for chastened Danzig in 1526, also presented *luteranismus* principally as a danger to civic peace in the city. Fully half of the lengthy *Statuta Sigismundi* text addressed urban constitutional issues, such as the dignity of the mayor, punishments against revolt, a ban on secret gatherings, restrictions on social groups heavily implicated in the 1525 uprising such as brewers, and an insistence that grievances be addressed to the King, and not the general populace.[97] The Crown's remedies were thus focused on preventing any future breakdown of social and political order. The *Statuta* present Lutheranism as a social-political crime, an epidemic of insolence and disobedience.

A second point to note is the Crown's repeated assertion that it was bad local government in Danzig which caused the revolt and entire crisis—that the causal prime mover was not a heretical movement, but ineffective local elites. In royal texts, heretical preaching functions as a mere catalyst for disorder, the result of bad government, like an opportunistic secondary infection. Specifically, the misrule of Mayor Eberhard Ferber was seen to have created a volatile situation in civic affairs which demagogic, Wittenberg-linked preachers simply exploited. Mayor Ferber himself was pointedly told by a royal orator in 1526, for example, that 'His Majesty is not ignorant of what was done in your city and from what origins all this evil has sprung.'[98] Reporting to Queen Bona Sforza from Danzig in 1526, Piotr Kmita confirmed that the lawsuit of the ejected mayor Eberhard Ferber had at last been settled, 'for this affair was the cause of all the bad things in this city'.[99] In the 1526 charter granting Danzig land in the Hel peninsula, the Crown declared, summing up the events of recent years, that 'in this our city of Danzig there *first* arose internal sedition, and *then* disturbances in all human and divine affairs'.[100] Bishop Ferber (the mayor's brother), writing in 1529, asserted that the real cause of the revolt had been political hatred of their family.[101] Even Marcin Kromer's 1548 funerary oration remembered the Danzig revolt as an entirely political affair: he referred to 'sedition' and 'rebellion', but not once to heterodoxy in the city.[102] The Polish Crown and leading senators thus depicted Lutheran heresy in Royal Prussia in 1525–6 not so much a source of political breakdown (a cause) as a result of bad government and a vehicle for political discontent (a symptom). Sigismund I's regime thereby seemed to deny Lutheran preaching a powerful intrinsic agency of

---

furcam et rotam in foro extructam contra privilegia et libertates civitatis...ecclesias parrochiales juris patronatus nostri externis sacerdotibus, sine scientia et consensu nostro, collates...'.

[96] For example, 7, p. 318; AT 8, pp. 31, 62.   [97] AT 8, pp. 76–83.

[98] AT 7, p. 393: 'ut vobis declararet, quam non incognita sit ejus Mti ea, que acta sint in civitate vestra et ex quibus initiis hec omnia mala processerint'.

[99] AT 8, p. 106: 'hec enim causa totius fomentum mali in hac urbe fuit'.

[100] AT 8, p. 88: 'Quod cum in civitate nostra gdanensi primum seditiones intestine, deinde omnium divinarum et humanarum rerum perturbationes exorte essent...'

[101] AT 11, pp. 107–8.   [102] Kromer, *De Sigismundo Primo*, fo. 145v.

its own—it became a problem only in the right social-political conditions. Whereas much recent scholarship on the Reformation has stressed the raw spiritual power of Luther's ideas as a prime mover in turning parts of Europe upside down from 1517, Sigismund and his counsellors sound disconcertingly like nineteenth-century historians, accounting for the success of the Reformation with reference to local political factors and leadership alone.

Also striking is the strangely anaemic religious language used by the Crown about Lutheranism, in which preachers and rebels are not much referred to as 'heretics'. Even in the twenty-seven regime documents produced about Royal Prussian Lutheranism in the active phase of royal policy (May 1525 to August 1526), in only five is any reference made to 'heresy', 'heretical' things, or to 'heretics'. Key texts from this time which shirk all reference to heresy include the May 1525 furious royal letter listing the crimes of the city of Danzig, the decree demanding the surrender of all Lutheran materials within the city walls, Primate Łaski's outraged memorandum about the 'seditious preachers' of Danzig, and the anti-Reformation statutes issued for Braunsberg.[103] Even the *Statuta Sigismundi*, a list of rules running to some twenty pages, refers to heresy only once, towards the end and in passing, in a clause ordering tavern keepers to check that any guests are free of 'heresies, and new and impious dogmas'.[104] Within the Danzig elite, Stegman's chronicle too referred to the rebels of 1525 not as heretics, but as 'the new council' or 'the storm-preachers'.[105] The well-established, colourful medieval rhetoric against heresy—as a weed, leprosy, devilish deception, Satanic work—is all but absent from the language of Sigismund I's regime in its response to Lutheran urban revolts in the 1520s.[106] The *Statuta Sigismundi* made a single reference to 'weeds': that is all.[107] This anti-Reformation intervention was characterized, then, by a certain rhetorical ambivalence about heresy; or, rather, about Lutheranism as heresy. In particular, the Polish Crown was not using the normative platform provided by its decrees and edicts—and its large-scale military intervention—to actively demonize Lutheranism itself. Put simply, it was treated in these royal sources as a local social and governmental problem, not as a major religious catastrophe for the wider monarchy.

The curious invisibility of any 'religious' sentiment in this major Crown intervention is clearest, however, when we focus on the actual restoration of the old church in Danzig by Sigismund I and his bishops in summer 1526, and how little it amounted to. Biskup dismissed it as 'superficial'.[108] Royal policy towards the 'religious' elements of Lutheranism can best be characterized as 'remove and replace'. The first pages of the *Statuta Sigismundi* set out how Lutheran things (objects, people) transmitting 'seditious' ideas would be removed from the

[103] AT 7, pp. 356–8, 387–9; AT 8, pp. 75–6, 114–19.

[104] AT 8, p. 79: 'hereses ac nova et impia dogmata'.

[105] Published in Hirsch, 'Forsetzung', pp. 569–75.

[106] See L. E. Sackville, *Heresy and Heretics in the Thirteenth Century: The Textual Representations* (York, 2011).

[107] AT 8, p. 77, 'zizaniam seminare'.

[108] Biskup, 'O początkach', p. 111: 'pozorna restytucja katolicyzmu'.

city—enforced exile for married clergy, and an import ban on Lutheran books, pictures, and songs. 'To ensure that this fire is not reignited', that rebel influences did not take hold again, the *Statuta* stipulated too that only non-suspect sea captains could dock at the port, and that tavern keepers must show a copy of the King's heresy edicts to all guests as they checked in.[109] Restoration of the old religion, meanwhile, lay in simply putting things back as they had been—'ad pristinam', in one of the Crown's favourite descriptions of its achievements in 1526 in Danzig, Elbing, and Braunsberg.[110] Royal decrees demanded that citizens return to churches looted liturgical plate, as well as images and service books which had been removed. Chronicles describe how monks were led back into their houses, one after another, by Bishop Drzewicki, undoing their expulsion.[111] This suggests a very limited religious anti-Reformation vision, where restoration of the old church was equated with a painfully literal 'putting back' of chalices, patens, liturgical books, images of saints and friars. Alaistair Duke has pointed out that in Europe in the 1520s, 'Lutheranism' was seen as a negative religion in that it essentially denied many everyday religious practices of the old church.[112] In Royal Prussia, the Polish Crown evidently shared this view of *luteranismus*—if Lutherans removed religious things, the pious could triumph simply by putting them back, on a shelf, in a niche, in a building. What occurred in Royal Prussian towns in spring and summer 1526 was therefore a physical reversal of Lutheran reforms, but not what we would normally understand as a 're-Catholicization'. In stark contrast to the Habsburg re-Catholicization of Prague a century later, Sigismund I ordered no preaching campaigns, no mendicants were sent in to win souls, no catechisms or confessions utilized.[113] It is important to note that the Crown did not see this restoration of the old church as in any way limited or modest—Bishop Tomicki boasted that the King had with all severity 'driven out' ('explosus') Lutheranism from Danzig.[114] With thousands of armed men at the King's disposal, this major mobilization of royal resources was not a half-hearted anti-Reformation action, but it was a pre-confessional one.

What religious purpose or understanding of the church, then, is revealed in Sigismund I's policies—in the identification of Lutheranism primarily with social disorder, the belief that heresy merely exploited a vacuum created by bad government, the lack of traditional anti-heretical rhetoric, the minimal and mechanistic restoration of the old church? When articulating catholicism to Royal Prussian subjects, the Crown placed a consistent emphasis on historic consensus and unity. The Crown's 1524 delegation and 1525 great letter to Danzig both told its citizens that the church embodied things agreed 'by the holy fathers, all ecclesiastical authorities and the whole Christian world throughout so many centuries'.[115] The *Statuta Sigismundi* too, in their very first clause, stressed that 'the traditions of the

[109] AT 8, pp. 78–9.   [110] AT 8, pp. 63, 76, 113–14.
[111] Lorkiewicz, *Bunt Gdańska*, p. 135; AT 8, p. 109.
[112] Duke, *Reformation and Revolt*, pp. 25–8, 41–57.
[113] Louthan, *Converting Bohemia*.   [114] AT 9, p. 30.
[115] AT 7, p.12, 'sanctorum patrum totiusque ecclesie auctoritas et universi orbis christiani per tot secula consensus'; the same sentiments expressed also at p. 357.

church were handed down to us as an orthodoxy by our glorious ancestors, and must be obeyed . . .', adding that the city must use 'the old religion and ceremonies, observed for all centuries in all Christian kingdoms and dominions, and handed down to us by our ancestors'.[116] Sigismund I's envoys had also told the Danzigers in 1524 that religion was the glue which bound the commonweal together, in a unified church-society.

By contrast, King Sigismund and his advisors did not seem very much interested in doctrine, either Lutheran or otherwise. Of the scores of royal documents pronouncing on the Reformation in Royal Prussia, only one engaged directly with doctrinal controversies. When the Danzig rebels presented their two, lengthy, heavily doctrinal-theological Apologias to the King in 1525, Vice Chancellor Tomicki was charged with replying in the King's name. In his oration, Tomicki attacked *sola fide*, iconoclasm, and the rejection of monasticism and saintly cults— but only after the first half of the oration had first offered a lengthy articulation of orthodoxy as lying in the unity (not in any specific teaching) of the universal church. The church was 'a perfect congregation', 'a firm rock', conserved in unity, its long history of Christian teaching juxtaposed with the sedition and sacrilege of the Danzigers.[117] Tomicki's oration apart, no other royal text relating to Lutheranism in Royal Prussia—not even those issued during the 1526 royal armed visit—contained an explicit defence of the papacy, monasticism, or salvation through works. The Crown's 'religious' goals in Royal Prussia in the 1520s and 1530s were instead, it seems, to restore the social-political order of local Christian society.

Read in this 'religious' (but not confessional) light, it is less surprising that, after 1526, King Sigismund I lost interest in the religious life of his Hanse towns. He had restored to power loyal patrician families, and it did not matter much if they were privately sympathetic to Martin Luther's teachings because these were not the 'Lutherans' whom the King had set out to remove by force in 1525/6. The Danzig 'Lutherans' whom the King could not tolerate were men such as Jakob Hegge or Jakob Knade: these, Sigismund I was in the end willing to execute, and scrupulous about exiling or imprisoning. These rebels posed a violent threat to the Crown's authority and social order. After 1526, the Crown's limited epistolary interventions took place only in those cases where bishops had briefly (but only briefly) convinced the King there might be a seditious Lutheran element still present on the ground—in Bartholomeus Vogt (whom Bishop Ferber painted as a rabble-rouser), in the peasants of the Vistula delta who no longer fulfilled their feudal obligations to their priest, or in Pancratius Klemme, persistently but unsuccessfully labelled by bishops as fermenting rebellion in Danzig. In 1535, when the Danzig Rat insisted on swearing an oath of loyalty to the 'Christian' rather than the 'Roman' church, Prussian bishops were aghast, but the King himself did not act and expressed only

---

[116] AT 8, p. 77: 'quia traditiones ecclesiastice, ut a majoribus nostris orthodoxis prodite sunt, servari debent . . . statuimus ut deinceps usus antiquus religionis et ceremoniarum, tot seculis in omnibus regnis et dominiis christianis observatus et a majoribus nostris nobis per manus traditus . . . in omnibus ecclesiis observetur'.

[117] AT 7, pp. 400–5.

limited censure. He was not in the business of imposing doctrinal uniformity on what remained controverted questions. If preachers such as Pancratius Klemme obeyed political authorities, adhered to the core creedal tenets of the *fides*, and operated within the social-institutional umbrella of the catholic church (preaching in its parish churches, nominally within its diocesan hierarchies), they and their controversial theological opinions could be accommodated within the notionally unified church inherited from the fifteenth century.[118] Patrician-led Lutheranism existing within the context of loyalty to the Crown and good civil order, and discreetly patronized by the social elite, as it was in Royal Prussia from 1526 onwards, might have been a source of personal disappointment to King Sigismund I, but it was not the end of the world, far less of the catholic church.

CONCLUSIONS

Is it possible to pull together these two parallel tellings of this story——the 'political' and 'religious'? King Sigismund's responses to Lutheran Reformation in Royal Prussia progressed from inaction, to a huge show of royal strength, to a longer-term passivity. Faced with a tide of urban Lutheranism in Royal Prussia which culminated in major city revolts in 1525, the Polish Crown initially did nothing at all because it feared that this prized province would secede wholesale to the pro-Reformation Grand Master of the Teutonic Knights. Finally freed to act by the Treaty of Kraków (1525), which deprived the rebels of Duke Albrecht's protection, Sigismund I and his councillors moved to end this defiance of royal authority, restore the patrician pro-Polish elite to power, end the breakdown of normal constitutional structures, and ensure that the physical and social fabric of religious life was returned to its former harmony, 'its pristine state'. Thereafter, local bishops and the King somewhat parted company. After 1526, a handful of Prussian bishops (Drzewicki, Ferber, Dantiscus) were keen to see continued action against Lutheran heresy in Royal Prussia. The Crown, seeing no overwhelming evidence of Lutheranism in the sense of demagogic preaching and popular unrest, would not intervene.

These events, especially those of 1525–6, occurred at one of the most violent and traumatic moments of the European Reformation, its communal social insurrection phase. It is often said that sixteenth-century princes had a determined confessional agenda—Berndt Hamm writes that princes saw the 'stability of their governments as founded upon the standardized authority of their creeds', and Scott Dixon that 'it became the goal of every European ruler to create the perfect confessional state, a union of ruler and ruled bounded by a single faith'.[119] Such statements—envisaging societies with complete agreement around precise

---

[118] Aspects of catholicism in Danzig did continue into the 1530s: convents functioned on some level, and Danzig counsellors might attend episcopal Masses when required to do so, *Corpus of Johannes Dantiscus' Texts*, nr. 4323.

[119] Hamm, 'Normative Centering', p. 316; Dixon, 'Introduction', *The German Reformation*, p. 18.

doctrinal positions—would have baffled Sigismund I, Piotr Tomicki, or Krzysztof Szydłowiecki. They sought to maintain the unity and peace of a fairly heterogenous late medieval church, not an as-yet-unimaginable rigorous theological uniformity among all the Crown's subjects. Throughout the 1520s and 1530s, in a major heartland of European Lutheranism, the actions of the King and his advisors were thus rooted in a pre-confessional and late medieval catholicism. One need not juxtapose politics (necessity) and religion (idealism) to understand the policies of the Polish Crown in Lutheranized Royal Prussia. This is because the King's earthly geopolitical priorities (retaining the province) were not actually in conflict with his sense of orthodoxy (peace and unity)—loyal Lutheran burghers could remain part of the *respublica* and the *ecclesia* alike. Just a few miles east, Sigismund I's willingness to accommodate good Lutherans was to be seen even more starkly.

3

A Difficult Nephew
The Polish Crown and Lutheran Ducal Prussia

The enigmatic relationship between the Polish Crown and the Duchy of Prussia is encapsulated in the friendship between two men, Albrecht of Brandenburg and Krzysztof Szydłowiecki. Albrecht, born in 1490 into the venerable line of Hohenzollern, was the third son of Margrave Frederick of Brandenburg-Ansbach and Princess Sophie of Poland, King Sigismund's older sister. Aged just 20, he had been elected Grand Master of the Teutonic Order in Prussia: a portrait by Hans Krell shows him wearing the black-and-white cloak of the Order, rosary in hand. Having waged war against his uncle from 1519–21, and converted to Lutheranism, under the terms of the 1525 peace Treaty of Kraków Albrecht became secular duke in Prussia and a vassal of the Polish Crown.[1] He was now painted by Lucas Cranach as a lay prince, in ermine collar and gold chain, a jewelled brooch pinned to his great black hat (Figure 3.1). Krzysztof Szydłowiecki was the close friend of Sigismund I's youth, and catholic Chancellor of Poland from 1518. In 1526, Szydłowiecki and Albrecht performed a ritual of eternal friendship.[2] Duke Albrecht sent gifts of medicine to Szydłowiecki, named him godfather of his first-born son, and invited the Chancellor and his wife to stay at the ducal castle in Königsberg. When the Szydłowiecki family suffered a string of deaths, Albrecht sent to 'my dearest brother' a letter of religious consolation, urging him to think on Christ.[3] The anti-Reformation bishop Andrzej Krzycki frowned on the Chancellor's intimacy with Lutherans, attacking it in his poetry.[4] Historians, too, have long portrayed Szydłowiecki as an unprincipled player in Sigismund I's regime, and his conspicuous friendship with one of Europe's leading Lutheran princes has played no small part in this posthumous image.

The creation, tutelage, and energetic defence of Ducal Prussia, Europe's first Lutheran principality, offers perhaps the starkest example of religious 'toleration' by the Polish Crown in the early Reformation period. From 1525, King Sigismund I enjoyed amicable relations with Albrecht, and was seemingly untroubled by the extensive contacts which soon grew up between Polish elites and the Lutheran

---

[1] See Chapter One, pp. 54–5.

[2] AT 8, p. 65; Mariusz Lubczyński and Jacek Pielas, 'Krzysztof Szydłowiecki', *PSB* 49 (Warsaw, 2014), pp. 551–6; Jacek Wijaczka, 'Kanclerz wielki koronny Krzysztof Szydłowiecki a książę Albrecht pruski', in Zenon Guldon (ed.), *Hrabstwo Szydłowieckie Radziwiłłów: Materiały sesji popularnonaukowej 19 lutego 1994 r* (Szydłowiec, 1994), pp. 23–38.

[3] AT 11, p. 318; AT 12, pp. 129–30; AT 14, p. 285.   [4] AT 8, p. 102.

Figure 3.1 Albrecht of Brandenburg-Ansbach, Duke of Prussia, by Lucas Cranach.
Herzog Anton Ulrich-Museum Braunschweig, Kunstmuseum des Landes Niedersachsen. Reproduced with permission.

court of Königsberg, as epitomized by his Chancellor. As Klaus Militzer has written, 'The transformation of Prussia into a Protestant duchy dependent upon Poland remains an astonishing development, when it is taken into consideration that the Polish king was a convinced opponent of the Reformation...'[5] This puzzling story forms the focus of this chapter. The religious relationship between Ducal Prussia and the Polish Crown has broader significance for the history of the early Reformation: it can, for example, provide an instructive parallel to Emperor Charles V's relations with his own Lutheran princes in the Holy Roman Empire. For those interested in the social history of sixteenth-century toleration, meanwhile, the border between Ducal Prussia and its catholic neighbours Royal Prussia and Mazovia was, from 1525, the first Protestant–catholic 'confessional' frontier in Christendom. The relationship between the Polish Crown and Ducal Prussia was for centuries studied primarily by scholars interested in the rise of the Prussian state, which in the partitions of Poland (1775, 1791, 1795) swallowed its former

---

[5] Klaus Militzer, 'Introduction', p. 5. Tazbir also notes that Sigismund I did nothing to protect catholics in Ducal Prussia during its Reformation: *Państwo bez stosów*, pp. 35–6.

parent.[6] In a new wave of work from the 1970s by Małłek, Szymaniak, Hartmann, and Benninghoven, the economic and diplomatic relations between Sigismund I's monarchy and Albrecht instead came to the fore.[7] Religious or confessional issues have, however, attracted less attention.[8]

This chapter seeks both to characterize, and account for, the nature of this religious relationship from 1525 to *c*.1540. It reconstructs nine principles of coexistence which one can detect in operation. These rules were improvised, and imposed, by King Sigismund I himself and by his royal council, although that council was not always united. The rules were rarely articulated explicitly, and they were typically discovered by Albrecht in the act of transgressing them. There was one set of rules regulating the Duke's relationship and interactions with the Polish Crown, his uncle, and the Kraków court, and a second set which dictated his behaviour with regard to nominally catholic Royal Prussia, on the borders of his own territory. There were rules about which religious actions were prohibited, and which were permitted. The chapter will ask how this relationship fits within our existing models, or typologies, of early modern toleration, suggesting that the ecclesiological perspectives of King Sigismund or Chancellor Szydłowiecki might further illuminate these events. As we shall see, the old king regarded Albrecht as a very dear kinsman, a man unfortunately interested in controversial religious teachings, but nonetheless a fellow Christian and member of the universal church.

NINE PRINCIPLES OF COEXISTENCE

1 The King Cannot Be Made Lutheran

The first rule, and the one most fiercely asserted by the Polish royal court from 1525 onwards, was that King Sigismund I himself could not and would not be made a follower of Martin Luther. The angriest epistolary and verbal clashes between the Crown and Ducal Prussia took place as a result of Albrecht's repeated attempts, in 1526–7, to convert his uncle to the new evangelism. The hapless rebel envoys from Danzig had already tried to accomplish a similar feat in their royal audiences in 1525—they had received an excoriating reply in the King's name from Bishop Tomicki, and later headed the Crown's 'most wanted' list of Danzigers.[9]

---

[6] Vetulani, *Lenno pruskie*; Pociecha, *Geneza hołdu*; Stephan Dolezel, *Das preussische-polnisch Lehnverhältnis unter Herzog Albrecht von Preussen (1525–68)* (Köln, 1967); Biskup, 'Geneza i znaczenie'; Hubatsch, *Albrecht von Brandenburg*. For the 1525 treaty in Polish historiography, see Natalia Nowakowska, 'Jagiellonians and Habsburgs: The Polish Historiography of Charles V', in M. Fuchs and C. Scott Dixon (eds), *The Histories of Emperor Charles V* (*Nationale Perspecktiven von Personalichkeit und Herrschaft*) (Münster, 2005), pp. 249–73.

[7] Małłek, *Prusy książęce*; Szymaniak, *Rola dworu* and *Organizacja Dyplomacji*; Benninghoven, *Die Herzöge in Preussen*, and Hartmann, *Herzog Albrecht*.

[8] See Janusz Małłek, 'Polska wobec luteranizacji Prus', *OiRwP* XLIX (2005): 7–16, recently printed in English as 'Poland in the face of the Lutheranisation of Prussia', in Militzer (ed.), *The Military Orders and the Reformation*, pp. 31–42.

[9] AT 7, p. 400; AT 8, p. 75.

Duke Albrecht made at least three attempts to persuade his uncle of Luther's teachings in 1526. When the royal entourage arrived at Marienburg, they were met by Bishop Erhard von Queis of Pomesania, who treated them to an exposition of Lutheran teaching, following this up later with letters.[10] Soon afterwards, joining his uncle in Danzig, Albrecht used a private audience to outline his religious views to the King.[11] And as the Polish royal entourage marched south out of Royal Prussia, Albrecht sent his chancellor, the Lutheran humanist Friedrich Fischer, after them with a 'theological' letter, in which the Duke openly invited the Polish King to embrace the Gospel.[12] King Sigismund responded to all three initiatives with distaste. In indignant written replies to Albrecht and Queis, the King marvelled that they sought to instruct him in the Gospel, which he heard read at Mass every day, and lamented the 'perpetual ignominy' which Albrecht had brought on their royal family through his adherence to condemned teachings. To Queis' suggestion that the Polish Crown should seize church lands, Sigismund answered that Queis must take him for 'an infidel'.[13] Whereas the default tone of Sigismund I's letters is measured and statesmanlike, these rebuffs of Albrecht and his co-reformers stand out for their tone of deep personal offence, and also for their use of (what today reads as) sarcasm, which is otherwise rare in the King's correspondence.

The old king's piety and catholic identity was not only asserted before Ducal Prussia's ruling elite, but also performed before them. In 1527, a ducal delegation to Kraków was kept waiting over a week for an audience. Both Bishop Tomicki and the King pointedly explained to Albrecht that he had sent his envoys in Holy Week, a time when it was known that Sigismund I enacted no public business, but spent his time entirely in contemplation of the Passion.[14] During Sigismund I's 1526 stay in Danzig the King attended Mass every day—Albrecht, arriving part way through the liturgy, was very publicly summoned by Sigismund to sit by his side in the pew.[15] The consistent message to Albrecht was that the King's catholic piety was a fundamental boundary, quite beyond negotiation, and any attempt to taint his person with heretical belief would not be tolerated.

Sigismund I's religious honour (as we shall see further in Chapter Four) was all-important, because it touched on a fundamental red line: in the King's eyes, it was the role of anointed monarchs to act as personal guarantors and defenders of the church. As he asked Albrecht, when kings and emperors leave the church, what happens? 'All who left the unity of the church, were either absorbed by the Infidels, or were involved in domestic revolts and perished ignominiously'—in short, the world as we know it will collapse and many will die.[16] This, then, was the only Lutheran scenario (besides revolt) which the Polish King saw as truly apocalyptic: if the precious society of crowned princes rejected the church. Whatever rules or rationales of toleration might apply elsewhere, the sacralized person of the king was a class apart.

---

[10] AT 8, pp. 34–5, 132.   [11] Szymaniak, *Organizacja*, pp. 39–40.
[12] *Elementa*, p. 15.   [13] AT 8, p. 132.
[14] AT 8, pp. 169–70.   [15] AT 8, pp. 56–8.
[16] AT 8, p. 51: 'omnes enim quicunque ab unitate ecclesie defecerunt, vel ab Infidelibus absorpti sunt vel domesticis saltem turbis et calamitatibus sese confecerunt et ignominiose perierunt'.

2 The Polish Crown Is Not Lutheran

The non-Lutheran character of the Polish Crown itself as an office and institution (as distinct from its human incumbent) was also firmly asserted. The 1525 Treaty of Kraków made no rhetorical concession to Albrecht's Lutheranism, but pretended that the new duchy would be catholic like the rest of the monarchy.[17] Thus Clause 4 of the Treaty of Kraków—which can still be seen in the Polish royal archives, seals appended—required the new duke to administer church lands as a true Christian prince. Clause 5 stipulated that Albrecht and his bishops would discipline any cleric in their lands who acted against the universal church, a delicately phrased injunction to act against heretics.[18] All parties signing the treaty knew that a Lutheran reform was already well advanced in Königsberg and its environs, but this was not officially acknowledged in the 1525 treaty. The Crown itself did not explicitly, in writing, sanction a Lutheran church in Ducal Prussia at any point. The ceremonies which concluded the peace deal and investiture were also impeccably in the old ecclesiastical style—King Sigismund, Duke Albrecht, and their 'huge' entourages of nobles and councillors processed from the city square, up the Wawel hill, and into Kraków cathedral, where the King and his Lutheran nephew 'kissed the relics of the holy saints, sang a "Te Deum Laudamus", and gave thanks to God'.[19]

As part of this insistence on the non-Lutheran character of the Crown, in the years which followed Albrecht was kept at arm's length from the royal succession, and also barred from voting in royal elections. As lay duke in Prussia, and the King's nephew, Albrecht was the monarchy's 'first senator'. From 1525 he positioned himself accordingly, seeking recognition as a future regent or guardian of the young heir Sigismund Augustus.[20] At the Sandomierz *sejm* of June 1529, the court surprised the nobility by presenting the 10-year-old prince for immediate election *vivente rege*—a daring political act which struck at the basic elective principles of the Polish monarchy. Queen Bona was named as future guardian of Sigismund Augustus, should the King die before the boy reached his majority.[21] These unprecedented actions barred Albrecht from the regency, denied him the chance to stand as a candidate for election after Sigismund's death, and also the opportunity to vote for his own future king—he had not been present at the rushed assembly. Albrecht now took action. He came in person to the 1530 *sejm*, seeking confirmation from the Crown that he would be entitled to vote in all future Polish royal elections. To his surprise, in a legally dubious interpretation, he was told by the senate that, while technically the most senior member of the royal council (the electoral body), he in fact had no right to vote at all.[22] Years of legal protest and representation by the Duke (1531–5) made no impact, and he was finally advised

[17] See Małłek, *Prusy Książęce*, p. 24.   [18] AT 7, p. 229.
[19] AT 7, p. 227, 'et ingressi ecclesiam cathedralem osculatisque sanctorum reliquiis, et dicto cantu: TE DEUM LAUDAMUS etc.'.
[20] Szymaniak, *Rola dworu*, p. 79. See also Chapter One, pp. 64–5.
[21] Sucheni-Grabowska, *Zygmunt August*, pp. 31–4; Szymaniak, *Organizacja*, p. 40.
[22] Discussed most fully by Vetulani, *Lenno pruskie*, pp. 127–67. See AT 12, pp. 389–93, 401, 404–6.

by Sigismund I not to raise the issue again because his refusal to take no for an answer was offending many.[23] In Poland's elective monarchy, its Lutheran duke had been entirely disenfranchised.

Historians have accounted for the humiliation of Albrecht in different ways, but there are grounds for reading this episode as an expression of the Crown's religious red lines. The 1529 election is often described as a semi-coup by Bona, the power-hungry Italian queen of popular cliché. In a different kind of nationalist-influenced reading, Pociecha argued that the Poles had closed ranks against Albrecht, a 'German' aggressor; recently Szymaniak concluded that it was 'raison d'état' which dictated that the national Crown should limit the influence of this foreign outsider.[24] Only Vetulani, writing in the 1920s, suggested in passing that Albrecht's status as one of Europe's leading Lutheran princes might have been a factor in excluding him from regency, succession, and even voting.[25] There is much in the sources to support this. Albrecht himself squarely blamed the bishops in the royal council for sabotaging his rightful claims, along with Sigismund I himself.[26] Bishop Andrzej Krzycki described a tense lunch he had hosted for two of the *korona*'s most high-profile evangelicals, Jan Łaski junior (the future Calvinist theologian) and magnate Andrzej Górka, as they returned from a trip to Albrecht's court. These guests declared that the Duke would fight hard for the right to vote in royal elections: young Łaski had turned to his catholic host and asked how on earth 'they' (Krzycki and his party) would stop him. There was no mystery to this evil endeavour, concluded Krzycki.[27] Krzycki praises the King for 'deducing how dangerous this thing is'.[28] The 1529–32 episode can thus be read as a battle over the confessional composition of the body which elected the King of Poland, and arguably a proxy electoral struggle in itself. As such, this legal and political clash within the Polish monarchy foreshadowed events in the Holy Roman Empire a century later, when the prospect of a Protestant majority among the German Electors triggered the murderous Thirty Years' War. In Poland, the King and council intervened early on to prevent any such scenario: a deep, defensive trench was dug between the office of the Crown and the Lutheran Reformation.

3 No Promotion of Lutheranism in Royal Prussia

The border between Albrecht's Lutheran duchy and nominally catholic Royal Prussia was one of the great proto-confessional frontiers of early modern Europe. This land of lakes, lagoons, and red-brick castles was the front line of the emerging new religious difference. The border was problematic—it formed a squiggly line, with enclaves of each territory projecting deep into the other, and it awkwardly separated what had until 1454 for centuries been one polity (the *Ordenstaat*), so

---

[23] AT 17, p. 173.
[24] The debates are discussed in Vetulani, *Lenno pruskie*, pp. 127–8 and Szymaniak, *Rola dworu*, p. 8.
[25] Vetulani, *Lenno*, p. 157.   [26] AT 14, p. 563.   [27] AT 14, p. 563.
[28] AT 12, p. 401: 'rem plenam esse periculi deducens'.

that kinship and economic ties did not stop at the frontier.[29] A third principle of coexistence was that Albrecht and his subjects were not permitted to promote, disseminate, or encourage Lutheranism in neighbouring Royal Prussia; they could not seek to openly Lutheranize their sister territory. As Dantiscus explained in a letter of 1533, 'His Majesty would not like Lutheranism to go on there'.[30]

The Ducal Prussian authorities were expected to assist with anti-Reformation action in turbulent Royal Prussia. In the wake of the pacification of Danzig (1526), King Sigismund looked to his nephew to round up the radical reformers who had fled to the new duchy. Having been sent the names of escaped Danzig preachers, Albrecht embarked on a policy of discreet non-cooperation.[31] In 1526, for example, an alleged radical, Mauritius the potter, was arrested in his native Danzig and during interrogation gave the authorities a list of fellow rebels now active in Königsberg. Albrecht's officials arrested these suspects at the King's request, but they were released without charge. Moreover, the lawyer sent to Königsberg to represent the Danzig council in the case was himself immediately imprisoned. King Sigismund accused Albrecht of breaking his word, and of letting dangerous rebels and radicals loose on Royal Prussia.[32] The King was crosser still in 1527, when a group of married priests from Danzig were released from custody in Königsberg, on the grounds that they enjoyed clerical immunity. 'My dear nephew!' replied Sigismund, in an epistolary equivalent of speechlessness. [33] The Duke's defiance of the Crown's sentences against Danzig Lutherans on the run was seen as reprehensible.

The active promotion of Lutheranism by individuals from Ducal Prussia, when visiting nominally catholic Royal Prussia, was also not tolerated. Albrecht was asked to punish Christoff Schnürlein, who had verbally abused old believers in Ermland as 'Mamelucks'; an artisan from Ducal Prussia who had blasphemed and mocked an image of the Virgin Mary situated outside Löbau in 1526; a noble who committed iconoclasm by breaking into the same town's Marian chapel and smashing up its pictures (1531); and Albrecht's own court architect Vogt, who was repeatedly accused of preaching Lutheranism in Elbing.[34] In 1531, Bishop Dantiscus complained bitterly to Albrecht that the Duke's envoy, the noble Adam Radziminski, had scandalized his episcopal household by drinking and feasting during Lent, laughing at the church and sacraments, and telling others not to confess or receive the Eucharist. Dantiscus expelled him from the episcopal residence.[35] Public Lutheran actions and speech by the subjects of Ducal Prussia on the wrong side of the confessional frontier, such as these, were thus regarded as hostile acts for which Albrecht was ultimately held responsible.

---

[29] For a meticulous reconstruction of the relations between the two Prussias in this period, see Małłek, *Dwie Części Prus.*

[30] Johannes Dantiscus, *Corpus of Ioannes Dantiscus' Texts*, IDL31, Dantiscus to Nikolaus Nibschitz (1533): 'Konigliche majestet szold ungern wellen das lutheri do gehalten wurd...'.

[31] *Elementa*, pp. 18–19.   [32] AT 8, pp. 141–3.   [33] AT 8, p. 143.

[34] Hartmann, *Herzog Albrecht*, p. 17; *Elementa*, p. 12; AT 13, p. 281; AT 17, p. 167.

[35] AT 13, p. 320.

4 No Lutheran Ecclesiastical Jurisdiction over Royal Prussia

The Crown also insisted that Duke Albrecht's Lutheran church and bishops could have no spiritual jurisdiction whatsoever over the peoples of Royal Prussia. The alarming possibility that Lutheran prelates might enjoy pastoral jurisdiction over catholic populations existed because of the shape of Prussia's late medieval dioceses. Created in the thirteenth century, these had failed to keep pace with the dizzying border changes wrought by successive wars and peace deals. The old diocese of Pomesania (f. 1243), one of the principal sees in the Teutonic Knights' *Ordenstaat*, after 1525 covered parts of both the Duchy of Prussia and Royal Prussia, around the town of Marienburg.[36] From 1523 (when Queis was appointed bishop to the see), the people of this part of Royal Prussia therefore found themselves under the rule of a catholic king, but under the canonical jurisdiction of one of Europe's first Lutheran bishops, Erhard Queis. Albrecht and his bishops sought to exploit this anomaly. In April 1526 Bishop Queis came to Marienburg, where Sigismund was gathering his army against Danzig, and requested the release of Lutheran preachers imprisoned in the town's castle by Bishop Drzewicki of Włocławek, on the grounds that he was their superior because the town lay within his own see. Queis' claims to (Lutheran) spiritual jurisdiction over Royal Prussian clergy were rebuffed—Queis was told bluntly in the King's name that he was only a pretended and false bishop, whom the Crown would not deal with until he had been properly consecrated.[37] This came as a painful surprise to Duke Albrecht, who protested that Queis was not only a highly virtuous churchman, but a leading negotiator of the Treay of Kraków, well known to the court.[38] Here, Albrecht was missing the point—the Crown had not performed a sudden *volte face* on the matter of whether Queis was a fit person to do business with. Rather, it had publicly humiliated Queis because of the audacious jurisdictional claims he had made over the peoples of its catholic territories. Following this incident, Sigismund I asked the papacy to approve a wholesale diocesan reorganization of Prussia, giving the parishes of the Pomesanian see to the bishop of Kulm (in Royal Prussia). This was necessary, he explained to Rome, because the apostate bishop of Pomesania was intent on spreading the 'infection' of Lutheranism throughout his entire diocese, including Royal Prussia, and denying his flock access to church sacraments 'and other necessities'.[39]

Even indirect and apparently innocuous jurisdictional contacts between Albrecht's Lutheran bishops and the inhabitants of Royal Prussia were resisted. In 1532, the Lutheran bishops Paulus Speratus and Georg von Polentz asked Johannes Dantiscus, as newly installed bishop of Kulm, to assist them with a routine ecclesiastical legal case which had arisen in Ducal Prussia, by collecting

---

[36] Zenon Nowak (ed.), *Państwo zakonu krzyżackiego w Prusach: podziały administracyjne i kościelne w XIII–XVI wieku* (Toruń, 2003) and Udo Arnold, 'Hochmeister Albrecht von Brandenburg-Ansbach und Landmeister Gotthard Kettler. Ordensritter und Terittorialherren am Scheideweg in Preussen und Livland', in Militzer, *Military Orders and the Reformation*, pp. 11–29, at p. 13.
[37] AT 8, p. 34.   [38] AT 8, pp. 36–7.
[39] AT 8, p. 133. Bishop Ferber agitated for the ex-Pomesanian lands to be attached to his own Ermland see: AT 12, p. 115.

witness statements from some of his flock. This was the sort of favour which late medieval bishops had routinely asked of one another. In the new Reformation context, however, Dantiscus refused any cooperation on the grounds that he was a servant of Rome, whereas Polentz and Speratus were married, illegitimate 'pseudo' bishops, with no claims whatsoever on him or his congregations—'I do not recognize them as bishops of our church.'[40] Again, the fear was that ecclesiastical interaction of any kind between Royal Prussians and Lutheran bishops might contaminate those involved.[41] Dantiscus was strongly backed up in his stance by Primate Drzewicki and Bishop Tomicki, who declared: 'it seems to me neither just nor honest' that the flock of Kulm diocese 'should be placed under an external, alien, inferior jurisdiction, contaminated with condemned heresy'.[42] The Lutheran bishops' request for technical assistance had, once again, raised the spectre of a Lutheran church with ecclesiastical rights over Royal Prussians. Duke Albrecht was offended. He took the ill treatment of his bishops as a slight against his own person, and failed to grasp why his Royal Prussian friends were reacting with such repugnance. Even after receiving gifts from Kulm to mollify him, Albrecht expressed his disappointment that the cosmopolitan Dantiscus had taken such a 'blunt' view of the matter.[43]

5 Duke Albrecht May Be a Lutheran

The simple rules of religious coexistence in the 1520s and 1530s—that the catholic King, Crown, and peoples of Royal Prussia should not have to suffer Lutheran proselytizing or ambitions—were relatively limited in scope, and their overall effect was to give Duke Albrecht a considerable amount of religious leeway. As well as restrictive rules, there were permissive rules.

The first of these permitted Duke Albrecht himself to follow a Lutheran faith without interference from the Polish Crown: he was not put under any sustained official pressure to convert. Sigismund's recorded exhortations to his nephew to return to the old church were rare and made chiefly in private (1526 in person, and in a letter of 1531). The 1531 request was made in a tone of resigned paternal disappointment, rather than censure or threat. Tellingly, the verb employed was 'consuluimus' (advised) not 'mandamus' (ordered)—'we advised you from our heart and with paternal affection...to follow the catholic church'.[44] There were

---

[40] AT 14, p. 840: 'non recognoscam pro episcopis ecclesiae nostrae'.

[41] For the correspondence of Polish bishops on this matter, see AT 14, pp. 822–4, 834, 853; AT 15, pp. 32–3, 36, 39.

[42] AT 15, p. 36: 'neque iustum, neque honestum mihi videtur, ut quae iurisdictionis DVR sunt, ad alienam externam, inferiorem et haeresi damnata contaminatam iurisdictionem ...'.

[43] AT 14, p. 824: 'stumff antwurt'; see also Dantiscus to Duke Albrecht (1533), *Corpus of Johannes Dantiscus' Texts* IDL5391, in which the bishop defended his actions, stressing he had had to follow direct orders.

[44] Szymaniak, *Rola dworu*, p. 39, based on an account in the royal registers; AT 13, p. 24: 'consuluimus illi ex animo et affectu paterno, ut potius vestigia majorum suorum et instituta ecclesiae catholicae recepta et approbata cum summatibus christianis, quam seditiosa apostatarum dogmata sequeretur'.

those in the regime who wished to see more pressure applied to Albrecht, but Sigismund I did not oblige. Maciej Drzewicki, Polish primate from 1531, repeatedly expressed the hope that Albrecht would return to the old rite.[45] Bishop Ferber of Ermland, entertaining Albrecht in his episcopal castle in Heilsberg, planned with eager trepidation to attempt a reconversion himself over dinner.[46] However, when the Polish *sejm* of 1534 noted that the entire royal council vehemently urged the King to act as a good physician to Albrecht's sickness, the royal reply was not encouraging: 'the King will warn the lord duke yet again, but he [Albrecht] is hardened in his purpose'.[47] The monarch himself seemingly placed no great hope, or store, in the conversion of the Duke of Prussia; that too was part of the modus vivendi.

The ceremonial and social treatment which Albrecht received from the Polish court was in no way diminished by his religious views. King Sigismund himself gave every appearance of holding Albrecht in respect and affection. Szymaniak has calculated that the two men spent no fewer than 200 days in one another's company, with the Duke granted dozens of private audiences. During Albrecht's two-month-long sojourn in Vilnius in 1535, for example, the King and Duke made it their habit to take long private walks together in the castle grounds.[48] Their mutual correspondence is also characterized by an emphatic use of the language of kinship and family sentiment—Sigismund regularly declared that his nephew was as dear to him as a son, and Albrecht professed similar emotions.[49] At major royal events, such as the Kraków coronation Mass of Sigismund Augustus in 1530 or the wedding of Princess Jadwiga in 1535, Albrecht participated as a senior member of the royal house.[50] After the festivities in 1530, an entertainment was thrown in his honour in the Wawel castle, and Albrecht participated in days of celebratory jousting with the cream of the Polish nobility.[51] Albrecht's wider Lutheran entourage were also received with honour by the Kraków court—his consort, the Danish princess Dorothea (who visited in 1530 and 1535), and his official envoys, who included the married Bishop Polentz (1530), the prominent pro-Luther scholar Jan Rubeanus (1528), and Chancellor Johannes Apel (1530), one-time rector of Wittenberg university.[52] Albrecht, in other words, was neither identified nor treated primarily as a heretic by King Sigismund I and his court. While Sigismund may have written (once) of the 'ignominy' of having heresy in the family, in practice there was no obvious stigma attached to Albrecht's person. Where the Duke and his closest associates were concerned, the simple fact of their Lutheranism was no barrier whatsoever to a warm welcome in Kraków.

---

[45] AT 12, p. 371; AT 16b, p. 172. See also Bishop Ferber on this possibility, AT 12, p. 135.
[46] AT 12, p. 397.
[47] AT 16b, p. 524: 'Admonebit quidem iterum M. regia dominum ducem, sed ille induratus est in proposito suo'.
[48] Szymaniak, *Organizacja dyplomacji*, pp. 41–2. An inventory of their diplomatic meetings is given in pp. 38–42.
[49] AT 12, p. 137; AT 13, p. 24, 'quam filio nostro'; *Urkundenbuch*, p. 154, 'domine et pater'; AT 17, p. 727; *Elementa*, p. 15.
[50] AT 12, pp. 56–7; Szymaniak, *Organizacja dyplomacji*, p. 41.
[51] Szymaniak, *Organizacja dyplomacji*, p. 40.
[52] Szymaniak, *Organizacja dyplomacji*, pp. 40–1, 45–6, 56–7.

6 Duke Albrecht May Impose a Lutheran Reformation in his Territories

In perhaps the most permissive, significant, and tacit rule of all, Duke Albrecht was left free by the Polish Crown to impose Lutheranism on the populations of Ducal Prussia, that is on the former subjects and monks of the Teutonic Order. From 1525, a Lutheran church was erected on the ruins of the *Ordenstaat*, with new forms of worship (in German and Latin), the secularization of episcopal lands, closing of monasteries, the active dissemination of Martin Luther's works to parish priests, and a programme of evangelical preaching and visitation designed to bring the Word of God to every village in the duchy.[53] To the great majority of this, and to the basic fact of a wholesale territorial Reformation, Sigismund I said not a word.

This silence was in spite of the fact that, as Vetulani showed, the 1525 Treaty of Kraków had given Sigismund I considerable legal scope to intervene in the internal affairs of the new duchy. Clause 18 allowed for the creation of a Polish royal commission which would hear complaints against Albrecht by his subjects, potentially curbing the Duke's authority in a way not normally suffered by other vassals, such as the Dukes of Mazovia or Pomerania.[54] Such a commission was convened, in the great test-case of Polish royal authority over Ducal Prussia, in 1532 to hear the petition of the noble Fasolt, who claimed to have been treated unjustly by Albrecht. In the Fasolt case, Sigismund I was uncompromising in asserting his overlordship, writing that he was the lord of Prussia and would defend 'superioritatem nostram'.[55]

These royal powers were not, however, used to impede the Reformation in Ducal Prussia. The minor instances where the Crown did intervene against religious change themselves illustrate how limited the scope of such intervention was. In January 1526, for example, Sigismund I complained that Ermland clergy had donated money to the beleaguered monastery of Saint Augustine in Ducal Prussia, only to see it secularized and the estate given to a layman.[56] Here, the King was objecting not to the abandonment of the monastery per se (the principle), but to the illegitimate appropriation of funds given in good faith—here, in essence, we see anxiety about the Reformation as theft. The second incident, also in 1526, occurred when Albrecht's Reformation in the see of Pomesania met with opposition from the cathedral canons of Marienwerder, whom he imprisoned for their resistance.[57] Sigismund I and Bishop Tomicki wrote repeatedly to Albrecht, demanding the canons' release.[58] The imprisonment of catholic clergy by a Lutheran prince scandalized the Polish King—his objection, however, was not to

---

[53] Stupperich, *Die Reformation*. See also Chapter One, pp. 55–6.

[54] Vetulani, *Lenno pruskie*, pp. 60–122, especially pp. 98, 120, 199.

[55] Vetulani, *Lenno*, pp. 206–7, 225–31, quote at p. 231. See also AT 8, p. 131, 'superiori domino'.

[56] *Elementa*, pp. 5–6.

[57] The episode is discussed by Helmut Friewald, *Markgraf Albrecht von Ansbach-Kulmbach und seine landständische Politik als Deutschordens-Hochmeister und Herzog in Preussen während der Entscheidungsjahre 1521–1528* (Kulmbach, 1961), pp. 195–6.

[58] AT 9, pp. 33–4, 169–70.

the preaching of the Reformation in the duchy per se, but rather to the forceful oppression of 'catholic men'.[59] Even this anti-Reformation protest, seen in context, recedes in size. The fate of the Marienwerder canons did not become a defining issue in Sigismund I's relations with Albrecht in the late 1520s—his paragraph on the issue within a longer letter ends with the sentence, 'but enough of this', before moving on to discuss matters of international relations and mutual diplomatic initiatives quite cordially.[60] The locking up of catholic priests was an unfortunate aspect of the Reformation in Ducal Prussia, but it was not, apparently, a deal-breaker. Moreover, in both these cases, the Saint Augustine monastery and the Marienwerder canons, Sigismund I only intervened when directly petitioned to do so—by a senior cleric of Ermland, and by the Marienwerder canons themselves. Aspects of the implementation of Albrecht's Reformation might draw critical letters from the Polish royal court, but its basic, groundbreaking trajectory was permitted.

7 Duke Albrecht May Cultivate a Network within the Wider Monarchy

The King's forbearance extended to allowing Duke Albrecht to cultivate a large network of clients within the monarchy, which exposed these families and powerful individuals to Lutheran ideas and practices. Noblemen from many parts of the Polish monarchy sent or hoped to send their sons to the court at Königsberg, in the Duke's service. These ranged from relatively junior figures such as Kacper Maciejowski, a royal official in the Sandomierz district,[61] to the noble Odrzywolski family,[62] to Stanisław Wolski and Wenceslaus Szydłowiecki, kinsmen of the Polish Chancellor.[63] Those noble boys who served in the ducal court in Königsberg would have lived among the Lutheran scholars and theologians whom that city attracted from the Reich like honey; they would have presumably witnessed or attended Lutheran services.[64] Königsberg was also a city of Lutheran books, strictly forbidden by law in the *korona*—Albrecht's private library contained silver-plated copies of works by Luther and Melanchthon.[65] This prospect did not, apparently, concern King Sigismund, who himself wrote a letter of recommendation for a high-ranking son, whose kin were keen to send him to Königsberg.[66] This stance is striking given the Crown's edicts of 1534 and 1540, which prohibited Polish nobles from studying at Wittenberg and similar establishments on the grounds that youth should

---

[59] AT 8, p. 131, on the King's shock; quote from AT 9, p. 34.

[60] AT 9, pp. 169–70: 'Sed de hoc satis.'

[61] AT 17, p. 658: See also Ludwig Kolankowski, 'Z archiwum królewieckiego, Polscy korespondenci Ks. Albrechta', *Archeion* 6–7 (1930): 102–8.

[62] AT 12, nr. 141, pp. 136–7.

[63] AT 12, p. 156; AT 13, p. 68. A further unnamed noble boy was recommended for Albrecht's service by Palatine Jan Tarnowski, AT 12, p. 137.

[64] For the everyday life of the ducal court, see Gundermann, *Herzogin Dorothea*.

[65] Małłek, *Dwie części Prus*, p. 176; see also Paul Schwenke and Konrad von Lange, *Die Silberbibilothek Herzog Albrechts von Preussen* (Leipzig, 1894), pp. 17–23.

[66] AT 12, p. 137.

not be exposed to bad influences.[67] Duke Albrecht also engaged nobles from Royal Prussia, such as Felix Allen from Graudenz and Fabian Lehndorff from Ermland, as his courtiers and diplomats.[68] Here again, Sigismund I did not remark on the fact that the ducal court was functioning as an alternative, Lutheran channel of patronage within his kingdom.

A blind eye was also turned when Albrecht sent Lutheran materials to top senators in the Polish royal court, in defiance of numerous royal edicts. In 1532, his agent Nipszyc distributed Lutheran books to Polish bishops, as gifts from the Duke.[69] Albrecht himself wrote to Bishop Chojeński, the King's influential private secretary, on the theology of salvation and in praise of the Augsburg Confession.[70] In 1531, Chojeński thanked Albrecht warmly for a copy of the first Polish printed translation of Luther's catechism, and in 1537 also received a Lutheran song-text.[71] Albrecht maintained a close friendship with Krzysztof Szydłowiecki, the royal Chancellor, as we have seen. All this the Crown tolerated—the flow of nobles to Königsberg, which made possible a degree of Lutheran acculturation among elite families in the *korona* and Royal Prussia, and Albrecht's direct proselytization of the royal senate. So long as Albrecht did not impose his beliefs on the royal house and the Crown itself, he was free to draw elite families to himself.

8 (Lutheran) Ducal Prussia and (Catholic) Royal Prussia Should Be Good Neighbours

On the ground, as part of the practice of religious coexistence, the twin territories of Ducal and Royal Prussia mostly enjoyed friendly neighbourly relations. The catholic bishops of Royal Prussia—Mauritius Ferber of Ermland (1523–37), Jan Konopacki of Kulm (1508–30), and Johannes Dantiscus of Kulm (1533–7)—all resisted the Reformation in their own dioceses to a greater or lesser extent, yet they all had cooperative, close relationships with Duke Albrecht, and even with his Lutheran prelates (so long as Rule 4, on pastoral jurisdiction, was obeyed). Dantiscus, for example, in his letters pledged Albrecht his friendship, promising to assist him in his quarrels with the Emperor and praying for his well-being.[72] The high clergy of Royal Prussia dispatched regular gifts to Königsberg. Dantiscus sent a work of biblical humanism to the Duke and a children's toy or book to Duchess Dorothea, Ferber a (possibly pedagogical) volume, and Canon Giese of Ermland a book on warfare.[73] Dantiscus exchanged paintings and painters with Albrecht and wrote him poetry, while the Duke would stay with Bishop Ferber at the episcopal

---

[67] Printed in Ignacy Chrzanowski and Stanisław Kot (eds), *Humanizm i Reformacja* (Kraków, 1927), pp. 317–18; Zakrzewski, *Powstanie i wzrost*, p. 236.
[68] Szymaniak, *Organizacja dyplomacji*, pp. 55–60. Szymaniak calculated that of the forty-one envoys whom Albrecht sent to Sigismund between 1525 and 1548, six were Royal Prussian nobles in his service.
[69] AT 14, pp. 521–3.   [70] AT 14, pp. 551–2.
[71] Władysław Pociecha, 'Jan Chojeński', *PSB* 3 (1937), pp. 396–9, at p. 397.
[72] Johannes Dantiscus, Corpus of Ioannes Dantiscus' Texts, IDL5391 (Dantiscus to Duke Albrecht).
[73] Benninghoven, *Die Herzöge in Preussen*, pp. 2, 26–7; Hartmann, *Herzog Albrecht*, pp. 57, 147.

stronghold of Heilsberg.[74] When Albrecht's first son was born, Bishop Ferber wrote him a fulsome letter of congratulation, wishing the baby a long life as a Christian prince.[75] The correspondence between Albrecht and Bishop Ferber in particular was vast, amounting to a letter every couple of days for almost two decades. It paints a vivid picture of close coordination in the management of Prussian trade, fisheries, legal affairs, and local politics—and engages in no direct discussion of the Reformation whatsoever on this, one of the first confessional frontiers in early modern Europe.[76] The highest catholic bishop of Royal Prussia and a Lutheran duke wrote to one another far more frequently on the subject of carp than they did about any aspect of Christian teaching.

Even where ecclesiastical issues did crop up, catholic–Lutheran cooperation was possible. When Bishop Dantiscus wished to build a new church, Duke Albrecht supplied the timber and his Lutheran prelate Polentz a helpful memorandum on church construction techniques.[77] In 1525, Bishop Ferber and Albrecht worked together to apprehend a rogue priest who had insulted church officials in both catholic Ermland and Lutheran Ducal Prussia; in 1527, Albrecht asked Ferber to send back to the duchy a woman who had fled from her pastor husband, and was now sheltering with her kin near Heilsberg.[78] He clearly felt that, out of neighbourliness, the catholic bishop would help to patch up this Lutheran clerical marriage. Perhaps most surprisingly, Albrecht regularly intervened in top ecclesiastical appointments in Royal Prussia, to the apparent contentment of its catholic clergy—he backed Dantiscus' campaign to be named co-adjutor (successor) of the see of Ermland, and used his permanent representative in Rome, von Reden, to secure the nominations of his own candidates to the Ermland cathedral chapter.[79]

9 King Sigismund Will Protect

The final rule, which provided a framework and context for all the others, was that the King of Poland would protect all parts of his monarchy. While Polish literature has stressed the vow of fealty which Albrecht made to his uncle in April 1525, at that ceremony Sigismund I also made a holy vow—to protect Ducal Prussia from its enemies, as its lord. We shall see, in Chapter Five, how much diplomatic capital the Polish Crown expended in trying to protect Albrecht from the Reich, and what kind of military risks it ran in doing so. As Sigismund I assured a nervous Albrecht in 1536, the health, safety, protection, and tranquillity of the Duke and every one of the duchy's

---

[74] AT 16a, pp. 25–7; AT 12, p. 397; Hartmann, *Herzog Albrecht*, p. 230. See also Tomasz Ososiński, 'Nieznane epigramy Dantyszka w liście tegoż do Albrechta I księcia Pruskiego', *OiRwP* 50 (2006): 245–55.

[75] Hartmann, *Herzog Albrecht*, p. 110.

[76] Correspondence published in summaries by Hartmann, *Herzog Albrecht*. Albrecht himself wrote of the importance of good neighbourliness, Hartmann, *Herzog Albrecht*, p. 25.

[77] Benninghoven, *Herzöge*, p. 41; AT 16b, p. 41.   [78] Hartmann, *Herzog Albrecht*, p. 37.

[79] Benninghoven, *Herzöge*, pp. 32–3; Hartmann, *Herzog Albrecht*, pp. 137, 160, 171–2; AT 12, p. 130.

subjects was his own great care and responsibility.[80] Duke Albrecht was assured that his person and duchy would be protected by the Polish Crown 'strenuously and with alacrity'.[81] Those promises were not made subject to doctrinal conformity; the religious difference represented by the monarchy's Lutheran territory was either of secondary importance to Sigismund I's regime, faintly perceived, or assumed to be remediable. In terms of the anointed king's duties towards his people, it did not matter in the end that the inhabitants of Ducal Prussia were Lutheran. This, then, was the bottom line of coexistence—the paternal care of Sigismund I as monarch.

Taken together, these nine principles meant that Duke Albrecht's Lutheran Reformation, within the dominions of the Polish monarchy, would proceed unmolested throughout the reigns of Sigismund I (d.1548) and Sigismund Augustus—even as Königsberg emerged in the 1540s as a centre of Polish-language Lutheran ministry and printing, and as Albrecht himself moved beyond the orbit of Wittenberg by embracing the controversial theology of Osiander (who was active in Ducal Prussia from 1549).[82] Albrecht successfully fended off the Counter-Reformation zeal of his neighbour Stanisław Hozjusz, Bishop of Ermland (1551–79), and died in 1568, leaving his son Albert Frederick as successor.[83] As in Royal Prussia to the west, the reign of Sigismund I had been decisive in witnessing and permitting a solid entrenchment of Reformation ideas in Ducal Prussia. There were, it is true, dissenting voices, but they were few, and they were in the minority: Krzycki who called the Chancellor a Judas for aiding Lutherans, or Bishop Ferber who feared terrible divine vengeance on all Prussia for Albrecht's acts of sacrilege.[84] The louder voice, and the voice which carried the day, was however that of the King and his chief counsellors. Albrecht's new polity emerged as a major centre of North European Lutheran culture and patronage, which evolved and flourished under the watchful eye of King Sigismund the Old. That king's relations with his Lutheran nephew were, from 1525, markedly smoother and warmer than those which the kings of Poland had enjoyed with any catholic Grand Master of the Teutonic Order in the preceding century—the Reformation notwithstanding.

A CASE OF TOLERATION?

How should we define this kind of multifaceted toleration, and where does this episode fit in our existing typologies of religious coexistence in the sixteenth century? Like many core concepts in early modern history, 'toleration' has so successfully established itself in our mental landscape that scholars often invoke it but rarely define it. There is in fact no consistent definition of religious toleration in the extensive literature on this phenomenon. Istvan Bejczy argued that in medieval

---

[80] *Elementa*, pp. 64–5.
[81] AT 12, pp. 405–6; AT 13, p. 132: 'tamquam vassalum, strenue et alacriter defendemus'.
[82] Hubatsch, *Albrecht von Brandenburg*, pp. 167–82.
[83] Hubatsch, *Albrecht von Brandenburg*, p. 159.
[84] AT 8, p. 102; AAWa, A1, fos. 15, 281–281(v); see also ASPK, vol. 8, p. 390.

Europe 'tolerantia' meant abstaining from the punishment of evil, and went on to stress that one should distinguish between tolerance, freedom of religion, pluralism, and relativism.[85] Benjamin Kaplan describes early modern toleration as 'a containment of religious conflict'.[86] Alexandra Walsham has argued that toleration and intolerance are not polar opposites, black and white, but 'dialectically and symbolically linked'.[87] Robert Scribner's work encourages us to think not of a single definition of toleration, but of its typologies. Writing on early modern Germany, Scribner offered nine types. His list, which is worth considering in full, included the permitting of religious diversity in private behind closed doors; the non-enforcement of heresy laws; religious compromise forced by political circumstance; the 'cuius regio, eius religio' German religious settlement formula; temporary toleration in the hope of imminent vanquishing of the religious enemy; pastoral latitude, i.e. requiring only minimal outward conformity to official religion; toleration necessitated by the authorities' political weakness vis-à-vis heretical groups; toleration of dissident groups because they are economically useful; and finally the 'toleration of practical rationality', that is everyday social coexistence without fuss.[88] Scribner's definitions capture a mish-mash of social and political actions, each implying more or less conscious toleration of religious difference. Here toleration emerges as a highly heterogeneous phenomenon, and a rather porous concept.

The coexistence of Ducal Prussia and the Polish Crown in the 1520s and 1530s chimes with many of Scribner's different 'toleration' scenarios and typologies. His category of (elite) 'social coexistence' fits the cordial relations between the catholic bishops of Royal Prussia and Albrecht's Lutheran regime in the Baltic region. A permitting of religious freedom in private, and a non-enforcement of royal heresy laws can be seen too in the courteous treatment of Lutheran Ducal Prussian visitors to Kraków. One might argue that Sigismund I adopted the principle of 'cuius regio, eius religio', the famous formula in the 1555 Augsburg Religious Peace for the Holy Roman Empire, which left every individual prince free to choose, and impose, his preferred form of Christianity on his territory. At first glance, it might appear as if the Polish Crown was indeed creating separate religious/confessional spheres within one polity, designating Ducal Prussia as a Lutheran zone, with the remaining parts of the monarchy as catholic—but doing so thirty years before the Augsburg Peace (1555). King Sigismund's concern that Lutherans from Ducal Prussia should not proselytize in 'catholic' Royal Prussia, or exercise clerical jurisdiction there, fits such a pattern of confessional 'zoning' within a monarchy. However, a Crown which entertained Albrecht so lavishly in Kraków and permitted him his client networks across the monarchy was hardly throwing up a religious *cordon sanitaire* around Königsberg. In the actions of Sigismund I's regime, in other words, there is a spirit of coexistence which seems to go beyond the mere territorial containment of heresy embodied by 'cuius

[85] Bejczy, 'Tolerantia', pp. 367–8.   [86] Kaplan, *Divided by Faith*, pp. 9, 11.
[87] Walsham, *Charitable Hatred*, p. 5.   [88] Scribner, 'Preconditions of Tolerance', pp. 32–47.

regio, eius religio'. There are, then, so many individual shades of coexistence present in the nine rules that it remains unclear what overall model of 'toleration' this Baltic episode provides us with—let alone the rationales which might have underpinned it.

How, then, might we explain the far-reaching religious 'toleration' which characterized Sigismund I's relationship with Ducal Prussia? As we saw in the Introduction, scholarship on early modern toleration tends to define it as pure pragmatism, politics winning out over religious idealism. However, in this case there is a dearth of convincing domestic or geopolitical calculations to explain the Crown's stance. Certainly, the acquisition of the lands of the Teutonic Order as a new vassal of the Polish Crown in 1525 was a stunning success for King Sigismund, completing a centuries-long campaign by Polish kings to regain control of the Baltic littoral (a kind of Polish *reconquista*). Perhaps this was so great a political triumph that religious considerations were sacrificed, in a Faustian pact with a Lutheran vassal? However, had he ardently desired religious uniformity in his monarchy, Sigismund I could probably have had Ducal Prussia without its Lutheran duke. This was not a simple case of forced toleration, arising from sheer political impotence of the 'orthodox' party. This was a royal regime in many respects at the height of its powers. In 1526, King Sigismund had in a sense reconquered Royal Prussia, marching an army of 6,000 men on Danzig and reasserting Polish rule over the province; it was not for nothing that Albrecht feared that that same army would later turn east and come for him, rushing to Danzig uninvited to have his ducal title reconfirmed once more.[89] In 1529, the King and council accomplished the incorporation of the vassal duchy of Mazovia into the Crown, despite local resistance. That same year, the royal family secured the semi-legal election of a child prince *vivente rege*; Sigismund I was the only Polish king successfully to accomplish such a feat in the entire 400-year lifetime of the elective monarchy (1360s to 1795).[90] Albrecht, meanwhile, was in a desperately weak position, as Bues and others have noted. He had little or no legitimacy domestically or internationally. Albrecht had very few allies (the King of Denmark, the Prince of Leignitz, the Margrave of Brandenburg), powerful enemies (the Teutonic Order, the pope, Emperor Charles V), and was entirely dependent on the Polish Crown for the survival of his new duchy.[91] His territory was small compared with the size and resources of the *korona*. Albrecht's letters to Sigismund never lost their tone of paranoia, panic, and occasional hysteria, and in them he constantly sought reassurance that his uncle would not desert him.[92] It would thus have been no great feat for the Crown to depose Albrecht himself (not least as a heretic), and install a new, catholic vassal duke in his place—internal opposition to Albrecht and his religion had existed in the Teutonic Order in Prussia in the 1520s, an opposition which

---

[89] Małłek, *Prusy Książęce*, pp. 37–41.

[90] On King John Casimir's attempted seventeenth-century *vivente rege* election, see Robert Frost, 'Initium Calamitatis Regni? John Casimir and Monarchical Power in Poland-Lithuania 1648–1668', *European History Quarterly* 16 (1986): 181–207.

[91] Bues, *Apologien*, pp. 22–8.   [92] For example, AT 16a, pp. 4–5.

the Crown chose to ignore.[93] Moreover, it is far from certain that maintaining a Lutheran Ducal Prussia within the monarchy was the most attractive option politically, or the path of least resistance. This toleration came with great geopolitical risk. In autumn 1534, King Sigismund warned the royal council to prepare for an imminent invasion of Ducal Prussia by the Teutonic Order and imperial forces; the local diet and Primate Drzewicki promised the King to do all they could towards defence of the duchy.[94] Indeed, Bishop Andrzej Krzycki's apologia for the original 1525 treaty described the royal councillors wavering and fretting over the peace deal, their chief worry being that it would bring down on Poland the wrath of the pope and emperor, leading not to peace but a much bigger future war.[95] If one wishes to read sixteenth-century royal government as a form of entirely rational power politics, therefore, by far the more logical choice for King Sigismund would have been to pacify the pope, emperor, and powerful headquarters of the Teutonic Order in Germany by finding an alternative, less controversial duke of Prussia. Politics alone, in a strict realpolitik understanding, does not account for the Polish Crown's stance.

An alternative angle is offered by other kinds of contemporary consideration. Benjamin Kaplan reminds us that in the Reformation period European elites operated with a range of values, which included a strong sense of the 'sacred bonds' which existed in their society.[96] These often fell somewhere between the 'moral', 'religious', and 'political'. Kinship is an important lens for understanding King Sigismund's commitment to Albrecht. The King repeatedly declared his affection for Albrecht as one of his own blood, his sister's son, a member of 'our house'. He addressed Albrecht as 'our very dearest relative', and as we have seen addressed the Duke as a son.[97] In discussions between the Crown and Royal Prussian diet about the 1525 treaty, it was stressed that the King and Grand Master were bound through blood.[98] If we take seriously this sense of an intimate kinship relationship, it becomes clearer why it was important for Sigismund I to have this particular prince (Lutheran or not)—rather than any other candidate—as his vassal in Ducal Prussia. Kinship and blood tied the former *Ordenstaat* more closely to the Crown than an ink-and-paper treaty alone.

Certain kinds of religious and intellectual convictions also played a part. While scholars long considered written defences of toleration as a moral good to be a rarity in the sixteenth century, Victoria Christman has shown that they can be found in unexpected quarters.[99] In common with the Antwerp city councillors of her study, King Sigismund in his interactions with Ducal Prussia made statements which sound very much like explicit endorsements of toleration for its own sake.

---

[93] Bues, *Apologien*, p. 24; Hartmann, *Herzog Albrecht*, p. 5.
[94] AT 16b, pp. 172, 184, 237–43, 341–2.   [95] AT 8, p. 250.
[96] Kaplan, *Divided by Faith*, p. 9.
[97] AT 12, pp. 137; AT 13, p. 24, 'quam filio nostro'; *Urkundenbuch*, p. 154, 'domine et pater'; AT 17, p. 727; *Elementa*, p. 15.
[98] ASPK, vol. 8, p. 388.   [99] Christman, *Pragmatic Toleration*, pp. 107–27.

The most celebrated of these was a cool royal reply to the Ingolstadt university polemicist Johann Eck:

> Centuries pass, and with them the mind of lawmakers in kingdoms. Knowledge which once was lost is found. . . . Let King Henry write against Martin. I wish you and Krzycki to be praise worthy writers. Permit me to be king of the sheep and the goats.[100]

This quote is one of the foundations of Sigismund I's reputation in Polish scholarship as an arch-tolerator, as a mild-mannered man who believed in freedom of conscience.[101] However, it is less well known that the Eck quote is not a one-off: the King made multiple statements about the undesirability, or impossibility, of forcing conscience in matters of belief. His most explicit pronouncements on freedom of conscience all occurred in the context of his contacts with Ducal Prussia. Protesting in 1527 about the imprisonment of the Marienwerder canons, Sigismund objected specifically to Albrecht's desire to force people to abandon a religion into which they had been born, or which they had followed from childhood.[102] This was wrong, the King wrote, because 'even among the *ethnici*, everybody is free to follow that religion, which he chooses for himself'.[103] The duchy had no right to compel its subjects to embrace Lutheranism, he continued, just as princes did not compel their Jewish subjects to become Christians.[104] In 1534, Sigismund I again put these points to Albrecht, claiming that the Duke injured his subjects by 'compelling them to embrace this new faith, which is something not even the Turks do to their prisoners'.[105] Forcing individuals in matters of religion is presented by the Polish King as a barbarian act. Freedom of individual conscience was in fact an established part of the discourse between the Polish Crown and Ducal Prussia—when Albrecht made a passionate appeal to his uncle to spare the lives of Lutheran preachers in 1526, he too based his argument on freedom of conscience. The Crown, wrote Albrecht, should not lift the sword of justice against those who had acted only out of religious conviction, based on their reading of Scripture.[106] Bishop Tomicki also employed this language, writing to the Queen's doctor Aliphio in 1525 that 'it is not for us to compel anyone in religion'. He stressed to his more militant nephew Bishop Krzycki that Christianity could never,

---

[100] The Eck letter is widely cited in Polish scholarship and popular histories, but there is no surviving contemporary copy. It was quoted by Tadeusz Czaski, who claimed to have 'a handwritten letter of Sigismund I which I have before my eyes', 'mam przed oczyma list w rękopiśmie od Sigismunda I', *Dzieła Tadeusza Czackiego*, vol. I (Poznań, 1843), p. 312: 'fluere saecula, et in illis mutantur regna mentis legumlatorum. Obsoletae erant nuper scientiae, nunc renascuntur. Antea crimina in sinu temeritatis ortum habebant, nunc facinora in umbra erudationis illustrentur. Scribat rex Henricus contra Martinum. Ego te et Cricium volo esse encomiis dignos scriptores. Permittas mihi fieri ovium et hircorum regem.' Pius II's fifteenth-century *Historia Bohemica* attributed a very similar speech to the Utraquist King George of Bohemia: see Thomas Fudge, 'Reform and the Lower Consistory in Prague, 1437–97', in Zdeněk David and David Holeton (eds), *The Bohemian Reformation and Religious Practice*, vol. 2 (Prague, 1998), pp. 67–96, at p. 82.

[101] For example, Tazbir, *Państwo bez stosów*, p. 40.

[102] AT 8, p. 131; AT 9, pp. 169–70.

[103] AT 9, p. 169–70, 'apud ethnicos etiam unicuique liceat eam religionem sequi, quam sibi quisque delegit'.

[104] AT 8, p. 131.   [105] AT 16a, p. 328.   [106] *Urkundenbuch*, pp. 153–4.

ever be spread by force.[107] There was, then, some articulated ethical basis for the Polish monarchy's 'toleration' towards Ducal Prussia, some discourse of freedom of belief/conscience.

It is possible, as in Chapter Two, to approach this problem of toleration by considering the underlying ecclesiological beliefs of Sigismund I and his top counsellors. If we as modern scholars do not find religious convictions which we recognize at work in this episode, that does not mean they were absent. A definition of catholic orthodoxy as a historic consensus permeates the writing of the Polish Crown and its top counsellors in their communications with Ducal Prussia. In 1526, Sigismund I informed Bishop Queis that he valued that 'which has been handed down from antiquity and observed by all Christian kings and princes', and in Danzig he told Duke Albrecht that true faith was rooted completely in 'the consensus and unity of the church', handed down by the church through the ages and embraced by all Christian kings and princes.[108] In autumn of that year, catholicism was yet again spelt out to Albrecht as the religion of the Fathers, and one's ancestors.[109]

By contrast, as in the Danzig episodes, the Crown was most reluctant to engage with the specific Lutheran doctrinal positions put to it by Ducal Prussia. If Bishop Ferber, in his vast correspondence with Duke Albrecht, talked often of fish but never of theology, the same lack of doctrinal engagement can be seen with Sigismund I and his council. In its interactions with Albrecht, the Polish Crown grappled with doctrine only when forced to do so—specifically in 1526, when Lutheran theological positions were repeatedly, publicly put to the King by the Duke and his bishops, and required some response. In these circumstances, Sigismund wrote to Bishop Queis that apostolic succession was necessary for high clerical office, that the church alone had jurisdiction over spiritual affairs, and that the seizure of its lands by princes was a great impudence.[110] In a subsequent letter to Duke Albrecht, Sigismund explained that Luther's doctrines did not *seem* to come from Christ, with their emphasis on the carnal (i.e. clerical marriage).[111] On the great theological question of the Reformation—salvation—Sigismund I expressed his views somewhat timidly, in no way presenting them as universal truths necessary for salvation. He himself, he wrote to Albrecht, placed his personal hope for reaching Heaven in good works.[112] To the Crown, there was of course such a thing as doctrinal error, doctrinal rectitude, or bad doctrine—but it engaged in doctrinal discussions very reticently, preferring always to talk of what was not controverted but to them absolutely clear, the historic consensus of the Christian people. The secondary role of doctrine in the Crown's concept of orthodoxy is well revealed by King Sigismund's declaration to Albrecht, in 1526,

---

[107] AT 7, p. 293: 'Nec nostrum est, aliquem ad religionem cogere' and AT 10, pp. 439–40. See also Chapter Six, p. 65.
[108] AT 8, p. 34, 'quam antiquitus traditum est et quam omnes reges et principes christiani observant'; AT 8, pp. 49–51.
[109] *Elementa*, p. 15.   [110] AT 8, p. 132.
[111] *Elementa*, p. 15.   [112] *Elementa*, p. 15.

that the entirety of religion could not consist of a single academic point won in a theological disputation.[113] Self-evidently, to the Polish King, *doctrina* was not *fides*.

In this reading, Lutherans in Ducal Prussia were tolerated because, ultimately, they were still regarded in the main as fellow members of the universal church. Luther himself was a wicked heretic who sinned against the wisdom of the church, but his followers might yet be part of it. As such, Ducal Prussia, its married bishops, and Lutheran duke were still Christians, even if they were goats rather than sheep. Even Krzycki referred to the 1525 treaty, between his King and Albrecht of Brandenburg, as a 'peace among Christians'—not peace between a catholic and a heretic.[114] Sigismund assured Albrecht that God was on their side, and would bring triumph against the machinations of the evil Teutonic Knights of Livonia—a comment which posits the catholic Teutonic Order as irreligious, but includes Albrecht within a Christian sphere of princely truth and justice.[115] Lutheranism thus sat on the edges of a church stretched so broad that it could, in a great paradox, encompass even followers of a heretic like Luther. Hubatsch suggested that the King saw Albrecht's church as another type of Christianity within the one kingdom, a local variant.[116] This is why a catholic such as Szydłowiecki could act as godfather to a Lutheran duke's son, for there was no widespread sense of an ultimate, sacramental, or metaphysical barrier between these two religious communities; what united them, as Latin Christians, was still far more powerful than what divided them. This is why we find awkwardness and occasional anger in the nine rules of coexistence, but no acute metaphysical terror—in fact, the Polish government was more afraid of Charles V's very earthly retaliation for the absorption of Prussia, than of any form of divine anger at local heresy. The Lutheran Reformation in Ducal Prussia, an early modern project which played out throughout the 1520s, 1530s, and 1540s, was thus permitted by elites operating with a late medieval ecclesiology. It was not a Lutheran Reformation taking place in defiance of an antagonistic, Catholic-confessional Crown, and Panek's description of the 'essential position of confessional absolutism' as seeing 'in the non-Catholic believer the enemy of the state' clearly does not describe Polish royal thinking in the first five decades of the sixteenth century.[117] King Sigismund thus models how the late medieval church could potentially reconcile itself to, and accommodate, Lutheranism without self-destruction.

This story has implications for how we approach the chronologies of toleration in sixteenth-century Europe. There are many celebrated, and many obscure, examples of religious coexistence between different Christian groups in sixteenth-century Europe: the brief permitting of multiple confessions in cities such as Basle, Strassburg, Lausanne, and Augsburg in the early Reformation, the 1555 Peace of Augsburg, the 1598 Edict of Nantes which allowed French Huguenots their own strongholds, the laissez-faire of a Venetian senate which could inform Pope

---

[113] AT 8, p. 51.   [114] AT 7, pp. 250–5.   [115] *Elementa*, p. 67.
[116] Hubatsch, *Albrecht von Brandenburg*, p. 247.
[117] Jaroslav Panek, 'Bohemia and Moravia in the Age of Reformation', in Grell and Scribner, *Tolerance and Intolerance*, pp. 231–48, at p. 244.

Clement VII that 'as for the Lutherans and heretics, our state and dominion is free; thus, we cannot prohibit them'.[118] Poland itself, at the end of the Jagiellonian era, produced the Confederation of Warsaw (1573), promising protection for 'dissidents in religion'. The story of Lutheran Ducal Prussia and Sigismund I suggests, however, that we should distinguish more clearly between pre- and post-confessional forms of toleration.[119] Where those in power operated with a pluralistic sense of a possibly variegated Christianity, religious coexistence was uncomfortable but a continuation of known trends and habits of mind. But where the Reformation vision of confessional-doctrinal churches had triumphed, toleration in the sense of living in peace with a religious Other became a challenging and indeed appalling prospect. Toleration in that brave new world might well be purely forced, or pragmatic, or cynical; or it might be, in the guise of irenicism, a survival of older ideas and habits of mind. Late medieval and early modern varieties of 'toleration' coexisted throughout the sixteenth century (paradoxically to us) with considerable chronological overlap; perhaps these labels do not so much denote historical periods, as different Christian cultures within Christendom. So in Krzysztof Szydłowiecki, Chancellor of Poland, close friend and ally of the Lutheran Duke of Prussia, we need not see a cynical Judas, a politician without religious conviction, but a man comfortable in a loose and variegated church, to whom his doctrinal differences with the educated, pious, loyal, suave Duke Albrecht mattered but little.

---

[118] These case studies are all discussed in Grell and Scribner, *Tolerance*; quotation from Salvatore Caponetto, trans. Anne and John Tedeschi, *The Protestant Reformation in Sixteenth-Century Italy* (Kirksville, 1999), p. 43.

[119] For possible chronologies of toleration see also Christman, *Pragmatic Toleration*, pp. 3–4 and Kreigseisen, *Stosunki wyznaniowe*, pp. 661–74.

4

Hollow Law?

Royal Edicts against Lutheranism

'We order that no book of Luther or his followers...will be imported or read in our kingdom and dominions...on penalty of death and the forfeiture of all goods and property.'[1]

Royal edict, September 1523

In the lands of the Polish Crown (*korona*), the king's chief instrument against the Reformation was the anti-Luther edict. These territories—Wielkopolska, Małopolska, Ruthenia-Podolia, and (from 1529) the Duchy of Mazovia, often problematically regarded as 'Poland proper'—saw persistent, bitty, and heterogeneous manifestations of pro-Luther sentiment. Sigismund I issued edicts at a prolific rate, remarkable in contemporary Europe, and they constitute yet another apparently contradictory aspect of Crown policy. Historians have puzzled over whether these edicts reveal the regime to have been, at heart, tolerant or persecutory. On the one hand, the edicts were sternly worded laws threatening draconian punishments, and many subjects perceived them as deadly serious in intent—on paper, as the 1523 edict above shows, King Sigismund's Poland was a dangerous place in which to even possess a Lutheran book. Polish historians who insist on the humane outlook of Sigismund I find these edicts awkwardly out of character, and present them as anomalies, forced on him by overenthusiastic Italian clerics or Primate Łaski.[2] For the Protestant Theodor Wotschke, the edicts were proof that the Polish Crown was a zealously persecuting catholic power from the outset of the Reformation.[3] On the other hand, the edicts openly acknowledged their own ineffectiveness; the Crown was coy about their enforcement, and by King Sigismund's death in 1548 not a single one of his subjects had been burnt as a Lutheran heretic. In practice, the Polish Crown lands were a very safe place in which to flirt with Wittenberg theologies, so long as one did not take up arms in their cause.[4]

---

[1] CIP, IV, p. 29: 'mandavimus, ne qui libri Lutheri cuiusdam eiusque sequacium...ad regnum et dominia nostra inferrentur et legerentur...sub poena capitis et confiscatione bonorum omnium'.

[2] Tazbir, *Państwo bez stosów*, pp. 34, 40; Budka, 'Przejawy reformacji', p. 188; Pociecha, 'Walka sejmowa', p. 164.

[3] Wotschke, *Die Reformation*, pp. 14–15.

[4] The thirteen men executed following the Danzig revolt were punished as rebels, through royal justice; they were not tried by church authorities as heretics.

Anti-Reformation edicts issued by European princes have been relatively little studied as a subject in their own right.[5] They are usually treated as part of the wider apparatus of religious persecution, a subplot in larger narratives of trials, executions, and martyrdoms.[6] There has been no systematic study of King Sigismund's anti-Luther edicts of 1520–40, and they have not yet been located within a comparative European framework. We do, however, have the impeccably scholarly editions of King Sigismund's edicts produced by the eminent legal historian Oswald Balzer in the early 1900s.[7]

This discussion will first reconstruct the history of the Polish Crown's eleven anti-Reformation edicts up to 1540—their drafting, dissemination, and the evolving prohibitions on Lutheranism in the *korona*—before attempting to account for their paradoxical nature. This paradox seem to run deeper than the straightforwardly political, i.e. conflict between the centre and non-cooperative officials in the localities. It will be suggested that these royal laws in part had a symbolic function, for both an international audience and a domestic one. Above all, however, their history makes more sense once we perceive that Sigismund I's edicts were not outlawing 'Lutheranism' as we normally understand it. As their wording and timings reveal, these edicts were intended to stave off social revolt—their chief target was 'luteranismus' in the sense of an uprising by the lower social orders, not elites discreetly interested in controversial teachings. This in turn can further explain why they were not actively enforced in the *korona*, where no peasant war or widespread Lutheran city revolts in fact manifested themselves.

THE EDICTS: EVOLUTION AND DISSEMINATION

An anti-heresy edict is a royal decree in which a prince announces his intention to punish followers of a new teaching condemned by the church. It was well established in medieval Europe that it was the role of the church authorities themselves to detect and judge heretics (e.g. via inquisitions), because they alone had the theological expertise to do so.[8] The role of the lay ruler was simply to provide the *bracchium saeculare*, the 'secular arm'—that is, to make available the coercive physical resources of the Crown to punish and specifically to execute heretics, which the church itself could not under canon law, as an institution forbidden

---

[5] Some exceptions are P. R. Cavill, 'Heresy and Forfeiture in Marian England', *Historical Journal* 56:9 (2013): 879–907; James D. Tracy, 'Heresy Law and Centralization under Mary of Hungary: Conflict between the Council of Holland and Central Government over the Enforcement of Charles V's Placards', *Archiv für Reformationsgeschichte* 73 (1982): 284–308.

[6] Edicts are a background presence, for example, in William Monter, *Frontiers of Heresy: The Spanish Inquisition from the Basque Lands to Sicily* (Cambridge, 1990) and *Judging the French Reformation*; Farge, *Orthodoxy and Reform*; N. M. Sutherland, *The Hugenot Struggle for Recognition* (New Haven, 1980); Grell and Scribner, *Tolerance and Intolerance*. For a study of heresy prosecutions as a social-legal phenomenon, see Ian Forrest, *The Detection of Heresy in Late Medieval England* (Oxford, 2005).

[7] CIP, III and IV.

[8] For introductions to the institutional and legal apparatus, see Forrest, *Detection of Heresy*, pp. 28–59; B. Bernard Hamilton, *The Medieval Inquisition* (London, 1981); Richard Kieckhefer, *The Repression of Heresy in Medieval Germany* (Liverpool, 1979).

from shedding blood directly.[9] In the Polish Crown lands, as in other parts of Europe, princely edicts against Lutheranism built on an existing body of legislation against the fifteenth-century heresies of Hussitism and Lollardy. Prior to the Martin Luther affair, the Polish Crown had only issued one anti-heresy decree— the Wieluń edict of 1424, modelled on the thirteenth-century heresy edicts of Emperor Frederick II.[10] In the Wieluń text, Sigismund I's grandfather, King Władysław-Jogaila, had declared that the Crown's officials would punish heretics, and that any subject who did not return immediately from Hussite Bohemia would see their property and noble privileges forfeited, and their children subjected to eternal infamy as the descendants of heretics.[11] This was the legal benchmark.

Anti-Luther edicts for the *korona* were produced in the Royal Chancellery, headed by Chancellor Krzysztof Szydłowiecki and Vice-Chancellor Tomicki, but we cannot know precisely who wrote or edited the texts themselves. Oswald Balzer has shown that some of these decrees underwent redrafting.[12] The master copy of an edict was entered in the royal register (*Metryka Koronna*), and sealed copies sent to one or more royal officials across the *korona*. A royal instruction to local captains on how to publicize an edict on coinage gives us some insight into how these manuscript anti-heresy commands might have been disseminated: 'they must be publicly proclaimed in the cities and towns of the captaincy on market days, and at parish churches on religious feast days'.[13] If the default model was one of oral dissemination in public places, the Crown also made use of printing. One of King Sigismund's anti-Luther decrees was printed in the 1532 official compendium of Polish law, *Statuta Inclyti Regni Poloniae*, for example.[14] Hieronym Wietor's 1535 printing of an Anabaptist decree likewise seems to have been a royal commission.[15] Certain anti-heresy decrees were also printed on individual/private initiative, at home and abroad—for example by Nuncio Ferreri and Bishop Andrzej Krzycki to accompany and frame their early 1520s polemics.[16] So although the city council of Thorn could claim in 1535, with a certain bravura, that it was unaware that the King had issued any decrees against Lutheran books, this was surely a claim with limited credibility.[17]

Sigismund I's first edict, issued in May 1520, was purely local in scope, barring the citizens of Danzig from possessing Lutheran texts (nr. 1).[18] An edict of July 1520 extended this prohibition to the entire *korona*—it stipulated that the books of an Augustinian friar named Martin Luther must not be imported, bought, or

---

[9] In this chapter, the term 'edict' is used, but other historiographies have different terms, e.g. 'plac-ards' in Holland, or 'ordinances' in England. See also G. R. Elton, 'Government by Edict?', *Historical Journal* 8:2 (1965): 266–71.

[10] See Paweł Kras, *Husyci w piętnastowiecznej Polsce* (Lublin, 1988), pp. 233–4.

[11] *Volumina Legum*, vol. I (St Petersburg, 1859), p. 38.

[12] CIP, IV, p. 27.

[13] AT 10, p. 122, 'ut per publicas proclamationes in civitatibus et oppidis capitaneatus sui diebus fororum et circa ecclesias parrochiales diebus festis...dilvugari'.

[14] *Statuta Inclyti Regni Polonie* (Kraków, 1532), fos. xcviii–xcviii(v).

[15] AT 17, pp. 612–13; printed as *Edictum contra Anabaptistas* (Kraków, 1535).

[16] Ferreri, *Oratio Legati*; Krzycki, *Encomia Luteri*, published 1524 in Speyer as *Epistola Andree Cricii et edictum Regis Poloniae in Martinum Lutherum*.

[17] AT 17, pp. 33–4.   [18] CIP, III, p. 579.

sold in the realm, on pain of confiscation of property and exile (nr. 2).[19] The ban on Lutheran books was reiterated in 1522 (nr. 3).[20] An edict of March 1523 addressed itself to problems in Kraków, stressing that Lutheran books would be burnt, and their owners' property seized (nr. 4).[21] That summer, penalties were stiffened. In August, the King and his councillors drew up their most infamous anti-Luther decree, addressed to all subjects and all visitors to the Polish monarchy (nr. 5). This edict for the first time announced the death penalty for spreading Lutheran dogmas, and also set out a number of anti-heresy measures for the royal capital of Kraków—an episcopal inquisition, house-to-house searches for prohibited books, and pre-print censorship by Kraków University (nr. 6).[22] This decree was reissued for the province of Ruthenia-Podolia in June 1524 (nr. 7).[23]

There followed a hiatus of seven years.[24] In April 1534 and September 1535, Sigismund I issued two new decrees against Anabaptists (nrs. 8, 9). These sought to prevent the settlement of Anabaptist exile groups in the monarchy—any social contact with these roving bands was strictly prohibited, and officials were urged to move them on as quickly as possible.[25] From Vilnius, in February 1535, Sigismund I issued his most contested anti-Luther edict, decreeing that any subject of the *korona* who studied at Wittenberg University would be barred from holding royal office on his return to the kingdom (nr. 10).[26] This was reiterated in a further edict of 1540, which extended the list of prohibited seats of learning to encompass Leipzig University and Goldberg College in Silesia (nr. 11).[27] It was relaxed in 1543, when travel abroad was permitted, but the ongoing complete ban on bringing Lutheran books into the kingdom was underlined.[28] Alongside the King's own edicts, the vassal duchies within this composite monarchy also issued their own decrees against heterodoxy: the Duke of Mazovia against Lutherans in 1525, and Duke Albrecht of Prussia against Anabaptists.[29]

In a European context, Sigismund I's anti-Reformation decrees are strikingly early. The May 1520 Danzig edict predated even the first papal bull condemning Luther's opinions, *Exsurge Domine* (June 1520). The July 1520 ban on Lutheran works across the entire *korona* was the first such general prohibition issued by a

---

[19] CIP, III, pp. 583–4.   [20] CIP, III, pp. 647–50.   [21] CIP, IV, p. 3.

[22] CIP, IV, pp. 21–30.

[23] CIP, IV, pp. 103–5. Balzer has speculated that the August 1523 edict was also reissued by the Chancellery in 1527/8, when it was again copied into the royal registers, CIP, IV, p. 25 and AT 9, pp. 287–8.

[24] Some of the documents issued during King Sigismund's armed intervention in Danzig in 1526 reminded the city of the prohibitions on Lutheran books, and sought to enforce them: AT 8, pp. 75–83. See Chapter Two, p. 81.

[25] AT 16a, pp. 490–1; AT 17, pp. 612–13.

[26] Printed in Chrzanowski and Kot, *Humanizm i Reformacja*, pp. 317–18. A similar ban on study at Wittenberg had already been issued in Bavaria in 1524—see Wolgast, 'Die deutschen territorialfürste', p. 422.

[27] Printed in Zakrzewski, *Powstanie i wzrost*, p. 236.

[28] Printed in Zakrzewski, *Powstanie i wzrost*, p. 47.

[29] Bogdan Sobel, 'O zaginionym druku mazowieckiego dekretu przeciwko luteranom 1525', *Przegląd Historyczny* 50 (1959): 81–5; Peter Klassen, *Mennonites in Early Modern Poland and Prussia* (Baltimore, 2009), p. 10.

prince anywhere in Christendom.[30] It was followed five months later by a ban in the Low Countries,[31] only after a year by the imperial Edict of Worms (spring 1521), and then by further anti-Reformation decrees issued by the Crown of Castile in April 1521, the Archduke of Austria in 1522, and the Scottish parliament in 1525.[32] The unusually early appearance of Sigismund I's edicts might be taken as further evidence that, as argued in Chapter One, the Polish monarchy was precocious in its experience of Lutheranism in the 1520s.

It is also the case that no other monarch in early Reformation Europe issued as many anti-heresy edicts in these decades as Sigismund I of Poland (eleven). Francis I's diverse royal decrees on the Reformation—which were as likely to include suspensions of heresy trials as edicts condemning them—included only a handful of explicitly anti-Luther edicts (e.g. 1521, 1535).[33] The English Crown under Henry VIII issued only one royal proclamation against Lutheran books (1529) before its own break with Rome.[34] The Emperor Charles V issued his single landmark edict against Luther, the Edict of Worms.[35] In issuing more than ten, his kinsman Sigismund I was behaving more like a German territorial prince—it is only in the individual territories of the Empire, and also in the Habsburg Netherlands, that we see sustained flurries of anti-Reformation law-making comparable to those produced by the Polish Royal Chancellery.[36]

HOLLOW LAW? THE PARADOXICAL NATURE OF THE EDICTS

There were plenty of reasons why contemporaries, and historians, have taken the Polish Crown's anti-Luther edicts as evidence of a persecutory instinct—starting with the fact that the texts themselves insist on the seriousness of the King's intent. The edicts were presented by the Crown as grave acts of law-making which by their nature were to be obeyed. An edict was, prima facie, a direct royal command which expressed the King's will, hinging on words such as 'mandavimus' and 'declaravimus', which carried coercive legal power. The 1522 edict was typical in explicitly

[30] For initial papal and imperial reactions, see Jared Wicks, 'Roman Reactions to Luther: the First Year (1518)', *Catholic Historical Review* 69:4 (1983): 521–62.

[31] Alistair Duke, ed. Judith Pollmann and Andrew Spicer, *Dissident Identities in the Early Modern Low Countries* (Farnham, 2009), p. 103.

[32] For Castile, see Hamilton, *Heresy and Mysticism*, p. 72 and Bataillon, *Érasme et l'Espagne*, p. 118; for Austria, see Chisholm, 'The Religionspolitik of Emperor Ferdinand', p. 555; for Scotland, McGoldrick, *Luther's Scottish Connection*, p. 33.

[33] For an overview of Francis I's policies, see Lauren J. Kim, 'Censorship, Executions and Sacrilege: The First Twenty Years of Protestant History in France', *Trinity Torch Journal* 13:2 (2010): 152–72.

[34] Paul L. Hughes and James F. Larkin (eds), *Tudor Royal Proclamations. Volume I: The Early Tudors (1485–1553)* (New Haven and London, 1964), pp. 181–5.

[35] De Lamar Jensen, *Confrontation at Worms: Martin Luther and the Diet of Worms* (Provo Utah, 1973).

[36] See Tracy, 'Heresy Law and Centralization'; Martin Brecht, 'Das Wormser Edikt in Suddeutschland', in Fritz Reuter (ed.), *Der Reichstag zu Worms von 1521* (Worms, 1971), pp. 475–89; Robert Stupperich, 'Vorgeschichte und Nachwirkungen des Wormser Edikt im deutschen Nordwesten', in Reuter, *Der Reichstag zu Worms*, pp. 459–74.

instructing royal officials, in the King's name, to execute the heresy law.[37] Likewise, in 1526 Sigismund I 'most strictly ordered' that the city council of Poznań obey his edicts and remove its Lutheran preacher.[38] Approaching Danzig with an army in 1526, the King declared to the city that it had held his edicts in contempt.[39] This insistence on compliance in the *korona* is a standard, unsurprising legal refrain in Sigismund I's edicts. This is not, at first glance, the language of a monarchy which saw its anti-Reformation edicts as purely rhetorical or decorative.

The edicts also describe precisely how they were to be implemented on the ground, adding to the sense that the Crown envisaged active enforcement. The August 1523 edict described the precise steps to be taken in the royal capital— episcopal inquisition, house searches, censorship.[40] Other cities and towns adapted these rules to local circumstances. Reprinting this edict for the Gniezno ecclesiastical province in 1527, for example, Archbishop Łaski stipulated that diocesan officials would check books in western Poland.[41] In 1524–5, the Crown empowered local officials in Wielkopolska to act as royal anti-heresy commissioners. In Kościan and Wschowa, nobles were required to identify those who had broken the edicts, and apply penalties.[42] Enforcement, and the expectation of enforcement, thus appeared to be very much on the cards in the *korona*.

Plenty of contemporaries read the edicts in just this spirit, as binding royal commands against the Reformation. Bishop Tomicki in 1535 expected the King to enforce heresy edicts in Kraków, because it would be a scandal if the guilty went unpunished in the face of these laws.[43] Bishop Ferber, in Prussia, also insisted to the monarch that those guilty of ignoring royal heresy edicts must face penalties; the law could not be a dead letter.[44] The polemicist Johann Cochlaeus praised Sigismund I's ban on studying at Wittenberg, declaring that this Polish edict enjoyed real force, unlike the ineffectual commands of German princes—he thus thought it a characteristic of Sigismund's edicts that they were (meant to be) obeyed.[45] The royal secretary Jan Zambocki reported in 1525 to his friend Johannes Danticus, in faraway Spain, that the King had 'prohibited the reading of Luther's books with a most severe edict'.[46] The humanist Andrzej Frycz Modrzewski too, reminiscing in the 1550s about his own student days in Kraków, claimed that university lecturers had burnt their copies of Luther in fear after they were outlawed.[47] Polemicists invoked royal anti-heresy edicts: in Poznań, Grzegorz Szamotulski stressed ominously in his pamphlets that his colleague Christoph Hegendorff had broken the 'iura regni' with his Lutheranism.[48] When the Kraków printer Wietor was arrested for Lutheranism in 1536, the episcopal warrant specified that he had

---

[37] CIP, III, pp. 647–50.   [38] AT 8, p. 151.   [39] AT 8, p. 39.
[40] CIP, IV, pp. 29–30.
[41] *Statuta provintiae gnesnensis antiqua et nova, revisa diligenter emendata* (Kraków, 1527). See also discussion by Balzer, CIP, IV, pp. 21–8.
[42] CIP, IV, pp. 114–16.   [43] AT 17, pp. 258–9, 266.   [44] AT 10, p. 160.
[45] AT 17, p. 325.   [46] AT 7, pp. 320–1, 'severissimo edicto'.
[47] Barycz, *Historia uniwersytetu*, p. 98. Modrzewski cites the 1520 papal bull, not royal edicts, as causing this panic.
[48] Szamotulski, *Vincula*, fo. C(v).

'disobeyed' royal heresy edicts.[49] The King's anti-Luther edicts were, in the eyes of many, prohibitions to be taken very seriously indeed.

It might seem, therefore, that Polish anti-Luther edicts were robust and intended to eradicate Lutheranism on the ground efficiently, but this would be an illusion for several reasons. Firstly, the edicts themselves candidly admit that they were not obeyed; that their main characteristic, even, was their inefficacy. Sigismund I's second edict for the *korona* (1522) already complained that subjects held the original edict (1520) in contempt, and 'do not cease to import little works by Luther and other work of that sort'.[50] The March 1523 decree likewise observed that people were still openly selling Lutheran books in Kraków, and the 1527 decree that earlier anti-Luther edicts were being ignored.[51] When in 1540 Sigismund I reissued the decree banning study at Wittenberg, he explicitly stated that the first decree on the matter had been ignored, and he was therefore issuing the command again.[52] The last comment is revealing—if a first attempt failed, the Crown's instinctive response was simply to issue another identical edict.

The edicts failed to trigger any sustained heretic crackdowns by either state or church. The concrete measures set out in Polish royal edicts—the house-searches, Wielkopolska anti-heresy commissions, and so on—have left no documentary trace, and there has to be a real suspicion that they did not take place. The generally well-preserved records of Polish sixteenth-century dioceses enable us to test whether the actions ordered by Sigismund I's edicts generated a wave of Lutheran-hunting in the dioceses of Kraków, Gniezno, Poznań, or Włocławek—and they did not. In Kraków, ecclesiastical prosecutions for Lutheranism took off abruptly only in 1525, two years after a royal edict had commanded Bishop Tomicki, Sigismund's most important and effective minister, to instigate an inquisition.[53] In Gniezno, an inquisition against Lutherans was launched only in 1534, by Primate Drzewicki.[54] P. R. Cavill has warned us that 'special commissions are among the worst documented processes of sixteenth-century government', yet even so the Wielkopolska anti-Lutheran commissions, if they ever took place, are not referred to in the paperwork of the bishopric of Poznań; they led to no heresy trials before diocesan officials.[55] Monter has observed a similar lack of correlation in France, where 'the history of sixteenth-century French heresy trials fits awkwardly with the history of sixteenth-century French heresy legislation'.[56] Now, heresy trials were the business of the clergy, and if none of Sigismund I's subjects were burnt as Lutheran heretics then the reasons for this must lie in large part within the church itself; ecclesiastical responses to the Reformation will be explored in Chapter Six. However, there is

---

[49] Ptaśnik, *Cracovia impressorum*, p. 147.
[50] CIP, pp. 647–50, 'non cessent opuscula eiusdem Lutheri et alia id genus invehere'.
[51] AT 9, pp. 287–8.
[52] Chrzanowski and Kot, *Humanizm i reformacja*, pp. 317–18. As Wotschke showed, the royal edict had no real impact on the number of Polish subjects enrolling at Wittenberg, 'Polnische studenten'.
[53] See Appendix 1.   [54] AAG, Acta. Cap., B18, fo. 248(v).
[55] Cavill, 'Heresy and Forfeiture', p. 886. Based on AAP, AC 97 (1522); AC 98 (1523); AC 99 (1524); AE VII.
[56] Monter, *Judging the French Reformation*, p. 5.

evidence to suggest that diocesan officials who did not act were simply taking their lead from the Crown.

The King ignored requests from some of his disgruntled clergy to enforce his own laws against Lutherans. In 1527, the cathedral chapter of Płock crossly asked its bishop to write to the King, demanding that the secular arm provide more assistance in fighting heresy in their region. In 1533 their bishop, Andrzej Krzycki, promised his canons that he would ask the King once more for help.[57] In a telling admission, Primate Drzewicki wrote in 1535 that bishops must take the lead in fighting Lutheranism, because the old king 'is distracted and busy with other business'—in other words, enforcing heresy law in the *korona* was known to be a low priority for the pious Sigismund I.[58] Collective bodies too grumbled that edicts were a dead letter. In 1532, the statutes of the Łęczyca synod (the parliament of Polish clergy) petitioned the Crown to enforce its own edicts against heretics.[59] The royal council too wrote to the King in 1534, from the Piotrków *sejm*, begging him in the name of his subjects to order royal officials ('capitaneos') to enforce existing laws against heresy.[60] None of these appeals had any discernible effect.

The disinclination among top figures in royal government to persecute religious dissidents is also attested to by the redrafting of one key edict. As Oswald Balzer demonstrated in 1910, the first draft of the August 1523 anti-Luther decree, probably drawn up by Bishop Andrzej Krzycki, stipulated that convicted heretics would be burnt at the stake.[61] This form of execution had not been specified in the Wieluń edict or in any earlier Polish anti-Reformation decree, even though in practice convicted Hussites had been burnt in the kingdom (on episcopal orders) as recently as the 1490s.[62] Krzycki's draft text, in the event, proved unpalatable to the King or council—the final version simply read 'death penalty' ('sub poena capitis'), with all reference to fire ('poena concremationis') expunged. This was a regime whose own chosen enforcement mechanisms on the ground were employed half-heartedly if at all, which ignored requests to implement its own heresy laws, and was very queasy at the prospect of burning Lutherans. How can we account for this?

ACCOUNTING FOR PARADOXICAL EDICTS

The most obvious explanation for this conflicted stance is a political one: that Sigismund I genuinely wished to move against his pro-Luther subjects in the *korona*, but lacked the authority or support to do so.[63] Writing to Bishop Tomicki,

---

[57] Bolesław Ulanowski (ed.), 'Acta Capituli Plocensis, 1514–77', *Archiwum Komisyi Historycznej*, vol. X (Kraków, 1916), pp. 153, 171.

[58] AT 17, p. 226.   [59] *Statuta provintiae gnesnensis* (1527).   [60] AT 16b, p. 525.

[61] CIP, IV, p. 27.

[62] Wojciech Kujawski, *Krzesław z Kurozwęk jako wielki kanclerz koronny i biskup włocławski*, Studia z Kościoła w Polsce 8 (Warsaw, 1987), pp. 118–21.

[63] For political explanations of the implementation or not of princely anti-heresy edicts, see Chisholm, 'The Religionspolitik', and Tracy, 'Heresy Law and Centralization'.

his nephew Andrzej Krzycki grumbled about obstruction from nobles, opining that issuing a new Crown decree 'will accomplish little, especially when you consider the protests of the deputies [at the *sejm*], and only ignominy and collusion will follow'.[64] Polish scholars since the nineteenth century have argued that the edicts were unenforceable, both politically and legally, because privileges granted to the Polish nobility in the late Middle Ages rendered them exempt from royal imprisonment and forfeiture, although high clergy such as Cardinal Fryderyk of Poland (d.1503) or Bishop Tomicki were able to summon noblemen before church courts.[65] It is by no means clear that Sigismund I was simply unable to impose his will on the crypto-Lutheran magnates in the council, or on shadowy populations of booksellers and clandestine readers in the *korona*, due to their political and numerical strength. 'Lutheranism' in the 1520s and 1530s in the *korona* was a complex, variegated phenomenon which did not amount to a movement in any normal sense of that term. There was no powerful group in the *korona* which openly adopted Martin Luther as their political cause, which can be shown to have beaten the King, or tied his hands. While we might consider Sigismund I's petulant reissuing of anti-heresy edicts to his subjects to be a not-too-tacit admission of political failure, of publicly compromised royal authority, in sixteenth-century terms (as we shall see) non-enforcement could in some circumstances be a token of a king's magnanimity and forbearance.

One way of reconciling the fierce language of the edicts with their persistent non-enforcement is if we judge them to have had a largely symbolic function, for example on the international stage. Bylina has suggested that Poland's 1424 anti-Hussite Wieluń edict had been chiefly 'declaratory and propaganda-like' in nature, while Henry VIII's anti-Reformation decrees have also been described as 'propaganda devices' first and foremost.[66] Kieckhefer too has suggested that the celebrated heresy edicts of Emperor Frederick II were mainly issued to placate Rome, for their international symbolism, and there is no evidence 'whatsoever' of their enforcement.[67] Sigismund I's anti-Luther decrees were a key feature of the regime's international image as a 'catholic' power.[68] In the 1520s, Chancellor Szydłowiecki eagerly sent copies of the royal edicts to Rome, where they met with papal approval.[69] When Bishop Krzycki's polemic *Encomia Luteri* was reprinted in Strassburg and Speyer, Sigismund I's 1523 decree was included alongside it, raising the King's international profile as an anti-Lutheran actor.[70] In the 1530s, Europe's top anti-Luther polemicists celebrated the Polish king's edicts. In Saxony, Johann Cochlaeus planned to reprint the anti-Wittenberg decree in Leipzig as an excellent

---

[64] AT 10, p. 85, 'id si fiet, profecto non servabitur, praesertim reclamantibus nuntiis terrarum, unde et ignominia sequetur et collusio videbitur'.

[65] Natalia Nowakowska, *Church, State and Dynasty in Renaissance Poland: The Career of Cardinal Fryderyk Jagiellon (1468–1503)* (Aldershot, 2007), pp. 63–4, 89–90. See also Introduction, p. 15.

[66] Stanisław Bylina, 'Wizerunek heretyka w Polsce późnośredniowiecznej', *OiRwP* 30 (1985): 5–24, at p. 13; Hughes and Larkin, *Tudor Royal Proclamations*, p. 294.

[67] Kieckhefer, *The Repression of Heresy*, p. 17.   [68] See Chapter Five, pp. 145, 148.

[69] Theiner, *Vetera Monumenta*, vol. II, p. 419.

[70] Krzycki, *Encomia Luteri* (Speyer, 1524) and printed in Strassburg 1524 as a supplement to Bartholomeus Arnoldi's *Sermo de Matrimonio*.

example of anti-heresy policy.[71] When in 1550 the Kraków funerary orations for Sigismund I were reprinted in Germany, Cochlaeus also supplied a preface, identifying as the chief feature of the reign how 'King Sigismund himself showed with many edicts with what zeal and study he resisted the sects new at that time, particularly the Lutherans, by issuing multiple Edicts'.[72] Dedicating his *Contra Ludderum* (1530) to the Polish king, another prominent German anti-Reformation writer, Johann Eck, wrote approvingly:

> It is thus apparent, most serene King, that since you are mindful of the virtue, piety and religion of your grandfather and father, as well as your own, you do not tolerate the pernicious heresy of Lutheranism to be divulged, spread or taught in your dominion and territories, publicly or privately, banning his and his followers' pestilential books from your lands, and decreeing well-deserved punishments for men addicted to and entangled in these errors.[73]

Eck went on to situate Sigismund I's Polish laws within a roll call of anti-Luther edicts by other princes, including Charles V, Francis I of France, and Henry VIII. Edicts, therefore, played a role in impressing foreign princes, authors, and the papal court, and were as such a diplomatic tool. It was not necessarily burning or jailing Lutherans which mattered, in this context, but rather being seen to condemn heresy loudly before all Christendom.

In a domestic context too, anti-Luther edicts can be seen as having a symbolic function in proclaiming the King's piety to his subjects. Sigismund I's anti-Luther edicts repeatedly stated that, as a Christian prince, he was entrusted with preserving concord and upholding divine law in his realm, and thus had a duty to stop heresy by the very nature of his office, 'officii nostri'.[74] A monarch's failure to do this, as he wrote to his nephew Ludwig, King of Hungary, in 1524, was a great indignity.[75] Issuing Crown edicts against heresy was, then, a mark of conscientious rule and in itself an act of public piety. The symbolic function of the edicts is reinforced if we recall that Sigismund I was not obliged to issue any anti-Luther edicts at all, because Poland, like most Latin kingdoms, already possessed a corpus of royal heresy legislation (the Wieluń edict). Most rulers, such as Charles V, found that one anti-Luther edict sufficed. Other kings were simply content to let high clergy proceed against Lutheranism on their own authority. In France, the theology faculty of Paris University and the Paris Parlement acted in concert, using existing law, to prosecute Lutherans—with or without the approval of Francis I.[76] In England, Henry VIII was long content to allow his episcopate, Archbishops Wareham and Wolsey, and Bishop Tunstall of London, to ban Lutheran books on

---

[71] AT 17, p. 325.
[72] Kromer and Maciejowski, *De Sigismundo Primo Rege*, fo. 4: 'Ipse vero Sigismundus Rex, quanto zelo & studio restiterit novis hoc tempore sectis, in primis Lutheranae, multis declaravit Edictus.'
[73] Johann Eck, *Prima pars operum Iohannis Eckii contra Ludderum* (place of printing uncertain, 1530/1), fo. Ai(v): 'Eo videlicet Rex Serenissime, ut cum avitae paternae atque adeo propriae virtutis, pietatis, ac religionis sis memor, perniciosam Lutheri haeresim…non patiaris per dominia et terras tuas, nec publice, nec privatim evvulgari, afferi aut doceri, libros eius pestilentes et sequacium a finibus suis cohibeas, homines huiusmodi erroribus addictos et irretitos, condigna poena afficias….'
[74] CIP, III, p. 584; IV, p. 29.   [75] AT 7, p. 76.
[76] See Monter, *Judging the French Reformation*; Farge, *Orthodoxy and Reform*.

their own authority.[77] Sigismund I, by contrast, saw value in issuing anti-heresy edicts in his own name, again and again.

Domestically, it is possible to read the function of these edicts as not just declaratory, but also admonitory in character. To read these sixteenth-century laws, we might need to disaggregate notions of criminalization, enforcement, detection, prosecution, and punishment. It is likely that the punishments stipulated in the edicts (while not completely notional) were not automatic penalties, but possible punishments for the worst offenders, to be applied at the King's discretion. This sense of Lutheran activity as *potentially* punishable can be detected in Crown communications with the towns of Royal Prussia. Approaching Danzig in 1526, King Sigismund announced that he had decided to 'suspend' its punishment for breaking the anti-Luther edicts, out of his mercy; in the 1530s, he informed the town of Graudenz that it too would escape punishment under the edicts, because its local bishop had interceded on its behalf.[78] An Ermland chronicle tells us that the ringleaders of the Braunsberg Reformation abjured before Bishop Ferber in 1526 with such humility, that they were promised remission from the rigor of the law.[79] Parallels elsewhere in sixteenth-century Europe reinforce the sense of stated legal penalties as merely the maximum punishment: Nicholas Davidson has shown that the savage punishments proscribed for sexual crimes in Renaissance Italy were virtually always commuted to lenient ones by 'flexible' courts, and in Tudor England local authorities which found subjects infringing royal heresy edicts did not automatically apply the stated penalties, but turned to the Privy Council for advice.[80]

Closer inspection of the Polish anti-Luther edicts suggests that they were concerned above all with preventing social revolt, with Lutheranism's potential to spark disorder forming the Crown's principal concern. The edicts place great stress on the risk that Lutheranism posed to civil order in the *korona*, as a movement particularly predisposed to triggering unrest. The first edicts for both Danzig and the *korona* (1520) thus stated that Luther's works were banned because they 'bring forth disturbances in civic life and religion'—in that order.[81] The 1522 edict declared that Luther's dogmas disturbed 'the general state of things'.[82] And the 1523 edict condemned Luther's followers as 'seditious men', declaring that it was the duty of a king to keep the peace.[83] Refusing to release Lutheran preachers to

---

[77] Craig d'Alton, 'The Suppression of Lutheran Heretics in England, 1526–1529', *Journal of Ecclesiastical History* 54 (2003): 228–53 and 'William Wareham and English Heresy Policy after the Fall of Wolsey', *Historical Research* 77:197 (2004): 337–57.

[78] AT 8, p. 39; AT 15, p. 170.

[79] *Monumenta Historiae Warmiensis*, vol. VIII, nr. II (Braunsberg, 1889), p. 491.

[80] N. S. Davidson, 'Theology, Nature and the Law: Sexual Sin and Sexual Crime in Italy from the Fourteenth Century to the Seventeenth Century', in Trevor Dean and J. K. P. Lowe (eds), *Crime, Society and the Law in Renaissance Italy* (Cambridge, 1994), pp. 74–98; R. W. Heinze, *The Proclamations of the Tudor Kings* (Cambridge, 1976), p. 254.

[81] CIP, III, pp. 579 and 584: 'quam etiam in perturbationem communis ordinis et status rei ecclesiasticae et religionis... pullularent'.

[82] CIP, III, p. 649: 'in peturbationem communis status...'.

[83] CIP, IV, p. 3: 'hominesque seditiosi'.

Bishop Queis' custody in 1526, the Crown stressed that these men had preached 'purely apostate and seditious teachings in breach of the King's orders and edicts'.[84] Banning his subjects from studying in Wittenberg in 1535, King Sigismund declared that the impact of Lutheranism on other kingdoms was plain to see, bringing 'such sedition, such slaughter, destruction of property, and disturbance in all things...'.[85] The senate, writing to the King in 1536, stressed that heretics were actively insulting the Polish monarch himself, threatening the *respublica* with sedition.[86] The kind of Lutheran that the Crown would not tolerate in any circumstances was the evangelical blacksmith attacking a town hall, or an armed and rebellious peasant quoting the Gospel—it is fear of these types which underpins Sigismund I's edicts. These edicts—just like the anti-Reformation *Statuta Sigismudi* for Danzig (1526)—can be read as anti-revolt instruments first and foremost, aimed at preventing mass disorder in the *korona*.[87]

The timing of Sigismund I's edicts reinforces the sense that they were intended to prevent Lutheranism-as-revolt. The years 1520 to 1525 saw intense edict activity in Poland—these are the years of the so-called communal Reformation, of the German Peasants' War, the Prussian peasant uprising, and urban revolts across Royal Prussia. When Bishop Tomicki finally held an inquisition in Kraków in 1525 (at the peak of the Luther-inspired uprisings in Europe), many of the accused were from the lower social orders—'insolent' tanners and tailors.[88] It is no coincidence that King Sigismund's heresy commission for Wschowa occurred in the wake of an urban riot and the violent deposition of the town's mayor (1523), in which it was suspected that Reformation preaching had played a role.[89] Similarly, Duke Janusz of Mazovia issued an anti-Luther edict modelled on that of the Polish king in 1525, directly following a major riot in Warsaw.[90] Once the communal Reformation was subdued from 1525/6, it was only the arrival of Anabaptist refugees from Münster in 1535, where they had conducted their radical experiment in communal living, which spurred the Crown to issue new edicts. While the 1536 edict on studying at Wittenberg was obviously aimed at the *korona*'s elites, its references to disobedience and disorder were probably inspired by the sight of the Holy Roman Empire fragmenting into armed religious leagues following the breakdown of dialogue at the Augsburg Diet of 1530; Lutheranism as eroding obedience, as political anarchy.

If the point of Sigismund I's heresy edicts—alongside their symbolic functions— was to outlaw Lutheranism as a vehicle for revolt, the fact that the Crown did not actively enforce this law in the 1520s and 1530s, or initiate large-scale hunts for Lutherans, makes more sense. Revolts by Luther-inspired peasants, butchers, and brewers never materialized on any scale in the *korona* (as they had done in the

---

[84] AT 8, p. 34: 'meram doctrinam apostaticam et seditiosam contra mandata et edicta Mtis sue regie...'.

[85] Chrzanowski and Kot, *Humanizm i Reformacja*, p. 317: 'quantae seditiones, quantae caedes, bonorum direptiones, et quanta rerum omnium perturbatio'.

[86] AT 16b, p. 525.   [87] For Lutheranism as mass disorder, see also Chapter Seven, pp. 187–9.

[88] See Appendix 1.   [89] Dworzaczkowa, *Reformacja i kontrreformacja*, p. 58; CIP, IV, p. 116.

[90] Sobel, 'O zaginionym druku'.

Reich, Royal Prussia, and Ducal Prussia), so there was no need to apply the potential punishments set out in the edicts; an anti-revolt law, in other words, was not enforced in the absence of attempted or actual revolt. The only Lutherans executed on royal orders, or actively hunted down, were the Danzig rebels after 1526.[91] Mazovian nobles who engaged Lutheran tutors in their households, furiously denounced by the senior clergy of Płock as heretics under the edicts, did not much alarm Sigismund I; it was not primarily to criminalize them that these laws had been framed.[92] In such cases the Crown turned a blind eye, and thereby appeared (but only appeared) to step away from its own edicts.

Anti-Reformation edicts, almost by definition, look to us like instruments of confessional struggle—the outlawing of one variety of Christian belief by adherents of another. Heresy edicts thus appear to be a defining feature of the Reformation as it is normally understood, a desperate contest between two rival theologies. However, the construction of Lutheranism as a form of (mass) social-political insurrection in King Sigismund's edicts reflects instead their pre-confessional instincts, where 'lutherani' were a threat to the coherence and peace of Christian society first and foremost, and their specific doctrinal claims of secondary importance. The edicts' language reflects this: the majority (90 per cent) do not label Luther or 'luteranismus' heretical at all, and in that sense it is perhaps misleading to call them anti-heresy edicts. The 1520 edict for the *korona* referred only to 'erroneous writings' by the Augustinian monk, the 1522 and March 1523 edicts to Luther's 'dogmas', the 1535 ban on study at Wittenberg to 'terrible doctrines'— but not explicitly to 'heresy'. In contrast to the Edict of Worms and papal bulls, Sigismund I's edicts had virtually no doctrinal content (as we would understand it)—they did not specify Luther's erroneous doctrines, noting only in passing (1520) that he disrespected the pontiff. Similarly, the contents of catholic belief or teaching are nowhere spelt out or defended in these Polish royal texts. Their rhetorical emphasis is not on the demonization of heresy and exposition of doctrine, but instead on the preservation of social-ecclesiastical peace and unity (these seen as indistinguishable from each other).[93]

Even in the short texts of these edicts, we can find clear definitions of orthodoxy as the unity and consensus of the Christian community over space and time— exactly as we do in royal communications with Royal Prussia and Ducal Prussia. Luther was in error, the 1522 edict tells us, because he had adopted positions which were 'against the customs and teachings of the Church Fathers and the holy mother church'—against consensus.[94] The 1523 edict stressed that Sigismund I was upholding 'the very religion which was directed by the Fathers and the Holy Roman Church, passed down to us by our ancestors'.[95] Edicts stressed that the King's aim was to preserve unity, concord, and tranquillity among his people; that Luther

---

[91] See Chapter Two, p. 80. [92] See Budka, 'Przejawy reformacji', p. 189.

[93] For the medieval church as focused on social harmony-unity, see John Bossy, 'The Mass as a Social Institution: 1200–1700', *Past & Present* 100 (1983): pp. 29–61.

[94] CIP, III, pp. 649–50: 'contra mores et instituta patrum et sanctae matris ecclesie'.

[95] CIP, IV, p. 29: 'ipsam religionem, a sanctis patris ordinatam ac per sanctam Romanam ecclesiam directam, nobisque a majoribus nostris per manus traditam...'.

disturbed the peace of the kingdom, the church and religion (these elided together), and the unity of Christian folk.[96] The Polish Crown's laws speak of a late medieval sense of a single universal church which could not be distinguished from society itself. As such, we should recognize Sigismund I's eleven anti-Luther edicts as a pre-confessional policy towards the Reformation, something we have long and incorrectly assumed to be a contradiction in terms.

In 1721, the coffin of Sigismund I was opened in the crypts of Kraków cathedral and found to contain the sword with which the old king had been buried. On its pommel (dated 1521) were images of the Virgin Mary, Saint Stanisław, and Saint Sigismund, but its centrepiece was Hercules vanquishing the hydra—a classic medieval image of the fight against heresy. Mossakowski has thus suggested that heresy-fighting could have been an important part of Sigismund I's self-image and self-understanding as king.[97] His reign saw no one executed for Lutheran heresy, and Lutherans walked free from church courts, but in a pre-confessional world view Sigismund I's claims to be a smiter of heretics could still make sense—where an anti-heretical king was one who defended peace, social order, and a broad Christian unity, rather than a prince who policed the inner doctrinal opinions of his subjects.

---

[96] CIP, IV, p. 3; CIP, III, p. 649.   [97] Mossakowski, *King Sigismund Chapel*, pp. 252–3.

5

'A Most Pious Prince'?
The Reformation Diplomacy of Sigismund I

In 1526, a single-sheet woodcut of King Sigismund I was printed in Kraków (Figure 5.1). The monarch is shown pensive in embroidered hat and furs: beneath his portrait a Latin verse praises his achievements in what we would today term foreign policy, lauding victories over the Wallachians, Tartars, Muscovites, and heretical Prussians.[1] This sheet captures in microcosm the ambiguities of Sigismund I's diplomacy, glossing religiously questionable acts as impeccably catholic, and presenting the King himself as an enemy of the enemies of God. The ambiguities, riddles, and paradoxes of Polish policy towards the early Reformation seen in so many spheres were, in Sigismund I's international relations, played out on a bigger and more conspicuous canvas. The substance of the King's diplomacy appeared basically pro-Lutheran, promoting leading Lutheran princes across northern Europe. However, Sigismund I also presented himself on the international stage as a pious prince and model defender of the old church, and protested at the progress of the Reformation in both neighbouring states and those further afield, such as England. Żelewski, writing in the definitive modern history of Polish diplomacy, has called foreign policy in the 1520s and 1530s a 'paradox' where the Reformation was concerned.[2] Certain contemporaries too struggled to make sense of it: an old Teutonic Knight from Livonia, interviewed by a Polish agent in the French town of Lusignan in 1526, grumbled that aspects of Sigismund I's diplomacy were 'reprehensible', but others 'most Christian'.[3]

If scholarship often explains princely toleration domestically (towards dissident subjects) as rooted entirely in pragmatic politics, scholarship on early modern diplomacy had made particularly heavy use of the notion of toleration-as-realpolitik. After all, much royal diplomacy of the sixteenth century looks contradictory, or openly cynical. In the 1540s, Francis I fiercely repressed the Reformation in France while channelling enormous sums to aid the Protestant Schmalkaldic League in the Reich against Charles V. David Potter has argued that, here, the French Crown

---

[1] See Feliks Koper, 'Dary z Polski dla Erazma z Rotterdamu w historycznym museum Bazylejskiem', *Sprawozdania komisyi do badania historyi sztuki w Polsce* 6 (1900): 110–38.
[2] Roman Żelewski, 'Dyplomacja polska w latach 1506–72', in Marian Biskup (ed.), *Historia Dyplomacji Polskiej*, vol. 1 (Warsaw, 1982), pp. 587–671, at p. 588.
[3] AT 8, p. 374.

Figure 5.1 Painted woodcut of King Sigismund I, 1526.
Historisches Museum Basel; photo: Ph. Emmel. Reproduced with permission.

prioritized 'external security': politics abroad, and idealism at home.[4] Describing the tangled politics of the Holy Roman Empire in the 1530s and 1540s, which saw Lutheran princes regularly joining Catholic leagues and vice versa, Joachim Whaley has concluded that German princes placed 'territorial interests' ahead of 'confessional loyalties'.[5] Elector John of Saxony (1525–32), sabotaged his fellow Protestants' early attempts to create a league against the Emperor *c*.1530. Here too, Carl C. Christiansen and others have concluded that the Elector simply put the political interests of his own territory ahead of those of the wider Reformation cause.[6] However, as Onnekink and Rommelse have warned us, applying realpolitik analyses to sixteenth-century diplomacy might be anachronistic, and its juxtaposition of 'politics' and 'religion' possibly too crude.[7] To understand foreign policy, in other words, we should not try to identify which logical, self-serving goals it pursued in the abstract, but rather seek to decode the underlying political culture and its operating values, to grasp the international relations of earlier centuries on

[4] D. L. Potter, 'Foreign Policy in the Age of the Reformation: French Involvement in the Schmalkaldic War, 1544–47', *Historical Journal* 20:3 (1977): 525–44. The same point is made by Monter, *Judging the French Reformation*, p. 56 and Sutherland, *The Huguenot Struggle*, pp. 19–20, 27.

[5] Whaley, *Germany*, vol. I, p. 310.

[6] Carl C. Christensen, 'John of Saxony's Diplomacy, 1529–30: Reformation or Realpolitik?', *Sixteenth Century Journal* 15:4 (1984): 419–30, see conclusion at p. 30.

[7] Onnekink and Rommelse, *Ideology and Foreign Policy*; discussed more fully in the Introduction— see p. 10.

their own terms. Understanding the foreign policy of Sigismund I is thus not a case of mapping how 'religion' and 'politics' were pitted against one another in the cauldron of the early Reformation (in a zero-sum game), but rather of capturing more fully *how* they were enmeshed with one another in the minds of ruling elites.

Here, we will reconstruct the Polish Crown's pro- and anti-Lutheran actions in the international arena in the 1520s and 1530s, suggesting that the characteristically sixteenth-century assumptions which animated Sigismund I's Reformation foreign policy were kinship, the politics of princely reputation, and a unity-focused concept of religious orthodoxy. Recent scholarship has tried to read Renaissance diplomacy afresh as a cultural activity: both high culture in the traditional sense (stressing the role of literature and the visual arts), and in an anthropological sense (focusing on gift giving, ritual, symbolic communication).[8] Recognizing the underlying ecclesiological concepts in play gives us another fruitful lens through which to view the diplomatic behaviour of princes. We cannot easily grasp the dynamics of early Reformation diplomacy until we have a clearer sense of how princes, and not just theologians, thought about the church and orthodoxy itself in their rapidly changing world. King Sigismund I's diplomacy towards Sweden and Silesia, Pomerania and England, Bohemia, Livonia, and the Holy Roman Empire was not, in that monarch's own eyes, contradictory or cynical; it was simply a diplomacy conducted in the belief that the universal, heterogeneous, unified church of the fifteenth century was still basically intact.

THE CHARGE SHEET: 'A FRIEND AND PROMOTER OF LUTHERANS'

During his draining twelve-year stint as Sigismund I's representative at the roving imperial court, Johannes Dantiscus was repeatedly told by Charles V and Ferdinand Habsburg that the Polish king 'held councils and hatched conspiracies with Lutherans', 'has Lutherans with him and favours them', 'promotes and defends Lutheranism'.[9] Modern readers might well reach a similar verdict. There are four items one might put on such a charge sheet.

First, and most embarrassingly, was the Polish Crown's creation of the Lutheran territory of Ducal Prussia as its vassal. Sigismund I's foreign policy was construed by contemporaries as pro-Reformation chiefly because of the 1525 Treaty of Kraków. Under the terms of this controversial peace, the King had invested his openly Lutheran nephew, Albrecht Hohenzollern, son of the margrave of Brandenburg-Ansbach and Grand Master of the Teutonic Order in Prussia (1510–25),

---

[8] John Watkins, 'Toward a New Diplomatic History of Medieval and Early Modern Europe', *Journal of Medieval and Early Modern Studies* 38:1 (2008): 1–14 and 'Ambassadors, Factors, Translators, Spies: Agents of Transcultural Relations in the Early Modern World', *Clio* 38:3 (2009): 339–47; Oren Margolis, *The Politics of Culture in Quattrocento Europe: René of Anjou in Italy* (Oxford, 2016).

[9] AT 12, p. 197: 'cum Lutheranis consilia aut conspirationes facere' and 'cum tamen rex vester Lutheranos apud se et sub se habeat et foveat'; p. 200: 'quod rex vester eum tueatur et defendat in Lutheranismo' (of Duke Albrecht).

as a lay duke in Prussia.[10] In early 1520s Europe, this audacious deal between Albrecht and the Polish Crown appeared to be a nakedly Lutheran act—because it dissolved the religious order of the Teutonic Knights and thus appeared to be an attack on the principle of monasticism; because it converted their ecclesiastical property (i.e. land) into the possessions of a secular prince; and because it sanctioned the Grand Master's high-profile rejection of his monastic vows, and elevated Albrecht himself, one of the most prominently pro-Luther princes at that date. The investiture ceremonies performed in Kraków square in 1525 appeared, moreover, to be implementing the will of Martin Luther himself, who had specifically called for the secularization of the Teutonic Order in a 1524 pamphlet addressed to its knights.[11]

As rumours of this event spread through the courts of Europe, the initial reaction was one of disbelief and, in Rome, panic. 'The pope and all the curia were in a state of agitation' reported the Gniezno cleric Myszkowski, who found himself summoned before the papal datarius, as the first Pole the papal court could locate, and required to explain how his king could create a secular duchy from church land, on his own authority.[12] Clement VII told Myszkowski that he expected an urgent explanation from Primate Łaski.[13] At Charles V's court in Toledo, Johannes Dantiscus was told by an amazed chancellor, Mercurino Gattinara, that 'if your king has done this thing, he will certainly have lost his authority and reputation with everybody'.[14] The 1525 treaty led European observers to conclude that Sigismund I and his chief councillors had themselves, like Albrecht, become disciples of Luther. Piotr Tomicki, for example, in 1525, wrote in exasperation that 'among certain of our enemies has emerged the suspicion, or rather the calumny, that I am a supporter of the Lutheran sect (to which the same duke of Prussia is said to be dedicated)'.[15] The papal legate, Johann Pulleo, wrote darkly to Sigismund I that Hungary, a kingdom which had failed to fight heresy, was being destroyed by the Ottomans in an act of divine vengeance, hinting the same fate might meet the Polish monarchy.[16] A few years later, in 1530, Johann Eck, dedicating his *Contra Ludderum* to Sigismund I, reminded the King that people had once thought him to be a follower of Luther because he had made a duke of Albrecht, a man who had thrown off his monastic habit.[17]

The Polish Crown's spirited international defence of Ducal Prussia after 1525, once Albrecht had implemented a full Lutheran reform in his territory, only strengthened the impression that Sigismund I was tacitly pro-Reformation. Duke Albrecht had many enemies—the pope, Emperor Charles V, and the international Teutonic Order, all of whom saw the 1525 secularization of the *Ordenstaat* as an

---

[10] See Chapter One pp. 54–5, and Chapter Three.

[11] Martin Luther, *An die Herren Deutschen Ordens* (Wittenberg, 1523).

[12] AT 7, p. 283: 'Ex rumore fuit papa turbatus et curia tota.'   [13] AT 7, p. 284.

[14] AT 7, p. 271: 'si hoc rex vester fecit, certe apud omnes autoritatem et opinionem suam amisit'. Dantiscus confessed himself also to be 'attonitus' at the news.

[15] AT 7, p. 292: 'Et deinde a quibusdam malevolis nostris nata est suspicio, immo calumnia, quasi nos luterane secte (cui idem dux in Prussia quadam ex parte deditus esse dicitur) faveremus...'.

[16] AT 7, pp. 333–4.   [17] Eck, *Prima Pars*, fos. Aii–Aii(v).

illegitimate usurpation of church land, and its new duke as a heretic.[18] Charles V's long absence in Spain and the Netherlands gave Kraków and Königsberg an initial five years' grace, which came to an end with Charles V's much anticipated return to the Empire in 1529. In a ceremony at the Augsburg Diet (1530), Charles V installed Walter von Cronenberg as Grand Master of the Teutonic Order and legitimate ruler of all Prussia, in a staged riposte to the 1525 Kraków investiture of Albrecht as *dux in Prussia*.[19] Thereafter Dantiscus, as Sigismund I's chief agent at the imperial court, was urged by Kraków to defend Duke Albrecht 'strenuously and prudently'.[20] In June 1532, Sigismund I demanded that Charles V revoke his edict banishing Albrecht from the Empire, decrying this as an affront to his own royal sovereignty ('superioritas'), Albrecht's princely dignity, and the Polish royal family.[21] Although Charles V initially suspended the banishment for two years, there followed a cat-and-mouse game of confirmations and suspensions which lasted until the late 1540s, each time prompting intensive waves of Polish petitioning of German princes, towns, imperial counsellors, and judicial bodies on Albrecht's behalf.[22] Throughout the 1530s, Prussia and the Polish court were awash with rumours that a German crusading army would imminently land on the Baltic coast, on high military alert.[23] From 1525, therefore, the principal object of Polish diplomatic activity in the Holy Roman Empire was to prevent the legal harassment, or full-scale invasion of, Lutheran Ducal Prussia as a land of heretics.

The pro-Wittenberg air of Polish diplomacy was reinforced too by Duke Albrecht's own subsidiary foreign policy, conducted with the permission of his royal uncle. Albrecht quickly became a keen participant in alliances among pro-Reformation princes in northern Europe. In 1526, he married Princess Dorothea of Denmark, in one of Europe's earliest Lutheran princely matches.[24] Dorothea's father, King Ferdinand I, had, from 1525, openly taken communion in both kinds and consumed meat on fast days, but King Sigismund gave his blessing to this match. While busily suppressing Danzig's Reformation revolt in 1526, he lavishly entertained Princess Dorothea's wedding party when it anchored in the Prussian port, 'with games, dance, music, various pastimes in their honour, [and] all acts of hospitality, liberality, and benevolence'.[25] The King gave direct guarantees to the Danish Crown that it would recognize Dorothea as holder of the Prussian landed estates with which Albrecht enfeoffed his bride (which included property seized from bishops).[26] From 1534, Dorothea's Lutheran brother, Christian, fought a major Baltic war against Danish supporters of the old church and their ally Lübeck, in order to claim his throne (the Count's War). Albrecht borrowed 10,000 marks

---

[18] For the Order's printed polemics against Albrecht, see Bues, *Apologien*.
[19] Wijaczka, *Stosunki dyplomatyczne*, pp. 58–61; Dantiscus' report from Augsburg, AT 12, p. 202.
[20] AT 12, p. 193.   [21] AT 14, p. 404.
[22] Wijaczka, *Stosunki dyplomatyczne*, pp. 58–98; AT 16a, pp. 331–6; AT 16b, pp. 90–1, 94–5.
[23] See Chapter One, pp. 110–11, 113–14.
[24] See the biographical study by Gundermann, *Herzogin Dorothea*; Grell, 'Scandinvia', p. 105.
[25] AT 8, p. 104, 'ludi, choree, musice, solatia varia ad eorum honorem acta, omniaque hospitalitatis, liberalitatis, benevolentie…'.
[26] Szymaniak, *Rola Dworu*, pp. 90, 102.

from royal officials in Royal Prussia to fund his brother-in-law's military effort, sending from Königsberg several hundred soldiers and a fleet of six warships commanded by Johann Pein, which participated in a decisive naval battle off Gotland in 1535.[27] All this Albrecht did with the expressed permission of Sigismund I, whose only (pragmatic) concern was that Albrecht did not find himself backing a candidate who might fail to win the Danish Crown.[28] When the Prussian Diet expressed anxiety about this campaign, Albrecht assured them that King Sigismund I was perfectly content.[29] Bishop Tomicki too worried that Albrecht had exposed his duchy to real danger by intervening in a civil war.[30] When King Christian took Copenhagen, the catholic King of Poland declared himself to be utterly delighted.[31] Via its vassal Albrecht, the Polish monarchy thus found itself indirectly on the Lutheran side of one of Scandinavia's decisive Reformation conflicts, a war which ended the old church in Denmark.

From 1525 to 1547, Duke Albrecht also cultivated diplomatic ties with pro-Reformation princes of the Reich. In Breslau in 1526, an amicable agreement was concluded between Albrecht and John, Elector of Saxony, as co-religionists.[32] In 1534, Ducal Prussia joined the Schmalkaldic League, an association of Reformation princes in the Empire against Charles V, and Sigismund I permitted Albrecht to send the League financial aid. Talks with the League were held in Königsberg.[33] Albrecht also corresponded on theological subjects with the Dukes of Württermberg and Brunswick-Lüneburg, and the Countess of Henneberg.[34] Keenly involved in international Reformation politics, all this Albrecht did as a vassal of Sigismund I: the catholic Polish monarchy permitted a satellite pro-Lutheran diplomacy to be run out of Königsberg.

Albrecht of Prussia was not the only theologically suspect member of the house of Brandenburg whom Sigismund I actively promoted before the eyes of Christendom. Albrecht's younger brother, Wilhelm of Ansbach-Brandenburg (1498–1563), had been invited by the King to reside as his guest at the Polish court, with suggestions of a match with a Mazovian duchess. In 1530, Wilhelm was elected Archbishop of Riga, a pivotal position in Livonia (present day Latvia/Estonia), a Baltic state still ruled by the Teutonic Knights.[35] Opposition from the Teutonic Knights prevented him from taking up this post. When Wilhelm was soon thereafter (1533) elected to another Livonian see, Ösel island, it led to skirmishes.[36] Albrecht looked to Sigismund I to back the career of yet another Brandenburg nephew, and the Polish king by and large complied—even though,

[27] Ekman, 'Albrecht of Prussia'; for reports by Danstiscus and Tomicki, see AT 16b, pp. 41, 104.
[28] AT 16b, p. 112.   [29] Ekman, 'Albrecht of Prussia', p. 28.   [30] AT 16b, p. 104.
[31] *Elementa*, pp. 66–7.   [32] Hubatsch, *Albrecht von Brandenburg-Ansbach*, p. 239.
[33] AT 16a, p. 692; Hubatsch, *Albrecht von Brandenburg-Ansbach*, pp. 237–41.
[34] Hubatsch, *Albrecht von Brandenburg-Ansbach*, p. 242. Hubatsch reports that there was a plan, with the death of Louis Jagiellon in 1526, for Albrecht to be elected Lutheran King of Bohemia, p. 244.
[35] Szymaniak, *Rola Dworu*, pp. 92–5.
[36] For the most recent study of Wilhelm von Brandenburg's career, see Thomas Lang, *Zwischen Reformation und Untergand Alt-Livlands: der Rigaer Erzbischof Wilhelm von Brandenburg im Beziehungsgeflecht der livlandischen Konfoderation und ihrer Nachbarlander*, 2 vols (Hamburg, 2014).

as Albrecht's agent Nipszyc reported, everybody in the Polish court believed that Wilhelm was a disciple of Luther.[37] Writing to Pope Clement VII, King Sigismund stressed that the see of Riga had been founded by his ancestors, and he wished his nephew's co-adjutorship to be confirmed by the Holy See.[38] Dantiscus was told to defend the causes and claims of both Brandenburg nephews at the imperial court 'publicly and privately, with diligence and dexterity'.[39] The Polish Crown sent legations to the Grand Master of the Teutonic Order in Livonia in 1530 and 1533, warning him not to oppose the ecclesiastical rights of Wilhelm Hohenzollern, beloved nephew of the King, with a thinly veiled threat of Polish intervention.[40] In 1534, Sigismund I dispatched an orator to Charles V to denounce the Livonians and stress the justice of Wilhelm's claims—pushing a suspected Lutheran into a catholic see.[41] Chancellor Szydłowiecki praised this Rigan endeavour, which in his eyes advanced 'the glory of the name of God and the prosperity of the church'.[42]

Wilhelm of Brandenburg's attempt to gain a dominant position in Teutonic Livonia looked to many observers like a plan to emulate what his brother Albrecht had already achieved in Teutonic Prussia—the creation of a secular, Lutheran lordship in lieu of theocratic rule. Dantiscus openly warned Piotr Tomicki that Wilhelm's actions in Livonia were a conspiracy to make the Baltic territory Lutheran.[43] Nonetheless, Sigismund I and his council lent their own diplomatic weight, and threats, to Wilhelm's campaign throughout the early 1530s, creating the impression that the Polish Crown was happy to see the controversial 1525 Treaty of Kraków replicated further east.[44] Queen Bona was recorded to have said how good it would be if Livonia could be incorporated into the Crown, by implication in the manner of Ducal Prussia.[45] Wilhelm's widely suspected Lutheranism, like Albrecht's openly professed Reformation beliefs, were no impediment to strong Polish diplomatic backing.

Sigismund I tied himself even more closely to the house of Brandenburg in August 1535, when Princess Jadwiga, the only surviving issue of his first marriage to Barbara Zapolya, was married to Joachim II Hector Hohenzollern (1505–71), Elector of Brandenburg, in Kraków cathedral. This match had been brokered by Duke Albrecht, a cousin of the Elector, and Joachim Hector himself was strongly

---

[37] AT 15, p. 673: 'der Herzog [Albrecht] yst luterysch und markfroff vylhelm yst seyn dyszczypul'. For Albrecht's correspondence with the Order in Livonia, see Ulrich Müller, *Herzog Albrecht von Preussen und Livland: Regesten aus dem Herzoglichen Briefarchiv und den Ostpreussischen Folianten* (Köln, 1996).

[38] AT 12, p. 94.

[39] AT 12, p. 229: 'ut omnia negotia praedictorum dominorum nepotum nostrorum istic in aula caesarea publice et privatim ea diligentia et dexteritate tractet et curet...'.

[40] AT 12, p. 212; AT 15, pp. 134–5.

[41] AT 16b, p. 419–20; see also Ekman, 'Albrecht of Prussia', p. 22.

[42] AT 12, p. 212: 'Dominus prosperet negotium hoc pro gloria nominis sui et augmento ecclesiae...'

[43] AT 15, p. 119.

[44] In the event, Sigismund I and the Teutonic Order in Livonia reached a peace agreement in 1536, by which Wilhelm resigned the see of Ösel, but was recognized as Archbishop of Riga, Szymaniak, *Rola Dworu*, p. 98.

[45] AT 16a, p. 12.

suspected of harbouring Lutheran sympathies—his father Joachim I (who died shortly before the Polish wedding) had made his son pledge to uphold the old church as a condition of his succession.[46] The bridegroom may initially have been more discreet than his cousin Albrecht with regard to his beliefs, but soon after his accession he issued a Reformation ordinance for his territories. The Brandenburg wedding entourage which came to Kraków contained many Lutheran luminaries, as Melanchthon enthusiastically pointed out to Jan Łaski the Younger.[47] These included Georg Sabinus (d.1560), who would, in 1536, become Melanchthon's son-in-law and, in 1544, the first rector of the Lutheran university of Königsberg, and Johann Carion (d.1537), Joachim II's personal astrologer and a significant early Lutheran historian. In spite of the ambiguous nature of Joachim II's theological stance, Sigismund I was delighted that the first wedding of any of his children linked the Polish royal family and Brandenburg more closely—this match, wrote the King proudly to his future (Lutheran) son-in-law was 'good, joyful, and auspicious, and for the greater good of Christendom'.[48] Tomicki too expressed his joy, writing to Dantiscus that 'I favour this honest and excellent husband.'[49]

Associations with yet more Lutheran princes also served to make Sigismund I's own foreign policy look anything but anti-Reformation. In 1534, Duke Albrecht was given a green light by the Polish court to hold talks with none other than Philip of Hesse, Elector-Palatine and the most powerful Lutheran prince in the Reich, about a possible dynastic match between Philip himself and a Polish princess.[50] In 1526, Sigismund I enfeoffed Barmin XI and George I, Dukes of Pomerania, with the territories of Bytow and Lebork.[51] Here too, the Polish Crown was seemingly unconcerned that Duke Barmin had recently graduated from Wittenberg University and was a follower of Luther. Matthias Franconius' account of the wedding of the junior king Sigismund Augustus and Elizabeth, Archduchess of Austria, in Kraków in 1543, contains a scene which would presumably have given the pope pause. Franconius described the young Polish king dressed brilliantly in cloth of gold and crown, flanked in church by three kinsmen: Duke Albrecht of Prussia, Margrave Georg of Brandenburg-Ansbach, and Duke Frederick of Leignitz.[52] The first of these had presided over a Lutheran territorial church since 1525, the second issued a Reformation Ordinance for his lands in 1533, and the third founded the first Lutheran academy in Silesia in 1526.

The religious reputations of some of Sigismund I's agents also raised eyebrows. The Habsburgs nursed persistent suspicions about Poland's top diplomat—Charles V personally interrogated Johannes Dantiscus about his visit to Martin Luther at

---

[46] Udo Krolzik, 'Joachim II Hector', in *Biographishe-bibliographisches Kirchenlexicon*, vol. III (Herzberg, 1992), pp. 110–15. For the pre-marriage talks, see AT 16b, pp. 43, 63–4.

[47] AT 17, p. 541.   [48] AT 17, p. 240.

[49] AT 16b, p. 84, 'maritum honestum et egregium'.

[50] AT 15, pp. 124–5, 842; AT 16a, pp. 432–6, 471.

[51] Vetulani, *Lenno pruskie*, pp. 108–9.

[52] Matthias Franconius, *Oratio in splendidissimas nuptias et foelicem hymenaeum potentissimi Sigismundi Augusti regis Poloniae* (Kraków, 1543), f. Biv(v).

Wittenberg in 1522, and members of Danticus' ambassadorial household were investigated by the Spanish Inquisition for Lutheranism.[53] One of those arrested in Castile was Fabian Damerau-Wojanowski, whom in the 1530s Sigismund I sent back to the imperial court as his envoy.[54] It was presumably the prominence of such men which led the Emperor to allege crossly that Sigismund I 'keeps Lutherans with him'.[55] The Polish king himself was also capable of ambiguous interventions. In 1526, he petitioned Henry VIII and Cardinal Wolsey on behalf of a group of Danzig merchants who had been arrested in the London Steelyard for possessing Lutheran books.[56] The Polish king—probably unaware that the Danzigers were meant to play starring roles in an abjuration ceremony at St Paul's Cross—asked the Tudor monarch to let the men go. Stressing his own opposition to the 'plague' of Lutheranism, Sigismund I nonetheless insisted that Joannes Molenbeck, Ulric Wise, and others were innocent, and must be released.[57]

We have already seen how the 1525 Kraków Treaty led stunned contemporaries to ask whether the King of Poland had become a Lutheran, but the cumulative effect of this foreign policy—the diplomatic defence of Lutheran Ducal Prussia and of Wilhelm Brandenburg's designs on Livonia, the marital alliance with Elector Joachim II, the indirect but explicit support for the ruling Lutheran house of Denmark, interventions for 'heretics' by the King—was to leave a permanent question mark over Sigismund I's own religious orthodoxy, and that of his court. There were many reasons why the old Teutonic Knight interviewed in Central France might have found the Polish monarchy's diplomacy 'reprehensible'.

THE DEFENCE: 'A MOST PIOUS PRINCE'

Protesting against the Reformation

Puzzlingly, alongside all this, the Polish Crown also pursued a proactive anti-Reformation diplomacy, mainly taking the form of royal letters censuring fellow princes. Sigismund I's epistolary interventions were directed, firstly, at neighbouring polities. As an ecclesiastical-geographical unit, the 'Polish province' of the church extended well beyond the sixteenth-century political frontiers of the Polish monarchy itself, encompassing areas such as Silesia, which had been part of the medieval Crown centuries earlier.[58] Sigismund I thus intervened as protector of catholicism in the (greater) Polish province of the Latin church. Sigismund, for example, lamented the Bohemian Crown's failure to stop the rise of Lutheranism

---

[53] AT 8, pp. 362–3.   [54] AT 16b, pp. 418–20.

[55] AT 13, p. 197, 'Lutheranos apud se habeat.'

[56] For the London Steelyard raid, see Celia A. Hatt, *The English Works of John Fisher, Bishop of Rochester (1469–1535): Sermons and Other Writings, 1520–35* (Oxford, 2002), p. 58.

[57] AT 8, pp. 64–5; *Letters and Papers, Foreign and Domestic, of the Reign of Henry VIII*, Vol. 4, Part I (1524–6), ed. J. S. Brewer (London, 1870), pp. 971–2.

[58] The metropolitan see of Gniezno included the sees of Poznań, Włocławek, Kraków, Płock (in the Polish monarchy), and Breslau, in Bohemian-ruled Silesia.

in Silesia, whose churches had been founded by his own predecessors as kings of Poland. In this spirit, he protested to his nephew King Louis II and Bohemian royal officials, urging them to protect the harassed monks of Breslau who were finding it impossible to sing divine office.[59] Further north, the Polish ecclesiastical province extended into the Duchy of Pomerania, the Electorate, and the Mark of Brandenburg. Here too King Sigismund bewailed the damage the Reformation was doing to the old church, specifically to those properties of his own bishops which lay beyond Polish royal jurisdiction—demanding that Duke Barmin, Elector Joachim II, and Margrave Georg variously restore the fishponds owned by the see of Włocławek, respect its bishop's privileges, and force nobles and commoners to pay the episcopal taxes they owed.[60] Sigismund I declared himself to be 'greatly astonished' that his princely neighbours had allowed such things to occur.[61] Sigismund could also pose as defender of the metropolitan see of Riga, in Livonia, which he claimed to have been founded by his Lithuanian ancestors.[62] In 1526, a Polish embassy to Livonia secretly assured the Archbishop of Riga, Johannes Blankenfeld, that the Crown had taken him under its protection. These envoys urged the Grand Master of Livonia, Walter von Plettenberg, to reverse the advance of the Reformation in his lands, warning that the King had already taken up his sword against Lutheranism (in Danzig), and would do so again if need be.[63]

The Polish king also wrote forcefully against the Reformation further afield, even where the Polish Crown had no jurisdictional connections. In 1526, he dispatched a passionate letter to King Gustav I of Sweden (reigned 1523–60), expressing astonishment at rumours that the Swedish monarch had been 'persuaded by the Lutheran dogmas'. Sigismund I urged his brother monarch to meditate on the evils which Lutheranism had caused.[64] When the Archbishop of Uppsala, Johannes Magnus (d.1544), and Bishop of Linkoping, Hans Brask (d.1538), fled Sweden and its Reformation in 1527, they not only enjoyed long-term refuge in Danzig, but found in Sigismund I and his councillors firm allies, who drew attention to their plight before the popes.[65] The Polish Crown, therefore, came out strongly in its diplomacy against the Swedish Reformation. In England too, the Polish monarchy interceded with Henry VIII for the (Italian) bishop of Worcester, who had lost his episcopal incomes with that kingdom's Reformation statutes.[66] Sigismund I thus acted before Europe's princes as a protector of those pious bishops, loyal to the old church, who had suffered as a result of the advancing Reformation.

The second anti-Reformation strand of Polish diplomacy in this reign was an energetic campaign to stress the catholic probity of King Sigismund I. The King

---

[59] AT 7, pp. 76–7; AT 14, p. 10.

[60] AT 9, p. 284; AT 11, p. 56; AT 15, p. 361; AT 16a, p. 529.

[61] AT 16a, p. 529, 'miramur etiam magnopere'.   [62] AT 12, p. 94.

[63] AT 8, pp. 53–5. For the Reformation in Livonia, see Juhan Kreem, 'Der Deutsche Ordern und die Reformation in Livland', in Militzer, *The Military Orders*, pp. 43–57.

[64] AT 8, p. 43.

[65] AT 10, pp. 58–9; AT 15, p. 18; Theiner, *Vetera Monumenta*, vol. II, pp. 455–6; Grell, 'Scandinavia', pp. 112, 114.

[66] AT 16b, p. 123.

and his councillors protested throughout the 1520s and 1530s that their own beliefs, and their dealings with fellow princes, were characterized by impeccable religious orthodoxy. The old king was aghast to find charges of Lutheranism levelled at him by other rulers, particularly when they fell from the lips of the Emperor or his brother Ferdinand. In 1530, he repeatedly urged Dantiscus to defend him from such calumnies, urging him to impress upon Charles V and his councillors that 'there is nothing whatsoever further from our mind than conspiracies with Lutherans... we have always remained in integrity and constancy and in the office of a Christian prince, [as] we remain up to this point, and will always remain so'.[67]

The Crown was strident, for example, in defending the 1525 Treaty of Kraków before an international audience as an act concluded for the greater Christian good. The definitive formulation of these arguments was set out by Bishop Andrzej Krzycki in an apologia commissioned by the Crown and printed in Kraków by Hieronymus Wietor's workshop in 1525. The *Ad Iohannem Antonium Pulleonum Baronem Brugij nuntium apostolicum in Ungaria, de Negotia Prutenico Epistola* stressed that the treaty was legitimate because it had been brokered by two external princes (Frederick of Leignitz and Georg of Brandenburg), and approved by the Polish royal council and parliament.[68] Along with Martin Luther in his 1522 pamphlet, Krzycki called for the destruction of the Teutonic Order—but whereas Luther's call had been rooted in a rejection of monasticism per se, Krzycki argued that the Teutonic Knights deserved to share the fate of the Templars because of their deviations from those very principles, for warmongering, violence, and illegal occupation of land. The Teutonic Order, in its corruption, was likened by Krzycki to the unrepentant Bad Thief at the Passion, a reference to the black cross of its heraldry. On the subject of Albrecht Hohenzollern's Lutheran heresy, 'that plague so pernicious to the catholic church', Krzycki pointed out that King Sigismund was no in way responsible for this—the Knights had embraced Luther's teaching long before the 1525 treaty, and if Charles V himself could not eradicate heresy in the Reich, the Polish Crown could not be held culpable for the presence of Lutherans in its lands, especially as the source of their error had been Germany itself.

The points made in Krzycki's *De Negotia Prutenico Epistola* became a mainstay of Polish diplomatic rhetoric. In 1525, King Sigismund defended himself to Pope Clement VII, arguing that in the Kraków accords he had simply acted on the papacy's long-standing plea for the princes of Christendom to make peace.[69] Bishop Tomicki stressed to Aliphio, the queen's secretary, that the 1525 negotiations had not touched at all on religious matters, and to Cardinal Campeggio that the peace treaty now freed up the Polish king to wage war on infidels.[70] The creation of Ducal Prussia, the first Lutheran polity in Europe, was therefore presented by the Polish Crown to the pope and Emperor and as a self-evident Christian good.

---

[67] AT 12, p. 230, quote at pp. 410–11: 'cum Turcis vel Lutheranis consilia vel conspirationes aliquas faciamus, quam res omnes longissime absunt a voluntate et cogitatione nostra.... nos simper in integritate, constantia et officio christiani principis mansisse, hactenus manere et perpetuo mansuros esse'.
[68] Printed in AT 7, pp. 249–56.   [69] AT 7, pp. 257–8.
[70] AT 7, pp. 292–3. See also AT 9, p. 118 and AT 12, p.191.

Throughout the 1520s and 1530s, the Polish Crown continued to stress in a variety of written and visual media that Sigismund I was an energetic opponent of all enemies of the faith, of Lutheran heresy, as well as the infidel or schismatic armies of the Ottomans, Tartars, and Muscovites. In 1527, the Minuzio workshop in Rome printed an oration given before the pope by Bishop Francesco Speruli, on Sigismund I's victory over a force of over 20,000 Tartars.[71] This speech painted the Polish king as offering his triumph over the infidel to God in pious humility, before seamlessly moving on to praise Sigismund's anti-Lutheran actions in Royal Prussia. Military action against Tartars and rebel Lutherans is here presented as two sides of one coin. The 1526 woodcut introduced at the start of this chapter (Figure 5.1) similarly included a panegyric verse praising King Sigismund's extreme piety and victories over enemies of the faith: Orthodox Moldavians and Muscovites, Muslim Tartars, and Lutheran Prussians.[72] While in Basel, Jan Łaski the younger gave a painted copy of this woodcut as a gift to Boniface Amerbach, Erasmus of Rotterdam's good friend.[73] At the coronation *vivente rege* of Sigismund Augustus in 1530, Andrzej Krzycki delivered an oration which characterized the Polish royal family as devoted to the Mass, with vivid descriptions of King Jagiełło (*c*.1434) prostrating himself before the elevated Host.[74] The closing pages of Krzycki's printed apologia for the 1525 treaty, meanwhile, featured a poem which concluded that Teutonic Prussia had been conquered not by armies, but by Sigismund I's 'pietas…et integritas'.[75]

If the Habsburg courts of Charles V and Ferdinand I were unpersuaded by such Polish rhetoric, others were more easily convinced. Pope Clement VII recovered promptly from his shock at the 1525 Treaty of Kraków and, in a signal that Rome would not consider it a stain on Sigismund I's character, honoured the Polish king with the gift of the ceremonial spear and ensign. These objects—traditionally given to honour a Christian prince who had fought for the faith—were presented to Sigismund I in Kraków cathedral by Gonsalvus de Sagro, a member of the papal household, 'in a great gathering of the royal council and the people'.[76] In 1526, Cardinal Campeggio reported that the entire curia was abuzz with praise for King Sigismund's glorious and 'holy work' in pacifying Danzig.[77] Three years later, when Dantiscus enjoyed an audience with Clement VII, he could relay that the pope was full of goodwill and affection towards the King of Poland.[78] Henry VIII too paid tribute to Sigismund I as a true Christian prince, 'so strongly committed to the extirpation of heresy', as did the Archbishop of Mainz, in an oration given at the wedding of Princess Jadwiga to Elector Joachim in 1535.[79]

---

[71] *Oratio Francisci Speruli, episcope S Leonis, habita in missa papae Clementis VII ob victoriam Sigismundi, Regis Poloniae, de Tartaris parta anno dni MCXXVII* (Kraków and Rome, 1527), printed in AT 9, pp. 90–3.

[72] Kopek, 'Dary', p. 134.   [73] Koper, 'Dary z Polski', p. 134.   [74] AT 12, p. 10.

[75] Printed in AT 7, p. 256.   [76] AT 7, p. 295, 'in maximo senatorum et populi concursu'.

[77] AT 8, pp. 135–6.   [78] AT 11, p. 332.

[79] AT 8, p. 71, 'tam strenuum fidei sancte cultorem et in Lutherana extirpanda heresi comitem…'; AT 17, p. 572.

It was not just popes, cardinals, and princes who were willing to praise the piety of the old Jagiellonian king before all Europe, but leading scholars and literary figures. In May 1527, Erasmus of Rotterdam composed a letter to Sigismund I, lauding the King's piety and prudence, but in particular his model foreign policy, characterized by a love of peace—here was a monarch who waged only necessary wars (against the infidel), and who made peace with Grand Master Albrecht in 1525, rather than shedding more blood by pressing on with an outright conquest of Prussia. This diplomacy Erasmus contrasted favourably with the bloody, self-serving wars waged by other kings in unhappy Italy.[80] A Wietor-printed edition of the letter quickly appeared in Kraków, dedicated to Vice Chancellor Tomicki.[81] Next into the fray was Johann Eck, Ingolstadt professor and one of Luther's most long-standing theological opponents. Dedicating a volume of his colossal oeuvre *Contra Ludderum* to King Sigismund in 1530, Eck offered his readers an account of the piety of generations of the Polish royal family, before presenting Sigismund I's anti-heresy edicts and his refusal to suffer Lutheranism in his territories as a natural continuum of this devotion.[82]

The (defensive) creation of Sigismund I's image as a pious monarch, before European courts and men of letters, was therefore a collaborative act, involving foreign luminaries as much as the Polish Royal Chancellery—texts written in Dresden, Vienna, Basel, and Ingolstadt as much as in Kraków. While the imperial court pointed its finger at Sigismund I and his councillors, popes, rulers, theologians, and scholars across Europe were happy to agree that the Polish king was indeed, in the verdict of that most celebrated of early sixteenth-century commentators, 'a most pious prince'.[83]

This foreign policy was, then, contradictory in its general impulses, and could be shockingly so also in its specifics. In Livonia in 1526, Sigismund I threatened military intervention against Lutherans who menaced the Archbishop of Riga, but by 1533 he threatened warfare if the Livonians did not accept his Lutheran nephew Wilhelm as bishop. When Andrzej Górka was sent as the King's representative to the Imperial Diet in 1527, the first part of his instruction set out how he should defend the creation of Lutheran Ducal Prussia as a new vassal territory of the Polish monarchy, and the second how to justify the closure of the trade route through Silesia as necessary to protect Sigismund I's lands from heresy.[84] Individual counsellors could also adopt strangely contradictory positions: Dantiscus, shortly after his bitterly humiliating anti-Reformation intervention in Danzig in 1535, urged the King to forge an alliance with the (Lutheran) King of Sweden.[85] How, then, are we to account for the contradictions in a foreign policy which actively supported Lutheran or reputedly Lutheran princes in Prussia, Livonia, Brandenburg, and Denmark, while protesting against the Reformation

[80] Erasmus, *Opus Epistolarum*, ed. P. S. Allen, vol. 7, pp. 59–65.
[81] Erasmus, *Des. Erasmi Roterodami Epistola ad inclytum Sigismundum regem Poloniae* (Kraków, 1527). For the royal reply, see Erasmus, *Opus Epistolarum*, ed. P. S. Allen, vol. 7, pp. 330–2.
[82] Eck, *Prima pars*, fos. A–Aiii.
[83] Erasmus, *Opus Epistolarum*, ed. P. S. Allen et al., vol. 7, p. 60.
[84] AT 9, p. 118.   [85] AT 17, p. 472.

in Silesia, Sweden, and England, and presenting Sigismund I universally as defender of the old church?

Principles: Kinship, Reputation, and the Church

Polish foreign policy clearly involved objectives or calculations which we would define as, in some sense, 'political', even if we wish to question whether sixteenth-century diplomacy was purely the pursuit of rational goals by any practical means. Sigismund I and his council placed a high premium, for example, on the preservation of peace. After a spate of wars in the first half of the reign, which had secured its borders (with Moldavia in 1509–10, Teutonic Prussia in 1519–21, and Muscovy in 1507–8, 1512–22), the Crown worked hard to maintain peace with the Crimean Tartar Khanate, the Ottomans, and the Habsburgs—to the extent of abandoning the kingdoms of Hungary and Bohemia to those latter powers in 1526, following the death of King Louis II, Sigismund's nephew.[86] The splendid Renaissance funerary chapel, which the King constructed from 1519 in Kraków cathedral, presented him in just this way, with its triumphal arches and inscriptions: as a military victor who had delivered a long peace.[87] Naturally, goals could come into conflict with one another, as for example when loyalty to his kinsman Duke Albrecht might endanger the King's prized reputation for piety. Accustomed to seeing modern diplomats navigate the multidimensional, fast-moving world of international relations, we might see some inconsistency in diplomacy as inevitable.

There are, however, three contemporary principles which might iron out some of the contradictions in Sigismund I's Reformation diplomacy, the first of them being (again) kinship—whether we classify that as a cultural belief, a political calculation, or something in between.[88] It was the Polish king's promotion of his sister Sophie's (d.1512) children—the Brandenburg nephews Albrecht and Wilhelm—which was responsible, above all, for the pro-Reformation appearance of Polish foreign policy. King Sigismund himself had just one legitimate son, and seemingly used his Brandenburg nephews as surrogate agents of Polish royal interest. In 1533, the Livonian Grand Master was told that King Sigismund was obliged to help Margrave Wilhelm because of their 'bond of blood'.[89] At the height of the banishment crisis, Sigismund I assured Duke Albrecht that he would defend him because they were of the same blood.[90] To Charles V, the Polish king stressed that Albrecht was 'his dearest nephew, by my sister'.[91] The 'Lutherans' whom Sigismund I promoted in north-central Europe were, first and foremost, his close kin. The ties of kinship which, as we saw in Chapter Three, gave Albrecht such a privileged position within the Polish monarchy, had amplified repercussions when played out on an international stage.

---

[86] For an overview of foreign policy, see Żelewski, 'Dyplomacja polska'.
[87] Mossakowski, *King Sigismund Chapel*, pp. 234–6.   [88] See also Chapter Three, p. 114.
[89] AT 15, p. 135, 'sanguinis vinculo'.   [90] AT 16a, p. 326, 'pro sanguinis necessitudine'.
[91] AT 14, p. 404.

A second contemporary concern was that of a prince's reputation for piety, which emerges as a central rather than peripheral diplomatic issue. 'Pietas' itself was an important buzzword in conduct literature and diplomatic texts alike. It had been a commonplace of 'Mirrors for Princes' literature since the Middle Ages that the prince must display 'pietas'. The frequency with which this refrain occurs in treatises and panegyrics on kingship has perhaps led us to treat 'pietas' as a hollow rhetorical trope, but it rewards closer attention. Erasmus, who had placed such emphasis on princely piety in his *Education of a Christian Prince*, repeated this point in his second letter to Sigismund I—presenting wisdom, constancy, and fear of God as the foundations of kingship, applying the adjective 'pius' to the Polish monarch repeatedly and unstintingly.[92]

A reputation for piety was a material political fact—Bejczy has written that princely virtue was a source of princely authority.[93] Others stress that a medieval individual's 'fama' was constantly shifting, affecting their honour and rank.[94] Acknowledged 'pietas' was a source of prestige, fame, and international influence (and thus, in effect, power). Piety here emerges as an important currency in early sixteenth-century diplomacy. A cardinal in Rome, on receiving news of the 1525 Treaty of Kraków, thus declared that he did not believe that Sigismund I could have performed this heretical act because he 'has always enjoyed an excellent reputation for virtue and wisdom, and taking after his ancestors, was most Christian'.[95] Sigismund I told Duke Albrecht that 'His Majesty must be above all suspicion where the Christian faith is concerned' because a prince's reputation was everything—'there is no greater endowment for kings and princes than unblemished glory and reputation'.[96] According to Krzycki, the senate initially baulked at the 1525 treaty because of the damage it would do to the Crown's reputation: it would be badly spoken of 'among all Christians'.[97] Dantiscus refused to show the imperial court the blatantly Lutheran apologia for Ducal Prussia penned by Duke Albrecht in 1534, on the grounds that it was not fitting ('non conveniet') for his royal master to be seen to defend religious error.[98] Pious reputation could equally be invoked to pressure or shame princes into action. Writing to Margrave Georg of Brandenburg and Elector Joachim, King Sigismund expressed his confidence that they would ensure tithes were paid to bishops because 'we know Your Illustriousness to be a good and just prince, most observant of the Christian religion'.[99] This kind

---

[92] Erasmus, *The Education of a Christian Prince*, ed. Lisa Jardine (Cambridge, 1997); Erasmus, *Opus Epistolarum*, ed. P. S. Allen, vol. 7, pp. 59–65.

[93] István Bejczy and Cary J. Nederman, 'Introduction', in *Princely Virtues in the Middle Ages, 1200–1500* (Turnhout, 2007), pp. 1–8, at pp. 1–2.

[94] Thomas Fenster and Daniel Lord Smail, 'Introduction', in *Fama: The Politics of Talk Reputation in Medieval Europe* (Ithaca, 2003), pp. 1–11, esp. pp. 3–4.

[95] AT 7, p. 282: 'tantus rex, qui virtutis et sapientie opinionem inclytam semper de se habuit, et ex predecessoribus suis alioquin christinissimus extiti…'.

[96] AT 8, p. 50: 'regum et principum nulla sit dos et facilitas major quam glora et fama inculpata'.

[97] AT 7, p. 250.

[98] AT 13, p. 164. Dantiscus also wrote to Albrecht, stressing that he risked bringing 'invidiam et vituperationem' upon the Polish king and his senators, AT 13, p. 321.

[99] AT 15, p. 361; 16a, p. 539: 'Cum autem sciamus Illtem. V. bonum et iussum esse principem et religionis christianae observantissimum.'

of threat, that a prince's pious reputation was on the line, was common in diplomatic exchanges. King Sigismund warned his nephew that a failure to issue anti-Luther edicts in Hungary and Bohemia risked his 'perpetual ill-fame'.[100] Cardinal-legate Campeggio urged Sigismund I to act against Bohemian heresies 'for your dignity' as a prince.[101] A prince who did not act against heresy, or who, worse still, embraced it, was 'un-pious' (as Rome labelled Henry VIII), with the implication that such men represented an inversion of princely virtues.[102] We can thus perhaps understand Sigismund I's own distress at the rumours of his Lutheranism circulating at the imperial court, and his pleas to Dantiscus to stop them at all cost.

In light of this, we can better grasp the logic behind the central claim made by Polish diplomacy: that Sigismund I's foreign policy was by definition pious, because the King himself was. Even if the content of the prince's actions towards Lutherans might appear dubious, such a conclusion was really a misunderstanding (or, on the part of the Habsburgs, a mischievous and deliberate misunderstanding)—if the prince was himself constant in the faith and pious, in his person and intentions, it followed that his policy was orthodox. To gauge the probity of a foreign policy, you need only look to the prince himself, the guarantor of its integrity. Sigismund I held up as joint evidence of his probity his own personal piety, and his anti-heresy edicts for the Polish monarchy. Put more simply, Sigismund I held that he was no Lutheran, so his foreign policy could scarcely be Lutheran either, in its ultimate goals and intentions.

Thirdly, there were also ecclesiological, or 'religious', reasons as to why Sigismund I's merry dealings with pro-Luther princes seem to us to be characterized by confessional contradiction, or even Machiavellian cynicism, although they likely made a certain pious sense to the Crown itself in the 1520s and 1530s. Here, we should ask again what notion of church and religious orthodoxy lay behind this foreign policy. When, in his diplomatic letters, Sigismund I patiently explained to other rulers why Luther should not be followed, he used the same definition of the Latin church as he had to his rebellious Lutheran subjects in Danzig, to Ducal Prussia, and in royal heresy edicts. As the Polish Crown informed the Hungarian and Swedish courts, this was 'the universal church which has been ordained and instituted in so many kingdoms and dominions, throughout so many centuries, by so many saints and councils', the church adhered to by all Christian princes and kings, a unified historic consensus.[103] Asking Henry III of Nassau-Breda to intercede with the Emperor on Albrecht's behalf, Dantiscus stressed that the Polish king's goal was to secure 'love and unity' between the Emperor and Duke, 'for the benefit of general Christianity and that peace may be maintained'—Christian unity here more important than doctrinal difference.[104]

---

[100] AT 7, p. 76.   [101] AT 7, p. 273: 'pro vestra dignitate'.   [102] AT 17, pp. 535–6.
[103] AT 7, p. 76: 'quam ecclesiam universam in tot regnis et dominiis tanto seculo tot sanctis totque conciliis ordinatam et institutam...' and AT 8, p. 43.
[104] Johannes Dantiscus, *Corpus of Johannes Dantiscus' Texts*, IDL1162: 'do mit lieb und einigheit zcwischen hochgedochten(n) unser(n) h(e)rn und der gemeynen cristenheit zu gut / fried mocht erhaltn(n) werden(n)'.

If he had to explain how this church might be defended on the ground, Sigismund often talked of very earthly practical measures—principally the restoration of church property and incomes which had been seized by Lutherans. Defending the church in his diplomacy, King Sigismund also defined it in large part as a property jurisdiction. To the pope, he pledged in 1525 that he would ideally like to reverse the Reformation in Ducal Prussia, a task he understood as amounting to restitution of the property of the church in those lands'.[105] Writing in protest to Duke Barmin of Pomerania, Sigismund I specifically demanded the restoration of episcopal property—tithes, estates, and a fishery in Lepszko lake.[106] The *ecclesia* is thus, in these diplomatic texts, defined as consensus, and the Reformation reversed by restoring church property; there is no engagement with what we often see as the heart of the Reformation, with doctrinal matters.

To Sigismund I and Bishop Tomicki, then, even as they grappled with competing imperatives, this was not a Latin Christendom with a red religious line drawn across it, not a Europe split into antagonistic Lutheran and Catholic camps. In this context, it was not unthinkable for King Sigismund to give his Lutheran nephew a duchy, or back another probably Lutheran nephew's claims to Livonia. These were fellow Christian princes, kinsmen, men of virtue and high birth, and not a religious enemy—they held dissident opinions in theology and recklessly flirted with schism, but were not outside the universal church. Hence Sigismund I, busy putting down the radical Reformation revolt in Danzig in 1526, could gladly receive the entourage of the Lutheran princess Dorothea of Denmark, and the court poet Andrzej Krzycki write poetry praising her ladies in waiting as fair mermaids sent by Neptune to visit the Polish king.[107] In 1527, a full decade after the indulgences controversy, Piotr Tomicki wrote with trepidation that if a permanent schism were to occur, peace and concord in Europe would be simply impossible, because no prince could trust another prince who believed differently in God—a universal church, in other words, was the *sine qua non* of diplomacy itself.[108] Tomicki, and his royal master, pursuing their diplomacy in the 1520s and 1530s, believed that moment had not yet come to pass.

King Sigismund and Vice Chancellor Tomicki likely experienced no binary conflict between 'religious' and 'political', 'confessional' and 'territorial' interests, in their Reformation diplomacy. This is because Lutheran dukes and palatines posed only a latent threat to the late medieval church as they understood it—doctrinal disagreement and debate was one thing, outright formalized schism quite another. Lutheranism's emergence on the European political scene did not, therefore, limit

---

[105] AT 7, p. 258: 'pro jurisdictione ecclesiastica et restitutione bonorum ecclesiasticorum in illis terris'.

[106] AT 9, p. 284.

[107] Quoted in Juliusz Nowak-Dłużewski, *Okolicznościowa poezja polityczna w Polsce: czasy Zygmuntowskie* (Warsaw, 1966), p. 88.

[108] AT 9, p. 120: 'Qua re una ad concordandos invicemque sibi concilandos principum Europae animos nihil potest esse efficacius, quod inter eos, qui Dei nomen aliter atque aliter agnoscunt, nulla unquam fida pax, nullum foedus sanctum potest intercedere, nec ullum majus dissidium atque odium inter mortales fieri potest, quam dissimilis de Deo immortali sententia.'

their diplomatic possibilities as much as might be expected—Princess Jadwiga might still, in good conscience, marry the Lutheran Elector Philip of Hesse, or Elector Joachim II of Brandenburg, for a prince-heretic was virtually a contradiction in terms.[109] For statesmen such as these who still mentally and spiritually inhabited a united Latin church, friendship with Lutheran princes could be honourable and even 'pious' (in the sense of catholic). The Polish Crown was running a late medieval, pre-confessional foreign policy in the early Reformation world.

---

[109] See Chapter Three, pp. 117. When the Reformation was formally introduced in Brandenburg in 1539, the Polish Crown did engage in diplomacy to seek assurances that Jadwiga would not be compelled to convert to Lutheranism. See Jolanta Dworzaczkowa, 'Jadwiga Jagiellonka (1513–1573)', *PSB* X (1962–4), p. 305.

6

A Smoked Pig, Monsters, and Sheep
The Polish Church and Lutheranism

In 1529, Maciej Drzewicki penned a letter to Dr Martin Luther. As Bishop of Włocławek in northern Poland, Drzewicki had for years banished Lutheran clergy from Danzig and its environs. Nonetheless, in his polite letter Drzewicki wrote enthusiastically to Luther of the Gospel and Christian faith, and expressed a keen desire to discuss the new theology in person with the Wittenberg doctor. As a token of his goodwill, Drzewicki sent an expensive present from Poland to Saxony, a side of smoked wild hog.[1] This letter—this apparent volte-face—has long perplexed historians, and it perplexed Martin Luther too, who wrote a skilfully equivocal reply. What are we to make of Maciej Drzewicki's smoked pig?

How did the institutional church in Sigismund I's Poland respond to the early Reformation? We have, so far, surveyed the policies of the Polish Crown towards the Reformation in Royal Prussia, Ducal Prussia, the *korona*, and abroad. Polish prelates were automatically members of the royal council (*senatus*), and as such were deeply implicated in those royal actions. Here, however, we will ask how Polish bishops responded to the Reformation not in their capacity as courtiers, senators, and councillors, but specifically as bishops—as pastors of their dioceses and ecclesiastical leaders. How did the institutional church in Royal Prussia and the Polish *korona*—with all its material, legal, and cultural resources—react to the advent of *luteranismus* in Sigismund I's monarchy, and why? Historians have not been kind to Sigismund I's high clergy. While men such as Piotr Tomicki, Andrzej Krzycki, and Maciej Drzewicki are lauded as great patrons of Renaissance culture, contributors to Poland's 'Golden Age', as clergy they have been judged failures, not least for their lax efforts against the Reformation. Chodynicki argued in the 1920s that the bishops of the early Reformation demonstrated 'the ruination of the clergy at the highest levels of the church'.[2] Janusz Tazbir, too, has claimed that Sigismund I's bishops were intellectually of low calibre, and simply failed to respond to the Reformation.[3]

---

[1] *D. Martin Luthers Werke: Briefwechsel*, ed. Joachim Karl Friedrich Knaake, vol. 5 (Wiemar, 1930), pp. 88–90.

[2] Kazimierz Chodynicki, *Reformacja w Polsce* (Warsaw, 1921), p. 9: 'zepsucie duchowieństwa na szczytach kościoła'.

[3] Tazbir, *Państwo bez stosów*, p. 33. For episcopal responses under Sigismund I, see Anna Odrzywolska-Kidawa, 'Stanowisko polskich dostojników kościelnych wobec idei reformacyjnych w latach 20 XVI wieku', in *Drogi i rozdroża kultury chrześcijańskiej Europy* (Częstochowa, 2003),

The responses of the church leadership to Lutheranism in the Polish monarchy up to *c.*1540 were apparently no less contradictory than those of the Crown. At a rhetorical level, Polish and Prussian high clergy were vehemently opposed to Luther's 'errores'—stern ecclesiastical statutes were issued prohibiting Lutheranism, inquisitions were announced, and clergy condemned the Saxon reformer in numerous printed polemics. In practice, however, a very different spirit prevailed. Church courts routinely treated Lutheranism as a minor offence: in only 3 per cent of cases was any recorded punishment handed down. This was the result of a marked lack of appetite for persecution among bishops and their clergy. Instead, bishops placed great emphasis on persuasion and reconciliation, on preaching campaigns, irenic treatises, and private initiatives, all intended to coax individuals away from theological error. This 'tolerant' Polish-Prussian picture is strongly in keeping with Craig D'Alton's findings for 1520s England, where he concluded that top clergy such as Thomas Wolsey and William Wareham much preferred 'gentlemanly chats behind closed doors' and private reconversions to trials, let alone burnings.[4]

The rich evidence from Polish diocesan archives, alongside episcopal correspondence, reveals that a lax approach towards 'luteranismus' was not just an eccentric position adopted by King Sigismund I and a coterie of Kraków courtiers; it can be found right across the Polish-Prussian church in the early Reformation, among many bishops, archdeacons, and even lowly scribes in church courts. This chapter will briefly set out the role of papal Rome in shaping local ecclesiastical responses, before exploring the condemnatory, and then the 'tolerant', areas of clerical activity. Here, we can capture from another angle the lack of cosmological fear provoked by Lutherans, and the deep impulse to reconcile them peacefully, thereby preserving the quintessential unity of the *ecclesia*.

ROMAN INPUT

It is important to stress that the anti-Reformation strategies of Polish and Prussian bishops were highly autonomous, in that the Roman papacy offered this part of the church only the most minimal leadership in the matter of early Lutheranism. Sigismund I's prelates did initially look to Rome for aid. In 1527, the Polish episcopate sent Canon Jerzy Myszkowski as its envoy to Rome, to seek papal assistance in the face of heresy.[5] Primate Łaski explained that he had 'asked the pope again and again, not only by letter but even orally with an envoy . . . not only persuading him, but begging His Holiness to call a council and save the universal church'.[6] The papacy's responses to these pleas from Sigismund I's Poland, a monarchy precariously

pp. 237–46; Bukowski, *Dzieje Reformacyi*, pp. 472–519; on Primate Łaski see Grad, *Kościelna działalność* and on Tomicki, see Gabryel, *Działalność kościelna*.

    [4] d'Alton, 'The Suppression of Lutheran Heretics' and 'William Wareham'.
    [5] Theiner, *Vetera monumenta*, II, pp. 426–7.
    [6] AT 7, p. 282: 'ego iterum iterumque pontifici jam non literis, sed ore tenus per nuncium proprium, eundem scilicet cancellarium, non solum suadebam, sed orabam, ut concilium esset celebratum, si sua Sctas salvare vellet ecclesiam universalem a summis periculis . . . '.

positioned in the midst of Europe's Lutheran tempest, proved limited, however —just as, in the eyes of many Poles, the papacy's reaction to a century of Ottoman encroachment had been scandalously limited.[7]

From 1520 to 1521, a papal nuncio to the Polish monarchy, Zacharias Ferreri, Bishop of Gardialfranco, briefly emerged as a vigorous Roman opponent of Luther on the ground.[8] Before the royal court at Thorn, Ferreri delivered a rousing anti-Lutheran oration in 1520, which was subsequently printed in Kraków.[9] In common with papal legates all over Northern Europe in the early 1520s, Ferreri went on to organize a public burning of Lutheran texts. In Thorn's main square, as Ferreri testified in his official deposition, 'all the writings of brother Martin Luther, diligently searched out, published copiously in Latin and German' were gathered up, the papal condemnation of Luther read before a large crowd, 'and with [an effigy of] their father the Devil, they were burnt in terrible fire'.[10] Bishop Międzyleski of Kamieniec assisted the nuncio 'strenuously and bravely', as Ferreri noted with approval.[11] Ferreri—whose brief had been to investigate the possible canonization of the Polish prince Casimir (d.1484)—had had no specific instructions from Rome with regard to the Reformation, and such anti-Lutheran actions were independent initiatives, the result of his own personal zeal. These events of spring 1520 were the most energetic 'Roman' anti-Reformation action that King Sigismund I's subjects would see.

The papal representatives subsequently sent to the Polish monarchy were low-ranking, some of them laypeople rather than clergy—Ioannes Francesco Cito (1525–7), Giovanni Antoni, Baron of Buglio (1524–5), and Nicholas Fabro (1526).[12] In the mid-fifteenth century, by contrast, senior cardinal legates had been dispatched to Kraków to negotiate on the key issues of the day. None of the nuncios seen in the 1520s or 1530s was sent to deal only, or even primarily, with the challenge posed by Lutheranism.[13] Instead, they went to the Polish monarchy for much the same reasons as nuncios had in the fifteenth century: to call for crusade against the Ottomans, to make peace between the Polish king and his enemies in Muscovy or Teutonic Prussia, to investigate candidates for possible canonization.[14] In Poland, nuncios pursued the papacy's own Italian diplomatic agendas—to keep the Ottomans away from Italian shores, or to broker matches

---

[7] Natalia Nowakowska, 'Poland and the Crusade in the Reign of King Jan Olbracht, 1492–1501', in Norman Housley (ed.), *Crusading in the Fifteenth Century: Message and Impact* (Basingstoke, 2004), pp. 128–47.

[8] E. Stöve, 'Zaccaria Ferreri', in *Dizionario biografico degli italiani*, 46 (Rome, 1996), pp. 808–11; his letters published in *Zacharias Ferreri*.

[9] Ferreri, *Oratio*.

[10] Wojtyska *Zacharias Ferreri*, pp. 118–19: 'omnia scripta fratris Martini Luteri diligenter perquisita, et latino ac germanico idiomate copiose edita…cum patre eorum diabolo terribiliter sunt concremata'; see also Chapter One, p. 52. Another book burning was organized by Primate Maciej Drzewicki in Gniezno in 1534, AT 16a, p. 537.

[11] Wojtyska, *Zacharias Ferreri*, p. 119, 'in hoc opere se admodum strenue et viriliter gerente'.

[12] In the 1530s, Rome sent as envoys Pamphilius of Strassoldo (1536) and Hieronymus Rorario (1539). See Wojtyska, *Zacharias Ferreri*.

[13] The closest such instruction is that given to Hieronymus Rorario in 1539: the main subject of his mission was the conflict in Hungary and Sigismund I's role in it, but its second purpose was to ensure the orthodoxy of Sigismund Augustus' entourage. Wojtyska, *Zacharias Ferreri*, pp. 321–2.

[14] Nowakowska, *Church, State and Dynasty*, pp. 127–53.

between Polish princesses and Italian princes loyal to the pontiff of the day.[15] This papal disengagement from the Reformation crisis is shown especially clearly, for example, by the Roman envoy Francesco Cito, who in spring 1526 found King Sigismund at Marienburg with an army, preparing to march on the Lutheran-held city of Danzig. Cito saw no reason to stay and witness that event, far less to involve himself in it—instead, he pressed on towards Moscow, where he hoped to persuade the Grand Duke to accept papal supremacy.[16]

One could read the correspondence between Sigismund I's bishops and the curia, which survives today in the Vatican archive, and never know that this was the era of the European Reformation. These contacts are entirely procedural, about taxes owed, appointments to sees, rights to benefices, dispensations from the 'ad limina' visit—identical in content, subject matter, and scope to the letters sent from Rome to Polish dioceses in the decades before 1500.[17] The administrative machinery of the curia simply rolled on, as it had for centuries. When bishops did ask for urgent papal advice, the answers they received were vague. In 1525, in response to Primate Łaski's appeal for assistance, Pope Clement VII simply urged the head of the Polish province to resist the Reformation and discuss it at local synods.[18] Writing to Bishop Ferber in Ermland, the pontiff agreed that heresy was a terrible Satanic evil from which the people must be protected, but gave no suggestions at all as to how this might be achieved—apart from a general invitation to the bishop and his clergy to resist Lutheranism.[19] Lutheranism was thus implicitly presented by Clement VII as a local Polish-Prussian problem, for local clergy to tackle.

OFFICIAL CONDEMNATIONS OF LUTHERANISM

Just as King Sigismund I issued anti-Reformation edicts for his subjects, the clerical leadership of the Polish church started its anti-heresy efforts by promulgating its own official condemnations of Martin Luther. The first such decree dates from December 1520, when Bishop Jan Konarski of Kraków (reigned 1503–24) ordered the printing of the papal bull *Exsurge Domine* for his diocese, prefaced with a brief pastoral letter in which he warned the faithful to avoid certain new 'books and errors' condemned by the pope.[20] In 1527, Primate Łaski summoned a provincial synod to Łęczyca, a gathering of bishops and high clergy from the Polish ecclesiastical province, declaring its purpose to be 'extermination of the Lutheran sect in all

---

[15] See for example *Zacharias Ferrari*, pp. 232–6 proposing a Mantuan match for Princess Jadwiga.
[16] *Zacharias Ferrari*, pp. 268–72.
[17] ASV, Reg. Lat. 1579, fos. 103v–106; Reg. Lat. 1470, fos. 171–3; Reg. Lat. 1297, fos. 181–182v; Reg. Lat. 1555, fos. 256–9; Reg. Lat. 1467, fos. 239(v)–240; Reg. Lat. 1599, fos. 47(v)–50(v); Armadio XL vol. 14, fo. 105, nr. 127 and fo. 106f; Armadio XL vols 24, 38; Camera Apostolica, Div. Cam. 83, fo. 251(v); Div. Cam. 74, fos. 10, 22(v), 80(v), 186(v).
[18] Theiner, *Vetera monumenta*, II, pp. 428–9.   [19] AAWa, D64, fos. 5–5(v).
[20] Konarski, *Bulla contra errores*.

the dioceses in the kingdom'.[21] The synod issued a full set of anti-heresy rules for the sees of Gniezno, Poznań, Kraków, Płock, Włocławek, and Breslau in Silesia. The Łęczyca statutes simply recycled earlier general remedies against heresy, requiring clergy to report suspected heretics, barring any parish clergy under suspicion from preaching, demanding that secular authorities support inquisitorial activity—and making regular reference to Jan Hus and Bohemia, but none to Martin Luther.[22] A second provincial synod organized by Łaski in 1530 stressed that clergy must diligently use the inquisition to find Lutheran heretics with their 'perverse doctrines'.[23] Łaski's successor as primate, Maciej Drzewicki, in 1532 printed a much extended set of synod statutes on Lutheran heresy, stipulating which texts parish clergy could preach from, the works students and youth should study, and in particular requesting that the King appoint a special anti-heresy preacher at court.[24]

In the prince-bishopric of Ermland, in Royal Prussia, prelates also issued stern prohibitions of Lutheranism, in their capacity as both pastors and temporal rulers. In January 1524, Bishop Ferber prohibited priests in Ermland from discussing the Wittenberg doctor's works or adopting new forms of liturgy.[25] At the Ermland diet of 1526, meanwhile, Ferber promulgated a general anti-heresy decree for the territory, banning Luther's works and threatening his followers with banishment.[26] Johannes Dantiscus, upon succeeding Ferber as Bishop of Ermland in 1539, also immediately issued edicts for the prince-bishopric against Lutherans and other 'sects'.[27]

PRINTED POLEMIC

The terse anti-Lutheran statements found in synod statutes were much elaborated on in the notable corpus of anti-Reformation printed polemic produced in King Sigismund's monarchy—all of it by clergymen—from 1520 to 1540.[28] In 1524, Piotr Rydziński, Canon of Poznań, composed two vituperative pamphlets against the Reformation in Breslau. These consisted of a string of personal attacks on

---

[21] AAWa, D66, fo. 146: 'pro exterminio secte Lutherane ex omnibus regni dioce' tractaturi sumus'. Kraków diocesan synods discussed heresy, but any statutes they might have produced do not survive. See Gabryel, *Działalność kościelna*, pp. 354–7.

[22] *Statuta provintiae gnesnensis. Antiqua et nova, revisa diligenteret emendate* (Kraków, 1527), fo. M–Mi, 'De Hereticis'.

[23] Printed in *Archiwum Komisyi Prawniczej*, vol. I (Kraków, 1895), pp. 378–9.

[24] *Constitutiones et articuli synodi Lanciciensis* (Kraków, 1532), 'Extirpatio heresium et sectae Lutheranae' (no page numbers).

[25] *Spicilegium Copernicanum, order Quellenschriften des Literaturgeschichte des Bisthums Ermland in Zeitalter des Nikolaus Kopernicus* (Braunsberg, 1873), pp. 321–4. See also Teresa Borawska, *Tiedemann Giese (1480–1550): W życiu wewnętrznym Warmii i Prus Królewskich* (Olsztyn, 1984), pp. 309–10.

[26] Borawska, *Tiedemann Giese*, p. 315.

[27] *Spicilegium Copernicanum*, pp. 329–33.

[28] For Polish anti-Reformation polemic, see Nowakowska, 'High Clergy and Printers'. For a wider overview, see John Dolan, 'The Catholic Literary Opponents of Luther and the Reformation', in Erwin Iserloh, Joseph Glazik, and Hubert Jedin (eds), *Reformation and Counter Reformation*, vol. 5 of *History of the Church*, trans. Anselm Biggs and Peter W. Becker (London, 1980), pp. 191–207.

Johannes Hess' Lutheran party, calling the heretics of Germany 'harpies' and merchants who sold spoiled goods. Rydziński warned that there would be religious anarchy if the reformers gave the Gospel, which had been communicated to the Apostles, to the vulgar people—that Lutherans would have Christendom 'live without law'.[29] That same year, in a far more celebrated intervention, Rydziński's uncle Andrzej Krzycki, Bishop of Płock, produced the *Encomia Luteri*, a letter addressed to King Sigismund I on Lutheranism.[30] The *Encomia* asserted that Luther made priests of laymen, whores of nuns, and incited acts of sacrilege and social disorder. This appeal was accompanied by satirical anti-Reformation verses by Krzycki and his circle, poems with titles such as 'In Praise of Luther', or 'Portrait of a Good Lutheran', which mocked Luther as a man who believed in nothing, a horned monster born to a Saxon cow, the heir to Wyclif and Hus. The *Encomia Luteri* enjoyed a certain international success, reprinted across the Holy Roman Empire and praised by Erasmus himself.[31] Krzycki followed it with his 1527 polemic *De Afflictione Ecclesiae*, which imagined the Reformation as the crucifixion of the church.[32] Here, Luther was mocked for having renounced everything he had formerly believed in, for tormenting the church/Christ with his attacks on the clergy, and his death-giving heresy. Krzycki pointed to a bleeding-Host miracle in Royal Prussia as miraculous evidence of the pain that Lutheranism was causing God in the kingdom.

In the 1530s it was Grzegorz Szamotulski, Archdeacon of Poznań, who emerged as the kingdom's most vocal anti-Lutheran writer in print. A 1531 printed sermon sought to refute Luther's attacks on indulgences by invoking Scripture and papal bulls.[33] Szamotulski also produced pamphlets furiously denouncing Christoph Hegendorff, his colleague at the Poznań Academy, as a heretic—in the *Anacephaleosis* (1535) and *Vincula Hippocratis* (1536).[34] Szamotulski stressed that the dogma of '*sola fide*' advocated by Hegendorff was Lutheran and heretical. Also in Poznań, Walenty Wróbel—Szamotulski's ally, and preacher at St Mary's parish church— composed the *Propugnaculum Ecclesiae* (1536), a 300-page rejection of 'heretical' teachings on fasting, papal supremacy, the cult of saints, and clerical celibacy, in a catalogue of contested areas.[35] In 1540, in the last major printed polemical intervention of the reign, the Lwów canon Andrzej Lubelczyk published against

---

[29] Rydziński, *In Axiomata*; *Petri Risinii* (unnumbered pages).

[30] Krzycki, *Encomia Luteri*.

[31] Reprinted in Regensburg (Paul Kohl, 1524), Dresden (Emserpresse, 1524), Strassburg (Johann Grüninger, 1524), Speyer (Konrad Hist, 1524), and Rome (Bachiensis, 1524); Erasmus, *Opus Epistolarum*, ed. P. S. Allen, vol. 6, pp. 193–5.

[32] Kryzcki, *De Afflictione Ecclesiae, commentarius in Psalmum XXI* (Kraków, 1527); Nowakowska, 'Lamenting the Church?'

[33] Grzegorz Szamotulski, *Sermo de indulgentiis* (Kraków, 1532). For his career, see Barycz, *Historia Uniwersytetu*, pp. 205–8.

[34] Grzegorz Szamotulski, *Anacephaleosis Flosculos monogrammos ex progymnasmatis Christophori Endorfini* (Kraków, 1535) and *Vincula Hippocratis* (Kraków, 1536).

[35] Walenty Wróbel, *Propugnaculum Ecclesiae adversus varias sectas* (Leipzig, 1536). Wróbel's later work, *Opusculum Quadragesimale* (Leipzig, 1537), also contained polemical passages about Lutheran rejection of fasting.

Philip Melanchthon.[36] Whereas anti-heresy statutes or episcopal pastoral letters were official institutional products of the Polish church, the status of polemics such as these was more nuanced. These books were the individual, independent contributions of high clergy, self-appointed spokespeople for the church who were nonetheless writing in their capacity as clergy.[37] The basic message of this group of texts, however, was the same as that of the decrees and statutes: that Luther himself was a heretic, his teaching (on Scripture, the papacy, fasting, saints, worship, Christian liberty) deeply erroneous, and his followers scoundrels.

To any contemporary who read the official statutes and decrees of the Polish-Prussian church, or the anti-Lutheran texts authored by canons, archdeacons, and bishops in the 1520s and 1530s, there would therefore seem little doubt that the church in Sigismund I's Poland had taken an uncompromising legal and rhetorical stance against Luther. It is perhaps no surprise then that leading international anti-Luther polemicists actively courted the Polish episcopate as potential literary patrons. Johann Cochlaeus commended his writings to Bishop Tomicki, and the Basel professor Johann Sichardt (d.1554) addressed a 1528 polemic to King Sigismund and his bishops.[38] Johann Fabri (d.1541), Bishop of Vienna, in a grand and hopeful gesture, dedicated an entire series of six anti-Reformation polemics to Sigismund I's bishops: refutations of Luther, Melanchthon, Anabaptists, and the Swiss Reformation.[39] Yet Bishop Dantiscus ignored all communication from the author, and for his pains Cochlaeus received only a paltry gift of 20 florins from Bishop Tomicki for the polemic dedicated to him—a clue that the anti-Lutheran stance of the Polish-Prussian episcopate was not perhaps all that it seemed to be.[40] Just as with Sigismund I's royal anti-Lutheran edicts, the rhetoric of these official and semi-official clerical texts turned out to be largely that—and sharply at odds with the policies which bishops and their clergy actually pursued on the ground.

CHURCH TRIALS FOR LUTHERANISM

The Polish synod statutes of 1527 had envisaged visitations-inquisitions in Polish dioceses. References to these in diocesan records are extremely sparse: Primate Drzewicki stands out, for example, in specifically ordering an inquisition into

---

[36] Andrzej Lubelczyk, *Tumultuaria responsio in libellum Philipi Melanctonis* (Kraków, 1540). For subsequent Polish polemic, see Rechowicz, *Dzieje teologii*, vol. II, pp. 49–68.

[37] For authorship, audience, and printing as a medium for clerical polemic, see Nowakowska, 'High Clergy and Printers'.

[38] AT 16b, pp. 543–5 and AT 17, pp. 324–5; Sichardt, *Antidotum*, fos. A2(v)–A3(v).

[39] AT 15, pp. 299–300. The titles are listed in AT 16b, p. 575: *De veneratione et invocatione sanctorum* (Leipzig, 1534), dedicated to Bishop Jan Latalski; *Adversus novam reformationem senatus Bernensis* (Leipzig, 1534), dedicated to Bishop Jan Chojeński; *Articuli Anabaptisarum Monasteriensium per doctorem Johannem Cochleum confutati* (Leipzig, 1534), dedicated to Bishop Jan Dantiscus; *Adversus impia et seditiosa scripta Martini Lutheri* (Leipzig, 1534), dedicated to Primate Drzewicki; *Philippicae quatuor Johannis Cochlei in Apologiam Philippi Melanthconis* (Leipzig, 1534), dedicated to Bishop Piotr Tomicki; and *Velitatio Johannis Cochlaei in Apologiam Philippi Melanchtonis* (Leipzig, 1534), dedicated to Bishop Andrzej Krzycki.

[40] AT 16b, pp. 543–5; AT 17, p. 545.

Lutherans in the 1530s in Gniezno.[41] Nonetheless, church court records show that Sigismund I's subjects were apprehended for Lutheranism in a highly intermittent way by diocesan authorities—typically by the 'instigator', the diocese's chief prosecutor. These cases are set out in Appendix 1. When we look more closely at these records, however, what we see is not a formidable persecutory mechanism at work, but something far more ambiguous and perplexing.

Hearings for Lutheran heresy before church courts in the reign of Sigismund I were treated, firstly, as low-profile events, and no longer as the courtroom dramas of the recent past. In the late fifteenth century, the Polish *korona* had seen three (known) trials for heresy. When the priests Adam and Matthias had been charged with Hussitism (1499) in Włocławek, Bishop Krzesław of Kurozwęki, Chancellor of Poland, had travelled to his remote diocese to preside in person over the hearing and Adam was sentenced to death.[42] Similarly, when in 1492 the Kraków printer Swajpold Fiol was accused of heresy for printing Orthodox liturgical books, a formidable panel of university canon-theologians acted as his judges.[43] Although trials for heterodoxy were far more numerous in the reign of Sigismund I than under earlier kings, they were seemingly taken less seriously. Under canon law, heresy was a crime so grave that it was 'reserved' for episcopal judges. This rule was ignored in early Reformation Poland. Of the fifty-nine heresy cases listed in Appendix 1, for example, only a quarter were presided over by the bishop himself—and most of those hearings (eleven) occurred in July 1535, when Bishop Jan Latalski of Poznań spent a couple of diligent days in court.[44] The norm was, instead, for suspected Lutherans to be dealt with by less senior figures. The one heresy case which came before the Gniezno church courts during Łaski's primateship (in 1524) was heard by his deputy, Archdeacon Wincenty Langnewski.[45] When Dantiscus, in 1535, asked Piotr Tomicki for details of a trial for Lutheranism held in Kraków a few years before, Tomicki had to explain that he knew little of it—'I know nothing about the Lutheranism of Lisman, because that year I was sick and mainly away from Kraków, but if there were disputes or controversies... I sent them to my vicar, so that I could take better care of my health.'[46] In Warsaw, meanwhile, trials for Lutheranism were instigated and heard by the canons of the city's collegiate church.[47] In early Reformation Poland, we can therefore see 'haeresia' slipping into the hands of lower courts, automatically delegated to deputies, no longer reserved solely for the reigning bishop.

---

[41] AAG, A. Cap. B18, fo. 248(v).   [42] AAWł, Abkp. vol. 1 (107), fos. 139(v), 150.

[43] AKMK, Acta Ep. 4, fos. 89–89(v).

[44] AAP, Acta Ep. 7, 331v–334v. Other examples are Drzewicki hearing the case of Bachmann the schoolmaster, and Tomicki the case of Jakub of Iłża: AAWł, Acta Ep. 2 (9), fos. 179v; BJ, MS 3227, fo. 74.

[45] AAG, A. Cons. A 84, fo. 39(v).

[46] AT 17, p. 510: 'Sacerdotem istum Lisman... sed de lutheranismo illius nihil comperti habeo et explorati, cum annus iste variis in morbis mihi sit consumptus maioremque illius partem Cracovia abfuerim et si quae fuerunt controversiae disceptandae, earum cognitionem iis mandavi, quorum in hac parte vicaria utor opera, ut tanto diligentius valetudinem curare meam.'

[47] Budka, 'Przejawy reformacji'.

In Polish church courts, hearings for Lutheranism also lacked the sense of occasion seen in earlier heresy trials. At the 1492 trial of Szawajpold Fiol, the Kraków court clerk had evidently judged the hearing to be a significant one, because he wrote 'In Causa Fidei' in large, portentous letters at the top of a fresh page.[48] The 1524 entry for the Gniezno diocese's first hearing for Lutheranism is, by contrast, remarkable for its ordinariness, sandwiched between loan registrations and tithe disputes. The Gniezno notary did not even label it as a heresy trial ('in causa fidei'), but simply as 'a case of the official versus a certain German named Pancratius'—as if it were a hearing like any other.[49] Any notion of heresy as a special—or extraordinary—crime is fading in these courts.

One might speak of a culture of non-punishment in these diocesan courts. Of the fifty-nine hearings for Lutheranism before ecclesiastical judges held in Polish and Prussian dioceses between 1520 and 1540 (Appendix 1), in fifty-six cases—or 97 per cent—there is no record of the accused receiving any kind of penalty whatsoever. In most cases (twenty-eight), the accused denied all the charges, often with elaborate explanations and excuses, and no further recorded action was taken. The illuminator Matthias, brought before the Kraków diocesan court in 1525 for 'being of the Lutheran sect', thus simply asserted that this was not true; there is no record of the court having contact with him again.[50] A group of seven citizens rounded up in Poznań in 1535 as suspected Lutherans—including a town consul—likewise protested that they were not heretics, and desired to live in peace with the Roman Church and Polish Crown.[51] Bishop Latalski ordered further questioning of these suspects, but they did not come before the court again in his reign. Church courts apparently let such cases drop, sometimes after giving the suspect an official warning (fourteen cases). In the great revolutionary year of 1525, the Kraków tanner Jeronimus Rubens was thus accused of preaching Lutheranism to the 'vulgar' in the city, and given a 'charitable warning' by the court to desist; as was, at the other end of the social scale, Andreas Salomon, son of one of Kraków's top banking dynasties (1532).[52]

Even in those cases where a diocesan court did hand down a sentence for Lutheranism, the penalty always fell far short of what royal edicts stipulated (execution). There are just three instances in Appendix 1 in which punishments were recorded by diocesan authorities. In Warsaw, the collegiate canons told the tailor Snyder in 1532 to abjure Lutheran error or face exile; he chose the latter, although Władysław Budka found evidence that he continued to live in the town.[53] The cleric Matthias was formally sentenced to a year in an episcopal prison, while the printer Wietor was briefly imprisoned by the Kraków city authorities pending further investigation.[54] In 1536, Bishop Latalski of Poznań declared the merchant Michael Werner a heretic for receiving communion in both kinds, despite earlier warnings. The court decreed that 'his goods, both mobile and immobile, both

---

[48] AKMK, Acta Ep., vol. 4., fo. 89.   [49] AAG, A. Cons., fo. 39(v).

[50] BJ, MS 3227, fo. 70, 'negavit, admonitus'; partly printed in Ptaśnik, *Cracovia impressorum*, p. 110.

[51] AAP, Acta Ep. VII, 331v–332f.   [52] BJ, MS 3227, fos. 70, 75(v).

[53] Budka, 'Przejawy reformacji', pp. 190–1.   [54] See Appendix 1.

within and beyond the city of Poznań be confiscated', including his townhouse, and given to the collegiate church of St Mary Magdalene.[55] Again, this was well short of the full penalties allowed under the law. Very occasional references to extrajudicial or ad hoc punishment of Lutherans can be found. In 1525, Bishop Drzewicki imprisoned in his episcopal castle Royal Prussian priests who had preached Lutheranism.[56] Bishop Ferber expelled from Ermland Simon Marchita, vicar of Wormditt, in 1526 for 'seducing many' to the Lutheran heresy—but here too there was seemingly no talk of actually executing the cleric.[57]

This lack of will to convict, and then to punish, is illustrated particularly clearly in the most widely cited conviction for heresy of Sigismund I's reign, that of the Kraków university lecturer Jakub of Iłża. The case demonstrates how hesitantly the wheels of Polish ecclesiastical justice ground when faced with followers of the Wittenberg Reformation. Jakub Iłża had been preaching Lutheran sermons in Kraków for 'several years' when Bishop Tomicki gave him a private warning in 1528, before creating an investigatory commission in 1534. Tomicki secured from the lecturer an undertaking that he would abjure his errors. However, in a change of heart, Iłża then penned a defence of Lutheran teaching and fled to Breslau in Silesia—no great feat, because the church authorities had taken no steps to apprehend him.[58] Tomicki confessed to colleagues his anxiety that a heresy trial might now become unavoidable, but tried to further postpone such an event by arguing that, given the gravity of the charge, a trial *in absentia* would be inappropriate.[59] When in 1535 Iłża declared his willingness to return to Kraków and perform a public abjuration, the bishop keenly embraced this plan, issuing the suspect with a letter of safe conduct.[60] As Tomicki explained to his Kraków heresy team (his deputy and canon-theologians), he was determined to proceed in a manner which accorded with his own character 'which is free of all bitterness', adding that if they did take the ultimate step (i.e. a capital sentence) it would not be out of any personal wish on his part. And if Iłża escaped corporal punishment, Tomicki reassured his colleagues, he would nonetheless suffer a spiritual wound.[61] In the event, Iłża did not appear for this new trial. He was convicted as a Lutheran heretic *in absentia* in May 1535, defrocked, and stripped of his university post.[62] In the final analysis, Iłża had lacked the appetite to become a Lutheran martyr, and Bishop Tomicki had lacked the appetite to make him one. This was as close as the Polish church under Sigismund I came to executing a condemned heretic in the early Reformation.

---

[55] AAP, Acta Ep. VII, fos. 330v–331, 333v–334v; at 347v: 'ab bona illius tam mobilia quam immobilia hic intra et extra Civitate posnan' consistentia confiscan' saluis t' censibus in lapidea domo illius ac quibusvis alijs bonis suis…ecclie' collegiate scte' Marie Magdalene in posnania…inscriptu, et resignatu'.

[56] *Urkundenbuch*, vol. II, pp. 175–6.

[57] *Monumenta Historiae Warmiensis*, vol. 2 (Braunsberg, 1889), p. 495: 'eo quod perniciosis et impiis sermonibus multos seduxerit …'.

[58] A clear summary of the case is given in Barycz, *Historia uniwersytetu*, pp. 102–5. See also BJ, MS 3227, fo. 74; AT 16b, pp. 433, 540–1; AT 17, pp. 134–5, 266, 286–7.

[59] AT 16b, pp. 539–41.   [60] AT 17, pp. 134–5.

[61] AT 17, pp. 134–5. Wacław Urban, in 1991, found new evidence that he ended his life as a Lutheran pastor in Upper Silesia, 'Jakub z Iłży', p. 212.

[62] Urban, 'Jakub z Iłży', p. 211; sentence recorded in BJ, MS 3227, fos. 74–74(v).

It is particularly instructive to compare the fate of those brought before diocesan courts for 'being of the Lutheran sect' with that of men and women accused of other crimes. For example, Polish diocesan courts and cathedral chapters in these same decades heard at least eighty-five cases of clergy accused of scandalous behaviour or neglecting their pastoral duties.[63] In contrast to those suspected of Lutheranism, these clerics were consistently punished: personally castigated by the bishop, fined, and/or incarcerated. In 1534, for example, the priest Simon of Myathokowo was fined 3 marks for a long-term sexual relationship with a woman, and told that any further contact with her would result in a perpetual jail sentence.[64] Kraków's 'instigator' demanded a prison sentence for the parish priest Albert, who had not heard his parishioners' confessions for many years due to his deafness.[65] Laypeople, too, could receive harsh treatment from church courts: the Poznań episcopal court ordered the immediate imprisonment of two women, both named Dorothea, suspected of divination (fortune telling).[66] In the view of Polish diocesan courts, it would seem that there were many crimes far worse than that of possessing Lutheran books, or advocating Luther's ideas to one's neighbours; sexually active priests and divining women felt the force of ecclesiastical justice far more strongly than even Jakub of Iłża.

The fifty-nine surviving recorded cases of alleged Lutheranism brought before church courts are, however, only one part of the picture of this culture of 'non-punishment'—there was also a large and prominent number of people accused of *luteranismus* whom diocesan authorities did not, or would not, initiate heresy proceedings against, indicating a wider culture of what we might term 'non-prosecution'. In many of these cases, leading bishops not only declined to prosecute, but actively patronized or protected those suspected of heterodoxy. The most high-profile such case was that of Christoph Hegendorff, invited to Poznań in 1529 by Bishop Jan Latalski to take up a lecturing post at the city's prestigious humanist academy. Hegendorff was the author of a number of successful pedagogic texts, such as his *Dialogi Pueriles*, but he had also published two defences of Martin Luther, a reformist commentary on the Gospel of Mark, and an early pro-Reformation catechism.[67] Once in Poland, he dedicated works to Latalski.[68] From 1533, the local archdeacon Grzegorz Szamotulski began to denounce Hegendorff from the pulpit as a heretic. Bishop Latalski, having received impassioned appeals for justice from both men, organized a formal theological disputation in Poznań, followed by a ceremony of reconciliation in which Hegendorff and Szamotulski were both required to burn the poison-pen letters they had been sending one another.[69] The bishop's priority was apparently to promote concord in his diocese, and retain his

---

[63] Trials before courts and disciplinary hearings before cathedral chapters recorded in AKMK, AE 7, AE 11, AE 12; AAWł, Acta Ep. 2 and 3; AAG, A. Cap. B17; AAP, CP 36, 37.

[64] AAP, AE VII, fo. 295(v). [65] AKMK, Acta Ep. VII, fo. 332 (1522).

[66] AAP, AE VII, fo. 322(v)–323.

[67] Christoph Hegendorff, *Dialogi Pueriles* (Hagenau, 1529). Mazurkiewicz, *Początki Akademji*, pp. 27–37; Franz Bierlaire, 'Christoph Hegendorff'.

[68] Christoph Hegendorff, *Oratio in artium liberalium laudem* (Hagenau, 1530). See Ignacy Zarębski, 'Hegendorfer, Krzysztof'.

[69] Mazurkiewicz, *Początki Akademji*, pp. 129–33.

famous lecturer at the academy—Latalski's protection ensured that at no point during Hegendorff's seven-year sojourn in Poland was a heresy trial for Lutheranism on the cards. In fact, the bishop's ire was reserved for Archdeacon Szamotulski, the catholic party in the dispute, whom Latalski lambasted at a chapter general for publishing polemics against Hegendorff, demanding that their author be severely punished.[70]

In an equally illuminating incident in Kraków, Piotr Tomicki was offended when the royal secretary Jan Zambocki in 1528 recommended to his service the young nobleman Andrzej Trzecieski, who had just returned to Poland from Germany. Tomicki explained that: 'We have heard, not through uncertain and differing rumours but through many speeches, that [Trzecieski] has perversely left our faith and with dedication and industry follows the dogma of the Lutheran sect.'[71] Trzecieski's apparently notorious Lutheranism barred him from entering the bishop's employ, yet sparked no immediate judicial process.[72] Put more starkly: the Bishop of Kraków knew he was a Lutheran, but felt no need to do anything about it. In Ermland, too, when the possibly pro-Luther monk Radike left his convent and roamed the countryside, diocesan authorities simply monitored the situation patiently over several years, with bemusement.[73] Even more strikingly, Johannes Dantiscus as Bishop of Kulm gave undertakings to local communities that he would not use his episcopal authority to harm Lutherans. Thus in 1535, when he investigated the preacher Pancratius Klemme for heresy on the orders of Primate Drzewicki, Danzig city council protested furiously at his behaviour.[74] Similarly, when at Tomicki's request Dantiscus removed the Lutheran parish priest of Graudenz in 1533, the town council wrote him a bluntly worded protest, claiming that he had broken his prior promises to them. Dantiscus smoothed over the affair by successfully petitioning the King to forgive Graudenz its heresy and not impose any punishment on its citizens.[75] Neither Hegendorff, Andrzej Trzecieski, Graudenz council, nor Radike ever faced a formal charge of Lutheran heresy before a church court. These cases were all amply well known to local bishops, whose first response was certainly not to reach for the levers of judicial investigation and suppression.

CONVERSION AND RECONCILIATION

When faced with suspected Lutherans, the most characteristic response of the Polish church under Sigismund I was to reconcile those who were in danger of breaking away from the universal church—through preaching, conciliatory

---

[70] AAP, CP 37 (Acta capituli), fo. 65; Nowakowska, 'High Clergy and Printers', pp. 61–2 .

[71] AT 10, p. 310: 'Est enim nobis non incerto et vario rumore perlatum, sed multorum sermonibus confirmatum, illum perverse admodum de fide nostra sentire et studia industriamque suam ad Lutheri sectam dogmataque ejus contulisse.'

[72] Trzecieski was later tried in Kraków diocese in April 1532, for blasphemy against the Virgin: see Appendix 1.

[73] AAWa, D39, fo. 4.   [74] AT 15, p. 833.   [75] AT 15, pp. 288–90.

polemic, and one-to-one conversion. Anti-Reformation preaching was energetically embraced by a number of senior clergymen. As Bishop of Poznań, in 1523 Piotr Tomicki founded a new cathedral canonry, specifically for a doctor of theology who would preach to clergy and laity alike.[76] On being installed as Bishop of Kraków, Tomicki also ordered an anti-Luther preaching campaign in the city's main German-speaking church, St Mary's. These sermons, preached by Martin Dobrogost, were addressed to university students and printed in the city.[77] Dobrogost was still regularly preaching in Kraków in 1529, when Duke Janusz of Oppeln, in Silesia, tried to poach him. Tomicki begged the King to ban the preacher from leaving the kingdom—Dobrogost's departure would be a 'great danger' to the people of Kraków diocese, he wrote, because with his German-language preaching he had kept the see free from infection by heresy, and was simply irreplaceable. If he left, Tomicki declared, heresy would decrease in Silesia but increase in Kraków.[78]

If a proportion of anti-Reformation tracts by high clergy were polemical in the fullest sense of that term—vituperative, polarizing, controversialist—others were, by contrast, conciliatory in their approach. The Ermland canon Tiedemann Giese, for example, wrote a major work entitled *De Regno Christi*, which survives only in fragments but paints a vision of a reformed, united, reinvigorated church as the outcome of the Reformation crisis.[79] Scholars have noted that Giese's 1525 *Anthelogikon*, while ostensibly refuting 110 Lutheran propositions, is accommodating and discursive rather than highly antagonistic.[80] In his response to the Lutheran articles published by the Prussian bishop Johannes Briesemann, Giese did not employ insult, or call the new teachings heretical. Instead, he posed friendly questions designed to awaken doubt.[81] The angel in Christ's empty tomb wore a white robe, Giese wrote, so probably there is no great sin in priests wearing vestments; tumults should be avoided because they did not advance the glory of Christ. The *Anthelogikon*—printed in Kraków, possibly at the instigation of Bishop Tomicki—was a learned conversation with Lutherans and an invitation to dialogue.[82] Another conciliatory Polish polemic, *Defensorium Ecclesiae*, by the archdeacon of Przemyśl, Stanisław Byliński, was printed in Kraków in 1531.[83] This text claimed to reproduce the texts of religious letters exchanged in the 1520s between Byliński and his friend, the Breslau reformer Laurentius Corvinus. In this correspondence, Byliński commended to his friend the universal church, while Corvinus explained

---

[76] AAP, AE VII, fo. 18v–19v. The first appointee was Dr Thomas Bedermann.

[77] Martin Dobrogost, *Orationes VI contra Martinum Lutherum* (Kraków, 1525), now lost. Catalogued by Karol Estreicher, *Bibliografia polska*, vol. xv (Kraków, 1896), p. 263.

[78] AT 11, pp. 156–8.

[79] For the history of this work, see Borawska, *Tiedemann Giese*, p. 319.

[80] Giese, *Anthelogikon*; discussed by Zins, 'The Reformation in Ermeland', pp. 591–2 and Borawska, *Tiedemann Giese*, pp. 305–9.

[81] Giese's lack of invocation of the Fathers was noted by Rechowicz, *Dzieje teologii*, vol II, p. 48.

[82] For Giese's wider writings, see Borawska, *Tiedemann Giese*, pp. 319–25.

[83] Byliński, *Defensorium Ecclesiae*.

the comforts of his own faith in the Word. These are letters between friends, not avowed antagonists—their disagreements about orthodoxy sit alongside expressions of mutual affection and concern, and Byliński sent his blessings to Corvinus' wife. At the end of his fifth and final letter, Archdeacon Byliński sadly concluded that his friend was at risk of heresy, but again this remained a publication free of personal insult.

The strong preference for reconciliation is seen above all, however, in attempts by bishops to bring Lutherans back to the *ecclesia*, ideally converting them in person. Primate Łaski, for example, secured permission from Pope Clement VII in 1526 for monks who had absconded from their houses and married to be able, on returning to the church, to become secular priests, rather than having to rejoin their monastic orders—a clear attempt to make reconciliation more palatable for defectors.[84] Bishop Latalski was in 1529 also granted a papal bull giving him special permission to reconcile heretics—Lutherans in Poznań diocese who repented of their errors, publicly abjured, and swore an oath would be free of all church penalties they might have incurred as a result of their heresy.[85] Stanisław Grad found evidence that Primate Łaski personally offered to convert Jan Hess, the leader of the Breslau Reformation.[86] During the Jakub of Iłża case, Tomicki asked Primate Drzewicki if he might like to attempt a reconversion of the lecturer in person.[87] Drzewicki himself claimed to have successfully reconciled a weeping Kaspar Lisman, a cleric who had earlier lost his preaching licence in Kraków diocese on account of his allegedly Lutheran sermons.[88] This is the same Drzewicki who, in Danzig in 1526, at the trial for Lutheranism of the city's schoolmaster Bernardus Baschmann, had treated the court to a speech on the desirability of bringing heretics 'to the sheepfold of the holy mother church and to the unity of the Christian religion'.[89] The zealous Bishop of Kamieniec, Wawrzyniec Międzyleski, when travelling through Royal Prussia met a Lutheran and 'for more than four hours disputed with him on the catholic faith and heresy', until the man declared himself convinced, and begged Międzyleski to write to him regularly with religious guidance.[90]

More audaciously, Andrzej Krzycki hoped to convert Philip Melanchthon himself. Krzycki sent an envoy to Wittenberg in 1530, carrying warm letters and gifts.[91] Melanchthon gave Krzycki a copy of the Augsburg confession, admitted his dismay at events in the Holy Roman Empire, and asked if the Pole might find for him some quiet corner to which he might escape.[92] Seizing on this with

[84] Theiner, *Vetera monumenta*, II, nr. 429, pp. 438–9. This was seen as a step too far even by Sigismund I, who asked Rome to reverse its decision: AT 9, pp. 120–1.
[85] AAP, Acta Ep. VII, fos. 161(v)–162(v).   [86] Grad, *Kościelna działalność*, p. 270.
[87] AT 16b, pp. 539–41.   [88] AT 17, pp. 444–5.
[89] AAWł, Acta Ep. 2, fo. 179(v): 'ad gremium sancte matris ecclesie unitatemque Christiana religione'.
[90] AAWa, D66, fo. 129, 'et ultra quam per quatuor horas secum disputari de fide katholica ac heretica'.
[91] AT 12, pp. 406–7; Bartel, 'Filip Melanchton'; Władysław Pociecha, 'Rzym wobec starań o sprowadzenie Melanchthona do Polski', *RwP* IX–X (1937–9): 418–22.
[92] AT 14, pp. 747–8.

excitement, Krzycki secured papal permission to welcome Melanchthon to Poland. The bishop explained his plans to his uncle, Piotr Tomicki: 'it is well known that he [Melanchthon] wishes to leave these factions... nothing would be more useful, or bring us more praise, than for me to do it, that is, dissuading him from heresy'.[93] It is also in this light that we should understand Maciej Drzewicki's contact with Martin Luther in 1529. As we have seen, the then Bishop of Włocławek sent the reformer a side of smoked pig. Just as Krzycki was keen to lure Melanchthon to Poland, Drzewicki's stated goal was to have a face-to-face meeting with Luther. Luther's reply implies that this was to have taken place on hostile ground in Poland: 'Therefore, as Your Excellency wishes to see me, thus I in turn earnestly desire in Christ—to see your venerable grey hairs confess Christ before that crowd, and hearing them disagree.'[94] Luther's reply is politely sceptical, with hints of sarcasm. The doctor of Wittenberg confesses his 'wonder' at this unlikely and 'miraculous' conversion of one who had long persecuted the Gospel, but bluntly declared that a meeting was not possible.

FREEDOM OF CONSCIENCE AND CHARITY

Finally, certain senior figures in the Polish episcopate explicitly advocated charity and a rejection of violence in the face of the early Reformation. Drzewicki, as primate of Poland, was challenged on his decision to promote the ex-Lutheran Kaspar Lisman. Drzewicki wrote that 'our office demands charity'—a bishop should be like the good shepherd, find the lost (heretical) sheep, place it on his shoulders, and bring it back to the fold.[95] However, it was Piotr Tomicki, the most pacifically inclined of all Sigismund I's bishops, who most explicitly rejected religious violence. 'It is not for us to compel anyone in religion', he wrote to Queen Bona's secretary Aliphio.[96] In a terse exchange of letters with his nephew Andrzej Krzycki in 1528, Tomicki argued passionately that the church of Christ was not permitted to use physical force in spiritual matters. The only weapons available, he wrote, were 'gentleness, tolerance, and the teaching of the Gospel'.[97] The teaching of the apostles and the Fathers was pacifist, Tomicki insisted, and all the church could hope to arm itself with were innocence, justice, clemency, and modesty. The fact that the church could not use force against its enemies is plainly shown, wrote Tomicki, by the fact that priests who took up arms were excommunicate under canon law.[98] Here, the bishop and vice chancellor is yet again very close in his statements to those expressed by his royal master on freedom of conscience.[99]

---

[93] AT 15, pp. 637–8: 'non ignorabat illum cupidum esse abdicandi se factionibus istis... nihil utilius laudabiliusque nobis contingere posse, quo faciam sedulo, modo ne haeretici disuadeant'.

[94] *D. Martin Luthers Werke*, vol. 5, pp. 88–90: 'Proinde sicut Tua Paternitas desiderat me videre, ita vicissim magna voluptas in Christo mihi esset, venerandos canos tuos videre confessores Christi in hac turba procerem hostilium, audientes illis dissentire.'

[95] AT 17, p. 444.

[96] AT 7, pp. 292–3: 'Nec nostrum est, aliquem ad religionem cogere.'

[97] AT 10, pp. 439–40: 'mansuetudine, tolerantia et doctrina evangelica'.

[98] AT 10, pp. 454–5.   [99] See Chapter Three, pp. 114–16.

Dantiscus too assured his fellow Danzigers in 1533 that he disapproved whole-
heartedly of the heated anti-Lutheran sentiments of Primate Drzewicki and Bishop
Krzycki, and that the King would too, 'who will not, as we believe, hold such vehe-
mence to be entirely good'.[100]

As Dantiscus' letter indicates, there were dissenting voices in these decades—the
voices of those clergy left aggrieved and appalled by their superiors' apparent laxity
in the face of a major new heresy. The Poznań cathedral chapter, for one, grew
increasingly exasperated with its bishops as the years passed. It urged Bishop
Latalski not to accept any intercessions on behalf of Hegendorff, 'who from certain
and legitimate causes is suspected of being of the Lutheran heresy'.[101] It was in the
absence of any judicial action against Hegendorff in Poznań that Szamotulski
seized on printed polemic as an alternative weapon, with which he attacked not
just heresy but his own bishop's passivity in his 1536 *Vincula Hippocratis:*

> O illustrious Frankfurt, always free and immune from Lutheran dogmas! Whereas you
> Reverend Bishop (in whose diocese a monster grazing in the field of stupidity is hiding)
> will tolerate so prominent a Lutheran and defender of Luther among your flock.[102]

In 1537, the Poznań chapter wearily petitioned its new bishop, the King's illegitimate son Jan of Lithuania, 'to appoint an inquisitor against heresy, and recall from
Germany those suspected of studying heresy'.[103] In Ermland, the cathedral canons
required all local boys setting off for study in Leipzig to take an oath in German,
swearing that they rejected Martin Luther and regarded themselves as catholics
and followers of the Roman church.[104] In Płock, the cathedral chapter regularly
asked Bishop Andrzej Kryzcki to provide them with resources which would enable
them to finally start arresting known heretics.[105] And Krzycki himself grew increasingly frustrated with the inaction of his fellow bishops, including his powerful
uncle and patron Piotr Tomicki. Violence, he informed his uncle in their angry
epistolary exchange of 1528, was required to defend the church. Christ, he wrote,
had told his apostles to sell their tunics and buy swords, and warned that he had
come to bring not peace but a sword. The bishop's own crozier, stressed Krzycki, was
fashioned in the shape of a hook as a symbol of the church's ultimate right to use
physical coercion—'compel them to enter!'[106] There were, then, high clergy who
were aghast at the prevailing culture of ecclesiastical indulgence towards Lutherans
in the church's midst. Figures such as Szamotulski and Krzycki were nonetheless
still in the minority in the Polish-Prussian church in the 1520s and 1530s.

---

[100] Johannes Dantiscus, *Corpus of Iohannes Dantiscus' Texts*, IDL4332.
[101] AAP, CP 37, fo. 55(v): 'pro Egendorfino, ex causis certis et legittimis...suspecta de heresi
Luterana'.
[102] Szamotulski, *Vincula*, fos. Bviii–Bviii(v): 'O insignis Francophordia semper a Lutheri dogmatibus
immunis & libera...Quamdum Reverend. Pontifex (in cuius diocesi haec bellua agrum stulticiae
depasta latitat) hunc tam egregium dogmatis lutherani fautorum & publicum defensorem in tuo
grege tolerabis.'
[103] AAP, CP 37, fo. 121: 'Item ut Inquisitor heretice pravitat, deputaretur. Item ut scholares de
studijs heresi suspect, in germania revocatur.'
[104] AAWa, Acta Cap. 1A, fo. 31.   [105] Ulanowski, 'Acta Capituli Plocensis', pp. 153, 170–1.
[106] AT 10, pp. 437, 449–52.

CONCLUSIONS

The Polish church may have published papal bulls condemning Martin Luther, and issued statutes designed to purge his teaching from Sigismund I's kingdom, but in practice those publicly suspected of Lutheranism were often left unmolested by diocesan authorities, people brought before church courts were almost never punished, and even in those few cases the full force of the law (execution) was never applied. The leadership of the old church in Jagiellonian Poland was thus happy to coexist with, tolerate, or turn a blind eye to Lutheranism—projects of religious reconciliation were embraced with enthusiasm in the 1520s and 1530s, while prosecution, persecution, and punishment were actively avoided. Those who disagreed, such as Archdeacon Szamotulski or Bishop Krzycki, were forced to vent their anger in printed polemics or private letters, to little effect.

Ian Forrest, in his study of heresy prosecutions in late medieval England, reminded us that heresy was in the final analysis a 'nebulous and a transitory legal state'.[107] A heretic, strictly speaking, was someone found guilty by an ecclesiastical judge, who had refused to abjure or had relapsed after an earlier abjuration, and was thus under a capital sentence. Sigismund I's monarchy, in the early Reformation, had only three Lutheran heretics in this strict legal sense—Jakub of Iłża in Kraków, the tailor Snyder in Warsaw, and Michael Werner in Poznań, all of whom received sentences and were officially declared anathematized heretics under canon law. Lutherans in the Polish monarchy did not become heretics, for the most part, because they were not systematically detected, prosecuted, and punished. The church in this kingdom in the 1520s and 1530s possessed the judicial and institutional structures required to prosecute heresy, and had employed them against Hussites in northern Poland in the fifteenth century (in one diocese, Włocławek in Kujavia). Where the early Reformation was concerned, however, there was simply insufficient institutional, cultural, or clerical will to deploy the formidable anti-heresy mechanisms of the Middle Ages against those who were now drawn to the teachings of Martin Luther.

How, then, do we account for the seemingly anomalous forbearance of the Polish-Prussian church, behind the official façade of rhetorical condemnation of Martin Luther—just at what historians normally see as a moment of intense religious struggle in Europe? Examining the similar reluctance of Thomas Wolsey and William Wareham to prosecute English Lutherans in these same years, Craig d'Alton presented these actions as arising out of the individual preferences (or even temperaments) of these venerable churchmen.[108] However, we might alternatively see the Polish church's conciliatory attitude towards local Lutherans as revealing a tenacious pre-confessional understanding of Christianity. Canon Giese thus ended his 200-page *Anthelogikon* with a prayer for unity: '[Christ] will give us the grace

---

[107] Forrest, *Detection of Heresy*, p. 241.
[108] D'Alton, 'The Suppression of Lutheran Heretics' and 'William Wareham'.

that all recognize the true light of his church in the spirit of perfect unity.'[109] The preferred response to the early Reformation was reconciliation rather than persecution, because Lutheranism (in the sense of theological dissent, rather than violent commoners' revolt) was not as alarming as we assume it to have been. People such as the Kraków schoolmaster Bartholomeus who read Lutheran books, or the King's master mason Benedikt who denounced the cults of saints, were ill-advised, mischievous, and making a social nuisance of themselves—but there is no sense whatsoever here that they constituted a threat so terrifying that it must be destroyed at all costs. Instead, the hearings in Appendix 1 seem to treat 'luteranismus' as a nuisance crime or, to use modern terminology, antisocial behaviour. Here we have the heretic as social miscreant, not as cosmological threat. This attitude is perplexing from a Counter-Reformation, or post-Reformation, perspective, in which we know that in the sixteenth century and beyond the Catholic and Protestant churches fought each other with such passion, spiritual conviction, and bloodshed. But it is more logical from a late medieval perspective, in which the Latin church had become so broad, so fuzzy at the edges, so devolved, diverse, and pluralistic that a movement like Lutheranism could no longer look (to many church leaders) like an entirely dangerous heresy. Instead, it looked more like another tricky minority opinion within the universal Christian church.

There was, in fact, one burning for religious crime under Sigismund I. It occurred in 1539, when the merchant's widow Katarzyna Melchiorowna was executed in Kraków, having being found guilty by a diocesan court of converting to Judaism. In 1529, Tomicki had warned her to take communion, to cease contact with 'the perfidious Jewish sect', and to share any spiritual doubts she had with learned clergy.[110] In 1530, she abjured before the episcopal court, swearing that her flirtation with Jewish belief had been down to her female curiosity and a 'debilitation' of the brain.[111] But under Bishop Maciejowski, she was later found guilty of having relapsed into Judaism, and in her old age was burnt at the stake. The Polish church *was* therefore capable of mustering the will and resources to execute those whom it identified as dangerous spiritual enemies. If the late medieval church had fuzzy boundaries, here was one which still commanded clear consensus—a Christian was not a Jew. In a figure such as Katarzyna Melchiorowna, the church in Sigismund I's Poland had finally found an Other whom it could convincingly define itself against.[112] Under Sigismund I, the great majority of clerical leaders in the Polish monarchy could not yet perceive such boundaries—absolute confessional fault lines—within the church itself. And perhaps the execution of an old woman for Judaizing in the early Reformation is no surprise, commanded as it was by a church which was increasingly desperately feeling for its own edges.

---

[109] Giese, *Anthelogikon* (unnumbered pages): 'donabit etiam gratiam ut corde unanimi et perfecto, eius verum lumen omnes ecclesiae agnoscant.'

[110] BJ, MS 3227, fos. 72f–72(v); Magda Teter, *Jews and Heretics in Catholic Poland: A Beleaguered Church in the Post-Reformation Era* (Cambridge, 2006), pp. 42–4.

[111] BJ, MS 3227, fos. 72(v)–73.

[112] For the role of Jews in later sixteenth-century confessional polemic and identity formation in Poland, see Teter, *Sinners on Trial*.

The boundaries of *doctrina* could no longer be policed with conviction, but the boundaries of the *fides* still could. Melchiorowna, in rejecting the Christian faith (the Trinity and Incarnation), had succeeded in putting herself definitively beyond the spiritual frontiers of the universal Christian *ecclesia*; Christoph Hegendorff, Kaspar Lisman, and Matthias Gutfor, by challenging positions in academic theology, had not.

PART 4

LANGUAGE ANALYSIS

7

Defining Lutheranism

All the royal and ecclesiastical responses to the early Reformation which we have explored so far—in episodes as diverse as Hanseatic town revolts, the birth of a Lutheran duchy, anti-heresy edicts, diplomacy with reformist princes, polemics, conversions, and trials—are underpinned by the vexing question of what, precisely, the ruling elites of the Polish monarchy understood Lutheranism to be in the years 1518 to c.1540. This chapter therefore takes a closer look at how contemporaries perceived Lutherans. Even modern scholarship can struggle to define religions or religious groups, both at a theoretical level and in the specific context of early Protestantism. In his lively 1983 work, *Imagining Religion*, Jonathan Smith pondered who had the moral and intellectual right to identify the boundaries of a religious group: its adherents, its opponents, or subsequent historians? Smith asked if historians, like zoologists, should adopt a Linnaean model whereby individuals are recognized as members of a group on the basis of one definitive characteristic (six legs, a belief in *sola fide*), or whether we should instead use a looser 'polythetic' approach, whereby we identify a spectrum of characteristics, some of which some members of the group will have.[1] These problems are certainly not new to historians of early Lutheranism. Some see the religious upheavals triggered across Europe in the 1520s as 'Lutheranism', a single ideological movement which looked to Wittenberg and Luther for leadership. Others, meanwhile, view the early Reformation as a wild outpouring of reform ideas on the ground, quite beyond Luther's control and linked to his own teachings only in the loosest possible sense—or even not united by 'any ideas at all', as Bernd Moeller has paraphrased it.[2] Risto Saarinen, for example, claims that Lutheranism did not exist as a 'church and confessional family' before the 1530 Augsburg Confession, which finally

---

[1] Jonathan Smith, *Imagining Religion: From Babylon to Jonestown* (Chicago, 1982), pp. 1–8. For a recent application of Smith's ideas to early modern history, see Michael Ostling, *Between the Devil and the Host: Imagining Witchcraft in Early Modern Poland* (Oxford, 2011).

[2] Bernd Moeller, 'What Was Preached in German Towns in the Early Reformation', in Dixon, *The German Reformation*, pp. 36–52, at p. 37 [originally published as 'Was wurde in der Frühzeit der Reformation in deutschen Städten gepredigt?', *Archiv für Reformationsgeschichte* 75 (1984): 176–93]; Susan Karant-Nunn, 'What Was Preached in the German Cities in the Early Years of the Reformation? *Wildwuchs* versus Lutheran Unity', in Philip N. Bebb and Sherrin Marshall (eds), *The Process of Change in Early Modern Europe* (Athens, OH, 1988), pp. 81–96; Hans-Jürgen Görtz, 'Eine "bewegte" Epoche: Zur Heterogenität reformatorische Bewegungen', *Zwingliana* 19:2 (1993): 103–25; Miriam Usher Chrisman, *Conflicting Visions of Reform: German Lay Propaganda Pamphlets, 1519–30* (Atlantic Highlands, 1996); MacCulloch, *Reformation*, stresses the fragmentation of the early Reformation from its first days, pp. 106–57; Rublack, *Reformation Europe*, implicitly paints a picture of a Wittenberg core and network at the heart of the early Reformation, pp. 12–64.

provided it with a codified set of doctrines.[3] The question of how one defines early Lutheranism is, then, both theoretically and historiographically knotty.

As the *Prussian Chronicle* (1529) by the Danzig Dominican Simon Grunau well illustrates, the question of what exactly Lutheranism was understood to be by contemporaries in King Sigismund I's Polish monarchy was, similarly, far from straightforward. Grunau's treatment of Lutheranism can look incomprehensible or simply bizarre. At first glance, his chronicle seems to handle Lutheranism in a straightforwardly hostile manner.[4] One of its leitmotifs is divine plagues sent to punish Prussians for their 'heresy'—plagues of ravenous mice, sweating sickness, poisonous fish, and terrible floods of the Vistula. Devils and demons lurk in the pages of his book. At the same time, however, Grunau praised Dr Alexander Svenichen—the cleric who led Danzig city council's religious reforms in 1524, and a man routinely identified in modern scholarship as an important local Lutheran.[5] Grunau approved too of the preacher Michael Meurer, who talked 'strangely and sweetly about the honour of God' and 'told the people how to understand the Lutheran doctrines'—also indubitably a Lutheran, sent to Danzig by Luther himself and, from 1526, a key figure in the implementation of Albrecht's Reformation in Ducal Prussia.[6] Even Duke Albrecht himself, unhesitatingly labelled 'lutterische' throughout the chronicle, in one scene declares Martin Luther to be a wicked man.[7] Simon Grunau's definition of Lutheranism is hard to fathom.

This chapter seeks to recover what Sigismund I and his subjects perceived Lutheranism to be—just as the next chapter examines what they understood catholicism to be—through close analysis of the religious language they used. 'Language analysis' can mean different things in different disciplines. The approach taken in these two final chapters could variously be described as discourse analysis, research into the semantic field of Lutheranism, lexicometry, the unearthing of a distinct contemporary language (Pocock), or an exploration of the construction of Lutheranism in the sources.[8] Broadly speaking, analysis of the language/discourse of historical sources has evolved out of early twentieth-century linguistics, the *Annales* school, Skinner and Pocock's Cambridge School in England, and the work of Michel Foucault.[9] Language analysis techniques were, from the outset, employed

---

[3] Risto Saarinen, 'Lutheran Ecclesiology', in Gerard Mannion and Lewis S. Mudge (eds), *The Routledge Companion to the Christian Church* (Abingdon, 2008), pp. 170–86, at p. 170.

[4] *Simon Grunau's Preussische Chronik.* On Grunau, see Jolanta Dworzaczkowa, 'Kronika Pruska Szymona Grunaua jako źrodło historyczne', *Studia Zródłoznawcze* 2 (1958): 119–46; Sławomir Zonenberg, *Kronika Szymona Grunau* (Bydgoszcz, 2009) and 'Wizerunek heretyka w Preussische Chronik', in Jacek Banaszkiewicz, Jacek Maciejewski, and Joanna Sobiesiak (eds), *Persona, gestus habitusque, insignium: Zachowania i atrybuty jako wyznaczniki tożsamości społecznej jednostki w średniowieczu* (Lublin, 2009), pp. 103–16; Możdżen, 'Miasto pod panowaniem diabelskim'.

[5] *Simon Grunau's Preussische Chronik*, vol. II, p. 782; Borawska and Reitz, 'Alexander Svenichen'; Bogucka, 'Walki społeczne', pp. 384–5.

[6] *Simon Grunau's Preussische Chronik*, III, pp. 177–8; Janusz Małłek, 'Michał Meurer: reformator Mazur', *Komunikaty Mazursko-Warmińskie* 3 (1962): 561–8.

[7] *Simon Grunau's Preussische Chronik*, III, pp. 176–7.

[8] For the distinction between discourse analysis and the German school of *Berichtsgeschichte* (concept history), see Peter Schöttler, 'Historians and Discourse Analysis', *History Workshop Journal* 27:1 (1989): 37–65.

[9] Quentin Skinner, 'Motives, Intentions and Interpretation', in *Visions of Politics. Vol 1: Regarding Method* (Cambridge, 2002), pp. 90–102; Pocock, 'The Concept of a Language'.

chiefly by historians of politics and political thought: on the French *cahiers de doléance* of 1789 (1975), on languages of republicanism and humanism in early modern Europe, or of class in modern Britain (1980s).[10] In the twenty-first century, language analysis is still most commonly embraced by historians dealing with political history and thought, and has been applied more rarely to religious or Reformation history.[11] Such scholarship has, over the decades, enhanced our appreciation that, as Schöttler puts it, 'language is more than a passive medium for carrying meaning'.[12]

A few words on methodology are thus in order. This and the following chapter analyse the language of the core corpus of sources used in this book. These amount to around 500 individual documents produced within the Polish monarchy which directly address the early Reformation: some 350 letters penned by the ruling elite (the King, royal council, courtiers), the records of sixty heresy trials, fifteen locally authored printed polemics, fifteen royal and episcopal heresy edicts, parliamentary materials, cathedral chapter acts, and dozens of poems, prefaces, and dedicatory letters found in Kraków-printed books from these decades. Geographically, these texts were composed all over Sigismund I's monarchy: from Poznań in the west, to Przemyśl in the east, in the cities of Prussia, in the royal capital of Kraków, and beyond. These documents are overwhelmingly, but not exclusively, in Latin—Pocock points out that early modern discourse was often polyglot (but was still a single discourse).[13] The list of texts used is given in Appendix 2. Each text was analysed individually (without the use of software), noting the words applied to the early Reformation/Lutheranism—i.e. nouns, adjectives, adverbs, metaphors, antonyms, as well more general statements revealing the characteristics attributed to Lutherans/Lutheranism, such as particular actions, beliefs, traits, or intentions. The aim was thus not just to recover how a single word ('luteranus') was used, but rather to establish its wider semantic field. The analysis has a quantitative element, in that the relative popularity/use of various terms was monitored.[14] In previous chapters, these sources were employed in a more traditional, empirical way, with reference to their individual context—i.e. establishing why particular actors might have said x in a given historical

---

[10] For an overview of the history of the field, see Schöttler, 'Historians and Discourse Analysis'. Régine Robin, 'Le champ sémantique de "feodalité" dans les cahiers de doléances généraux de 1789', *Bulletin du Centre d'Analyse du Discours* 2 (1975): 61–8; Anthony Pagden (ed.), *The Languages of Political Theory in Early Modern Europe* (Cambridge, 1987); Gareth Steadman Jones, *Languages of Class: Studies in English Working Class History, 1832–1982* (Cambridge, 1983).

[11] Pablo Sánchez León, 'Conceiving the Multitude: Eighteenth-Century Popular Riots and the Modern Language of Social Disorder', *International Review of Social History* 56 (2011): 511–33; Joanna Innes, '"Reform" in English Public Life: The Fortunes of a Word', in Joanna Innes and Arthur Burns (eds), *Rethinking the Age of Reform: Britain 1780–1850* (Cambridge, 2007), pp. 71–97; Innes and Phelp, *Re-imagining Democracy* contains multiple essays on language/language analysis. For Reformation-related language analysis, see Zoltán Csepregi, 'The Evolution of the Language of the Reformation in Hungary (1522–26)', *Hungarian Historical Review* 2:1 (2013): 3–34.

[12] Schöttler, 'Historians', p. 54.   [13] Pocock, 'The Concept of a Language', p. 21.

[14] The number of *texts* in which a particular phrase or statement about Lutheranism occurred was counted, rather than the total number of *references* across all these sources. In polemical treatises, for example, the main treatise, any dedicatory letters, and any poems printed alongside the text were each counted as a separate textual unit.

moment. Here, the same texts are instead viewed collectively, as a single, evolving, panoramic body of discourse in a two-decade window. Studying the sources thus, we can see the aggregate image of Lutheranism, or the early Reformation, held by Sigismund I's political, intellectual, and clerical elites in the 1520s and 1530s—a picture which enables us to see subtle shifts over time in the terminology used and ideas invoked.[15]

The findings of this analysis are summarized in Figure 7.1, which sets out the forty features most commonly associated with Lutheranism in these Polish-Prussian sources. This chapter explores, in turn, four principal themes which emerge. Firstly, Lutheranism was not very consistently, securely, passionately, or vituperatively identified as a 'heresy' in these texts, taken as a whole. Instead, the sources display a tendency to view the early Reformation as an epidemic of famil-iar, older forms of religious malfaisance such as blasphemy or sacrilege. While the doctrines of Martin Luther and his followers (on *sola fide*, *sola scriptura*) were rou-tinely identified as incorrect, interest in them was relatively limited, even in some 'theological' texts such as polemics. The focus, instead, was on Lutheranism's lamented schismatic and disruptive tendencies—its chief problematic feature was the (sometimes violent) threat it posed to the unity of local communities, realms, and the universal church itself. In elite catholic discourse in the Polish monarchy, Lutheranism was, then, a heresy of schism. The chapter concludes by examining how a separate body of texts produced by Reformation supporters (not included in Figure 7.1) defined their movement—here, by contrast, specific doctrines are lynchpins of reformers' self-understanding.

It is worth noting at the outset that King Sigismund and his elites did believe something called 'Lutheranism' existed—the term is not an anachronism or modern neologism. At least thirty-eight texts from this collection, from 1525 onwards, refer directly to *luteranismus*, Lutheranism. King Sigismund promised Bishop Ferber, for example, that he would ensure that *luteranismus* was eradicated from the episcopal towns occupied by Albrecht in the 1519–21 war; in 1535, Danzig council were invited to swear that they 'did not in any way adhere to Lutheranism', while Canon Grzegorz Szamotulski warned in his polemic *Vincula Hippocratis* of the dangers of 'luteranismus' in Poznań (1536).[16] 'Lutheran' was also employed extensively as an adjective, found in a third of these sources (154 texts). Bishop Tomicki could thus complain of 'the Lutheran trouble' in Europe,[17] while in the *Prussian Chronicle* Grunau talks of a 'Lutheran council', 'Lutheran Gospel', 'Lutheran pictures', 'Lutheran mass', and even a 'Lutheran paradise'. The insistent use of these labels suggests, prima facie, that King Sigismund and his sub-jects possessed a functional concept of Lutheranism as a tangible entity. What then did they understand 'the Lutheran cause', as Bishop Ferber described it in one letter, to be?[18]

---

[15] See also Schöttler, 'Historians', p. 43.
[16] AT 7, p. 33; AT 16b, p. 432; Szamotulski, *Vincula*, fo. Aiii.
[17] AT 10, p. 59.   [18] AT 11, pp. 107–8.

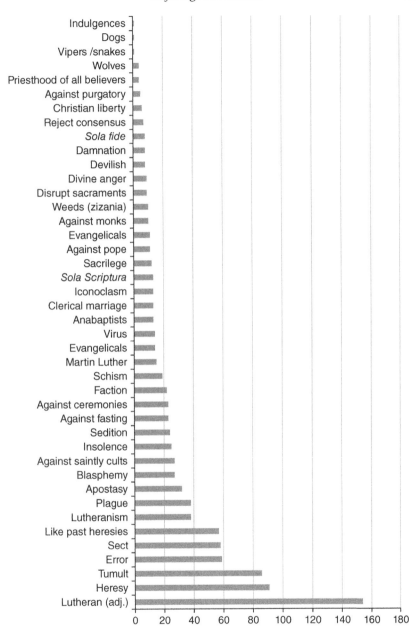

Figure 7.1 Construction of the early Reformation in sources from the Polish monarchy (1518 to *c.*1540).

HERESY?

At first glance, the sources from Sigismund I's Polish monarchy appear to characterize Lutheranism—both explicitly and implicitly—as a 'heresy', as that is the single term most commonly used in relation to *luteranismus* and *luterani*. Lutheranism was persistently referred to a heresy, or heretical, its followers as 'heretics': ninety-one texts (18 per cent) make this link unequivocally. King Sigismund, for example, warned Poznań in 1526 that the entire city would be suspected of 'the Lutheran heresy' unless its town preacher was dismissed.[19] Archdeacon Byliński gave his polemic the unambiguous title *Against Laurentius Corvinus, a Follower of the Lutheran Heresy*.[20] In 1534, Canon Giese of Ermland could note that a local monk had 'lapsed into the Lutheran heresy', while the Poznań chapter similarly stated that the scholar Hegendorff was 'suspected of the Lutheran heresy'.[21] In a slightly different way, a further fifty-seven texts (9 per cent) indirectly identified Lutheranism as a heresy by discussing 'haeresia' in the abstract in their accounts of early Reformation events—as a general historical phenomenon, a supernatural force, or a feature of the Christian past. Krzycki's anti-Luther polemic, *De Afflictione Ecclesiae*, for example, reproduced a passage attributed to Origen, which called heresy a three-horned devil, a death-giving fountain.[22] Byliński's *Defensorium* offered his readers a page-long list of ancient heretics and heresies.[23] Where writers presented heresy as 'timeless', the reader was meant to draw the obvious inference that Lutherans (even if not named as such in the text, or the passage) stood in this dark tradition.[24]

However, in context the identification of Lutheranism as a heresy was not at all so clear-cut: over two-thirds (68 per cent) of Polish-Prussian texts did not use the word 'heresy' (or its derivatives) at all when discussing the early Reformation. The word was more often absent than present. These include the first string of royal anti-Reformation edicts (May 1520, July 1520, February 1522, March 1523).[25] When King Sigismund came to Danzig, his royal command to surrender all Lutheran books in the city (1526) did not refer to these texts as heretical, but only as 'insolent', 'seditious', and 'insulting'.[26] Tiedemann Giese's major treatise against Lutheranism, *Anthelogikon* (1525), does not employ the word heresy either.[27] Throughout these decades, the word 'heresy' rarely featured, even in the trials of those accused of Lutheranism.[28] Many scholars have stressed the unique and terrible power of that one word 'haeresia' in medieval and early modern Europe—as a word which 'inspired violence', and 'horror', a word with 'corporeal consequences'.[29]

---

[19] AT 8, p. 151.

[20] Byliński, *Defensorium Ecclesiae adversus L Corvinum Lutherane hereseos sectatorem.*

[21] AT 16a, p. 606, 'haeresim Luteranam lapsum'; AAP, CP 37, fo. 55(v): 'suspectus de heresi Luterana'.

[22] Krzycki, *De Afflictione*, fos. E–Ei.   [23] Byliński, *Defensorium*, fo. 41v.

[24] On the rhetoric of heresy as diachronic, see Henderson, *The Construction of Orthodoxy*, p. 134.

[25] CIP, III, pp. 583–4, 579, 647–9; CIP, IV, p. 3.   [26] AT 8, pp. 75–6.

[27] Giese, *Anthelogikon.*   [28] See Appendix 1.

[29] Wandel, *Reformation*, p. 9; Hunter, Laursen, and Nederman, 'Introduction', *Heresy in Transition*, p. 5.

Susan Brigden writes that in Tudor London, to be called a heretic was the most damaging, and by implication dangerous, insult.[30] In the Middle Ages and beyond, in other words, great spiritual, legal, and metaphysical weight was placed on the term 'haeresia'. In this light, it is all the more striking that Polish-Prussian elites could write about Luther's followers without, in the clear majority of cases, choosing to utilize this highly resonant term. In this, our texts are similar to the letters of Charles V, who in the 1530s spoke little of heretics, preferring the term 'dévoyés'—those who have strayed.[31]

It is not the case that word 'haeresia' was so often absent because 'Lutheranism' itself functioned as a synonym for heresy. One might speculate, for example, that Lutheranism was so self-evidently heretical in the minds of these contemporaries that it was not necessary to spell out its heretical nature. Perhaps 'Lutheran heretic' was a tautology, like 'Sahara desert', and the two terms were simply interchangeable. But that would still not explain why 40 per cent of these texts (184) make no reference whatsoever to *either* Lutheranism *or* heresy when writing about the early Reformation. For example, the royal citation against the town of Braunsberg, in the wake of its 1525 Reformation revolt, made reference to violence, sects, and apostates, but not to heresy or to Lutheranism.[32] When King Sigismund wrote in alarm about the Gospel-quoting peasants who revolted in Ducal Prussia in 1525, he did not label them as either Lutheran or heretical—simply as dangerous robbers.[33]

It is not just the low use of 'haeresia' which is noteworthy in these sources, but also the near absence of an entire field of words which the medieval church had routinely used in the context of religious dissidents—i.e. graphic insults, and the invocation of diabolical forces, damnation, divine anger, and the apocalypse.[34] The medieval church had a sophisticated repertoire of negative metaphors about heresy, which themselves dated back to the church Fathers.[35] Heretics were routinely labelled as little foxes in the vineyard, as agents of Satan, as the weeds in the New Testament parable which would be cast into eternal flames, as a plague or virus, a leprosy. Bernard of Clairvaux, that leading anti-heretical voice of the Middle Ages, called them dirty as vomit, masturbators, a cancer, homosexuals.[36] Other Cistercian preachers of the thirteenth century declared that wherever heresy occurred, Satan and the Antichrist were at work.[37] In the Polish monarchy, only documents issued by the papacy or its nuncios employed such terms as standard.[38] This vituperative

---

[30] Susan Brigden, *London and the Reformation* (Oxford, 1989), p. 162.

[31] *Correspondenz des Kaisers Karl V. Aus dem königlichen Archiv und der Bibliothèque de Bourgogne zu Brüssel*, ed. Karl Lanz, vol. I, pp. 429, 456 (Leipzig, 1844) and vol. II, pp. 140, 269, 287 (Leipzig, 1845).

[32] *Monumenta Historiae Warmiensis*, vol. 8, pp. 487–9.   [33] ASPK, 8, p. 398.

[34] The lack of apocalyptic sentiment in the chronicle of Simon Grunau has been noted by Sławomir Zonenberg, 'Wizerunek heretyka'.

[35] Sackville, *Heresy*; Beverly Mayne Kienzle, *Cistercians, Heresy and Crusade in Occitania, 1145–1229: Preaching in the Lord's Vineyard* (Woodbridge, 2001), pp. 11–12; Stanisław Bylina, 'Wizerunek heretyka'.

[36] Kienzle, *Cistercians*, pp. 88–9.   [37] Kienzle, *Cistercians*, pp. 199–200.

[38] Wojtyska, *Zacharias Ferreri*, pp. 119, 133, 145; Konarski, *Bulla contra errores*; AAWa, D64, fo. 5.

language—the stock-in-trade of medieval anti-heresy edicts, liturgy, and theological writing—is, however, very muted in Polish-Prussian documents about the early Reformation, deployed in only 14 per cent of texts in total (sixty-eight). The Saxon doctor and his followers were, for example, called dogs, serpents, wolves in the sheepfold, a virus or a plague, but these direct insults were found chiefly on the pages of printed anti-Reformation polemic. Walenty Wróbel, in a preface to Grzegorz Szamotulski's polemic *Vincula Hippocratis*, for example, declared that 'many among us seek truth, but there are also vipers.'[39] Similarly, a poem by Leonard Cox printed on the frontispiece Bishop Krzycki's 1527 polemic, *De Afflictione Ecclesiae*, wrote of 'wolves' seizing sheep.[40] Even within this genre of text, then, the metaphors employed for Lutheranism were not at the same vituperative pitch as in much medieval polemic.

If ancient and medieval rhetoric had strongly associated heretics with demons and the Devil, in the Polish monarchy this link was again made in only a handful of texts (eight). The Crown linked Lutheranism with the Devil only once, when the King told Łukasz Górka in 1526 that reformers in Poznań were following 'their master, the Devil'.[41] It was again chiefly polemicists who did so: Krzycki's 1524 *Encomia* described Luther as demonically inspired.[42] Byliński, in his *Defensorium*, prayed that Corvinus be kept free from 'the doctrines of demons'.[43] Walenty Wróbel referred to contemporary heretics as 'apostles of the Devil' in his 1536 polemic, and Szamotulski in his *Vincula* (1535) suggested that Hegendorff was turning Christ's teaching into that of the Devil. These, however, were all very much passing remarks or insults—no polemicist in Sigismund I's Poland made it a major feature of his argument that Lutheranism was a Satanic product.

Similarly, Lutheranism was only very rarely linked explicitly with damnation (eight texts). The episcopal sentence handed down on Michael Werner in Poznań in 1535 was a rarity when it noted that he had taken Communion in two kinds 'to the damnation of his soul'—here, of course, employing a standard, long-standing formula from canon law.[44] Again, it was polemicists who were most likely to make stark statements about the spiritual consequences for Luther's followers—the noble Lachowski, in his polemical exchange with a Ducal Prussian correspondent, said plainly, 'heretics lead people to eternal damnation', while a ghost in Grunau's chronicle explains (more equivocally) that it has been damned to hell for its Lutheran belief and other sins. Byliński quoted Ireneus on hellfire as the consequence of heresy.[45] In other words, only a sliver of texts from this entire corpus of early Reformation material tell us explicitly that Lutherans will go to hell.

[39] Wróbel, in Szamotulski, *Vincula*, prefatory letter.
[40] Krzycki, *De Afflictione*, frontispiece: 'nam pelles ovium quibus hi latere rapaces/ante lupi...'.
[41] AT 8, p. 147.   [42] Krzycki, *Encomia*, fo. 4.
[43] Byliński, *Defensorium* (unnumbered page).   [44] AAP, AE 7, fo. 334.
[45] AT 10, Byliński, *Defensorium*, fos. 21(v), 29; *Simon Grunau's Preussische Chronik*, II, pp. 695–7.

It has been argued that heresy aroused cosmological fear in premodern societies because its presence in the community would provoke divine anger, and trigger terrible collective punishments.[46] However, one needs to look quite hard to find references to any such concerns in Sigismund I's Poland (nine texts). Professed fear of divine anger is invoked more often in fifteenth-century diocesan pronouncements on liturgical reform (divine displeasure at uncoordinated worship), than in Polish-Prussian texts about the early Reformation.[47] In the 1530s, Bishops Ferber and Dantiscus openly claimed that Lutheranism in Danzig risked provoking divine anger.[48] Dantiscus' unpublished polemical poem, *Jonah*, imagines the divine destruction of the city which had rejected both him and the Roman church.[49] Bishop Ferber worried too that Albrecht's (Lutheran) seizure of church land in Ducal Prussia would bring down vengeance from heaven.[50] Grunau's *Prussian Chronicle*, as we have seen, used plagues, divine retributions for heresy, as a key narrative device.[51] The notion that heresy was feared because it posed an existential threat to society, placing everyone in the path of God's retribution, is thus a background echo, but only that.

As for apocalyptic language about heresy, of the sort which Kienzle sees as characteristic of medieval Cistercian anti-heretical writing, this is virtually absent in early Reformation Poland.[52] The only, highly circumstantial, evidence that Lutheranism might have provoked apocalyptic sentiments is found in the 1527 Kraków reprinting of Vincent of Ferrara's *Prophetie Danielis*, an early fifteenth-century text which foretold 'the ruin of the spiritual life, the collapse of ecclesiastical dignity, the ruin of the catholic faith, the advent of the Antichrist and the end of the world', with a suitably alarming frontispiece of a crumbling citadel.[53]

Two papal bulls, and the imperial Edict of Worms, had condemned Luther and his teachings before all Christendom as a heretic. While 'heresy' might have been the single most commonly used term in Polish-Prussian writing on the early Reformation, and one much utilized in modern textbooks on the sixteenth century, that powerful word was a long way from dominating, or penetrating, discourse on Lutheranism among Sigismund I's subjects. The King and his elites consistently failed, or demurred, to deploy the polemical force of 'haeresia' against local Lutherans—not even in the powerful normative vehicles provided by edicts, trials, or (in some cases) polemical tracts. Lutheranism was thus only weakly, and often ambivalently, identified as a heresy.

[46] Henderson, *Construction of Orthodoxy*, p. 9.
[47] Natalia Nowakowska, 'From Strassburg to Trent: Bishops, Printing and Liturgical Reform in the Fifteenth Century', *Past & Present* 213 (2011): 3–39.
[48] AT 16a, p. 389; AT 17, p. 112. [49] Nowak, 'Antryreformacyjna elegia Dantyszka'.
[50] AAWa, AB A1, fo. 15. [51] *Simon Grunau's Preussische Chronik*, III, p. 25.
[52] Keinzle, *Cistercians*, p. 12.
[53] Vincent of Ferrara, *Prophetie Danielis tres horribiles et de casu videlicet et ruina vite spiritualis. De lapsu ecclesiastice dignitatis et de ruina catholice fidei ac adventu Antichristi et mundi consumatione* (Kraków, 1527).

MORE OF THE SAME? LUTHERANISM
AS A CONTINUATION OF TRADITIONAL
RELIGIOUS CRIMES

The second principal feature of Polish-Prussian discourse of Lutheranism was its strong focus on the illicit religious actions of its followers, which were not viewed as shockingly new, but slotted instead into traditional frameworks of irreligious behaviour (other than heresy). These texts often associated the early Reformation, for example, with acts of apostasy (thirty-two texts), blasphemy (twenty-seven), and sacrilege (twelve). These crimes were presented not just as a negative outcome of Lutheranism, but as actually constitutive of it. This demonstrates that 'haeresia' or 'luteranismus' were only one of several parallel lenses through which one could read—or interpret—the early Reformation from a late medieval perspective. An action such as destroying a statue of a saint was often identified primarily as the well-established crime of sacrilege or blasphemy, and only secondarily (if at all) as 'Lutheran' or explicitly heretical. In the high proportion of sources which make no reference to either heresy or Lutheranism in discussing the Reformation in the 1520s and 1530s (184 texts), it was normally apostasy, blasphemy, and sacrilege which contemporaries reached for to describe what was happening around them.

The first of these alternative lenses was apostasy. Apostasy—the crime of renouncing the Christian religion—in Sigismund I's Poland, tended to have the more specific meaning of leaving the priesthood or a religious order. 'Apostate' was a common term for a Lutheran preacher, freely applied to men such as the bishops of Ducal Prussia, the ex-friars, such as Jakub Hegge, who led the popular Reformation in Danzig and Elbing, the ex-Teutonic Knight and monk Albrecht, or indeed to Martin Luther himself. Canon Rydziński's pamphlets denounced the reformers of Breslau in Silesia as 'apostates', while Bishop Ferber noted the 'congresses of apostates' taking place in Elbing.[54] Sigismund I too could refer to the Swedish Reformation as 'the madness of apostates'.[55] Hence, the new religious trend could be referred to as 'apostates' dogmas', identified as the creation of a distinct (dishonourable) group of men who had broken their clerical or monastic vows.

The early Reformation was also associated with blasphemy—the crime of irreverence towards God—particularly in speech.[56] In a run of early heresy trials in the Kraków episcopal court (1525), individuals such as the schoolmaster Bartholomeus were accused of 'being of the Lutheran sect *and* blasphemy' against God, the saints, and church Fathers.[57] Some sources use 'blasphemia' as a simple synonym for the early Reformation—Primate Drzewicki complained in 1531 of the many 'blasphemies' (not heresies, not Lutheranism) present in Danzig, and King Sigismund wrote in similar terms to Elbing.[58] A Crown legation to Livonia

---

[54] Rydziński, *Petri Risinii*; AT 10, p. 409.   [55] AT 10, p. 58.
[56] See Francisca Loetz, *Dealings with God: From Blasphemers in Early Modern Zurich to a Cultural History of Religiousness*, trans. Rosemary Selle (Farnham, 2009).
[57] BJ, MS 3227, fo. 71(v).   [58] AT 8, p. 112.

referred to this as being a time 'of blasphemers of the name of God'.[59] In one of his chronicle anecdotes, Simon Grunau asserted that 'Christ endures blasphemy and scorn for a long time but the blasphemy and scorn directed towards his mother Mary would soon be ended.' Here, the Prussian friar sees what we call the Reformation as simply one great blasphemous act.[60]

Sacrilegium, in the ancient world, had meant specifically theft from a temple, but from the early medieval church onwards sacrilege could include magic, physical injury of clergy, Host desecration, or the seizure of church land.[61] Sacrilege had been occasionally prosecuted in Polish canon law courts in the first decades of the sixteenth century, but became part of the standard vocabulary around the early Reformation.[62] The courtier Jan Zambocki could write, for example, that Luther's teaching was considered to be 'an error and a sacrilege'.[63] Bishop Ferber commiserated with the exiled Bishop of Linkoping about the Swedish Reformation, where 'sacriligious men' of the 'Lutheran heresy' had spilt Christ's blood.[64] 'Sacrilege' was chiefly used, however, to describe the actions of Danzig's Lutheran rebels in 1525–6. Bishop Tomicki's oration to Danzig's envoys thus deplored the sacrilege committed in that city—the looting of churches, iconoclasm, and expulsion of monks.[65]

Blasphemy, apostasy, and sacrilege were therefore offences which 'lutherani' were likely to commit, but the relationship between this trio of religious crimes and Lutheranism runs deeper than that. In the 1530s, a canon of Kulm reported that a group of nobles had crossed from (Lutheran) Ducal Prussia into his diocese, and destroyed an image of the Virgin in the town of Löbau. The canon described this incident as sacrilege, but made no reference to either heresy or Lutheranism.[66] Bishop Tomicki's great oration to the Danzig envoys in 1525 might have lambasted their acts of sacrilege and blasphemy, but made no reference anywhere to Luther, Lutherans, or Lutheranism. Complaining to Cardinal Campeggio in 1527 that monks in his monarchy were leaving their convents in large numbers, King Sigismund I referred to them as apostates, but not as Lutherans or heretics—even though we may recognize flight from monasteries as a well-known early Reformation phenomenon.[67]

The authors of these texts were, in a sense, disaggregating early Reformation events into a series of long-standing crimes against religion, of which heresy was just one. In April 1513, a certain Petrus had been punished by the Kraków episcopal court for blasphemy, for discussing the Eucharist irreverently in a tavern, possibly

---

[59] AT 8, p. 54.
[60] *Simon Grunau's Preussische Chronik*, II, p. 655: 'So wirdtt von anbegin in der schrieftt gefunden und gelesen, wie die lesterung und hohnrede, Christo gethan, von ihm lange zeitt gedulgett istt, aber die lesterung und hohnrede auf Mariam, seine mutter, wurde balde geschendett.'
[61] Patrick Henriet, 'Sacrilege', *Encyclopedia of the Middle Ages*, vol. 2 (Rome, 2000), pp. 1273–4.
[62] Early trials include AKMK, AE5, fos. 26(v) (1505), 125 (1509). For sacrilege in later sixteenth-century Poland, see Teter, *Sinners on Trial*.
[63] AT 7, p. 321.
[64] AAWa, AB A1, fo. 82(v): 'Quibus errorem Lutherane hereseos in regno Swecie, aliaque mala illic increbuisse horrendumque facimus in effusione sanguinis Christi per sacrilegos homines perpetratum esse...'.
[65] AT 7, pp. 400–5.   [66] AT 13, p. 281.   [67] AT 9, p. 121.

while drunk; throughout the fifteenth century, nobles who damaged the interiors of Polish churches while pursuing vendettas against local clergy had been charged with sacrilege.[68] In the 1520s and 1530s, apparently similar Lutheran actions were often presented in the same way, as essentially the same crimes: not as a new kind of attack on the church with a different kind of intent behind it, but as recognizable acts of recklessness and vandalism. This becomes, therefore, a tale of continuities. Thus what mattered to and perturbed these writers was the fact that disruptive acts had been committed in religious life. Their Lutheran cause or inspiration was not necessarily important enough to note in every case. As with the King's diagnosis of the 1525 Danzig revolt, in the foreground was the crime itself (revolt, sacrilege), with its Lutheran cause or inspiration only secondary. This, then, is one way in which the disturbances of the 1520s and 1530s appeared to late medieval contemporaries, who did not know they were living through the European Reformation, and did not have that particular concept at their disposal.

BAD TEACHINGS

A third feature of this body of sources is the insistence, by a quarter of them (107 texts, using a variety of different phraseologies), that the teaching of Luther and his followers was bad. Lutheranism was described as an 'insane', 'depraved', 'pestiferous', or 'new' dogma—an 'impious' doctrine. Sigismund I, for example, wrote angrily to Łukasz Górka in 1526 about 'Luther's pestiferous doctrines'; the Polish synod statutes of 1527 declared Lutheranism to be a 'perverse doctrine'.[69] These religious opinions were not only bad, but explicitly said to be wrong—erroneous (fifty-nine). Sigismund I could complain to the Bishop of Linkoping about the 'errors' of the Scandinavian Reformation, about 'errors in the faith' in Braunsberg, or the 'errors' of Royal Prussian nobles who refused to pay tithes on religious grounds.[70] Bishop Drzewicki could refer to the 'errors' of the Lutheran priests whom he had incarcerated, and Bishop Tomicki to the 'Lutheran errors' of Jakub of Iłża.[71]

However, as Figure 7.1 shows, the Lutheran teachings which registered most highly in the Polish-Prussian 'catholic' sources were not the ones we might expect. Modern scholarship on the Reformation and its theology—and, indeed, sixteenth-century Protestant writings themselves—present as the core of Luther's teaching his novel theological propositions, such as *sola fide*, *sola scriptura*, and the priesthood of all believers.[72] Yet the mental picture of Lutheran teaching we find in Figure 7.1 is quite different, with Polish-Prussian catholic sources focusing instead

[68] AKMK, Acta Ep. 5, fo. 249; Nowakowska, *Church, State and Dynasty*, pp. 87–90.
[69] AT 8, p. 147; *Statuta provintiae gnesnensis*, fo. 36.
[70] AT 10, p. 59; AT 8, p. 114; AT 8, pp. 35–6.
[71] AT 9, p. 243; AT 17, pp. 262, 266, 286.
[72] Bernard Reardon, *Religious Thought in the Reformation*, 2nd edition (London, 1995); Cameron, *European Reformation*; Alister McGrath, *Luther's Theology of the Cross: Martin Luther's Theological Breakthrough*, 2nd edition (Oxford, 2011).

on those teachings which Lutherans had rejected (and not the distinctive ones they espoused). From this perspective, elites in Sigismund I's Poland seemed to be looking at Luther's teaching through the wrong end of a telescope; and, indeed, Dr Martin Luther himself would likely be exasperated by this table. Luther's celebrated core, new doctrines—and perhaps indeed doctrine as we understand it—were very much a secondary feature of the Reformation in the eyes of Sigismund I and his elites.

For example, *sola scriptura*—the proposition that what was contained in Scripture was more authoritative than any human teaching—occurs surprisingly infrequently in these sources (thirteen texts). The 1526 Danzig Statutes stated that people did not have the right to interpret Scripture for themselves, and that same year Sigismund I told Duke Albrecht that *sola scriptura* was 'an inept and impious doctrine'.[73] In their printed polemics, Rydziński (1524), Giese (1525), and Byliński (1535) noted the Lutheran position on Scripture, and rejected it on the grounds that the Gospels did not contain the entire Christian faith or all the works of Christ; but it was not for them a focus of sustained argument.[74] Meanwhile, Luther's notion of spiritual equality between all Christians, laity and clergy alike, i.e. the priesthood of all Christian believers (four texts), was known (albeit in slightly garbled form) to Simon Grunau in Royal Prussia, and engaged with chiefly by the nobleman Lachowski in a epistolary polemical exchange with a Prussian Lutheran, and Grzegorz Szamotulski, who vehemently disputed the notion that any Christian could grant any other absolution of sins.[75]

More surprisingly, the hallmark doctrine of *sola fide* was referred to in only eight texts (1 per cent of the total corpus). The fullest engagements are found in polemics, such as Tiedemann Giese's 1525 *Anthelogikon*, and Wincenty Wróbel's 1536 *Propugnaculum*, both of which devote substantial early chapters to tackling *sola fide* as a key Lutheran error—although, even then, Wróbel does not identify it as Luther's primary error.[76] *Sola fide* is referred to only in passing, in the many writings of the kingdom's arch polemicist, Andrzej Krzycki.[77] Archdeacon Byliński's 1535 polemic devoted only two paragraphs, in over 100 pages, to the question of *sola fide*.[78] Piotr Rydziński, in his bitter 1524 polemic with the Breslau Lutheran party, did not refer to it at all.[79] The Crown itself referred to *sola fide* in just one official pronouncement, when Tomicki delivered the King's response to the Danzig Lutheran envoys in 1525, stating simply that *sola fide* led to terrible crimes (eliding it, apparently, with the doctrine of Christian liberty).[80] Lucy Sackville has drawn our attention to the importance of genre in writing on heresy: that the same author

---

[73] AT 8, p. 77; AT 8, p. 51: 'doctrina inepta et impia'.

[74] Byliński, *Defensorium*, fo. 39(v); Rydziński, *Petri Risinii*; Giese, *Anthelogikon* (unnumbered pages).

[75] *Simon Grunau's Preussische Chronik*, II, pp. 645–6; AT X, p. 215; Szamotulski, *Anacephaleosis*, fo. 16, and *Vincula*, fo. Cv(v).

[76] Giese, *Anthelogikon*; Wróbel, *Propugnaculum*, Book 2.

[77] Krzycki, *De Afflictione*, fo. Civ(v).

[78] Byliński, *Defensorium*, fo. 46. Fabri's 1528 polemic too discussed the theological errors of the Lutherans and Anabaptists over several paragraphs in his preface, giving *sola fide* just one line, *Adversus doctorem Balthasarem*, fo. Aiij(v).

[79] Rydziński, *Petri Risinii*.   [80] AT 7, pp. 402.

might use different terminologies, depending on whether he was presiding over a courtroom, preaching, or writing a polemical treatise.[81] However, even if we allow for the fact that Crown decrees, or the letters of the King and counsellors, were not deemed an appropriate textual locus (or did not provide an adequate technical language) in which to engage in complex theological debates, it is striking how little interest even those writing in theological genres, such as polemic, took in Luther's position on justification by faith alone.

These doctrinal silences do not simply reflect a lack of information on the part of King Sigismund I and his elites about the novel theologies of Wittenberg. The King and his council were not, after all, on the far geographical fringes of the early Reformation—they were exceptionally well informed, among European royal regimes, about Lutheran theology. The King himself had, grumpily, sat through what was reputedly a three-hour exposition of Lutheran teaching when he received the envoys of rebellious Danzig at an audience in 1525.[82] In 1526, Duke Albrecht tried privately to convert the old Polish king to the new doctrines, and thereafter sent Bishop Queis to preach a Lutheran sermon before his royal uncle.[83] The Dukes of Pomerania also attempted to convert King Sigismund, issuing him with a theological defence of their reforms in 1528 (much to his distaste).[84] Lutheran theological writings circulated in the court, and were closely studied—the two lengthy Danzig Apologias of 1525, with their defence of the new evangelism and its doctrines, were read and commented on by members of the royal council.[85] In the 1530s, Albrecht sent books by Melanchthon and the Augsburg Confession to Polish bishops.[86] Polemics produced in Sigismund I's monarchy were often dialogues with Lutheran activists, inspired by their locally circulating theological materials: Polish-Prussian clergy wrote against Johannes Briesemann in Ducal Prussia, Laurentius Corvinus and Jan Hess in Breslau, or Luther himself in Wittenberg. The Polish king, his royal council and clergy were not, therefore, ignorant of Lutheran doctrine—they did not doubt that it was bad, and likely a repetition of historic heretical errors, but they lacked the appetite or interest to engage with (what we now see as) its distinctive intellectual substance.

THREAT TO ORDER AND UNITY

The main weight of anxiety provoked by Lutheranism, in these sources, lay elsewhere—in the threat it posed to the cohesion of Christian society (i.e. peace and unity) at every level, parish, polity, and international church. In its most extreme forms, Lutheranism was said to do this through the violent social unrest it unleashed, but even outside that context 'lutherani' were associated with factions, splitting off from the Christian community, and a potentially dangerous sectarianism.

[81] Sackville, *Heresy*, pp. 199–200.
[82] *Simon Grunau's Preussische Chronik*, III, pp. 57–8.   [83] See Chapter Three, pp. 99–100.
[84] AT 10, p. 52.   [85] AT 7, pp. 387–9.
[86] AT 14, pp. 521–3, 550–2; Pociecha, 'Jan Chojeński'.

Half a century ago, John Bossy argued that the medieval Mass was principally a visible enactment of social unity: an act which kept Christian society together and the cosmos intact.[87] It is perhaps in this light that we should read Polish-Prussian alarm at Lutheranism, as a phenomenon distinguished above all (to them) by its capacity to divide and disrupt, as a deliberate rejection of unity and community itself. As the King's envoys spelt out to Danzig's Lutherans in 1524, religion was the essential bond which kept the *Respublica* (state-society) together.[88] This section will explore how Figure 7.1 (with its references to tumult, sects, sedition, schisms, iconoclasm, denial of saints, ceremonies, and fasting) reveals Lutheranism to have been, from the perspective of our Polish-Prussian texts, primarily a heresy of schism.

For Sigismund I and his elites, a pronounced characteristic of Lutheranism was its tendency to cause major social-political disturbances: tumults, disorder (eighty-six texts), insolence (twenty-five texts) and sedition (twenty-four texts), the sixteenth-century language of revolt. It threatened anarchy and mass disorder, the great nightmare of sixteenth-century men and women.[89] Almost a quarter of texts (110) explicitly make this link. Throughout the Middle Ages, it had been a standard trope that those who resisted ecclesiastical authority as heretics were also rebels against the Crown, but in Sigismund I's Poland the link between *luteranismus* and 'tumults' was particularly intimate and pronounced.[90] Summoning the *sejm* in 1524, the King stated that 'Lutheran errors' had led to 'the furore of the multitude' in Prussian towns.[91] To the Prussian nobility in 1526, he declared that the new religious movement was causing 'sedition and tumult all over the world'.[92] The Crown's anti-Reformation edicts of 1520, 1522, and March 1523 all cited the risk of disturbances in the commonweal as the prime reason for banning Lutheran books and preaching.[93] King Sigismund's bishops concurred, Primate Łaski thundering in his 1525 memorandum on Danzig that 'the only fruit of their doctrine is tumult'.[94] Polemicists too placed great emphasis on disorder as the inevitable fruit of *luteranismus*.[95] The language of the archdeacon of Poznań, Grzegorz Szamotulski, in his *Vincula Hyppocratis* pamphlet, was quite typical when he accused the alleged Lutheran, Christoph Hegendorff, of bringing to their city 'a time of sedition and confusion, contamination with error, tumults, and factions.'[96] In Grunau's chronicle, we have a picture of near anarchy—the Lutheran rebels of Danzig, plotting to blow up the King and murder 700 fellow citizens, are so violently inclined that even Duke Albrecht tells them: 'I have the impression that

---

[87] Bossy, 'The Mass as a Social Institution'.   [88] AT 7, p. 11.

[89] For disorder as the great fear of sixteenth-century Western society, see Stuart Clark, 'Inversion, Misrule and the Meaning of Witchcraft', *Past & Present* 87 (1980): 98–127.

[90] See for example Alexander Patschovsky, 'Heresy and Society'.

[91] AT 7, p. 155.   [92] AT 8, p. 16.

[93] CIP, III, pp. 579, 649; CIP, IV, p. 3. See also Chapter Four, on edicts and disorder.

[94] AT 7, p. 389.

[95] Rydziński, *Petri Risinii* (unnumbered pages); Krzycki, *Encomia*; Leonard Cox, dedicatory letter, in Erasmus, *Hyperaspistes* (Kraków, 1526).

[96] Szamotulski, *Vincula*, fo. Avii(v), 'tempus seditiosius et confusivus…erroribus contaminare, tumultibusque ac factionibus'.

your Gospel does not want anything else except bloodshed, and that it causes discord and outrage.'[97]

Lutheranism was seen in these sources to lead to anarchy, not just because heresies always do, but because of two specific features it possessed: Martin Luther's irresponsible teaching on Christian liberty (i.e. spiritual equality), and also the mischievous preaching of this idea to the 'vulgar' by his followers. The draconian anti-Reformation edict of summer 1523 noted that Luther's words inspired people to act 'on the pretext of Christian liberty'.[98] To the royal court, Christian liberty was not just a threat to order, but to the very idea of monarchy itself. The King blamed the 1525 peasants' revolt in Ducal Prussia squarely on the preaching of Christian liberty, warned Poznań that this teaching was simply a licence to sin, and declared in 1527 that 'evangelical liberty' upset human laws, destroyed social order, caused seditions, tumults, and sacrilege, and meant that kings were no longer kings.[99] These claims were echoed in the correspondence of Polish bishops.[100] Andrzej Krzycki in both his polemics, *Encomia* and the *De Afflictione*, stressed in vivid terms that Christian liberty released people from all law and obedience to civil authority, presenting 'kings and princes as tyrants'.[101] The ruling elite of Poland-Prussia had no doubt, moreover, that Lutheran preachers deliberately targeted the lowest social groups. As the August 1523 edict grimly noted, 'on the pretext of Christian liberty... they spread their virus among the *vulgi*'.[102] Primate Łaski, in his 1525 memo, could barely mask his contempt at the Danzig radical preachers who targeted their message at 'the vilest plebeians'.[103] Krzycki's *Encomia Luteri* also warned the Crown that Lutheranism led to the 'insolence of the *vulgi*'.[104]

In their equation of Lutheranism with revolt, Polish-Prussian elites had much in common with commentators in the Holy Roman Empire, or even faraway Iberia, in these years. In the Empire, Thomas Murner's anti-Luther tract had, as early as 1522, featured a woodcut in which the Saxon held aloft a shoe (*Bundschuh*), the traditional symbol of peasant revolt.[105] Fabri wrote furiously in 1528 that Lutheranism was sedition, tumult, discord, and faction: 'This church of yours is tumultuous, muddling everything with sword and fire, sweating with the blood of poor [peasants].'[106] The Spanish Inquisition linked Castile's *comuneros* revolt of the 1520s with Lutheranism.[107] To Sigismund I, a 'Luteranus' was an armed blacksmith, peasant, or apprentice brewer. Writing to Duke Albrecht in 1527, Sigismund I described an underground conspiracy of 'Lutherans' at work in Prussia, dangerous plebeians travelling across borders in disguise, fermenting rebellion—a counter-society of the sort that witches and vagrants were accused of inhabiting later in the century.[108] For the old king, this nightmare vision (far more than, say, *sola fide*) came close to capturing the essence

---

[97] *Simon Grunau's Preussische Chronik*, III, pp. 172, 184–5.   [98] CIP, III, p. 29.
[99] AT 8, p. 151; AT 10, p. 41. See also Zins, *Powstanie*, p. 133.
[100] AT 7, pp. 210, 387–9.   [101] Krzycki, *De Afflictione*, dedicatory letter.
[102] CIP, III, p. 29, 'virus suum in vulgus spargunt'.   [103] AT 7, pp. 387–9.
[104] Krzycki, *Encomia*, fo. F.
[105] R. W. Scribner, 'Images of the Peasant, 1514–25', *Journal of Peasant Studies* 3:1 (1975): 29–48.
[106] Fabri, *Adversus doctorem Balthasarum*, fos. Aij(v), Aiii(v), F: 'Haec illa vestra est tumultuaria ecclesia, ferro flammaque omnia miscens, sanguine caesorum miserorum agrestium exudans.'
[107] Hamilton, *Heresy and Mysticism*, p. 72.   [108] *Elementa*, p. 10.

of Lutheranism in the 1520s. Martin Luther famously distanced himself from social rebels, and he would have approved warmly of the fact that modern scholarship identifies these commoners and their leaders, such as Thomas Müntzer, as 'Anabaptists' or participants in a 'radical Reformation'. Nonetheless, the elites of Poland-Prussia were very clear—all such people were 'Lutherans'.

If we look at how our sources label Lutheranism throughout the period, the vocabulary of schism is pronounced, occurring in a quarter of them: 'lutherani' are a 'faction', 'schism', or 'sect' (ninety-two texts). Lutheranism was persistently called a 'sect', both by the Crown and church (fifty-eight texts). Sect was originally a non-pejorative term, meaning in the ancient world a group, but in the epistles of the New Testament it took on more negative connotations of wilful division of the Christian community.[109] King Sigismund, Tomicki, and members of the royal council regularly complained of the 'Lutheran sect' in Danzig, Poznań, and Thorn, particularly in the mid-1520s.[110] In 1534, Tomicki was still grumbling about 'the Lutheran sect in Danzig' and 'the Lutheran sect in Kraków'.[111] Notably, in the trial records of those brought before church courts for alleged Lutheranism, in only a mere six cases did the official charge include any reference to heresy. Instead, the principal charge—in over 50 per cent of cases, i.e. thirty-one—was 'being of the Lutheran sect'.[112] Thus, Jacobus the Kraków tailor (1525), and two Poznań 'workers', Henricus Falkner and Thomas Stanski (1535), were tried for 'being of the Lutheran sect'. A private tutor from the household of a Kraków consul was charged likewise with 'being of the Lutheran sect'.[113]

The label 'faction', a splinter group, was also favoured. Bishop Tomicki could write in 1525 that the 'factione luterana' was strong across Prussia, going on to describe it more precisely as 'this faction in the Christian church'.[114] Bishop Krzycki, when planning to effect the conversion of Melanchthon in Poland, wrote that it was well known the Saxon wished to leave 'this faction'.[115] Faction did not have an exclusively ecclesiastical meaning in sixteenth-century Poland. The Crown, for example, complained regularly in 1525–6 about 'factions' in Danzig, meaning divisions and divisive groupings in civic government. 'Factions' meant the act of splitting into troublesome little groups, disturbing concord, a phenomenon which affected, and cut across, both spiritual and earthly affairs. Sigismund I could thus describe the Danzig Reformation revolt simply as the actions of factious men.[116]

Lutheranism was also defined explicitly in terms of religious schism (nineteen texts). In the fifteenth century, 'schismatic' had been used in the Polish monarchy mainly as a pejorative reference to the Orthodox church, and particularly to its great rival Muscovy.[117] These meanings continued in the 1520s and 1530s—Sigismund

---

[109] N. Weber, 'Sect and Sects', in *The Catholic Encyclopedia*, vol. 13 (New York, 1912).
[110] AT 7, pp. 11, 160; AT 8, pp. 147, 151; AT 10, pp. 191, 310.
[111] AT 16b, pp. 432–4. [112] See Appendix 1.
[113] BJ, MS 3227, fos. 70, 71; AAP, AE VII, fo. 331(v).
[114] AT 7, p. 210; AT 8, pp. 35–6, 62; AT 14, pp. 229–30. [115] AT 15, pp. 637–8.
[116] AT 8, pp. 76, 113, 153: 'factiones intestinas', 'autores et patratores factionum et seditionum intestinarum'.
[117] See for example the polemical tract by Johannes Sacranus, *Elucidarius Errorum Ritus Rutenici* (Kraków, c.1505).

I could thus sign a treaty of alliance against the 'infidel and schismatics' with Mecklenberg in 1524, and Duke Albrecht too referred to the Muscovites as schismatics.[118] A schismatic could, more loosely, be anybody who defied church authority. Andrzej Krzycki, embroiled in a bitter dispute with local elites in his Płock diocese, could refer to these men as 'my afflictors and schismatics'.[119] From *c.*1523, however, 'schismatic' came to also mean a supporter of the Reformation. A royal anti-Lutheran edict talked of 'schismatics', while an organist and manuscript illuminator arrested by the Kraków diocesan authorities in 1525 were both accused in court of partaking in 'the Lutheran schism'.[120] Byliński, in his *Defensorium*, openly wrote of 'Luther the schismatic'.[121] Prince-bishop Ferber, in his major 1524 decree against Lutheran heresy in Ermland, concluded that those disregarding his prohibitions would be regarded as 'schismatics' (this term used instead of 'heretics' in the crucial legal clauses requiring pastoral obedience).[122] In medieval Christian rhetoric, heresy and schism were close siblings: although, under canon law, heresy was a different, graver category of offence. Significantly, these Polish-Prussian sources often referred to the early Reformation as schism, *without* also labelling it a 'haeresia'. This arguably placed Lutheranism in a rhetorical or mental category similar to that occupied by the Orthodox church.

In addition to an explicit language of splitting and schism, however, many of the beliefs and behaviours attributed to Lutherans convey the same message, being apparently sectarian in nature. At first glance, Figure 7.1 would seem to suggest that Lutheran rejection of catholic teaching was (as we might expect) the problem: rejection of saintly cults, fasting, traditional liturgy, and use of devotional images. Finding a similar pattern in the Netherlands, Alistair Duke suggested that authorities there saw the early Reformation as an epidemic of religious denial, a withdrawing of belief in the quasi-magical power of saints, holy water, and miracle-working images.[123] However, if we look more closely we might posit that Polish-Prussian catholics were offended by Lutheran rejection of such practices not necessarily because they perceived them as non-negotiable catholic theological dogmas per se, but rather because they saw these practices as being integral to the functioning of Christian social unity on the ground.

The single 'belief' position most commonly associated with Lutheranism in these Polish-Prussian sources was, for example, rejection of the cult of saints (twenty-seven texts). A whole generation of scholarship has established that late medieval saintly cults were central reference points in urban, regional, and national identity—as foci for civic and parish ritual, shared patrons, heavenly protectors.[124] Their rejection scandalized many observers in King Sigismund's

---

[118] AT 7, p. 10; AT 13, p. 118.   [119] AT 13, p. 56, 'mei turbatores ac scismatici'.
[120] CIP, IV, p. 29; BJ, MS 3227, fo. 70.
[121] Byliński, *Defensorium*, fo. 40(v). For invocations of schism by other polemicists, see Krzycki, *De Afflictione*, fo. Cii(v); Wróbel, *Propugnaculum*, fos. 218, 297, 299; Szamotulski, *Vincula*, fo. B.
[122] *Spicilegium Copernicanum*, p. 324.   [123] Duke, *Reformation and Revolt*, p. 41–57.
[124] See, for example, Richard Trexler, 'Lorenzo de' Medici and Savonarola: Martyrs for Florence', *Renaissance Quarterly* 31:3 (1978): 293–308; Donald Weinstein and Rudolph Bell, *Saints and Society: The Two Worlds of Western Christianity, 1000–1700* (Chicago, 1982); David Rosand, *Myths of Venice:*

monarchy. In June 1525, Benedictus Byenek and the preacher Andreas were accused before the Kraków episcopal court of attacking local saintly cults—Byenek for claiming that local relics were calf bones and not the remains of the 11,000 virgins, and Andreas for preaching in St Mary's church that it was more useful to kiss an ass than the head of Poland's patron St Stanislas, the kingdom's most venerated relic.[125] In Simon Grunau's *Prussian Chronicle*, we hear of a Danzig mayor calling Mary (the traditional patron of Prussia) 'a whore of heaven', monks from Wittenberg claiming she had broken her oath to God by not remaining a virgin in the temple in Jerusalem, and Lutheran noblemen refusing to use coins of the realm which carried an image of the Virgin, declaring these a blasphemy against God.[126] When Jakub of Iłża became the first person to be legally condemned for Lutheran heresy in the kingdom, the first article of the sentence stated that he had declared that the cults of the Virgin Mary and saints were not essential to salvation.[127] Dantiscus refused to accept Kaspar Lisman as a canon of Chełmno, because he had earlier preached against saintly intercession 'and other Lutheranisms'.[128] Wróbel's *Propugnaculum* dedicated a whole chapter to the Lutherans' denial of saintly cults and intercession. Saints and their relics were prominent in the mental, social, and spatial worlds of late medieval city communities such as Kraków, as Aleksandra Witkowska has shown, and reformers' attacks thus shocked.[129]

The non-observance of late medieval church fasts (Fridays, Advent, and Lent) also greatly exercised many observers in Sigismund I's kingdom (twenty-three texts). Walenty Wróbel dedicated the very first chapters of his weighty anti-Reformation work to the question of Lutheran denials of fasts, as a primary Lutheran offence.[130] Stanisław Byliński too opened his 1535 polemic by pointing out with outrage that Lutherans condemned fasting, preferring to serve their stomachs rather than Christ.[131] In the church courts of Kraków, non-observance of fasting was the single most common basis for an accusation of Lutheranism in the 1520s and 1530s alike. Hannus Lembork, a member of the household of the leading merchant Johannes Haller, was one of five men accused in 1532 of 'being of the Lutheran sect and eating meat on prohibited days'.[132] A poem by Andrzej Krzycki described floods of the Vistula as Neptune's punishment on the Prussians for eating meat on fast days.[133] Simon Grunau too found such actions deeply shocking. In Lutheran Königsberg, he told his readers there were no fast days, and he felt compelled to spell out what this meant: 'they ate the same things on Sundays as

The Figuration of a State (Chapel Hill, NC, 2001); Gerald Parsons, *The Cult of Saint Catherine of Siena: A Study in Civic Religion* (Aldershot, 2008).
    125 BJ, MS 3227, fo. 71. See also the trial of the King's builder, fo. 75.
    126 *Simon Grunau's Preussische Chronik*, II, pp. 655, 760; III, p. 193.
    127 BJ, MS 3227, fo. 74.   128 AT 17, p. 128.
    129 Aleksandra Witkowska, *Kulty pątnicze piętnastowiecznego Krakowa: z badań nad miejską kulturą religijną* (Lublin, 1984).
    130 Wróbel, *Propugnaculum.*
    131 Byliński, *Defensorium*, fos. 2(v), 10–19(v), and dedicatory letter. See also Krzycki, *Encomia.*
    132 BJ, MS 3227, fo. 75.   133 Discussed in Nowak-Dłużewski, *Poezja*, p. 88.

they ate during the week'.[134] Fasts were also a key, visible part of the community's shared religious life—people ate fish on Fridays, and abjured meat throughout Lent, in a collective devotional act. Work on early medieval and medieval Europe has shown how central a facet of social interaction both feasting and fasting were.[135]

Also high in Polish-Prussian elite consciousness was Reformation disruption of aspects of collective worship in parish churches—sacraments, iconoclasm, and ceremonies (forty-five texts in total). The polemicists Canon Rydziński and Wróbel complained that Lutherans had dispensed with vestments and church decorations, like Judas despising things designed to bring glory to God.[136] Grunau's chronicle recounted with wonder how the Lutheran bishop Queis had told the canons at Marienwerder to use no crucifixes, and to sing no Masses.[137] Acts of iconoclasm— of violence against parish churches—also lurk in the background of the *Prussian Chronicle*: stained-glass windows smashed in Elbing, pictures urinated on in Braunsberg.[138] In Danzig, the Crown objected strongly to the looting of churches, to the removal of plate, pictures, liturgical books, and relics. Traditional liturgy, as fifteenth-century episcopal letters tell us, was an enactment of unity: a uniform set of service books, and uniform workshop, mirrored the unity of the *ecclesia*.[139] The parish church was a focal point for local social identity, and this too was deemed threatened by Lutheranism.

The cumulative effect of all this—revolt, faction, denials of traditional communal rites—was to make Lutheranism look like a series of public acts of secession, from a church which was strongly identified with society itself. As Primate Łaski warned King Sigismund, Lutherans 'separate themselves from the rites and observances of the ecclesiastical community of the faithful'.[140] In 1527, the Crown announced that the new Lutheran sect threatened 'the holy catholic church' and 'the peace and unity of the kingdom'.[141] Bishop Ferber warned in 1532 that Dutch Lutherans and Zwinglians in Elbing imperilled with their conventicles 'the unity of the faith and civil concord'—his letter thus equating religious unity and social peace.[142] The Kraków citizens who did not fast along with their fellow Christians in the city, or the Danzig zealots who destroyed images of saints in parish churches, were engaging in public acts of separation from Christian society and their neighbours. This reached its logical culmination when Reformation supporters took the radical step of forming their own religious meeting groups (if not yet formally

---

[134] *Simon Grunau's Preussische Chronik*, II, p. 718: 'und war in Konigsberg kein fasttagk noch fiertagk; gleichswie man ass am sontage, so ass man auch am freitage'.

[135] For anthropologically influenced readings of fasting in the medieval world, see Caroline Walker Bynum, *Holy Feast and Holy Fast: The Religious Significance of Food to Medieval Women* (Berkeley, 1987) and Bonny Effros, *Creating Community with Food and Drink in Merovingian Gaul* (New York, 2002), who argues that fasting/feasting was a key facet of social interaction.

[136] Rydziński, *Petri Risinii* (unnumbered pages); Wróbel, *Propugnaculum*, dedicatory letter, fo. Av(v).

[137] *Simon Grunau's Preussische Chronik*, vol. III, pp. 110–11.

[138] *Simon Grunau's Preussische Chronik*, vol. III, pp. 213–17.

[139] Nowakowska, 'From Strassburg to Trent', pp. 15–16.

[140] AT 7, p. 389: 'ob ritus et observationes quasdam a communi fidelium ecclesia se separare'.

[141] AT 9, p. 287.   [142] AT 14, p. 229: 'in unitate fidei ac civili concordia'.

congregations)—such as the Elbing reformers who met in the city armoury, or the Danzigers who assembled to hear sermons outside the city walls.[143] Lutheranism, then, was constituted by acts which individually and collectively repudiated the fabric and patterns of everyday religious life on the ground, of the things in which Christians publicly, collectively, and piously participated. This echoes the Inquisition in Castile, which policed with such ferocity not the inner theological beliefs of converted Jews and Muslims, but their external cultural conformity with catholic society in matters such as dress and food: couscous eating and avoidance of pork, acts of secession, and difference.[144] This was, therefore, a heresy above all of (social) schism. This is highly reminiscent of Rowan Williams' findings on the early church—where he argues that heretics were alarming and above all anomalous, not for the content of their beliefs per se, but for their willingness to split from the community of Christians, in social schism.[145]

THE PRO-REFORMATION PERSPECTIVE

What, however, did Reformation supporters in Sigismund I's Poland understand Lutheranism to be? This body of texts is smaller (around twenty) because fewer have survived, but they speak in an entirely different voice. Firstly, followers of the Reformation were adamant about what they were not, firmly resisting the labels Lutheran, rebel, and schismatic (and indeed any labels at all). Only Duke Albrecht self-identified as a Lutheran, writing to his agent at the Polish court that it was well known 'that we are...Lutheran'.[146] It was more common for people to deny that their Word-based faith had anything to do with Martin Luther—Laurentius Corvinus declared, for example, that he had no opinion 'on the person Luther', and that the beliefs he held were those of the Gospel, not doctrines devised by a single human being.[147] The prolix Danzig Apologias presented to King Sigismund in 1525 made no reference whatsoever to Luther or Wittenberg, calling themselves simply 'the church of Danzig'.[148] Similarly, the mayor of Danzig reassured his local bishop in 1535 that the evangelical preacher Pancratius Klemme had nothing 'de Lutereye' about him.[149]

Reformation texts rejected too the charge that they disobeyed civil authority. The Danzig Apologias explained that violence in the city was the result not of Reformation doctrines, but of the seditious provocations of monks.[150] In 1526, Duke Albrecht conceded that the Reformation revolts in Prussia might have put the Polish king off Lutheranism, but tried to distance 'my faith' from those

---

[143] Waldoch, 'Początki reformacji', p. 17.

[144] Wandel, *Reformation*, pp. 17–18, and Deborah Root, 'Speaking Christian: Orthodoxy and Difference in Sixteenth-Century Spain', *Representations* 23 (1988): 118–34.

[145] Williams, 'Defining Heresy'.

[146] AT 15, p. 713: 'das wir nit allein Luterisch, sonder Evangelisch und dem unwandelbarenn, allein heylmachenden, wortt gods...anhenging'.

[147] Byliński, *Defensorium*, fo. B13(v).

[148] AT 7, pp. 358–66, subtitled as 'ratio doctrine ministrorum ecclesie Dantiscane'.

[149] AT 17, pp. 67–8.   [150] AT 7, p. 370.

events.[151] He drew a careful distinction between 'criminals' and peaceful married clergy.[152] Similarly, Albrecht did not recognize the peasants who had revolted against his regent and nobles in 1525 as fellow Lutherans, any more than did evangelical princes in the Reich. Supporters of Luther across the social spectrum therefore insisted, with Luther himself, that the new teaching was no threat to civil order.

These texts also deny the charge of schism. Just as the rebelling peasants of the Holy Roman Empire stressed that their faith was one of 'peace, patience and unity', the Danzig Apologias declared that they had brought 'pax christiana', concord, and religious unity to the port.[153] In 1535, Danzig's pro-Reformation council refused to swear an oath of loyalty to the 'Roman church', but was willing to swear fealty to the Polish Crown and (a broader) 'Christian church'.[154] Laurentius Corvinus asserted that he was a true member 'of the holy mother church'.[155] These claims closely echoed developments in the Holy Roman Empire where, as Dantiscus reported, at the Augsburg Diet of 1530 the Lutheran princes refused to be described as 'a new sect or dogma', or as anything other than members of the Christian church.[156]

The Reformation in Sigismund I's Polish monarchy was, unsurprisingly, not theologically homogenous. Ringleaders of the 1525 Danzig revolt, such as Jakub Knade, studied at Wittenberg, but later became involved in sacramentarian circles.[157] Their iconoclasm in Danzig, and the repeated reports that their followers profaned the Eucharist when looting churches, suggest that these more 'radical' elements already played a role in the 1525–6 revolt.[158] Pancratius Klemme, Danzig's chief preacher from *c*.1529, spent time with Luther in Wittenberg, but his library also contained works by other reformers such as Bugenhagen, Bullinger, Hutten, and Dorp (all stamped with Danzig's city arms).[159] Duke Albrecht himself would break with Luther in 1549, when he invited Osiander to Königsberg to take the Reformation in a new direction.[160] Nevertheless, when defining themselves in positive (rather than defensive) terms, Sigismund I's pro-Reformation vassals and subjects spoke as one.

Pro-Reformation supporters defined themselves above all, and unanimously, with reference to a single doctrine of salvation—*sola fide*. The Danzig Apologia, for example, painstakingly explained the Fall, the sinful nature of man, the futility of good works, and faith in Christ alone as the sole path to salvation—this was 'nostra doctrina' and anyone who thought otherwise had been persuaded by false faith, and was a heretic.[161] The Danzig texts presented the advent of *sola fide* in sixteenth-century Europe as a dramatic divine intervention in history: a precious pearl, born

[151] *Urkundenbuch*, II, pp. 153–4.   [152] AT 8, p. 143.
[153] Peter Blickle, *The Revolution of 1525: The German Peasants' War from a New Perspective* (Baltimore, 1981), p. 195; AT 7, p. 370.
[154] AT 17, p. 456.   [155] Byliński, *Defensorium*, fo. 54.   [156] AT 12, p. 285.
[157] *Urkundenbuch*, II, pp. 294–5, 328.   [158] See Chapters One and Two.
[159] Nowak and Urban, 'Pankracy Klemme', pp. 117, 121–4.
[160] Martin Stupperich, *Osiander in Preussen* (Berlin, 1973).   [161] AT 7, pp. 359–60.

on a divine wind, which appeared simultaneously in many languages.[162] Laurentius Corvinus informed Archdeacon Byliński that *sola fide* was the truth, which alone could lead people into the kingdom of light.[163] Christoph Hegendorff, lecturer at the Poznań Academy, expounded the doctrine of *sola fide* in his inaugural lecture and sought to prove its veracity by expressing it as a syllogism: either we are justified by faith in Christ, or Christ died in vain, but as Christ did not die in vain, we are therefore saved by faith.[164] Bishop Briesemann too made *sola fide* the centrepiece of his 110 Articles, stating that it led to justification, and to teach salvation by works was a 'pernicious doctrine', an 'error', and 'impious'.[165] The true Christian knew this, and he alone was 'a king in the spiritual kingdom'.[166] Pro-Reformation texts composed in the Polish monarchy presented *sola fide* as constituting the essence of Christian orthodoxy.

If catholic sources from Sigismund I's Poland betray a marked ambivalence towards Lutheranism—it's Otherness an open question—pro-Reformation texts, as we shall see more fully in Chapter Eight, had no doubt about the depraved nature of the late medieval church. The Danzig Apologias characterize the old church as a darkness from which God had turned his face, a place of 'errors, deceptions, and seductions', a long-lasting Phariseical age, a time of heresies inspired by the Devil.[167] The 1525 Ducal Prussian Reformation Ordinance declared that those who had declared themselves to be Christians (the old church) had been 'alienated from Christ' for many years.[168] Similarly, the Lutheran theses published by Bishop Briesemann stated that those in the old church were not Christians, but 'servile and vile, not priests', hypocrites, lost in darkness. The old church is described as a place of the spiritually dead, where faith, grace, and Christian liberty have been extinguished.[169] From this pro-Reformation standpoint, the late medieval church was thus a place of acute spiritual danger and an implacable opponent.

In other words, pro-Reformation texts (unlike a majority of catholic texts) are characterized by their binary view of religious difference, their sense of two irreconcilable polar opposites. Here, then, we find an overarching paradox. Polish royal and ecclesiastical 'toleration' or non-persecution of Lutherans in the 1520s and 1530s was, the evidence suggests, rooted in a world view in which those subjects of the Crown were (potential) schismatics who held bad doctrines, did naughty and sometimes reprehensible things, were associated with heresy, but were not an Other. King Sigismund would likely have agreed with Johann Fabri's brusque comment to his Anabaptist interlocutor in Prague in 1528: you may be in error, but you are still nonetheless in the one church.[170] Lutherans inspired bemusement, serious anxiety, but not genuine terror or a thoroughgoing hatred

[162] AT 7, p. 367.
[163] Byliński, *Defensorium*, fos. 13–13(v).
[164] Hegendorff, quoted in Szamotulski, *Vincula*, fo. Dij(v): 'aut fide in Christum iustificamur, aut Christus frustra mortus est. Sed Christus frustra mortus non est, ergo fide in Christum iustificamur'.
[165] Printed in Giese, *Anthelogikon* (articles 15–44, 77, 80, 100–1).
[166] Giese, *Anthelogikon* (article 44).   [167] AT 7, pp. 359, 364–9.
[168] Stupperich, *Die Reformation*, p. 109.
[169] Printed in Giese, *Anthelogikon* (articles 57, 67, 69, 85).
[170] Fabri, *Adversus doctorem Balthasarem*, fo. Ggi(v).

(a small minority of commentators aside, such as Grunau who had likely experienced Danzig's anti-clerical violence of 1525). To King Sigismund and Bishop Tomicki, 'luteranismus' was more akin to the naughty comedy devils who populate Luther's own German writings, than the mighty Satan who stalked the anti-heresy sermons of the thirteenth century.[171] The spectre invoked by Lutheranism in this monarchy was more akin to the chaos of the Great Schism of 1378, than to the twelfth-century Cathars with their terrifying, non-creedal dualist beliefs. In contrast, Reformation supporters did emphatically perceive the late medieval Latin church as an enemy, and Other. For a community or society to split, of course, it only takes one side to decide they no longer have enough in common with the other.

---

[171] For devils as figures of mischief in Luther's work, see Lyndal Roper, 'Martin Luther's Body: The "Stout Doctor" and his Biographers', *American Historical Review* 115:2 (2010): 351–84.

8

Defining Catholicism

INTRODUCTION

What did the catholic elites living in Sigismund I's Polish monarchy in the turbulent 1520s and 1530s understand the church to be? Scholars such as Pelikan, Hendrix, and Yves Congar have examined how late medieval theologians answered that question, in an explosion of treatises on ecclesiology produced in Latin Christendom from *c*.1300.[1] This chapter takes an alternative approach. Employing the same methodology as Chapter Seven, it analyses the language used in a diverse corpus of around 500 texts to see how the *ecclesia* (or what we might call catholicism) was labelled, described, explained, and constructed in the context of the early Reformation.[2] Such language analysis enables us to capture the pre-confessional self-understanding of the catholic church in this monarchy, with its often unfamiliar reference points, and also a slow shift in the definition of catholicism in Poland-Prussia, as small steps were taken towards a more confessionalized standpoint. This chapter and the previous one form two parts of one whole, because the discourses of *luteranismus* and *ecclesia* were necessarily interrelated in the context of the early Reformation. These were not two separate clouds of language and ideas sitting alongside one another, but systems which (as we shall see) were intermeshed, and acted upon one another.

The first part of this chapter will discuss Figure 8.1, which illustrates the findings of the language analysis. It shows that *ecclesia* had a broad, diffuse, or even fragmented semantic field—so much so that there was precious little agreement even on what this church was called. Three key aspects of catholicism, as it is constructed in these sources, emerge from that chart. The church was defined with insistent reference to the past, on which its unity and consensus rested; to key leadership figures within it (the pope notable by his extremely faint presence); and to a range of practices which Lutherans had attacked and rejected. Moving away from the still snapshot provided by Figure 8.1, we then examine the important changes in catholic self-definition detectable in these sources by the 1530s, before considering how supporters of the Reformation themselves defined this late medieval church. As such, discourse analysis provides an important plane on which to plot the impact of the Reformation, and the dramatic changes it wrought on thought, language, and articulations of identity in a society such as Sigismund I's Polish monarchy.

---

[1] Pelikan, *The Christian Tradition*, vol. 4; Hendrix, 'In Quest of the Vera Ecclesia'; Congar, *L'Ecclésiologie*.

[2] For methodology, see Chapter Seven, pp. 174–6.

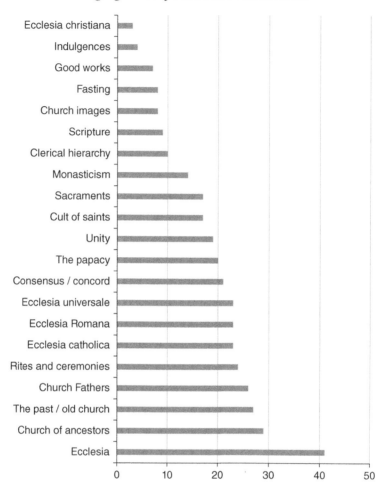

Figure 8.1 Construction of the church in sources from the Polish monarchy (1518 to *c.*1540).

Defining the Church from Within

The wide variety of names given to the church in these sources, and indeed the frequent absence of any name at all, is a useful entry point into Polish-Prussian views of the *ecclesia* at the very outset of the Reformation. In the majority of these texts the late medieval church is not even directly invoked—it is simply there, in the background, so big, all-encompassing, and institutionally enormous that it was often unnecessary to talk of it as an abstracted whole, or explain what it was.[3] It

---

[3] This is why Figure 8.1 has fewer entries than Figure 7.1 in Chapter Seven: while many texts in this sample of around 500 define Lutheranism in some way, explicit and implicit definitions of catholicism are rarer.

was perfectly possible to write about Lutheranism without juxtaposing its teaching explicitly with 'the church' as an entity—in 1525–6, for example, the Crown could accuse a Lutheran-led town like Danzig of ejecting monks, installing wicked preachers, and looting monastic buildings, without specifically labelling all this as an attack on 'the church' as an international institution, or as a concept.[4] The church, when invoked, usually referred to the local and specific—a bishop like Mauritius Ferber in Ermland was much more likely to talk of '*ecclesia mea*' (meaning his diocese) than he was of the international, eternal '*ecclesia*'.[5] Figure 8.1 shows that even where the church in general was referred to, it was given a wide variety of possible names. The most common label used was, tellingly, 'the church', '*ecclesia*', suggesting a perception that there was by definition only one church, which required no qualifier or name. They talked too of the 'universal church' and, in a label perhaps more familiar to us, of the 'catholic church'.

This Polish-Prussian vagueness in nomenclature is worth setting in context, as it was far from unique. Imprecision also characterizes the writings of Charles V and his brother Ferdinand Habsburg on the Reformation, who wrote in very general terms, in descending order of frequency, of 'nostra sancte foy', 'the Christian religion', and referred to the church variously as the church, the 'universal church' (*gemeine*), and only sometimes the 'Roman church'.[6] French royal texts on the Reformation in the 1520s and 1530s also tend to describe the thing under threat as 'la foi catholique', 'l'esglise', or the 'ecclesiastical polity'.[7] In marked contrast, the papal pronouncements on the Reformation addressed to the Polish monarchy employed a much tighter vocabulary, in which the church was consistently called 'Sancta Romana Ecclesia'—a formula so familiar that it was regularly abbreviated and also capitalized for emphasis, appearing simply as 'S. R. E'.[8] In late medieval Latin Europe, outside Rome, it seems a low premium was placed on giving the church a precise, agreed name.

In articulating the church's actual characteristics, the Polish-Prussian sources define it principally with reference to the past. The *maiori* or *patri* (ancestors) of early sixteenth-century Latin Christians were, for example, regularly invoked (twenty-nine texts), featuring as one of the very top categories in Figure 8.1. As early as 1522/3, a Crown delegation to Danzig urged its citizens to accept 'the religion they had accepted, the one used by their fathers'.[9] The anti-heresy legal settlements imposed on Danzig, Elbing, and Braunsberg by the Crown in 1526 all insisted these towns return to the faith which had been handed down to them by 'ancestors', as a benchmark of orthodoxy.[10] The Lutheran princes Duke Albrecht

---

[4] AT 7, pp. 318–19.   [5] AAWa, Acta Ep. 1, fo. 270v and *passim*.

[6] Based on an analysis of texts about the early Reformation in *Correspondenz des Kaisers Karl V*, vols. 1 and II; RTA II and V–X.

[7] Printed in Herminjard, *Correspondence*, III, pp. 300–1; *Recueil générale des anciennes lois fran- caise*, ed. A. Jourdan et al., 29 vols. (1822–33), vol. 12, pp. 676, 681, 405–7, i.e. Edicts of Fontainebleu and Coucy.

[8] Wojtyska, *Zacharias Ferreri*, pp. 42, 87, 113, 133; Konarski, *Bulla contra errores* (1520); AT 7, p. 295; AT 17, p. 536–7.

[9] AT 7, p. 10, 'religionem, uti illam a patribus suis acceperunt'.

[10] AT 8, pp. 77, 109–10.

and Gustav of Sweden were also urged by Sigismund I to accept the church 'as your ancestors did'.[11] To papal Rome, the King declared that he honoured the holy see because this is what had been handed down to him by his own ancestors.[12] Charles V's 1524 imperial edict addressed his German subjects much as Sigismund I had the Danzigers, ordering them to hold onto the religious teaching, law, and practice observed by their ancestors, 'unsere volaltern'.[13] Johann Fabri too opened his Leipzig-printed polemic dedicated to George of Saxony by describing 'the orthodox faith' as that of 'our ancestors'.[14]

The church was also defined with reference to history, to the past itself (twenty-seven texts). The Christian historic past was presented in general terms as a largely undifferentiated block of time. Only Archdeacon Byliński, in his 1535 *Defensorium*, presented anything approaching a historical narrative or framework, with his lists of church doctors and councils.[15] Time and centuries, stacked up on one another in the abstract, were key refrains when discussing the church. Primate Łaski wrote of the teaching 'embraced by the universal church from the times of the apostles to our own day', and Sigismund I in similar terms of 'the norms of the universal church observed for so many centuries'.[16] Duke Albrecht was told he was wrong to dismantle the shrine of St Dorothy at Marienwerder because it had been a holy place for so many centuries.[17] As such, catholicism could be called 'the old church' or religion. The royal secretary, Jan Zambocki, explained that Sigismund I's edicts were there to 'vindicate the old religion', the Danzig Statutes of 1526 set up the 'old religion' as the proper norm, and a poem written for Sigismund Augustus' coronation talked of 'the very old religion'.[18] Similarly, Elbing was told by the Crown that wills must be done 'in the old way', without any anti-ecclesiastical sentiments recorded in them, and the ruler of Oppeln in Silesia that his subjects must pay the St Peter's pence tax 'in the old way'.[19] The church, in other words, was commonly understood simply as the church which was, and which had been. This too was a theme embraced by two other prominent, if very different, catholic actors of the early sixteenth century, Charles V and Erasmus of Rotterdam, who stressed that the church had held its teachings 'for over a thousand years, to the present day', or '1500 years'.[20]

Another reference point for church identity firmly located in its past were the church Fathers (invoked or discussed in twenty-three texts). The Fathers were a corpus of late antique theologians, presented here as central interpreters of Scripture

---

[11] AT 12, p. 12; AT 8, p. 43.   [12] AT 16b, p. 257.

[13] RTA IV, pp. 496–8 (1524 imperial edict).

[14] Fabri, *Adversus doctorem Balthasarum*, fo. Aij, 'orthodoxae fidei … maioribus nostris'.

[15] Byliński, *Defensorium*, fos. 22(v)–26.

[16] AT 7, p. 389, 'doctrinam ab apostolis nostra usque tempora universa ecclesia est amplexa'; AT 8, p. 53, 'norma universalis ecclesie tot seculis observata'.

[17] AT 9, p. 171.

[18] AT 7, p. 320, 'vindicandam veterem religionem'; AT 8, p. 77; AT 12, p. 412. See also AT 9, p. 170; AT 10, pp. 159, 409; AT 12, p. 371.

[19] AT 14, p. 667; AT 15, p. 361.

[20] RTA II, p. 595 (1520 edict); Erasmus, *De Libro Arbitrio*, CWE 76, p. 88; *Hyperaspistes*, CEW 76, pp. 139, 142, 201, 240, 254; CWE 78, pp. 229, 242.

and Revelation, listed by Archdeacon Stanisław Byliński for his Lutheran opponent as 'John of Thessalonica, Theophilus, Planudes, Theophilicatus, Origen, Christostom, Basil, Jerome, Augustine, Ambrose and Gregory and others.'[21] The Fathers are presented in these sources as an unimpeachable authority and tradition. In a plea to Duke Albrecht, Bishop Tomicki defended 'the old and holy rite, instituted by the holy Fathers', an anti-Lutheran poem by Leonard Cox praised the authority of the 'holy Fathers', and the Danzig Statute of 1526 ordered that the Word of God be preached in that city 'according to the sense and understanding of the holy doctors and the catholic church'.[22] Sigismund I spelt out that the Fathers' holiness was testified to by their pious lives and miracles.[23] The Fathers—and their works written before the seventh century CE, these holy and long-deceased scholars—were thus a historic anchor point for catholic identity statements in the Polish monarchy in the early sixteenth century.

The consensus which the church embodied reflected this long past (twenty-one texts). As Palmer Wandel put it, in the late medieval church catholic self-understanding was rooted in a sense of 'multiple voices who formed a consensus over time...not a single note as of a rigidly enforced orthodoxy'.[24] A delegation from rebellious Danzig were told by the Crown in 1525, for example, that they had violated 'the rites and institutes of the church, confirmed for so many centuries, by so many miracles, by the authority of the councils, popes, emperors, kings, kingdoms, and Christian nations...'—that is, historic consensus.[25] The Polish Royal Chancellery defined the church in this same way in interactions with King Gustav of Sweden, Duke Albrecht, or his bishops, the definition or defence automatically reached for.[26] Primate Łaski too wrote, in 1525, of the universal church 'as confirmed by the consensus of so many centuries'.[27] The Crown told Bishop Queis, of Ducal Prussia, that the church was characterized by the observance of 'unity and consensus', and this was what Christ had prayed for.[28] Clerical polemics, well beyond the court, also stressed consensus. Archdeacon Byliński pointed out that consensus was made visible in church councils: the first church council in Jerusalem had worked on a principle of 'unanimous consensus', and recent councils had gathered up to 600 learned men.[29] 'A general council', he wrote, is 'the consensus of the community of the faithful.'[30] Walenty Wróbel's *Propugnaculum* (1536) stated that ceremonies and the Mass were correct, because they were recognized by

---

[21] Byliński, *Defensorium*, fo. 40(v).

[22] AT 9, p. 170; Cox poem in Krzycki's *De Afflictione*, frontispiece; AT 8, p. 77, 'iuxta sensum et intellectum sanctorum doctorum et ecclesie catholice'.

[23] AT 8, p. 151.   [24] Palmer Wandel, *Reformation*, p. 6.

[25] AT 7, p. 404, 'vos ritum et instituta ecclesie, tot seculis, tot miraculis, tanta auctoritate conciliorum, pontificum, imperatorum, regum, regnorumque et nationum christianarum confirmata...violasse'.

[26] See Introduction, pp. 23–4.

[27] AT 7, p. 389: 'majorum autoritati, quorum doctrinam vita probata et universalis ecclesie per tot secula usus et consensus confirmavit'.

[28] AT 8, p. 132: 'utque in omnibus unitas et consensus observeratur, pro cujus fide orasse Christum, ut non deficeret'.

[29] Byliński, *Defensorium*, fos. 22v–23.

[30] Byliński, *Defensorium*, fo. 42(v): 'concilium generale representat cum omnium fidelium communi consensu et ita universalis ecclesie nomine celebretur'.

'the whole Christian world'.[31] Martin Luther, in his 1520 treatise on the papacy, attacked this universalist definition of the church early on, pointing out its obvious historical and geographical flaws. The pope's church could not be the universal church, he wrote, because of the many types of Christians in the world who did not accept the primacy of Rome, 'the Muscovites, the white Russians, the Greeks, the Bohemians, and many other great nations in the world are some examples'.[32] King Sigismund I, who lived in far greater proximity to these populations than did Luther himself, and who ruled so many Orthodox subjects within his own realms, clearly did not see them as an obstacle to his equation of catholicism and universalism.

Resting on this church's consensus, generated by it, was one of the church's quintessential characteristics as articulated in these sources, its unity (nineteen texts). Joseph Lecler observed that, in late medieval thinking, the unity of the church was essential because without it 'the breakdown would be complete'.[33] A royal edict of 1522 warned that 'the dogma of a certain Luther' endangers 'the unity of the Christian people'.[34] In Grunau's chronicle, the King is shown telling Albrecht that he cannot be a Lutheran, 'otherwise there won't be any peace or unity on this earth'.[35] In his *De Afflictione Ecclesiae*, Krzycki quoted Ephesians IV—'one body, one spirit, one faith, one baptism, one God'—to stress that 'the church is one', and that this was a basic tenet of Christian faith.[36] He who does not believe in church unity, Krzycki wrote, cannot be of the faith.[37] Byliński too made unity a major theme of his polemic: the church is a single light, universal in the whole world, he wrote. 'He who breaks the peace and concord of Christ, is against Christ'—again, being Christian means being in a unified church.[38] Gregorz Szamotulski, in Poznań, declared too that the church was not a building, but Christians united in one baptism and the sacraments; that is a single sacral community.[39] A church without unity, in this world view, had no claim to orthodoxy—a church which was not universal could not be catholic.

The images chosen to represent the *ecclesia* in Kraków-printed polemics reinforce this point. Whereas Lutheran imagery, such as Cranach's famous excreting donkey-pope, focused on the pontiff, in Polish works the church is instead represented with reference to the Holy Spirit—by a dove printed at the end of Giese's 1525 irenic *Anthelogikon*, and in the more elaborate woodcut in Byliński's *Defensorium* (Figure 8.2) as the Apostles and Mary huddled together in a crowd at Pentecost, the Holy Spirit hovering above them. This composition conveys the key message: the Holy Spirit as guarantor of unity, and the church itself as a harmonious community with its roots deep in the past.

---

[31] Wróbel, *Propugnaculum*, fos. Avii(v) and Pi(v).   [32] LW 39, p. 58.
[33] Lecler, *Toleration*, p. 71.
[34] CIP, III, p. 649: 'in regno nostro Lutheri cuisdam dogmata…in perturbationem communis status et unitatis populi christiani'.
[35] *Simon Grunau's Preussische Chronik*, vol. III, p. 170: 'sonstt wurde kein friede, noch einigkeitt auf erden sein'.
[36] Krzycki, *De Afflictione*, fos. Dii, Cii(v).
[37] Krzycki, *De Afflictione*, fo. Cii(v): 'hanc ecclesiae unitatem, qui non tenet, tenere se fidem credit?'
[38] Byliński, *Defensorium*, fos. 58(v)–60(v), at 60(v): 'Qui pacem Christi et concordiam rumpti, adversus Christum facit'.
[39] Szamotulski, *Vincula*, fo. 29.

Figure 8.2 Woodcut, *Defensorium Ecclesie adversus Laurentium Corvinum Lutherane hereseos sectatorem editum* by Stanisław Byliński. Printed in Kraków in 1531.

Biblioteka Jagiellońska, Kraków (Poland). Reproduced with permission.

An alternative point of reference in defining the church was its contemporary leadership—presented not so much as clergy, in these texts, as the princes of Europe (twenty-two texts). In explaining why Martin Luther was not to be listened to, Sigismund I routinely invoked European princely edicts, stressing that this teaching had been condemned by 'all Christian kings and princes'.[40] Kings and princes were depicted as embodying the values of the church—it is easier to find explicit explanations of what a catholic prince is like, than of what the catholic church is like. Sigismund I is said, in royal documents, to be a Christian prince in that he brings peace, ends discord, protects the Christian people, hears the Scriptures, and protects the church.[41] Princes, therefore, have tutelage over the church, and in some sense represent it and act for it. Perhaps a Royal Chancellery, and an anointed king, were especially likely to think in this flattering, prince-centred way about the church. Perhaps it reflected the experience of many European princes who were, by the 1520s, in effect largely running the church in their lands themselves, regardless of its international legal independence and structures.[42] Either way, this prince-focused vision of the universal church evokes a world before Gregory VII's (d.1085) bold programme of a church where all secular power was seen as inferior to the power of the pontiff. This church is both universal, and highly devolved in its self-understanding.

The pontiff and his great city of Rome, so important in catholic identity by the end of the sixteenth century, appear only halfway up Figure 8.1 (invoked in twenty texts). The Crown's anti-Reformation edicts, of 1520, gave as one of two reasons for banning Luther's works the fact that they 'contain much against the Holy See'.[43] In his correspondence with King Gustav and Duke Albrecht, King Sigismund specifically urged them to follow 'the apostolic see', while to Clement VII he promised that he was willing to shed his own blood for the good of Christendom 'and this holy apostolic see'.[44] Treatises and polemics sometimes asserted the pope's authority, and his power to loose and bind—over several paragraphs in Grzegorz Szamotulski's *Sermo de Indulgentiis*, in the nobleman Lachowski's letter to a Lutheran correspondent, in Bishop Międzyleski's correspondence with Hieronynm Łaski.[45] Piotr Tomicki too, trying to resist a petition from Queen Bona, stressed that as a bishop he owed special allegiance to the pope, 'the head of our religion'.[46] Walenty Wróbel, the Poznań lecturer, could write by 1536 that salvation required a belief in Peter as the one true pastor.[47]

These sources, however, present us overall with a highly limited vision of a papacy, one not central to catholic identity and, moreover, reliant on the goodwill of princes. Wróbel's 1536 anti-heresy treatise, for example, reaches the papacy only in

---

[40] AT 8, pp. 16, 78; *Simon Grunau's Preussische Chronik*, vol. III, p. 170.
[41] AT 7, pp. 277, 383; AT 8, pp. 131, 400.
[42] See John Thomson, *Popes and Princes, 1417–1517: Politics and Polity in the Late Medieval Church* (London, 1980); Nowakowska, *Church, State and Dynasty*.
[43] CIP, III, p. 579, 'in quibus multa continentur contra Sedem Apostolicam'.
[44] AT 8, pp. 43, 51; AT 7, p. 258.
[45] Szamotulski, *Sermo*; AT 10, pp. 213–15; AT 9, pp. 243–5.
[46] AT 17, p. 421, 'religio capitis nostri'.   [47] Wróbel, *Propugnaculum*, fo. Ff(v).

book 9, long after it has articulated a catholic identity with reference to fasting, faith, good works, penance, the Mass, communion in one kind, clerical celibacy, and saintly cults.[48] Krzycki, even as he was defending the Petrine succession in *Encomia Luteri*, conceded the possibility that the popes had abused their power.[49] As for the Crown, the contingent nature of its pro-papal sentiments was sharply revealed in 1534, when Sigismund I and Clement VII quarrelled badly in a benefice dispute. 'The authority of the holy apostolic see', wrote Tomicki to Cardinal Pucci, 'rests on the veneration of kings and princes.'[50] A church with a purely symbolic pope, with churches run locally by kings, was therefore one which Sigismund I could easily imagine, without feeling himself less catholic as a result; all this, in the very year that the English Crown broke with Rome with the Act of Supremacy.

In fact, many of the statements about the pontiffs in these sources emphasize one point—that the primary purpose of the papacy was to provide Christian unity. The pontiff was not an end in himself, not there to reign as a grand papal monarch, but a mechanism to safeguard the church's essential characteristic, its oneness. The envoys from rebel Danzig were thus told in a royal audience in 1525 that one of the apostles was given the keys of heaven 'to conserve unity'.[51] Anti-Reformation polemics echo the point. In his *Encomia Luteri* (1524), Andrzej Kryzcki used the classic Gospel quotes to defend the Petrine supremacy, concluding that this served to ensure that there was only one sheepfold.[52] He expanded upon this in *De Afflictione Ecclesiae* (1527), quoting the church Fathers and Pope Cornelius (d.253).[53] The young canon of Poznań, Piotr Rydziński, offered similar quotes from Cyprian on papacy and unity to the Breslau Lutherans.[54] The subtitle of Byliński's *Defensorium* (1535), meanwhile, stated that it would treat of papal power, the Fathers, and church councils—whereas the latter two are discussed at length as aspects of catholicism, the papacy is reached only on folio 51, where the Petrine commission is summarized with the quick observation that God gave the pope power 'pro unitate ecclesie'.[55] Perhaps the lengthiest surviving treatments of papal power written in Sigismund I's Poland is found in Wróbel's *Propugnaculum*: yet his chapter on papal supremacy is an essay on the indispensability of church unity, rather than a defence of papal power per se.[56] Thus its chapter nine, 'On the Primacy of Peter', impresses on the reader its main conclusion that 'in no sense can something be said to be a church in which there exists Schism'.[57]

This Polish-Prussian catholic discourse of church shows starkly how far the popes were from being its centre of gravity. When the German theologian, Johannes Eck, dedicated one volume of his anti-Lutheran great work *On the Petrine Supremacy* to Sigismund, therefore, its spirited defence of papal supremacy would

---

[48] Wróbel, *Propugnaculum.*   [49] Krzycki, *Encomia*, fo. 3.

[50] AT 16b, p. 252: 'Ita enim . . . intelligere videor sanctae Sedis apostolicae auctoritatem ex maxime pendere, si ea, qua par est, veneratione reges, eam et prinicipes prosequantur . . .'.

[51] AT 7, p. 401, 'ad eam unitatem conservandam'.   [52] Krzycki, *Encomia*, fo. 3.

[53] Krzycki, *De Afflictione*, fos. Cij(v)–Ciii.   [54] Rydziński, *Petri Risinii* (unnumbered pages).

[55] Byliński, *Defensorium*, fo. 51(v).

[56] Wróbel, *Propugnaculum*, chapter 9.

[57] Wróbel, *Propugnaculum*, fo. 299: 'quod si nullo modo recte poterit dici Ecclesia in qua Scisma est'.

have felt rather foreign in the Polish royal court.[58] In 1505, Professor Jan Sacranus' polemic against the Orthodox church had carried an image of the pope, in triple tiara, on its frontispiece—in woodcuts accompanying Polish Reformation polemic, by contrast, the pope is not depicted at all.[59] It was therefore important, in this part of Christendom, for the papacy to exist, but it was not necessarily important for it to have much power. This rather reticent vision of the papacy's role within the church is perhaps not surprising in the Polish monarchy, where relations between the Crown and Rome had been diplomatically strained for much of the fifteenth century, particularly over crusading, and where concilarism (with its vision of a papal constitutional monarchy) had enjoyed a stronghold in Kraków University and court in the 1420s and 1430s.[60] Nonetheless, there are indicators that, here too, Sigismund I's realm was not radically unusual in its ambivalence about the papacy. In the letters and edicts of the famously pious Charles V and his brother Ferdinand on the Reformation, only a handful of texts made any reference to the pope, chiefly to identify him as the subject of Luther's attacks, and by the 1530s he has virtually disappeared from this writing altogether, as if the pontiff were a distant memory. [61] Likewise Lucy Wooding, writing on early Reformation England, argued that we should not assume the Roman papacy to have been central to catholic self-understanding in the early sixteenth century.[62] Certainly, Fabri's pious and learned dialogue against Anabaptists (1528) did not find it necessary to devote any of its thirty chapters to the subject of the papacy.[63]

Alongside its past and its leaders, the church was also defined through its religious practices. Unsurprisingly, the features of church life which register prominently in these texts from the 1520s and 1530s are precisely those which were coming under attack from Luther-inspired reformers. As Rowan Williams has written of heresy crises in early Christianity, the process of a church splitting results in 'a heightened self-consciousness all round of distinctive and distinguishable beliefs'.[64] Likewise, Bedouelle observed that, from the 1530s, old beliefs and practices 'came to constitute a Catholicism', a necessary parallel to Lutheranism.[65] Certain aspects of late medieval church life came into sharper focus, in the act of defending or even debating them. Rites and ceremonies (i.e. liturgy, forms of worship) are, for example, an important reference point in defining the church (twenty-four texts). The Crown warned the Danzig rebels in 1525 that they had rejected the venerable

---

[58] Johann Eck, *Prima pars.*

[59] Sacranus, *Elucidarius.* Byliński aside, the only other Polish printed Reformation polemics to carry woodcuts (portraits of the authors) were Ferrarius' *Oratio* and Giese's *Anthelogikon.*

[60] See Natalia Nowakowska, 'Diplomatic Relations between the Jagiellonian courts of Poland-Lithuania and Papal Rome, 1492–1506', in Urszula Borkowska and Markus Hörsch (eds), *Hofkultur der Jagiellonendynastie und verwandter Fürstenhäuser* (Leipzig, 2010), pp. 119–25 and Thomas Wünsch, *Konziliarismus und Polen: Personen, Politik und Programme aus Polen zur Verfassungsfrage der Kirche in der Zeit der mittelalterlichen Reformkonzilien* (Padeborn, 1998).

[61] Based on an analysis of texts about the early Reformation in *Correspondenz des Kaisers Karl V*, vols. 1 and II; RTA II and V–X.

[62] Wooding, *Rethinking Catholicism*, p. 5.   [63] Fabri, *Adversus doctorem Balthasaram.*

[64] Williams, 'Defining Heresy', p. 316.

[65] Guy Bedouelle, *The Reform of Catholicism, 1480–1620*, trans. James K. Farge (Toronto, 2008), p. xii.

rites of the church set down by the Fathers; a decade later, the oath required by the Crown from the city council still stressed that they should adhere to 'the ecclesiastical ceremonies' set down in the past.[66] In 1535, Danzig Council assured the King that it would bar any innovation in ceremonies, recognizing that traditional wording in worship was part of belonging to the (old) church.[67] In Grunau's chronicle, the abolition of 'Christian ceremonies' is one of the leitmotifs of Lutheran activity, and he specifies what this means—priests dressed without chasubles, no bell-ringing.[68] It is notable how ceremonies are presented as so inherent to the church, that they are indistinguishable from it. The Crown's capital sentence on the Danzig rebels in 1525, as reported by Grunau, declared that the guilty 'had denied the good ceremonies and Christian church', while the *sejm* in 1534 talked of 'the religion and rite of the universal church' as the same thing.[69] Ferdinand Habsburg too, writing to his brother in Spanish in 1521, identified religious ceremonies as a central aspect of catholicism denied by 'los luteranos'.[70]

The veneration of saints and belief in their intercessory power emerges in these sources as another important (defended) aspect of catholicism from early on (invoked in seventeen texts). In 1520, for example, Andrzej Krzycki joked in his letters with his uncle Piotr Tomicki that if Saint Appollonia did not heed his prayers and cure the vice chancellor's toothache, he would join the Lutherans, thereby positioning intercessory prayer as a feature of the church.[71] As Simon Grunau bluntly put it, the Wittenberg monks mocked the Virgin, but the 'good' monks of Elbing taught people to honour her in the rosary and seek her aid.[72] As we saw in Chapter Seven, it was a common charge against alleged Lutherans in church courts that they had denied the power of the saints, or mocked them in allegedly blasphemous ways.[73] Venerating and praying to the saints was, thus, a sign of piety, a mark of orthodoxy. Sustained theological defences of the cult of saints were, nonetheless, rare in Sigismund I's monarchy. Only Walenty Wróbel set his pen to this task in his 1536 polemic, arguing that it was a hallmark of heresies throughout history to deny the miracles performed by the saints.[74]

The sacraments were also claimed as an aspect of catholic identity. In 1525–6, a persistent feature of Sigismund I's accusations against Danzig was that its citizens had blasphemed 'the most holy sacrament', and 'treated it badly, in a shameful and abominable way'.[75] In 1535, Bishop Ferber lamented that, in its (catholic) past, Danzigers had piously attended Mass, but now people simply got up and left church after the Sunday sermon, while those who stayed did so only in order to

---

[66] AT 7, p. 357; AT 16b, p. 432; AT 17, p. 18.   [67] AT 17, p. 345.
[68] *Simon Grunau's Preussische Chronik*, vol. II, p. 698; vol. III, pp. 214–17.
[69] *Simon Grunau's Preussische Chronik*, vol. III, pp. 185–7; AT 16b, p. 525.
[70] *Correspondenz*, I, p. 426.   [71] AT 5, pp. 158–9.
[72] *Simon Grunau's Preussische Chronik*, vol. II, p. 655.   [73] See Chapter Seven, pp. 190–1.
[74] Wróbel, *Propugnaculum*, chapter 8. There is also a brief defence of saintly intercessions in AT 7, p. 402, the Crown reply to the Danzig envoys.
[75] AT 7, p. 318; AT 8, p. 110, 'indignis et abominandis malis tractassetis'.

mock this sacrament at the elevation with unrepeatable insults.[76] Utraquism, as well as disrespect for and non-participation in the Mass, was seen as a sign of non-catholic behaviour. Polish bishops grew agitated when Pancratius Klemme started giving communion in two kinds in Danzig *c*.1535, and in Poznań Michael Werner was convicted of heresy for the same act, in the same year.[77] Wróbel, in his *Propugnaculum*, included a chapter-long attack on utraquism, as a revival of Hussite heresy.[78] Mockery of the Mass, or innovations in the distribution of Communion, were seen as non-catholic acts. Simon Grunau, for example, knew that Michael Meurer preached Lutheran dogmas in Danzig, but found him perfectly acceptable 'because he didn't say anything against the sacraments'.[79] Only Grzegorz Szamotulski, in his *Anacephaleosis* pamphlet, explained why sacraments were so important, linking them explicitly to doctrines of salvation—sacraments as well as faith were needed for salvation, he wrote.[80]

The church was defined too with reference to monasteries and the clerical hierarchy. For Sigismund I in particular, monastic life was an important feature of a dignified Christian society. He chastised the Danzigers, the burghers of Breslau, and Silesian princes for permitting attacks on monks, the demolition of houses, the interruption of their prayer, and their incarceration.[81] A royal letter to the Abbot of Tyniec contains a particularly strong defence of the monastic life. Just as Wróbel would do in the preface to his *Propugnaculum*, the King claims that it is the accumulated prayers of monks which defend Poland from its infidel enemies (like a kind of Trojan palladium)—and that the abbot's abuses put in jeopardy this all-important monastic prayer.[82] The clerical office, and its jurisdiction, is also defended as a feature of the church—Sigismund I was adamant, in an exchange with the Lutheran bishop Queis, that 'the keys to the kingdom of heaven' and pastoral care had been given to the clerical caste and not to princes, and insisted to his Royal Prussian subjects that they must pay taxes to their clergy, who offered sacrifices for sins.[83] Meanwhile, writers engaged in polemical exchanges, such as Lachowski and Krzycki, defended the idea of a clerical hierarchy, with lower and higher forms of ministry.[84]

The Polish Crown and episcopate were highly offended by suggestions that the universal church was not rooted in Scripture. In 1525–6, at the most turbulent point of the Prussian Reformation, the King and counsellors stressed repeatedly, in the face of Lutheran assertions to the contrary, that their church was Scriptural. Sigismund I took it as a slight against his personal honour as a catholic prince to be told, as in the Danzig Apologias, that he did not know the true meaning of the Gospels—the Danzig envoys were told that the King heard the Word every day at Mass, 'kissing and adoring it', and that he had drawn his own sword (against the

---

[76] AT 17, p. 112.   [77] AT 17, p. 237; AAP, AE VII, fo. 334.
[78] Wróbel, *Propugnaculum*, chapter 6.
[79] *Simon Grunau's Preussische Chronik*, III, pp. 177–8.
[80] Szamotulski, *Anacephaleosis*, fos. 29(v)–30.
[81] AT 6, pp.110–11; AT 7, pp. 318, 383; AT 8, pp. 29, 109; AT 9, p. 165; AT 14, p. 10.
[82] AT 13, p. 373; Wróbel, *Propugnaculum*, dedicatory letter.
[83] AT 8, p. 132; AT 10, p. 42.   [84] Krzycki, *De Afflictione*, fo. D; AT 10, pp. 211–13.

infidel) 'for the Word of God, for the holy catholic faith', eliding these two concepts.[85] Primate Łaski too grumbled that the Danzigers talked about the 'Word of God...from which the catholic church has never departed'.[86] The leaders of the Reformation in Ducal Prussia were told by an increasingly exasperated King Sigismund that neither he nor any other Christian had ever resisted or oppressed the Word of God, that he heard the Bible every day, adding nonetheless that 'we are not so dense, that we cannot see how much lies between your Gospel and Christ's Gospel', thereby claiming for the universal church a correct reading of Scripture.[87] These exchanges were known to and reproduced by Simon Grunau, as a lowly Dominican in Royal Prussia, who added vivid details in his chronicle— after hearing the Lutherans Georg von Polenz and Paulus Speratus preach for three hours, claimed Grunau, the old king began to weep on his throne, saying, 'You treacherous men, you have stolen the Word of God from us!'[88] Polemicists in the Polish monarchy rejected Lutheran teaching by juxtaposing it with apparently contradictory quotes from Scriptures—a high percentage of Wróbel's *Propugnaculum*, Byliński's *Defensorium*, and Krzycki's works are strings of quotes, particularly from the Gospels. Those defining and defending the church in Sigismund I's monarchy were not prepared to concede that Scripture was not a part of its identity.

Indulgences, which have an iconic status in Reformation history as the subject of Luther's opening salvo of 1517, registered only very occasionally in these sources' articulations of the church. Grzegorz Szamotulski was almost uniquely exercised by this topic, composing a sermon in defence of indulgences against Luther, printed in 1532 in Kraków as *De indulgentiis*.[89] Simon Grunau reported, with disapproval, that in the early 1520s, actors in an Elbing carnival had dressed up as devils, teaching monks how to sell indulgences.[90] At the very end of the list of heretical charges against Jakub of Iłża was the accusation that 'on indulgences...and purgatory, he agrees with Luther'.[91] Indulgences, so important in the development of Luther's own theological thinking, were something of a footnote in this monarchy.

Looking at Figure 8.1, one might be struck by how little these sources have to say about what modern scholarship (with Luther) tends to present as the core doctrinal-theological controversy of the Reformation—justification. References to salvation by good works (as opposed to *sola fide*) can be found at the very edge of Figure 8.1, referred to explicitly in only eight texts. There is minimal discussion of good works as a distinctive, uniquely salvific 'catholic' theology of salvation. Royal documents dealt with the topic just twice, and gingerly. In a paternal letter

---

[85] AT 7, pp. 384, 400.

[86] AT 7, p. 389: 'dei verbo sincero...a quibus catholice ecclesie presides nunquam dissenserunt'.

[87] AT 8, pp. 51, 132: 'obtusi simus, ut non intelligamus, quantum intersit inter vestrum et Christi evangelium'.

[88] *Simon Grunau's Preussische Chronik*, vol. III, p. 137: 'O ihr vorreterischen buben, wie behendiglich habett ihr uns dass wortt gottes gestolen...'.

[89] Szamotulski, *Sermo*.

[90] *Simon Grunau's Preussische Chronik*, vol. II, pp. 646–7.

[91] BJ, MS 3227, fo. 74, 'de indulgentiis...et purgatoria idem sentit cum Luthero'. The same charge was also made against Kaspar Lisman by Dantiscus, AT 17, p. 128.

to Duke Albrecht in 1526, for example, Sigismund I wrote that he himself hoped that with works ('opera') and the support of others, he might reach the kingdom of heaven.[92] A handful of polemics explored good works more fully. Archdeacon Szamotulski's polemic *Anacephaleosis* included the demolition, through logic-dialectic, of his opponent Christoph Hegendorff's syllogism on *sola fide*.[93] Tiedemann Giese's *Anthelokigon* was subtitled 'on works and faith', rhetorically positioning a clear division over theologies of salvation—although the work itself concluded the difference was not really very important. Taking a more forceful approach, Walenty Wróbel's 1536 *Progulaculum* dedicated two chapters to 'faith and works' and 'good works', saying this was the biggest error of the heretics.[94] Modern scholarship positions the argument over salvation as the absolute core of the Reformation, yet these sources in the Polish monarchy clearly did not perceive the 1520s and 1530s in this way—before concluding that these voices were ill-informed or unperceptive, we might ask ourselves what this might suggest about the Reformation itself.

The near absence of classic doctrinal controversies in these Polish-Prussian definitions of the church is less surprising in light of the Crown's tacit acceptance of what Paulus called '*Unklarheit*'—theological fuzziness. Susan Schreiner has argued that the early modern period was characterized by a quest for certainty, particularly in religion, and others have proposed that the Reformation appealed to sixteenth-century Europeans precisely because it offered clear pathways to salvation.[95] The strongly anti-Lutheran Bishop Krzycki appeared to frown on catholic confusions, writing that it was no surprise heretics abused holy things, when everything was full of 'variety and confusion' and even 'to us' things were not 'sufficiently certain or clear'.[96] However, Sigismund I of Poland, the senior member of one of Europe's most powerful royal houses, had a more nuanced view. Royal envoys to Danzig in 1524 were told to remind the Luther-reading Danzigers that 'nothing is certain in human or divine affairs'.[97] This was not just a passing glib comment—that royal instruction document went on to spell out that it is precisely because of this lack of certainty that, if everyone devises a religious truth (certainty) for themselves, social and spiritual anarchy will ensue. The Danzig Statutes issued by the King in 1526 made identical statements.[98] To insist too much on this kind of doctrinal clarity was, for the Polish Crown, self-evidently catastrophic for Christendom. Such world views would not, and could not, survive the age of confessionalization.

---

[92] *Elementa*, p. 15. *Sola fide* was mentioned in one line in the 1525 royal reply to the Danzig envoys: AT 7, p. 402.

[93] Szamotulski, *Anacephaleosis*, fo. 29(v).　　　[94] Wróbel, *Propugnaculum*, chapters 2 and 3.

[95] Schreiner, *Are You Alone Wise?*; Cameron, *The European Reformation*.

[96] AT 10, p. 163: 'nunc apud omnia varietatis et confusionis plena sunt, neque mirum est sacra nostra improbari ab haereticis, cum neque nobis ipsis satis certa et probata esse videntur, ut apparet in Ardelione nostro, rerum omnium novatore et chao confussissimo'.

[97] AT 7, p. 10: 'nihil enim in mundo certi aut firmi tam in divinis quam humanis rebus haberetur'.

[98] AT 8, p. 767.

Changing Names: From Christian to Catholic?

Under the sheer pressure of the events unfolding across Latin Christendom in the 1520s and 1530s, the serene definitions of church found in the Polish-Prussian sources began (but only began) to warp. Before the eyes of the Polish King and his subjects, large and possibly enormous numbers of people (and princes) embraced the Reformation and rejected unity—in the Holy Roman Empire, Sweden, Denmark, the Low Countries, England, and more locally throughout Prussia and in towns, academies, and noble households across the Polish monarchy. In the face of this shock—the slow splitting of a church which understood its unity to be the benchmark of its orthodoxy—the language of catholicism was forced to evolve. This process was surprisingly subtle, yet far-reaching. Some words managed to retain something of their original sense, in an adapted form; some chaotically began to develop a range of different meanings; others emerged from the background to the foreground of discourse about the church.

The word 'Christendom' proved itself flexible, perhaps showing the enduring appeal of unity- and universalism-focused understandings of *ecclesia*. During the early Reformation, the concept of the '*respublica Christiana*' survived in the Polish monarchy, and simply adapted itself tacitly to include followers of Luther. Tomicki could thus speak of the German Peasants' War (1524–5) as a disturbance within Christianity, rather than an attack upon it.[99] From *c*.1530, Sigismund and his councillors unanimously expressed the hope that the Augsburg Diet (1530), or a church council, would bring concord between Christian princes (pro-Luther and anti-Luther), and tranquillity within Christendom.[100] The Reformation is thus seen as an internal conflict, paralysis, within Christianity, and Protestants not as extrinsic to it.

However, it was more common for key words—such as '*christianus*' and '*catholicus*'—to start fragmenting, acquiring right from the early 1520s multiple, parallel, and incompatible meanings. It is a sign of how slippery this groping for new vocabularies was that one individual (such as the King, Tomicki, or Simon Grunau) might use one word in two entirely different senses, sometimes in the same text. The word '*christianus*', for example, as adjective or a noun, could still be used in a universal way—in roughly 50 per cent of these texts, '*christianus*' encompassed both Lutherans and non-Lutherans. In 1524, a royal delegation warned the Danzigers that their heretical ideas would bring them shame 'among other Christians'—clearly including the port's citizens in that category.[101] Tomicki defended the 1525 Kraków Treaty to Rome by arguing that it was necessary in order to secure peace 'between Christians'—i.e. the Lutheran Grand Master of the Teutonic Order and the pious King of Poland.[102] Sigismund himself addressed Albrecht as 'a Christian prince', and wrote to the pro-Reformation Georg of Brandenburg of 'our Christian religion as princes'.[103] When a bishop such as Maciej Drzewicki rejoiced that a huge army had defeated an Ottoman force to

---

[99] AT 7, p. 275. [100] AT 12, p. 164; AT 13, pp. 92, 126; AT 14, p. 95.
[101] AT 7, p. 12. [102] AT 7, p. 293. [103] *Elementa*, pp. 60–1; AT 15, p. 361.

the great benefit of Christians, he was using the term in a general way, almost as a code for 'European'.[104] This kind of language—present consistently through-out the 1520s and 1530s—implied that the church was still at heart one; that any apparent schism was merely superficial and had not changed its underlying unified nature.

However, the word '*christianus*' simultaneously began to take on narrower, alternative meanings, as a rhetoric of 'good' and 'bad' Christians emerged. In the 1520s, 'good Christian' emerged as a label for a member of the universal church who was not a follower of the Reformation, and 'bad Christian' (not necessarily, *nota bene*, heretic) to mean Lutherans. Sigismund I, in 1526, expressed the hope that a Warsaw tailor arraigned for Lutheran heresy would now be reconciled to the church and live like a 'good Christian' ('*bonus christianus*').[105] Simon Grunau's chronicle recounted how Bishop Drzewicki had marched into Danzig in 1524 'to the delight of many good Christians, frightening the Lutherans'.[106] Grunau described how, during King Sigismund's armed sojourn in the city, no ship could leave unless its crew had letters testifying that they were all 'good Christians'.[107] Dantiscus, in 1533, assured the King that kinsmen of his who had abjured Lutheranism were now 'good Christians'.[108] As late as 1540, when five men from the Wielkopolska town of Śmigiel were seized by the Inquisition for owning vernacular Bibles, they swore on oath that they were not Lutherans, but lived like 'good Christians'.[109] The term 'bad Christian' (whether used explicitly, or implicitly) was not confined to Lutherans—from Castile, Johannes Dantiscus wrote to Tomicki that in Spain there were Moors and Jews who had been forced to convert to Christianity 'and many other bad Christians'.[110]

Some texts went further, and used '*christianus*' where today we might use 'Catholic'. 'Christian', in other words, began to function as an early label for a member of the Latin-Roman church which, it was now just conceivable, was not the only church, and even in some places not the church of the majority. Simon Grunau, for example, uses 'Christian' in many places in his chronicle, where we (with our post-Tridentine perspective) would say simply 'Catholic'. In Lutheran Königsberg, he writes, 'Christians had to hide themselves, and were oppressed.'[111] Lutherans in his story repent on their deathbeds, receive the sacraments of the church, and die 'like Christians'.[112] Dr Alexander Svenichen, writes Grunau, 'followed the Christian truth against the Lutherans'.[113] In 1534, Sigismund I warned Albrecht that other princes saw him as having 'deserted' the Christian religion.[114] In 1535, Tomicki stated that he, 'like all Christians', was loyal to the pontiff.[115]

---

[104] AT 14, p. 723.   [105] AT 8, p. 145.
[106] *Simon Grunau's Preussische Chronik*, vol. II, p. 702: 'her kam manchem gutten christen zur freude und allen offentlichen Lutteristen zur furcht'.
[107] *Simon Grunau's Preussische Chronik*, vol. III, p. 182, 'ob sie gutte christen weren'.
[108] AT 15, pp. 126–7.   [109] AAP, AE VIII, fo. 117.   [110] AT 10, p. 282.
[111] *Simon Grunau's Preussische Chronik*, vol. II, pp. 718–19.
[112] *Simon Grunau's Preussische Chronik*, vol. II, p. 755.
[113] *Simon Grunau's Preussische Chronik*, vol. II, p. 782, 'und folgete der christlichen wahrheitt wieder die Lutteraner'.
[114] AT 16a, p. 327.   [115] AT 17, p. 421.

The word '*catholicus*' underwent a similar set of bifurcations. It too could be used as a term for any believer in the Latin West, in its literal meaning of 'universal'—as when the widow Melchiorowna in Kraków was forced to abjure Judaism and embrace the 'catholic' and 'Christian' faith in 1530, the two concepts were apparently interchangeable.[116] However, from *c*.1526, some of these sources started to employ '*catholicus*' not only as a code for 'orthodoxy', but as a religious identity to juxtapose with Lutheranism. In 1526, Sigismund I instructed the radically pro-Luther council of Braunsberg to install 'a catholic preacher', and upbraided the Lutheran bishop Queis for 'oppressing catholic men'—i.e. the canons of Marienwerder.[117] Some texts started to use catholic-Lutheran together as a set of polar opposites, explicit antonyms—implying that Lutheranism was not a variant, but incompatible with catholic identity.[118] Dantiscus, in 1526, wrote that Charles V was zealous in 'castigating Lutherans and upholding the catholic faith'; Krzycki, in a 1527 polemic that Lutherans laughed at 'the catholic faith'.[119] In Grunau's chronicle (1529), Bishop Drzewicki tells the Danzigers in 1524 to 'hold onto Catholic belief and abandon Lutheran heresy'.[120] In 1532, founding a new preaching post in Elbing, the Crown specified that the man appointed must be 'not a Lutheran, but of the true catholic faith'.[121] These examples form only an undercurrent in the sources, a steady trickle, but they were the sign of what was to come. '*Catholicus*', once juxtaposed with '*Luteranus*', was the language of serious schism, the emergence of confessional identities.

In a context where the meanings of important words were shifting and destabilizing, it is no surprise that some reached for clearer labels, with 'Roman Church' emerging as the preferred name among the Polish clergy. The abjuration oath sworn by a Danzig schoolmaster accused of Lutheranism stated that he had returned to 'the unity of the church and Christian religion' and 'the holy mother Roman apostolic church'—a list of alternative formulations, which clearly tried to elide Christian and Roman church.[122] Dantiscus, forced in the 1530s to interact with openly Lutheran parishioners in Kulm diocese, referred insistently to a 'Holy Christian Roman Church' in his correspondence with them.[123] However, a specific incident seemingly spurred a wider shift to a language of a 'Roman' church among the episcopate—Johannes Dantiscus' failed mission to Danzig in 1535. The oath text which Dantiscus, in the name of the Crown, presented to the Danzig councillors required them to swear loyalty to the 'Roman church'; they refused, and substituted this phrase for 'Christian church'.[124] This incident prompted a flurry of correspondence, and it seems the Danzigers' rejection of the '*ecclesia romana*'

---

[116] BJ, MS 5357, fo. 72 ('in fide christiana') and fo. 73 ('fidem catholicam').

[117] AT 8, pp. 110, 131.

[118] On antonyms, see Innes, '"Reform" in English Public Life'.

[119] AT 8, p. 347, 'castigandis Luteranis et tuenda fide catholica'; Krzycki, *De Afflictione*, dedicatory letter.

[120] *Simon Grunau's Preussische Chronik*, vol. II, pp. 702–3.

[121] AT 14, p. 666: 'non lutherano sed verae et catholicae fidei'.

[122] AAWł, Acta Ep. 2, fo. 179–179(v).

[123] Johannes Dantiscus, *Corpus of Johannes Dantiscus' Texts*, ID937 (1533, to Graudenz clergy).

[124] See Chapter Two, p. 83.

encouraged Polish bishops to adopt it as a label for their own anti-Lutheran church.[125] Bishop Tomicki, for example, who had not used the term 'Roman church' in his correspondence at all before 1535, in that final year of his life, after being debriefed by Dantiscus about events in Danzig, asked Sigismund I to stop actions against 'the Roman church' in Kraków. His will employed this same vocabulary, specifying that he wished to be buried according to the rites of 'the Roman church', and that he had followed the faith of 'the holy Roman church'.[126] Polemicists too made this move in the mid 1530s: Archdeacon Byliński, in his often conciliatory polemic, wrote that there was only one universal church beyond which there was no salvation, and this was the 'church of the city of Rome'.[127] In seeking to find a terminology for a smaller, surviving church, Polish and Prussian clergy here adopted the distinctive language long used by the papal curia, of a 'Holy Roman Church'.

These linguistic shifts might appear small, but their implications were large, because they reveal the very concept of a universal church being reformulated. Our sources capture the basic contradiction faced by the late medieval church in the early Reformation, squeezed as it was between incompatible impulses—a deep conviction that the universal church was by definition one, and included Lutherans, and the urgent need to find new ways of articulating what catholic identity might be in a fragmenting Europe. Put simply, the *ecclesia universale* could not be both pan-Christian, and one of several competing European churches. This paradox was resolved through a tacit recalibration of the 'universal' claim. Universal had long meant a church consistently present in time and space—universal across the centuries, across the territories of Europe.[128] But now if the Roman church was to be 'universal', with Prussia, Scandinavia, and much of the Holy Roman Empire having rejected it, universal would have to mean a universal spiritual authority, in a more metaphysical sense. This meaning had always been latent in the phrase 'universal church', but it now came to the fore. The church was universal, the genuine church, despite the misleading appearances created by the Reformation, whereby the Roman church itself might look like a minority, or even a sect. Universal thus became less of an (exaggerated) historical and geographical statement of fact, and more of a truth claim. Thus Walenty Wróbel, in his 1536 treatise, could state uncompromisingly that the universal church which did not err 'was the Roman Church', and that anybody who left the universal church was an enemy, who would languish in the fire prepared by the Devil and his angels.[129] This was a concept of universalism adapted for the emerging confessional age, the stark end of the fifteenth-century 'church of options'.

---

[125] AT 16b, p. 432.   [126] AT 17, pp. 258, 562–3.
[127] Byliński, *Defensorium*, fo. 45(v).
[128] See Fabri, *Adversus doctorem Balthasarum*, fo. Ciii(v), who says the universal church is that of Europe, Asia, and Africa, making a grander geographical–historical claim.
[129] Wróbel, *Propugnaculum*, chapter 9.

THE PRO-REFORMATION VIEW

How did Reformation supporters in the Polish monarchy talk of the church they criticized, or rejected, so stridently? In general, pro-Luther writers avoided being drawn into ecclesiological debates. Thus Laurentius Corvinus, in his correspondence with Byliński, stressed his devotion to God and Christ, but made no reference to the institutional church—Byliński's lengthy expositions on the nature of the church could not draw Corvinus onto this discursive territory.[130] Christoph Hegendorff's pedagogic text *Stichologia* (Kraków, 1534), which was accused of promoting Lutheranism to Polish schoolboys, placed much emphasis on Christian virtue, holy wisdom, and devotion to God, but did not refer to the church—any church—at all.[131]

Where pro-Lutherans in the Polish monarchy did talk about the majority church, its corrupt personnel was a prime point of reference. In the 110 articles written by Johannes Briesseman, one of Albrecht's top Lutheran theologians in Ducal Prussia, articles 53 to 67 complained about the priests and prelates 'of our own time', declaring them to be vain, pompous, ambitious, and avaricious.[132] The 1525 Danzig Apologias complained about the inadequate pastoral care provided by the port's parish clergy, and lambasted their bishop (Maciej Drzewicki, Bishop of Włocławek) for oppressing widows and orphans with his taxes, and depopulating the countryside by driving it into poverty.[133] The Apologias reserved their real venom, however, for monks, that 'proud and impatient species of man'.[134] Monks were attacked as lazy troublemakers, arch hypocrites.[135] These Lutheran texts thus tended to identify (or conflate) the old church with its allegedly failing hierarchy—parish clergy, bishops, monks.

Pro-Reformation texts also present theological error as a key characteristic of the old church, applying against the medieval church the language it had long used of heretics. Corvinus describes this error as a darkness, leading to spiritual death. People, he informed Archdeacon Byliński, had walked with their eyes closed for the longest time, in darkest night, the blind leading the blind, moving away from the fountains of life. God has now saved his people from this error, and led them back to the kingdom of light.[136] He does not explicitly name the Roman or catholic church as a kingdom of darkness, but it is clear what he is referring to. Briesemann too suggested that the 'Christian people' had long wandered in darkness, the Christian faith and grace having been extinguished.[137] Error, and false doctrines, were also a refrain of the Danzig Apologias, which asserted that the preaching of monks was a 'virus', and that it was the Devil himself who had led people to erect images of saints in their churches.[138]

Lutheran writings were much concerned with Christian history and the past, but in an entirely different way to their opponents. Reformation texts were more

---

[130] Printed in Byliński, *Defensorium*. [131] Christoph Hegendorff, *Stichologia* (Kraków, 1534).
[132] Reproduced in Giese, *Anthelogikon*. [133] AT 7, pp. 367, 374–5.
[134] AT 7, p. 365, 'ut est superbum et impatiens hominum genus'.
[135] AT 7, pp. 364–5. [136] Byliński, *Defensorium*, fos. 12–13.
[137] Giese, *Anthelogikon* (article 67). [138] AT 7, pp. 364, 371.

historicizing than the Crown, its council, or Polish-Prussian polemicists, in that they identified different phases of church history—a pure origin in the days of the Apostles, an extended period of corruption and error which had ended in their own time, and the advent of a renewed, true church. The Danzig Apologias and Briesemann contrasted the primitive church favourably with the church they saw around them. Moreover, these texts located the contemporary catholic church firmly in the past, talking of it in the past tense, as something which had already been destroyed.[139] This cycle of golden age, decay, and rebirth was, of course, a pattern of thought characteristic of the fifteenth and sixteenth centuries, providing a template for talking about 'progress' in scholarship and artistic production. Its application to the church pushed that church, in Lutheran writings, back into a 'medieval' space.

Contrary to the initial diagnoses of many in the Polish monarchy, the Reformation was not just a brief epidemic of revolt, or a new Great Schism, or the advent of an ultimately contained heresy such as Utraquism. Instead, in a fundamental way, it confronted a late medieval understanding of the church as the unified community of Christians across time and space, with a Lutheran world view in which the criteria for the 'true' church were very much narrower and based in specific correct doctrines. As such, the early Reformation forced in Sigismund I's monarchy a gradual re-articulation of catholic identity, and conceptual redefinitions. These played out in profound linguistic shifts, often in the meaning of individual words, whose older meanings groaned under the weight of early sixteenth-century events. It is precisely at this microscopic, linguistic level that we can capture the first birth pangs of polarization and confessionalization, of a new Europe which saw, to quote Peter Marshall, 'the formation of identity by means of division and conflict'.[140]

At King Sigismund's funeral Mass in Kraków in 1548, Bishop Marcin Kromer, that future star of the Polish Counter-/Catholic Reformation, lavishly praised the late King's catholicism: 'See therefore this wisest king of our religion', a religion passed down through Christ and the Apostles, their successors, the holy Councils, 'and retained for so many centuries by the Christian world in consensus'.[141] Kromer, in this eulogy, used the King's own late medieval language of catholicism, a language once widely shared by his subjects and scholarly and princely contemporaries, but increasingly embattled in the face of powerful new ideas and realities. Sigismund I's death after a forty-two-year reign was, for the Polish monarchy, the end of an era, in very many ways. His primate and close contemporary, Maciej Drzewicki, had perceived some years earlier the possibility that theirs would be the last generation to see a unified church in the Latin West. In summer 1526,

---

[139] Byliński, *Defensorium*, letters by Corvinus, fos. 12–13; Giese, *Anthelogikon* (articles 66–7); AT 7, pp. 366–7.

[140] Peter Marshall, *The Oxford Very Short Introduction to the Reformation* (Oxford, 2009), p. 9.

[141] Kromer and Maciejowski, *De Sigismundo Primo rege*, fos. 157–157(v): 'Vidit enim sapientissimus rex in religione nostra nihil melius, nihil exactius hoc tempore a quoque inveniri posse, q' ab ipsis Christi servatoris nostri discipulis, eorumque successoribus proximis, santissimisque patrum Concilijs constitutum, et publico Christiani orbis consensu tot saeculis retentum esset.'

celebrating Mass in St Mary's parish church in Danzig after the flight of the radical preachers, Drzewicki had reportedly wept at the altar with joy and relief.[142] In 1530, he and Andrzej Krzycki discussed together the latest news from the Diet of Augsburg, so anxiously followed in Poland, where Charles V and his Lutheran princes were on the verge of making their historic religious split. Drzewicki, 'very eager for religious concord', reportedly became agitated—he exclaimed that it would have been better had the Emperor not returned to Germany, and he broke down, and bitterly wept.[143] It would be for the generation which followed these late medieval Christians to reimagine catholicism.

[142] AT 8, p. 40.   [143] AT 12, p. 318, 'concordiae est avidissimus'.

Summary and Conclusions

The importance of the Polish monarchy of Sigismund I (ruled 1506–48) in the early Reformation was well known to scholars from the nationalist late nineteenth century to the Stalinist 1950s, but the intellectual and geopolitical fallout of World War II pushed this story below the radar of international scholarship. This study has offered a fresh telling of Lutheranism in this polity: the urban revolts of Danzig and Elbing (1525–6), the emergence of a Lutheran vassal state in Ducal Prussia (1525), a Reformation peasant rising (1525), widespread support for Wittenberg reform in the royal court, Polish cities, educational institutions and noble households throughout the 1530s, and the real possibility of a Lutheran regent of Poland (the royal kinsman Albrecht of Prussia). Placed in a comparative context, this story is in many ways remarkable—the Danzig Reformation revolt was entirely without precedent in Christendom until the Anabaptist seizure of Münster (1534), Ducal Prussia was Europe's very first officially Lutheran territory, and Sigismund's was the only monarchy outside the Empire to experience urban, peasant, and princely forms of Reformation in the 1520s. This story can help us recover the full geographical scope of early Lutheranism, as well as its international character, preached as it often was in this monarchy in languages other than German.

This study has taken as its focus the (to us) perplexingly tolerant responses of Polish-Prussian catholic elites to the Lutheranism in their midst. Thirteen Danzig rebels were beheaded, and one Kraków widow burnt for Judaizing. Yet 90 per cent of the around sixty individuals tried for 'being of the Lutheran sect' in this reign walked free, with just a verbal warning; most were not tried at all, studiously ignored by the authorities. In Danzig, Sigismund I restored catholicism (of a sort) by force in 1526, but thereafter did not intervene as local elites enacted a de facto Lutheran reform across the wider province of Royal Prussia. In 1525, the king accepted as a vassal his Lutheran nephew Albrecht of Brandenburg-Ansbach—the Crown sanctioned the creation of a new duchy, in which Albrecht immediately rolled out a full-scale territorial Reformation. King Sigismund, deeply personally pious, nonetheless enjoyed a close political and social relationship with his nephew and his Lutheran entourage. On the international stage, Sigismund made alliances with Lutheran princes, and contemplated marrying his daughter to Elector Philip of Hesse. The eleven anti-Luther edicts issued for the Polish Crown lands made ominous threats, but went entirely unenforced by royal government. Among Polish high clergy and diocesan officials too, the emphasis was firmly on private conversions of Lutherans. Despite fiercely worded episcopal statutes, and some vituperative printed polemics by clergy, church courts across the kingdom treated

Lutheranism as a mild offence, a social mischief. By contrast, those caught fortune telling, or priests found with mistresses, routinely went to jail.

This would seem to be a straightforward, if unusually thoroughgoing, example of sixteenth-century religious tolerance. However, this study has questioned current models of early modern toleration, which diagnose both princely policy and every-day coexistence as simple political calculation (e.g. realpolitik, pragmatism), involving a deliberate sacrifice of religious idealism. We have questioned whether the conscious juxtaposition of 'politics' and 'religion' this formula requires might be anachronistic when applied to the sixteenth century. Instead, approaching the problem of non-persecution from another angle, this investigation has focused on what King Sigismund and his elites understood catholicism or Christian ortho-doxy itself to be, reconstructing their ecclesiology through analysis of both their words and actions.

Acknowledging there to be such a thing as *luteranismus*, the Polish-Prussian sources (viewed panoramically, as a body of discourse) meant two different things by this term. 'Luteranus' as an armed commoner—blacksmith, peasant, or sailor—stirred up by radical preachers in revolt was entirely intolerable: such people were executed and deeply feared by Sigismund I, his counsellors and clergy (and by Duke Albrecht). 'Luteranus' could alternatively mean a loyal, educated subject interested in controversial teachings. In general, Lutherans were not consistently labelled heretics; heretic-demonizing rhetoric was rarely deployed against them; *luteranismus* was viewed through the prism of its constituent acts, that is as instances of religious malfaisance already well known to the late medieval church such as sacrilege or blasphemy; minimal interest was shown in Luther's theological content, and this phenomenon was constructed above all as a sin of schism, a will-ingness to split the urban, regnal, or universal Christian community. There was, conversely, no word for 'catholicism', only a wide variety of terms to talk about the 'fides Christi' and the universal church. This was defined as the church which had always been, the church of the Fathers and one's own forefathers. Its key character-istic was its claimed universality across time and space, embodying a long-term consensus of councils, emperors, kings, scholars, peoples, popes, with unity as its *sine qua non* (the papacy registering sparingly and chiefly as a tool of unity). Only gradually did encounters with Protestants force the articulation of a narrower, more specific identity in some quarters in the 1530s—a move in Polish-Prussian sources from 'pious' versus 'bad' catholics, to Lutheran versus Catholic, and more tentatively from 'the church' to 'Roman church'.

These findings lead this study to the conclusion that King Sigismund and most of his catholic elites 'tolerated' non-violent Lutherans because, as late as 1540, they did not see them as a dangerous Other—as bad Christians, exasperating, lacking piety, but still part of the universal, catholic church. This aligns with M. S. Chisholm's research on Tyrol, where Austrian contemporaries did not see 'Lutheran' and 'Catholic' as entirely separate categories in the 1520s and 1530s. As the German scholar, Johann Fabri, told a leading Anabaptist in Prague in 1528: you might be in error, but you are still a member of the universal church. For Sigismund I, loyal burghers, discreet scholars, his beloved kinsman Albrecht, his fellow

Christian princes, were all likewise perceived and treated as fellow members of Latin Christendom. This stance was possible because in the Polish court's unity-centred understanding of the church, disagreement over specific teachings could be tackled through debate and the pursuit of consensus: unity and concord (in realm, society, politics, church) were obviously more important than doctrinal minutiae. King Sigismund declared to Duke Albrecht that a single doctrinal point, scored in a theological disputation, simply could not constitute the whole of Christian religion. For Poles, the Bohemian Utraquists, who had been negotiated back into the church in the 1430s, provided an obvious model for where Lutherans were heading.

Early modern Poland is often said to be uniquely tolerant, not least by Polish historians such as Janusz Tazbir—uniquely experienced in handling medieval religious diversity, uniquely influenced by Erasmus, ruled by a uniquely humane royal family, with a uniquely assertive parliament. Few of these arguments are watertight when subjected to comparative analysis (with Castile, France, German princes, England, etc.). The statistics tell a more complicated story, whereby the Polish monarchy in the reign of King Sigismund was entirely mainstream within Latin Christendom in executing Reformation-inspired rebels (ranking after only Germany, Austria, and Switzerland in the 1520s) without compunction, but balked at executing peaceful Lutherans for dissident belief alone, Monter pointing out that 'executions of Lutherans were everywhere rare'. It is only in the second half of the sixteenth century, as waves of religious persecution engulfed parts of Europe, that the Polish monarchy began to look more obviously unusual in the reign of Sigismund's son, Sigismund Augustus (1548–72).

This therefore raises the question of whether Sigismund I's 'eirenic' ecclesiology was a more widespread catholic phenomenon in the early Reformation, and not a purely Polish local oddity. To borrow from J. G. Pocock, the distinctive historic 'language' or discourse of catholicism as unity-consensus which so dominates Polish-Prussian literary, judicial, royal, episcopal, and theological texts, was also present more widely across the late medieval and early sixteenth-century church. Charles V, Henry VIII (before 1530), Ferdinand of Austria, prominent polemicists such as Johann Eck, Johann Fabri, or Jose Clichtove of France all consistently defined catholic orthodoxy (along with Sigismund I and his subjects) not as a set of teachings, but as the consensus of councils, popes, universities, princes, and kingdoms across space and time, a historic unity lasting centuries which was the guarantor of orthodoxy itself—echoing word for word the definitions articulated by the Council of Constance back in 1415, as well as sentiments expressed by William of Ockham, Jean Gerson, and Nicholas of Cusa. This ecclesiology is, of course, also that of Erasmus of Rotterdam—celebrated in scholarship as a lone voice for peace—but this book invites us to consider that it did not originate with him, even if he was its most eloquent speaker. In Poland, England, and Germany princes and scholars had already articulated this ecclesiology against the Reformation in the early 1520s, well before Erasmus himself ventured out in print against Luther (autumn 1524). What we call this understanding of the church, its language and ecclesiology, is a moot point: premodern Christian, pre-confessional catholic (ultramontane) late medieval, or fifteenth-century conciliar?

The late medieval church has long been viewed in scholarship as quietly chaotic, either fruitfully or reprehensibly so. Its diverse pieties—mystics, confraternities, proliferating saintly cults—have led John van Engen to call it a carnivalesque 'church of options'. Its equally diverse theologies have been labelled '*Unklarheit*' by historians, a Babylonian confusion of biblical humanism, sub-schools of scholasticism, Christian Neoplatonism. Little surprise that scholars routinely call it a church without an agreed or shared orthodoxy, a wild garden of unregulated religious experimentation. This book argues that, on its own terms (the terms of the discourse outlined above), the late medieval church did not in fact lack orthodoxy, but simply had a different understanding of this concept. Whereas we today routinely conflate religious orthodoxy with doctrine (correct belief), the sources discussed above reveal a strong sense that orthodoxy lay in universality-unity itself, rather than in a fixed body of theological positions. The *fides Christi* of the creeds and early councils could be augmented by evolving new teachings in the course of theological speculation, debate, and disputation—'doctrina' in the fifteenth century was, tellingly, interchangeable with academic 'opinion' (*sententiae, opiniones*).

This book, taking the Polish riddle as a springboard, outlines a broader hypothesis about what happened when this late medieval variegated, unity-focused catholicism entered the 1520s, and how those events shaped language for centuries to come. On the face of it, a church with flexible and only partly defined doctrinal boundaries, accustomed to a degree of heterogeneity, should have coped rather well with yet another devotional-academic tendency, patiently absorbing it (as some catholics were of course still attempting to do at the colloquy of Regensburg, or the Council of Trent). We are told that it was Luther's sheer theological novelty which made him unabsorbable: a new teaching on salvation acquired through faith in Christ alone, which in effect blew up a late medieval world of Masses, priests, and theologians. However, it is suggested here that Luther's central idea of *sola fide* revolutionized not just the content of Christian orthodoxy (teaching), but also the underlying concept and language of orthodoxy (the locus of religious truth). *Sola fide* was a doctrine about doctrine, a second-order belief in philosopher's terms, which claimed for itself unique insight and salvific power—rejecting consensus or the Christian majority as a source or form of orthodoxy, definitively conflating *doctrina* with *fides* (belief), and changing the meaning and status of the word 'doctrine' so powerfully that we still use Luther's redefinition of it today. Armed with this super-doctrine of the Reformation, Luther vividly reimagined the late medieval church itself as his own photo-negative image, as an institution constructed around one, wrong doctrine. As Pocock stresses, a language innovator of such power draws his opponents into his own discourse: in response, catholic polemicists, in Poland and beyond, slowly began to redefine catholicism as a set of distinctive doctrines, until the Tridentine Catechism consisted of a list of fixed beliefs, with no reference now to unity or the church as a historic universal consensus. In King Sigismund's Poland, where late medieval, pre-confessional catholics confronted Lutherans in print and orations and royal audiences, in the raw clash between Erasmus and Luther of 1524–5, we find these two parties talking right past one another—in different languages, using the same words (*doctrina, ecclesia*) to mean entirely different things. This thesis builds on John Bossy's suggestion, in the 1980s, that the Reformation involved a wholesale reconceptualization of Christianity in the Latin West, from a focus on society to a focus on belief, involving a major linguistic shift. John Henderson has argued that neo-orthodoxies diligently cover their tracks, masking their thought-revolutions by presenting them as part of a historic continuum, appropriating the language of those whom they defeat. This book suggests that the Reformation, in the Polish monarchy and well beyond, can be read as a collective defeat, and rejection, of a mildly pluralistic, unity-focused late medieval catholicism by both the Protestant and Catholic Reformations—and as their appropriation, and remoulding, of its very language.

The hypothesis gives us an interpretive lens through which to view the churches of the modern world. The Reformation generated three (principal) rival churches which all understood orthodoxy as rooted in correct doctrine, and themselves as possessing a unique and uniquely true set of belief-teachings—Lutheran, Calvinist, and Roman Catholic. One conclusion to draw from this study, for ecumenicalists, might be that so long as a majority see Christian orthodoxy as resting in doctrinal truth, rather than in unity itself, no institutional reconciliation of the churches produced in the Reformation is readily possible; doctrine is, after all, their *raison d'être*, and they were born in the sixteenth century out of a historic rejection of universalism and unity. The Christian consensus since the sixteenth century has, paradoxically, shifted away from consensus.

More broadly, the reading of the Reformation as a paradigm shift in thought, a revolution in the very concept of orthodoxy, represents a lesson in the origins of conflict. It is a case study in how a society, or a civilization, with shared beliefs can, in the space of a few decades, collapse into two polarized cultures, causing exile, inquisition, cultural conflict, and war. The late medieval church warns us that highly pluralistic societies or entities, which define themselves loosely with reference to very broad values or slogans, in their diversity are places of great cultural and intellectual creativity. However, precisely by defining their identity in the broadest possible terms (unity, the church) they are also inherently vulnerable to external shocks, or internal thought-revolutions, which might force them to redefine themselves in different, narrower terms, thereby destroying their fragile shared self-understanding and, in the process, their social cohesion. The late medieval church suggests that such pluralistic entities are broadly pacific, intellectually and culturally fertile, but that when they implode—like an atom being split—the forces they generate can prove unexpectedly destructive.

This book suggests too that we should take the medieval character of the Reformation period seriously, however difficult this is in an academic culture which still institutionally splits up the 'medieval' and 'early modern' periods. To treat these as different fields, rather than as deeply interpenetrating cultures, risks obscuring much. To recover the world view of late medieval catholics such as Sigismund I, as it emerges over thousands of pages of sources, is to see, with some surprise and discomfort, just how radically different that world view was to those of the Protestant and Counter-Reformation churches which emerged in the sixteenth century, and to our (Reformation-inherited) modern assumptions about religion. The Reformation is thus not only the *splitting up* of the late medieval church, as recently stressed by Mark Greengrass, but also the vanquishing of older concepts of religion and religious difference in Latin Europe so thoroughly, that they remain today unfamiliar and hard to read.[1] Their voices are hard to hear. Sigismund I's experiences thus help us to recapture afresh the Reformation as Europe's journey from a fragile but fertile late medieval world, to the more violent and heady one of the Reformation; from Christian pluralism in unity, to Christian pluralism in deadly conflict.

---

[1] Mark Greengrass, *Christendom Destroyed: Europe, 1517–1648* (London, 2014).

APPENDIX 1

Legal Proceedings against Followers of the Early Reformation in the Polish Monarchy, 1517–35

	Date	Source	Name of accused	From	Status of accused	Case heard	Charge	Outcome
1	1522	Barycz (1935), p. 99	Joachim of Loewenberg	Loewenberg (Lwówek Śląski)	University student	University court		
2	1522	Bukowski (1883), vol. 1, p. 165 Urban (1961), p. 149	Marcin Bayer	Biecz in Carpathians	Priest	Kraków episcopal court	[Manuscript lost]	
3	8 July 1524	AAG, A. Cons. A84, fo. 39(v)	Pancratius the German			Gniezno, court of the diocesan official	For being follower of 'sectam hareticam Martini Luther'; preaching as a lay person.	Denies charges
4	11 Feb 1525	BJ, MS 5357, fo. 70	Johannes called Hanus Pruss	Kraków	-	Kraków episcopal court	Suspected of being of Lutheran sect.	Denies charges; official warning
5	11 Feb 1525	BJ, MS 5357, fo. 70	Balthasar	Kraków	Organist of the collegiate church of All Saints, Kraków	Kraków episcopal court	Suspected of being of Lutheran sect.	Denies charges; official warning
6	11 Feb 1525	BJ, MS 5357, fo. 70	Jacobus Laudanus	Kraków	Tailor	Kraków episcopal court	Suspected of being of Lutheran sect.	Official warning
7	11 Feb 1525	BJ, MS 5357, fo. 70	Jeronimus Rymecz	St Anne's Street, Kraków	-	Kraków episcopal court	Suspected of being of Lutheran sect.	Official warning

(continued)

	Date	Source	Name of accused	From	Status of accused	Case heard	Charge	Outcome
8	11 Feb 1525	BJ, MS 5357, fo. 70	Andreas	St Anne's Street, Kraków	Tailor	Kraków episcopal court	Suspected of being of Lutheran sect.	Official warning
9	12 Feb 1525	BJ, MS 5357, fo. 70	Dorothea Laslowa	Kraków, Castle Street (Grodzka)	Widow	Kraków episcopal court	Eating meat in Lent; associating with cleric Kraszowski from All Saints' Church.	Official warning
10	12 Feb 1525	BJ, MS 5357, fo. 70 Ptaśnik, p. 110	Mathias	Arrested in the house of Kraszowski	Illuminator/ bookmaker	Kraków episcopal court	Being of Lutheran schism.	Denies charges; official warning
11	13 Feb 1525	BJ, MS 5357, fo. 70	Simon	Kraków	Tanner	Kraków episcopal court	Saying prayers for dead are useless; associating with Valentinus, a Lutheran.	Denies charges
12	13 Feb 1525	BJ, MS 5357, fo. 70	Gregyer Woythowycz de Cerdo	Kraków	Scholar in the house of Sthano, citizen and consul of Kraków	Kraków episcopal court	Being of Lutheran sect and heretical; blasphemy in saying prayers for dead useless.	Denies charges
13	13 Feb 1525	BJ, MS 5357, fo. 70		Kraków	Tanners (?)	Kraków episcopal court	Being of Lutheran sect; saying confessions useless; denying purgatory.	Denies charges
14	13 Feb 1525	BJ, MS 5357, fo. 70	Valentinus, son of Offnas, and Lucas	Kraków	Tanner (?)	Kraków episcopal court	Lutheran sect.	Denies charges
15	13 Feb 1525	BJ, MS 5357, fo. 70	Jeronimus Rubens Cerdo	Kraków	Tanner (?)	Kraków episcopal court	For spreading Lutheran sect among the vulgar people.	'Charitably' warned
16	15 May 1525	BJ, MS 5357, fo. 70(v)	Bernardus Czech	Kraków	Psalterista priest	Kraków episcopal court	Inappropriate behaviour with women, and being of the Lutheran sect.	Denies charges

	Date	Source	Name	Place	Description	Court	Charges	Outcome
17	8 June 1525	BJ, MS 5357, fo. 71	Benedictus Byenyek	Kraków	A German of Kraków's Garbary district	Kraków episcopal court	For being part of heretical Lutheran sect, and blasphemies against God, saying relics of the 11,000 virgins are bones of calves.	Denies charges; stood bail by neighbours
18	30 June 1525	BJ, MS 5357, fo. 71	Andreas	Kraków	Deputy German preacher at St Mary's Church	Kraków episcopal court	For a sermon mocking the relics of St Stanisław; declaring that listening to sermons and Word more useful than pilgrimages.	Denies charges; explains what he actually said in sermon
19	30 Dec 1525	BJ, MS 5357, fo. 71(v)	Bartholomeus	Kraków/Kazimierz	Rector of Corpus Christi school in Kazimierz, a town outside Kraków	Kraków episcopal court	Lutheran sect and blasphemy; associating with the Lutheran Johannes Hess in Breslau, possession of Hess' books.	Denies charges; told not to leave Kraków
20	22 Jan 1526	BJ, MS 5357, fo. 72(v)	Mathias of Ropczycze	Kazimierz	Cleric in minor orders at school of Corpus Christi, Kazimierz	Kraków episcopal court	On Boxing Day in Garbary in front of large crowd blasphemed against the saints.	Sentenced to one year in Lipowiec jail, 'in pene doloris et aquae', and then exiled from Kraków diocese
21	23 March 1526	BJ, MS 5357, fo. 71(v)	Michael	Kraków	Bookseller	Kraków episcopal court	Importing an edition of Christostom prepared by heretics.	Denies all knowledge of heretical content of books; told to cease such imports or face a fine of 300 florins

(continued)

	Date	Source	Name of accused	From	Status of accused	Case heard	Charge	Outcome
22	[spring] 1526	Budka, p. 188 AT 8, p. 145	[–]	Warsaw	Tailor	Court of collegiate church of Warsaw	Lutheranism and blasphemy.	Given bail
23	[before June] 1526	AAWł, Acta Ep. 2 (9), fos. 179–179(v)	Bernardus Baschman, rector of Danzig St Mary's parish school	Danzig	School master	Włocławek episcopal court	Already once abjured 'the damned Lutheran sect'; charged with relapse.	
24	1526	Bukowski (1883), vol. 1, p. 167; Gabryel, p. 383	Marcin Czech	Kraków		Kraków episcopal court	Denies presence of Christ in Eucharist.	
25	11 May 1528	BJ, MS 5357, fo. 72	Jakub of Iłża	Kraków	University lecturer and preacher at St Stephen's	Kraków episcopal court	Preaching on certain heretical Lutheran articles.	Denies charges
26	May 1529	Urban 1991, p. 210	Barbara and Gabriel Giebart	Kraków	Merchants	Kraków official's court	Lutheranism.	Renounce Lutheranism before diocesan officials
27	June 1529	Gabryel, p. 384	Szymon Zacjusz of Proszowice	Kraków	Psalterista in cathedral	Kraków episcopal court	For spreading Lutheran teaching, and immoral behaviour.	
28	6 Feb 1530	BJ, MS 5357, fo. 73(v); Ptaśnik (1922), p. 125	Petrus	Kraków	Bookseller	Kraków episcopal court	Bringing to Kraków heretical books of Lutheran sect, publicly selling them, especially heretical catechism for boys.	Admits importing six copies, denies knowing that they were heretical
29	21 April 1532	BJ, MS 5357, fo. 74	Andrzej Trzecieski	Kraków	Noble	Kraków episcopal court	Blasphemy, saying prayer to the Virgin does not work, must pray directly to Christ.	Denies charge

	Date	Source	Name	Location	Occupation	Court	Charge	Outcome
30	10 Dec 1532	BJ, MS 5357, fo. 75(v)	Perrus Danigiel	Kraków	Consul of Kraków	Kraków episcopal court	Lutheran sect, reading Lutheran books, eating meat.	Official warning
31	10 Dec 1532	BJ, MS 5357, fo. 75	Andreas Salomon	Kraków	Citizen (son of leading banker)	Kraków episcopal court	Lutheran sect, reading Lutheran books, eating meat.	Official warning
32	10 Dec 1532	BJ, MS 5357, fo. 75(v)	Johannes Eckler	Kraków	Citizen	Kraków episcopal court	Lutheran sect, reading Lutheran books, eating meat.	Official warning
33	10 Dec 1532	BJ, MS 5357, fo. 75(v)	Andreas Fogelweder	Kraków	Citizen	Kraków episcopal court	Lutheran sect, reading Lutheran books, eating meat.	Official warning
34	12 Dec 1532	BJ, MS 5357, fo. 75(v)	Mathias Gutfor	Kraków, Grodzka Street	Citizen	Kraków episcopal court	Eating meat; Lutheran 'conventicula'.	Official warning
35	19 Dec 1532	BJ, MS 5357, fo. 75	Stanislaus Schadek	St Nicholas Street, Kraków		Kraków episcopal court	Eating meat in Lent.	Denies charge
36 and 37	19 Dec 1532	BJ, MS 5357, fo. 75	Bartholomeus Almanus and his wife Barbara	Kraków	King's builder	Kraków episcopal court	Suspected of Lutheran sect; his wife Barbara for blaspheming against Virgin.	Denies charge
38	19 Dec 1532	BJ, MS 5357, fo. 75	Stanislaus Zelner	Slawkowski St.		Kraków episcopal court	Eating meat in Lent.	Denies charge
39	19 Dec 1532	BJ, MS 5357, fo. 75	Johannes/Hannus of Lembark	Haller house, Kraków		Kraków episcopal court	Lutheran sect, eating meat on prohibited days.	Official warning
40	1532	Budka, pp. 190–1	Synayder the German	Warsaw	Tailor	Warsaw	Spreading Lutheranism among town dwellers, attacking cult of saints.	Refuses to abjure, given one month to go into exile

(continued)

	Date	Source	Name of accused	From	Status of accused	Case heard	Charge	Outcome
41	1532	Bukowski (1883), vol. 1, p. 169	Sebastian Kuncz	Kraków		Kraków episcopal court		
42	c.1532	Bukowski (1883), vol. 1, p. 168	Matthias Goldszlagier	Kraków		Kraków episcopal court	[Lutheranism]	
43	c.1532	Gabryel, p. 384	A cluster of unnamed clergy	Kraków	Clergy	Kraków episcopal court	Accused of taking part in secret meetings, at which non-catholic doctrines professed.	
44	Jan 1533	Bukowski (1883), vol. 1, p. 170	Wolfgang Wolff			Kraków episcopal court		
45	April 1534	Budka, pp. 191–2	Jan Burbach	Warsaw	Son of Mayor of Warsaw	Warsaw	Avoiding holy water, like a Lutheran.	
46	10 Sep 1534	BJ, MS 5357, fo. 74	Jakub of Iłza	Kraków	University lecturer	Kraków episcopal court	Lutheran articles.	Denies it; will undertake canonical purgation
47	24 Nov 1534	BJ, MS 5357, fo. 74	Jakub of Iłza	Kraków	University lecturer	Kraków episcopal court	In absentia, list of heretical views he held presented to court—denial of cult of saints, church festivals, ceremonies, indulgences, purgatory; possession of Lutheran books, preaching Lutheranism.	(Fled)

No.	Date	Source	Name	Place	Status	Court	Charge	Outcome
48	July 1535	AAP, Acta Ep. VII, 331(v)–332f	Stanislaus	Poznań	City consul	Poznań episcopal court	Lutheran sect.	Denies charges; further investigation ordered
49	July 1535	AAP, Acta Ep. VII, 331(v)–332f	Andreas Schenkner	Poznań	Citizen	Poznań episcopal court	Lutheran sect.	Denies charges; further investigation ordered
50	July 1535	AAP, Acta Ep. VII, 331(v)–332f	Anna Wochowa	Poznań	Citizen	Poznań episcopal court	Lutheran sect.	Denies charges; further investigation ordered
51	July 1535	AAP, Acta Ep. VII, 331(v)–332f	Andreas Bruchman	Poznań	Citizen	Poznań episcopal court	Lutheran sect.	Denies charges; further investigation ordered
52	July 1535	AAP, Acta Ep. VII, 331(v)–332f	Conradus Pamirida	Poznań	Citizen	Poznań episcopal court	Lutheran sect.	Denies charges; further investigation ordered
53	July 1535	AAP, Acta Ep. VII, 331(v)–332f	Bartholomeus Cross	Poznań	Citizen, tailor	Poznań episcopal court	Lutheran sect.	Denies charges; further investigation ordered
54	July 1535	AAP, Acta Ep. VII, 331(v)–332f	Wlossek	Poznań	Citizen	Poznań episcopal court	Lutheran sect.	Denies charges; further investigation ordered
55 and 56	July 1535	AAP, Acta Ep. VII, 331(v)–332f	Henricus Falkner, Thomas Maritus Stanskij	Poznań	Citizen, worker	Poznań episcopal court	Lutheran sect.	Deny charges; further investigation ordered
57	July 1535	AAP, Acta Ep. VII, 331(v)–332f	Mauritius Cosch	Poznań	Citizen	Poznań episcopal court	Lutheran sect.	Denies charges; further investigation ordered

(continued)

	Date	Source	Name of accused	From	Status of accused	Case heard	Charge	Outcome
58	July 1535	AAP, Acta Ep. VII, 330(v)–331f; 333(v)–334v; 337(v)	Michael Werner	Poznań	Citizen, merchant	Poznań episcopal court	Confessed to utraquism.	Condemned as heretic; property confiscated
59	1536	Ptaśnik (1922), p. 147, fn. 1	Hieronym Wietor	Kraków	Printer		Importing books and images offensive to church; breaking episcopal and royal edicts on heresy.	Imprisoned in civil jail; inquisition will proceed against him when King back in Poland

APPENDIX 2

List of Texts Referring to and/or Discussing the Early Reformation Used in Language Analysis (Chapters 7 and 8)

MODERN SOURCE EDITIONS

AT 5 (1519–21)
  CLIII, Andrzej Krzycki to Piotr Tomicki
  CLIV, Andrzej Krzycki to Piotr Tomicki
AT 6 (1522–3)
  LXVII, Bishop Piotr Tomicki to Chancellor Krzysztof Szydłowiecki
  XCVI, King Sigismund to King Ludwig of Hungary
  XCVI, King Sigismund to the lords of Bohemia
AT 7 (1524–5)
  IX, Instruction for royal envoys travelling to Danzig
  XXXIII, King Sigismund to Bishop Erhard von Queis of Pomesania
  XXXIV, King Sigismund to Bishop Mauritius Ferber's envoy
  LXVIII, Bishop Tomicki to Łukasz Górka
  LXXII, King Sigismund to Georg, Margrave of Brandenburg
  CXL, King Sigismund to Pope Clement VII
  CXLI, King Sigismund to his cardinal protector
  CLIX, Johannes Dantiscus to King Sigismund
  VI, Bishop Tomicki to the Poznań cathedral chapter
  XIII, Johannes Dantiscus to King Sigismund
  XXIII, King Sigismund to Danzig
  I, Royal summons of a parliament
  III, Royal envoys to the Prussian diet
  IX, The King
  III, King Sigismund to Thorn
  XXV, Bishop Tomicki to Bishop Ferber
  XXII, Bishop Tomicki to Łukasz Górka
  XXVIII, Contemporary account of the 1525 investiture ceremony and treaty text
  XXX, King Sigismund to Bishop Tomicki
  XXXIII, Bishop Andrzej Krzycki, epigrams
  XXXIII, Bishop Krzycki, *Epistola de Negotio Prutenico*
  XXXV, King Sigismund to Pope Clement VII
  XXXVIII, Johannes Dantiscus to Bishop Tomicki
  XL, Bishop Tomicki to Johannes Dantiscus
  XLII, King Sigismund to Bishop Ferber
  XLIV, King Sigismund to King Louis of Hungary
  XLVIII, Primate Łaski to King Sigismund, report from his envoy in Rome

LVII, Bishop Tomicki to Ludovico Aliphio
LVIII, Bishop Tomicki to Cardinal Campeggio
LIX, Bishop Tomicki to the Captain of Bohemia
LX, King Sigismund to Duke Albrecht of Prussia
LXI, Ensign sent to King Sigismund by Pope Clement VII
LXIX, Bishop Krzycki to Bishop Tomicki
LXX, Bishop Krzycki to Bishop Tomicki
LXXXVI, King Sigismund to Bishop Ferber
LXXXVII, Jan Zambocki to Johannes Dantiscus
C, Instructions for royal envoys to Thorn
CI, Edict against heretics in Marienburg
CII, Bishop Tomicki to Bishop Maciej Drzewicki
CV, King Sigismund to Danzig Council
CXII, Bishop Tomicki to Bishop Drzewicki
CXIII, King Sigismund to the citizens of Danzig
CXIV, The Danzig Apologia (1)
CXV, The Danzig Apologia (2)
CXVI, Royal response to the Danzig envoys
CXVII, King Sigismund to his bishops and senators
CXVIII, Bishop Tomicki to Bishop Krzycki
CXIX, Primate Łaski's memorandum on Danzig
CXXII, Royal decree against Danzig
CXXIII, Royal letter to Danzig
CXXVI, Royal response to Mayor Ferber
CXXVII, Bishop Krzycki to Bishop Tomicki
CXXVIII, Bishop Krzycki to Bishop Tomicki
CXXIX, Bishop Tomicki to Bishop Krzycki
CXXX, Bishop Krzycki to Bishop Tomicki
CXXXIV, Second royal response to Danzig envoys (oration)
CXXXV, Royal decree on Danzig city officials
CXXXVI, Royal letter declaring innocence of named Danzigers
CXXXVIII, Royal letter declaring innocence of named Danzigers
CXL, King Sigismund to the Grand Master of Livonia
CXLI, King Sigismund to neighbouring princes
CXLII, Royal decree on circulating Danzig printed pamphlets
CXLIII, Dismissal of the Danzig envoys
AT 8 (1525–6)
I, Royal summoning of parliament
IV, Instruction of the Poznań delegation to parliament
V, Royal letter to officials of Royal Prussia on the payment of tithes
VI, Royal decree on the payment of tithes in Royal Prussia
X, King Sigismund to Bishop Ferber
XII, Royal summons/citation against the city of Danzig
XIII, King Sigismund to Danzig
XVI, King Sigismund to his Royal Prussian counsellors
XVII, King Sigismund to royal officials and nobles in Royal Prussia
XIX, Royal reply given to Bishop Queis
XX, Royal decree against Royal Prussian withholding tithes
XXI, Duke Albrecht to Chancellor Szydłowiecki

XXIII, Royal edict summoning Royal Prussian nobles for march on Danzig
XXVII, Bishop Krzycki to Bishop Tomicki
XXVIII, King Sigismund to King Gustav of Sweden
XXXV, Royal reply to Duke Albrecht
XXXVI, King Sigismund to Walter of Plettenburg, Grand Master of the Teutonic Order in Livonia
XXXVII, Royal delegation to John, Bishop of Riga
XXXVIII, Mikołaj Szydłowiecki to Queen Bona Sforza
XLIII, King Sigismund to Dukes George and Barmin of Pomerania
XLIV, King Sigismund to Dukes George and Barmin of Pomerania
XLVI, King Sigismund to King Henry VIII of England
XLVIII, Piotr Kmita to Queen Bona
XLIX, Mikołaj Szydłowiecki to Queen Bona
L, Bishop Tomicki to Bishop Krzycki
LIII, Bishop Tomicki to King Sigismund
LIV, King Sigismund decree for Danzig
LVII, Royal edict on surrender of Lutheran materials in Danzig
LVIII, *Statuta Sigismundi* for Danzig
LXX, Royal decree on the Hel peninsula and recent events in Danzig
LXII, Royal decree appointing Philip Bischof as new *burgrabius* in Danzig
LXXXIV, King Sigismund to Elbing
LXXXV, King Sigismund to Braunsberg
LXXXVI, LXXXVII, and LXXXVIII, King Sigismund to Elbing
LXXXIX, Appointment of royal commissioners for Elbing
XC, Royal decree on royal commissioners for Braunsberg
XCIV, XCV, and XCVI, King Sigismund to Bishop Queis
XCVII, King Sigismund to Cardinal Campeggio
XCIV, Bishop Tomicki to Jan Balinski, castellan of Danzig
CV and CIX, King Sigismund to Duke Albrecht
CXL, King Sigismund to Martin Oborski, captain of Warsaw
CXIII, King Sigismund to Łukasz Górka
CXVI, Bishop Tomicki to Achacy Czema
CXVIII, Bishop Tomicki to Philip Bischof
CXXI, King Sigismund to Poznań [wrongly labelled Danzig]
CXXIII, King Sigismund decree on resettling Danzig prisoners
CXXIV, King Sigismund to Achacy Czema
CXXV, Royal decree for city of Thorn
CXXVI, Royal decree on prisoner Joannes Ottendorp
CCXXXII, Johannes Dantiscus to Bishop Tomicki
CCXLIII, Jan Zambocki to Johannes Dantiscus
CCXLIX, Johannes Dantiscus to King Sigismund
CCLII, Johannes Dantiscus to Bishop Tomicki
AT 9 (1527)
9, Instructions for royal envoys to local assemblies (sejmiki)
12, Royal delegation to Royal Prussia assembly in Thorn
32, Bishop Tomicki to Johannes Dantiscus
35, King Sigismund to Bishop Queis
81, Royal reply to Duchy of Mazovia
106, King Sigismund to Chancellor Szydłowiecki

115, Instruction for Andrzej Górka, royal envoy to Imperial Diet
116, Bishop Tomicki to the Archbishop of Riga
117, King Sigismund to his Cardinal Protector
155, King Sigismund to Breslau
158, Bishop Krzycki to Cuthbert Tunstall, Bishop of London
161, King Sigismund to Duke Albrecht
162, Bishop Tomicki to Duke Albrecht
205, Johannes Dantiscus to Queen Bona
208, Hieronymus Łaski to Wawrzyniec Międzyleski, Bishop of Kamieniec
216, Royal decree on Jacobus Flynk, Danzig prisoner
238, Bishop Drzewicki to Duke Albrecht
239, Bishop Międzyleski to Hieronymous Łaski
248, Jan Zambocki to Johannes Dantiscus
276, King Sigismund to Dukes George and Barmin of Pomerania
277, Chancellor Szydłowiecki to Duke Albrecht
307, Bishop Tomicki to Cardinal Campeggio
AT 10 (1528)
33, Bishop Drzewicki to Bishop Ferber
35, King Sigismund to Johannes Baliński, treasurer of Prussia
45, King Sigismund to royal officials in Royal Prussia
46, Polish senators and bishops to the nobility of Royal Prussia
51, Bishop Drzewicki to Bishop Ferber
59, King Sigismund to the Archbishop of Uppsala
60, King Sigismund to the Bishop of Linkoping
61, Bishop Tomicki to the Bishop of Linkoping
87, King Sigismund reply to orator from Ferdinand Habsburg
101, Royal response to envoys from Danzig
127, Polish royal delegation to the Imperial Diet
138, Bishop Tomicki to King Sigismund
150, Bishop Ferber to King Sigismund
155, Bishop Krzycki to Bishop Tomicki
196, Bishop Tomicki to Queen Bona
209, King Sigismund to the palatine of Kulm
210, 266, and 304, Bishop Drzewicki to Bishop Ferber
306, King Sigismund to George, Duke of Saxony
321, Bishop Tomicki to King Sigismund
326, Bishop Tomicki to Jan Zambocki
361, Jan Zambocki to Bishop Tomicki
404, King Sigismund to Jerzy Konopacki, Palatine of Pomerania
405, Bishop Drzewicki to Bishop Ferber
426, Bishop Ferber to King Sigismund
451, Bishop Krzycki to Bishop Tomicki
455, Bishop Tomicki to Bishop Krzycki
470, Bishop Krzycki to Bishop Tomicki
AT 11 (1529)
59, Royal delegation to the Polish parliament
120, Bishop Ferber to Jan Chojeński, royal secretary
133, King Sigismund to Royal Prussia
195, Bishop Drzewicki to Bishop Ferber
204, Bishop Tomicki to Janusz, Duke of Oppeln

206, Bishop Tomicki to King Sigismund
232, Bishop Ferber to Jan Chojeński
354, Bishop Drzewicki to Bishop Ferber
412, Bishop Krzycki to Christoph Hegendorf
432, Chancellor Szydłowiecki to Duke Albrecht
AT 12 (1530)
10, King Sigismund to Duke Albrecht
111, Bishop Ferber to King Sigismund
136, Bishop Drzewicki to Bishop Ferber
137, Bishop Ferber to King Sigismund
138 and 150, Bishop Ferber to Jan Chojeński
164, Chancellor Szydłowiecki to Johannes Dantiscus
168, Kulm cathedral chapter to Johannes Dantiscus
177, Chancellor Szydłowiecki to Duke Albrecht
213, Johannes Dantiscus to King Sigismund, from Augsburg Diet
217, Johannes Dantiscus to Bishop Tomicki, from Augsburg
234, Johannes Dantiscus to King Sigismund
244, Bishop Tomicki to Johannes Dantiscus
288, Stanisław Rzeczyca, Polish agent in Rome, to Bishop Dantiscus
292 and 314, Bishop Dantiscus to King Sigismund
325, Royal envoy to parliament
348, Bishop Krzycki to Bishop Tomicki
378, Bishop Dantiscus to Bishop Tomicki
385, Bishop Drzewicki to Bishop Ferber
413, Bishop Ferber to Bishop Tomicki
427, King Sigismund to Bishop Dantiscus
429, Poem for the coronation of Sigismund Augustus
AT 13 (1531)
17, King Sigismund to Duke Albrecht
37, Bishop Krzycki to Bishop Tomicki
93, Bishop Tomicki to Bishop Krzycki
98, Jan Chojeński to Duke Albrecht
127 and 128, King Sigismund to Pope Clement VII
132, King Sigismund to Duke Albrecht
133, Bishop Drzewicki to Bishop Ferber
137, Bishop Tomicki to Dr Stanisław Rzeczyza
142, Bishop Tomicki to Bishop Drzewicki
165 and 241, Bishop Dantiscus to King Sigismund
248, King Sigismund to Bishop Dantiscus
256, Bishop Tomicki to Bishop Ferber
297, Martin Czema, Canon of Kulm, to Bishop Dantiscus
342, Bishop Krzycki to Duke Albrecht
351, Jan Chojenski, Bishop of Przemyśl, to Duke Albrecht
363, Bishop Dantiscus to King Sigismund
399, Oration by Bishop Tomicki
406 and 408, Bishop Tomicki to Bishop Krzycki
AT 14 (1532)
5, King Sigismund to Charles, Captain of Silesia
34, King Sigismund to Duke Albrecht
53, Primate Drzewicki to Bishop Dantiscus

128, Letter of Nicholas Pfluger
146 and 170, Bishop Ferber to King Sigismund
178, Bishop Tomicki to Bishop Ferber
337, Bishop Chojeński to Duke Albrecht
361, Bishop Tomicki to Jan Karnkowski, Bishop of Włocławek
442, Royal foundation of a new benefice in Elbing
462 and 470, Primate Drzewicki to Bishop Dantiscus
492, Bishop Krzycki to Duke Albrecht
525, Bishop Dantiscus to Danzig Council
535, Bishop Dantiscus to Bishop Tomicki
534, Bishop Tomicki to Bishop Dantiscus
550, Bishop Dantiscus to King Sigismund
AT 15 (1533)
4, Bishop Karnkowski to Bishop Dantiscus
10, King Sigismund to Clement VII
18, Primate Drzewicki to Bishop Dantiscus
24, Bishop Chojeński to Bishop Dantiscus
25, Joannes Tressler, citizen of Danzig, to Bishop Dantiscus
85, Bishop Dantiscus to Bishop Tomicki
87, Bishop Dantiscus to King Sigismund
143, King Sigismund to Bishop Dantiscus
147, Bishop Tomicki to Bishop Dantiscus
203, Bishop Dantiscus to the citizens of Graudenz
238, Bishop Tomicki to Bishop Dantiscus
260, King Sigismund to Georg, Margrave of Brandenburg
463, Bishop Krzycki to Bishop Tomicki
484, Nicholaus Nipszyc, royal secretary, to Duke Albrecht
525, King Sigismund to Clement VII
554, Bishop Krzycki to Queen Bona
AT 16a (1534)
54, Delegation to King Sigismund from parliament
97, Bishop Tomicki to King Sigismund
165, King Sigismund to Emperor Charles V
170, Royal delegation to Duke Albrecht
192, Mikołaj Działyński, Castellan of Kulm, to Bishop Dantiscus
210, Primate Drzewicki to Bishop Ferber
222, Johannes Werden of Danzig to Bishop Dantiscus
249, Jostus Ludovicus Decius, royal secretary, to Bishop Dantiscus
286, King Sigismund to Joachim, Margrave of Brandenburg
290, Primate Drzewicki to Bishop Ferber
328, Canon Tiedemann Giese to Bishop Ferber
333, Bishop Ferber to Bishop Dantiscus
361, Primate Drzewicki to Bishop Ferber
379, Bishop Ferber to Bishop Dantiscus
AT 16b (1534)
385, Bishop Dantiscus to Bishop Tomicki
396, Achacy Czema, Castellan of Danzig, to Bishop Dantiscus
399, Bishop Dantiscus to Bishop Tomicki

419, Bishop Tomicki to Bishop Dantiscus
430, Bishop Tomicki to Bishop Chojeński
431 and 441, Bishop Tomicki to King Sigismund
475, Primate Drzewicki to Bishop Ferber
480, King Sigismund to the royal council
522, King Sigismund to papal datarius
527, Bishop Tomicki to a Camera Apostolica official
548, Primate Drzewicki to Bishop Dantiscus
566, Royal delegation to Polish parliament
574, Bishop Tomicki to King Sigismund
589, Joannes Werden to Bishop Ferber
614, Bishop Tomicki to King Sigismund
651, Bishop Dantiscus to Bishop Tomicki
658, Bishop Kryzcki to Bishop Tomicki
668, Bishop Tomicki to Primate Drzewicki
671, Bishop Tomicki to Dr Stanisław Borek
672, Bishop Tomicki to Johann Cochlaeus
AT 17 (1535)
7, King Sigismund to Bishop Dantiscus and Georg Baisen
9, Bishop Tomicki to King Sigismund
55, Primate Drzewicki to Bishop Dantiscus
86, Bishop Ferber to Bishop Dantiscus
97, Bishop Dantiscus to Bishop Tomicki
104, Bishop Tomicki to Mikołaj Bedleński, his vicar
123, King Sigismund to Duke Albrecht
141, King Sigismund to Danzig Council
142, King Sigismund to Bishop Ferber and others
153, Bishop Chojeński to Bishop Dantiscus
160, Primate Drzewicki to Bishop Dantiscus
177, Instructions for Bishop Tomicki's envoy to King Sigismund
180 and 186, Bishop Tomicki to Mikołaj Bedleński and others
201, Bishop Tomicki to Stanisław Rzeczyca
204, Bishop Tomicki to Jan and Jakub Ostroróg
253, Danzig Council to King Sigismund
328 and 344, Primate Drzewicki to Bishop Dantiscus
355, Bishop Dantiscus to Bishop Tomicki
360, Bishop Tomicki to Mikołaj Bedleński
365, Bishop Dantiscus to Bishop Tomicki
368, Bishop Tomicki to Bishop Dantiscus
573, King Sigismund to Piotr Kmita
595, Bishop Dantiscus to Bishop Ferber
Theiner, *Monumenta Poloniae*, II
Nr. cccxlvii, King Sigismund to the pope (1524)
Nr. ccccxli, Chancellor Szydłowiecki to the pope (1524)
Nr. cccli, Polish episcopate to the pope (1525)
Nr. cccxc, Polish episcopate to the pope (1528)
Nr. dlxiii, King Sigismund to the pope (1534)
Nr. dlxxxvi, Johannes Dantiscus to the pope (1539)

Opus Epistolorum, ed. P. S. Allen,
  Bishop Krzycki to Erasmus, vol. 6, nr. 1652
  J. Antonius to Erasmus, vol 6, nr. 1660
  King Sigismund to Erasmus, vol. 7, nr. 1952
  Jan Łaski junior to Erasmus, vol. 7, nr. 1954
  Bishop Tomicki to Erasmus, vol. 10, nr. 2861
Zakrzewski, *Wzrost*,
  Royal ruling on accusation of heresy against Jodocus Ludovicus Decius
  Royal edict on study at Wittenberg
  Royal letter on study at Wittenberg
'Acta Capituli Gnesnensis', Ulanowski, B., ed.
  Two entries (nrs. 3015, 3045)
'Acta Capituli Plocensis, 1514–77', Ulanowski, Bolesław ed.
  Thirteen entries (nrs. 36, 38, 58, 61, 68, 75, 99, 104, 110, 113, 149, 158, 173)
Elementa,
  Seven letters of King Sigismund to Duke Albrecht
  One royal decree for Kulm
Spicilegium Copernicanum,
  Two episcopal decrees for Ermland
Simon Grunau's Preussische Chronik
CIP III and IV
  Eight royal heresy edicts
'Ferber Chronicle', *Monumenta Historiae Warmiensis* VIII
Ptaśnik, Jan (ed.), *Cracovia impressorum*, one heresy charge
Urkundenbuch II, nr. 505, list of clergy expelled from Danzig for Lutheranism
Warmiński, *Andrzej Samuel*, appendix, banishment decree for Lutheranism (1541)

SIXTEENTH–CENTURY PRINTED TEXTS

Jan Konarski, Bishop of Kraków, preface
  In *Bulla contra errores* (Kraków, 1520)
Mark Scharffenberg and Hieronym Wietor, preface
  In *D. Erasmi Roterodami opus de conscribendis epistolis* (Kraków, 1523)
Poem, 'In imaginem Lutheri'
Andrzej Krzycki, letter to the King
Poem, 'Conditiones boni luterani'
Poem, 'De monstro cucullato'
Poem, 'Vacca cucullatam'
Poem, 'De Lutero'
Poem, 'Cum semper maledicta'
Poem, 'Petrus Sadorius ad Luteram'
Poem by Johannes Tirvesius
Poem, 'In quendam luteranum'
Poem by Iohannes Ostrorius
Poem by Stanislaus Schlomonius
  In *Encomia Luteri* (Kraków, 1524)
Canon Piotr Rydziński, treatise

Canon Piotr Rydziński, poem
 In *Petrii Risinii* (Kraków, 1524)
Canon Tiedemann Giese, letter to Canon Felix Reich
Felix Reich, letter to Tiedemann Giese
Tiedemann Giese, letter to Canon Leonard Niderhoff
Tiedemann Giese, treatise
 In Giese's *Flosculorum Lutheranorum* (Kraków, 1525)
Hieronymus Wietor, preface
Leonard Cox, poem
Stanislaus Hosius, poem
 In Erasmus *Hyperaspistes* (Kraków, 1526)
Stanislaus Hosius, dedicatory letter
 In *Erasmi Roterodami Epistola* (Kraków, 1527)
Leonard Cox, poem
Andrzej Krzycki, letter to Queen Bona
Andrzej Krzycki, treatise
 In Krzycki, *De Afflictione* (Kraków, 1527)
Statuta provintiae gnesnensis (Kraków, 1527)
Gregory Szamotulski, preface
Gregory Szamotulski, sermon
 In his *Sermo de indulgentiis* (Kraków, 1531/2)
Stanisław Byliński, dedicatory letter
Stanisław Byliński, three letters to Laurentius Corvinus
 In his *Defensorium Ecclesiae* (Kraków, 1531)
Gregory Szamotulski, letter to reader
Gregory Szamotulski, treatise
 In his *Anacephaleosis* (Kraków, 1535)
Walenty Wróbel, dedicatory letter
Walenty Wróbel, treatise
 In his *Propugnaculum Ecclesiae* (Frankfurt, 1536)
Gregory Szamotulski, letter to Walenty Wróbel
Walenty Wróbel, letter to Szamotulski
Gregory Szamotulski, treatise
 In Szamotulski, *Vincula* (Kraków, 1536)

MANUSCRIPTS

Twenty-four Kraków court hearings for Lutheranism (BJ, MS 5337)
Fifteen letters of Bishop Ferber (AAWa, AB A1)
Five Poznań court hearings for Lutheranism (AAP, AEVII)
Four entries, cathedral chapter acts of Poznań diocese (AAP, CP37)
Three letters of Canon Tiedemann Giese (AAWa, D29)
Two entries, cathedral chapter *acta* of Włocławek diocese (ADWł Acta Cap. 2)
Two entries, cathedral chapter acts of Ermland diocese (AAWa, Acta Cap. A1)
Entry, cathedral chapter *acta* of Gniezno archdiocese (AAG, B18 Acta Cap.)
Trial, court of Gniezno official (AAG, A Cons. A 84)
Trial for Lutheranism (ADWł Acta Ep. 2)

Letter of Bishop Międzyleski (AAWa, D66)
Letter of clergy of Danzig parish church (AAWa, D66)
Letter of King Sigismund on Danzig (AAWa, D66)
Letter of Primate Łaski to Bishop Ferber (AAWa, D66)
Letter of Bishop Chojeński to Bishop Ferber (AAWa, D66)

Bibliography

MANUSCRIPT SOURCES

Cambridge
University of Cambridge Library
  MS Ee.4.27

Gniezno
Archiwum Archidiecezjalne w Gnieźnie (AAG)
A. Cap. B18
A. Cons. A84

Kraków
Archiwum Kurii Metropolitalnej (AKMK)
  Acta Ep. vol. 4
  Acta Ep. 5
  Acta Ep. VII
Biblioteka Jagiellońska (BJ)
  MS 5337, vol. 9, papers of Żegota Pauli
  Marginalia, inc. nr. 2636

London
British Library
  Cotton Vitellius B/VII

Olsztyn
Archiwum Archidiecezji Warmińskiej (AAWa)
  A1
  AB A1
  Acta Cap. 1A
  Acta Ep. 1
  D39
  D64
  D66
  Doc. Kap. Z4
  Doc. Varia I

Poznań
Archiwum Archidiecezjalne w Poznaniu (AAP)
  AE VII
  AE VIII
  CP 37 (Acta capituli)

Vatican
Archivio Segreto Vaticano (ASV)
  Armadio XL, vol. 14

Armadio XL, vol. 24
Armadio XL, vol. 38
Reg. Lat. 1297
Reg. Lat. 1467
Reg. Lat. 1470
Reg. Lat. 1555
Reg. Lat. 1579
Reg. Lat. 1599
Camera Apostolica, Div, Cam, 74
Camera Apostolica, Div, Cam, 83

Włocławek
Archiwum Diecezjalne we Włocławku (AAWł)
Abkp, vol. 1 (107)
Acta Cap. 1A
Acta Cap. 2
Acta Ep. 2
Acta Ep. 2 (9)
Acta Ep. 2 (19)
AKK 2 (216)
Dok. 383, 384

PRINTED PRIMARY SOURCES

Acta Tomiciana, 18 vols, ed. Władysław Pociecha, Wacław Urban, Andrzej Wyczański et al. (1852–1999).
Akta Aleksandra, ed. F. Papée (Kraków, 1927).
Akta Stanów Prus Królewskich, 8 vols, ed. Marian Biskup et al. (Toruń, 1955–93).
Archiwum Komisyi Prawniczej, Akademja Umiejętności w Krakowie, vol. I (Kraków, 1895).
Aurifaber, Andreas, *Schola Dantiscana* (Danzig, 1539).
Benninghoven, Ursula (ed.), *Die Herzöge in Preussen und das Bistum Kulm (1525–1691): Regesten aus dem Herzoglichen Briefarchiv und den Ostpreussischen Folianten* (Köln, 1993).
Byliński, Stanisław, *Defensorium Ecclesiae adversus Laurentium Corvinum* (Kraków, 1531).
Calvin, John, *Ioannis Calvini Commentarii in Epistolam ad Hebraeos* (Geneva, 1549).
Clichtove, Josse, *Propugnaculum adversus Lutheranos* (Paris, 1526).
Cochlaeus, Johann, *Confessio fidei exhibita invictiss. imp. Carolo V. Cæsari Aug. in comicijs Augustæ* (Wittenberg, 1531).
Cochlaeus, Johann, *Adversus novam reformationum senatus Bernensis* (Leipzig, 1534).
Cochlaeus, Johann, *Adversus impia et seditiosa scripta Martini Lutheri* (Leipzig, 1534).
Cochlaeus, Johann, *Articuli Anabaptisarum Monasteriensium per doctorem Johannem Cochleum confutati* (Leipzig, 1534).
Cochlaeus, Johann, *De veneratione et invocatione sanctorum* (Leipzig, 1534).
Cochlaeus, Johann, *Philippicae quatuor Johannis Cochlei in Apologiam Philippi Melanthconis* (Leipzig, 1534).
Cochlaeus, Johann, *Velitatio Johannis Cochlaei in Apologiam Philippi Melanchtonis* (Leipzig, 1534).
Correspondenz des Kaisers Karl V. Aus dem königlichen Archiv und der Bibliothèque de Bourgogne zu Brüssel, 2 vols, ed. Karl Lanz (Leipzig, 1844–5).

Corpus iuris Polonici, vols 1–4, ed. Oswald Balzer (Kraków, 1906–10).

Constitutiones et Articuli Synodi Lancicien[sis] Anno domini Millesimo quige[n]tesimo vigesimo septimo celebratae, Jte[m] Synodi Piotrkovien[sis] Anno domini Millesimo Quingentesimo tricesimo die Lunae ante festum sanctae Margaretae celebratae, Jtem Synodi Piotrcovien[sis] Anno domini Millesimiquingentesimo tricesimo secundo celebratae (Kraków, 1532).

Cusa, Nicholas of, *The Catholic Concordance*, ed. Paul E. Sigmund (Cambridge, 1996).

Dantiscus, Johannes, *Corpus Tekstów i Korespondencji Jana Dantyszka/Corpus of Ioannes Dantiscus' Texts & Correspondence* [website], http://dantiscus.ibi.uw.edu.pl

Decius, Jostos Ludovicus, *De Sigismundi Regis Temporibus* (Kraków, 1521).

Decrees of the Ecumenical Councils, ed. Norman Tanner, vol. I (London and Washington, DC, 1990).

Deutsche Reichstagsakten Jüngere Reihe: Deutsche Reichstagsakten unter Kaiser Karl V. Zweiter Band, ed. Adolf Wrede (Gotha, 1896).

Deutsche Reichstagsakten Jüngere Reihe: Deutsche Reichstagsakten unter Kaiser Karl V. Dritter Band, ed. Adolf Wrede (Gotha, 1901).

Deutsche Reichstagsakten Jüngere Reihe: Deutsche Reichstagsakten unter Kaiser Karl V. Vierter Band, ed. Adolf Wrede (Gotha, 1905).

Deutsche Reichstagsakten Jüngere Reihe: Deutsche Reichstagsakten unter Kaiser Karl V. Siebenter Band 1527–1529, ed. Johannes Kühn (Stuttgart, 1935).

Deutsche Reichstagsakten Jüngere Reihe: Deutsche Reichstagsakten unter Kaiser Karl V. Achter Band. Die protestierenden Reichsstände und Reichsstädte zwischen den Reichstagen zu Speyer 1529 und Augsburg 1530, ed. Wolfgang Steglich (Göttingen, 1970–1).

Deutsche Reichstagsakten Jüngere Reihe: Deutsche Reichstagsakten unter Kaiser Karl V. Zehnter Band. Der Reichstag in Regensburg und die Verhandlungen über einen Friedstand mit den Protestanten in Schweinfurt und Nürnberg 1532, ed. Rosemarie Aulinger (Göttingen, 1992).

Deutsche Reichstagsakten Jüngere Reihe: Deutsche Reichstagsakten unter Kaiser Karl V. Zwölfter Band. Der Reichstag zu Speyer 1542, ed. Silvia Schweinze-Burian (Munich, 2003).

Deutsche Reichstagsakten Jüngere Reihe: Deutsche Reichstagsakten unter Kaiser Karl V. Fünfter/Sechster Band. Der Reichstag zu Augsburg 1525, der Reichstag zu Speyer 1526, Der Fürstentag zu Esslingen 1526, ed. Rosemarie Aulinger (Munich, 2011).

Eck, Johann, *Epistola ad Carolum V de Luderi causa* (Ingolstadt, 1521).

Eck, Johann, *Prima pars operum Iohannis Eckii contra Ludderum* (place of printing uncertain, 1530/1).

Eck, Johann, *Edictum contra Anabaptistas* (Kraków, 1535).

Elementa ad Fontium Editiones XXX: Documenta ex archivo Regiomontano ad Poloniam spectantia, ed. Karolina Łanckorońska, part 1 (Rome, 1973).

Eyn statlicher unnd feyerlicher Actus der holdigund sso . . . Sigmundt . . . yn seiner Künglicher Stadt Dantzigk . . . enthpfangen hat (Kraków, 1526).

Erasmus of Rotterdam, *Des. Erasmi Roterodami Epistola ad inclytum Sigismundum regem Poloniae* (Kraków, 1527).

Erasmus of Rotterdam *Opus Epistolarum Des. Erasmi Roterodami*, 12 vols, ed. P. S. Allen et al. (Oxford, 1906–58).

Erasmus of Rotterdam, *Collected Works of Erasmus*, vol. 76, ed. Charles Trinkaus, trans. Peter Macardle and Clarence H. Miller (Toronto, 1999).

Erasmus of Rotterdam, *Collected Works of Erasmus*, vol. 78, ed. James D. Tracy (Toronto, 2011).

Fabri, Johann, *Adversus doctorem Balthasarem Pacimontanem, Anabaptistarum nostri saeculi* (Leipzig, 1528).

Ferreri, Zaccaria, *Oratio Legati Apostolici Habita Thorunij in Prussia ad Serenissimum Poloniae Regem contra Errores Fratris Martini Lutheri* (Kraków, 1521).

Ficino, Marsilio, *Platonica theologia de immortalitate animorum* (Florence, 1482).

Franconius, Matthias, *Oratio in splendidissimas nuptias et foelicem hymenaeum potentissimi Sigismundi Augusti regis Poloniae* (Kraków, 1543).

Giese, Tiedemann, *Flosculorum Lutheranorum de fide et operibus anthelogikon* (Kraków, 1525).

Hartmann, Stefan, *Herzog Albrecht von Preussen und das Bistum Ermland: Regesten aus dem Herzoglichen Briefarchiv und den ostpreussischen Folianten*, 2 vols (Köln, 1991–3).

Hegendorff, Christoph, *Dialogi Pueriles* (Hagenau, 1528; Paris, 1529; Antwerp, 1529).

Hegendorff, Christoph, *De instituenda vita et moribus* (Hagenau, 1529; Paris, 1529).

Hegendorff, Christoph, *Oratio in artium liberalium lauden coram frequenti* (Kraków, 1530).

Hegendorff, Christoph, *Stichologia* (Kraków, 1534).

Henry VIII, King of England, *A copy of the letters, wherin the most redouted [and] mighty pri[n]ce, our souerayne lorde kyng Henry the eight, kyng of Englande [and] of Frau[n]ce, defe[n]sor of the faith, and lorde of Irla[n]de: made answere vnto a certayne letter of Martyn Luther, sente vnto him by the same and also the copy of the foresaid Luthers letter, in such order, as here after foloweth* (London, ?1527).

Henry VIII, King of England, *Henry VIII Fid. Def. His Defence of the Faith and its Seven Sacraments*, ed. Richard Rex (Sevenoaks, 2008).

Herminjard, Aimé Louis, *Correspondance des reformateurs dans les pays de langue française*, ed. A. L. Herminjard, vol. 3 (Geneva, 1870).

Komjáthey, Benedict, *Epistolae Pauli lingua hungarica donatae* (Kraków, 1533).

Konarski, Jan, *Bulla contra errores Martini Luterij* (Kraków, 1520).

Kromer, Marcin and Maciejowski, Samuel, *De Sigismundo Primo rege Poloniae etc duo panegyrici funebres, dicti Cracoviae in eius funere* (Mainz, 1550).

Krzycki (Cricius), Andrzej, *Encomia Luteri* (Kraków, 1524).

Krzycki, Andrzej, *Ad Iohannem Antonium Pulleonum Baronem Brugij nuntium apostolicum in Ungaria, de Negotia Prutenico Epistola* (Kraków, 1525).

Krzycki, Andrzej, *De Afflictione Ecclesiae, commentarius in Psalmum XXI* (Kraków, 1527).

Letters and Papers, Foreign and Domestic, of the Reign of Henry VIII, Vol. 4, Part I (1524–6), ed. J. S. Brewer (London, 1870).

Lubelczyk, Andrzej, *Tumultuaria responsio in libellum Philipi Melanctonis* (Kraków, 1540).

Luther, Martin, *Resolutiones disputationum de virtute indulgentiarum* (Wittenberg, 1519).

Luther, Martin, *Ein kurtz fruchtbars Beicht büchlein auss den tzehen Gebothen gottes genugsam aussgelegt yre erfüllung uñd ubertretung von Doctor Martino Luther gemacht* (Danzig, 1520).

Luther, Martin, *An die Herren Deutschen Ordens* (Wittenberg, 1523).

Luther, Martin, *D. Martin Luthers bisher grossentheils ungedruckte Briefe* (Leipzig, 1784).

Luther, Martin, *D. Martin Luthers Werke: Briefweschel*, ed. Joachim Karl Friedrich Knaake, vol. 5 (Wiemar, 1930).

Luther, Martin, *Luther's Works*, vol. 36, ed. Abdel Ross Wentz and Helmut Lehmann (Philadelphia, 1959).

Luther, Martin, *Luther's Works*, vol. 44, ed. J. Atkinson and H. Lehmen (Philadelphia, 1966).

Luther, Martin, *Luther's Works*, vol. 39, ed. Eric W. Gritsch and Helmut Lehmann (Philadelphia, 1970).

Luther, Martin, *Luther's Works*, vol. 33, ed. Philip S. Watson and Helmut Lehmann (Philadelphia, 1972).

Mazzolini, Silvestro da Prierio, *Egregium vel potius diuinum opus in Iohannem Capreolum Tholosanum Sacri Predicatorum Ordinis: A Fratre Siluestro Prieriani eiusdem Ordinis. Sacre theologie baccalario rarissimis conferendo cu[m] nonnullis appendicibus seu additamentis complectentibus ad omnem in theologicis materiam accutissimoru[m] doctorum pene omnium clarissimas opiniones* (Cremona, 1497).

Monumenta Historiae Warmiensis, vol. 8 (Braunsberg, 1889).

Passerinus, Valentinus, *Propugnaculum ecclesiae adversus varias sectas* (Frankfurt, 1536).

von Polentz, Georg, *Ein Sermon am Ostertage geprediget* (Königsberg, 1524).

Ptaśnik, Jan (ed.), *Cracovia impressorum XV et XVI saeculorum* (Kraków, 1922).

Recueil générale des anciennes lois francaise, ed. A. Jourdan et al., 29 vols (Paris, 1821–33).

Regesta Copernicana, ed. Marian Biskup (Wrocław, 1973).

Rydziński (Risinius), Piotr, *In Axiomata Ioannis Hessi Wratislaviae edita* (Kraków, 1524).

Rydziński, Piotr, *Petri Risinii in Iohannis Hessi Cachinni Sycophantias Responsio* (Kraków, 1524).

Sacranus, Johannes, *Elucidarius Errorum Ritus Rutenici* (Kraków, c.1505).

Scotus, Duns, *Scotus pauperum vel abbreviatus in quo doctorum et Scoti opiniones in quattuor libris sententiarum compendiose elucidantur* (Speyer, 1492).

Scriptores Rerum Prussicarum, 6 vols, ed. Theodor Hirsch, Max Töppen, Ernst Strehlke, and Walther Hubatsch (Leipzig, 1861–1968).

Sichardt, Johannes, *Antidotum contra diversas omium fere seculorum haereses* (Basel, 1528).

Simon Grunau's Preussische Chronik, 3 vols, ed. Max Perlbach, R. Philippi, and P. Wagner (Leipzig, 1875–96).

Spicilegium Copernicanum, order Quellenschriften des Literaturgeschichte des Bisthums Ermland in Zeitalter des Nikolaus Kopernicus, Historischer Verein für Ermland (MAINZ) (Braunsberg, 1873).

Statuta Inclyti Regni Polonie (Kraków, 1532).

Statuta provintiae gnesnensis antiqua et nova, revisa diligenter emendata (Kraków, 1527).

The Statutes at Large from Magna Charta to the end of the Last Parliament, ed. Owen Ruffhead, vol. 1 (London, 1758).

Stupperich, Robert (ed.), *Die Reformation im Ordensland Preussen 1523/4: Predigten, Traktate und Kirchenordnungen* (Ulm, 1966).

Szamotulski, Grzegorz, *Sermo de indulgentiis* (Kraków, 1531/2).

Szamotulski, Grzegorz, *Anacephaleosis Flosculos monogrammos ex progymnasmatis Christophori Endorfini* (Kraków, 1535).

Szamotulski, Grzegorz, *Vincula Hippocratis* (Kraków, 1536).

Testamentum Novum. Z niemieckiego przekładu M. Lutra (Kraków, 1540/41).

Ulanowski, Bolesław (ed.), 'Acta Capituli Plocensis, 1514–77', in *Archiwum Komisyi Historycznej*, vol. X (Kraków, 1916).

Urkundenbuch zur Reformationsgeschichte des Herzogthums Preussen, 3 vols, ed. Paul Tschackert (Leipzig, 1890).

Vetera Monumenta Poloniae et Lithuaniae Gentiumque Finitimarum Historiam Illustrantia, 4 vols, ed. Augustin Theiner (Rome, 1860–4).

Vincent of Ferrara, *Prophetie Danielis tres horribiles de casu videlicet et ruina vite spiritualis. De lapsu ecclesiastice dignitatis et de ruina catholice fidei ac adventu Antichristi et mundi consumatione* (Kraków, 1527).

Volumina Legum, vol. 1, ed. Jozafat Ohryzko (St Petersburg, 1859).

Wróbel (Passerinus), Walenty, *Propugnaculum Ecclesiae adversus varias sectas* (Leipzig, 1536).

Wróbel, Walenty, *Opus Quadragesimale* (Leipzig, 1537).

Wojtyska, H., ed., *Zacharias Ferreri (1519–1521) et nuntii minores (1522–1553)*, ed. Henryk Wojtyska, Acta Nunciaturae Polonae (Rome, 1992).

PRINTED SECONDARY SOURCES

Abray, Lorna Jane, 'Confession, Conscience and Honour: The Limits of Magisterial Tolerance in Sixteenth-Century Strassburg', in Ole Grell and Robert W. Scribner (eds), *Tolerance and Intolerance in the European Reformation* (Cambridge, 1996), pp. 94–107.

Achremczyk, Stanisław, *Warmia*, 2nd edition (Olsztyn, 2011).

Achremczyk, Stanisław and Szorc, Alojzy, *Braniewo* (Olsztyn, 1995).

d'Alton, Craig, 'The Suppression of Lutheran Heretics in England, 1526–1529', *Journal of Ecclesiastical History* 54 (2003): 228–53.

d'Alton, Craig, 'William Wareham and English Heresy Policy after the Fall of Wolsey', *Historical Research* 77:197 (2004): 337–57.

Arnold, Udo, 'Luther und Danzig', *Zeitschrift für Ostforschung* 21 (1972): 94–121.

Arnold, Udo, 'Hochmeister Albrecht von Brandenburg-Ansbach und Landmeister Gotthard Kettler. Ordensritter und Terittorialherren am Scheideweg in Preussen und Livland', in Klaus Militzer, Johannes A. Mol, and Helen J. Nicholson (eds), *The Military Orders and the Reformation: Choices, State Building, and the Weight of Tradition* (Hilversum, 2006), pp. 11–29.

Backvis, Claude, 'La fortune d'Erasme en Pologne', in *Colloqium Erasmianum* (Mons, 1968), pp. 173–202.

Bagchi, David, *Luther's Earliest Opponents: Catholic Controversialists, 1518–25* (Minneapolis, 1991).

Barszcz, Leszek, *Andrzej Krzycki: poeta, dyplomata, prymas* (Gniezno, 2005).

Bartel, Oskar, 'Filip Melanchton w Polsce', *OiRwP* 6 (1961): 73–90.

Bartel, Oskar, 'Marcin Luter w Polsce', *OiRwP* 7 (1962): 27–50.

Barycz, Henryk, *Historia uniwersytetu jagiellońskiego w epoce humanizmu* (Kraków, 1935).

Barycz, Henryk, 'Udział Teodora Wotschkiego w rozwoju badań nad dziejami ruchu reformacyjnego w Polsce', *Reformacja w Polsce* XI (1948–52): 115–22.

Bataillon, Marcel, *Érasme et l'Espagne: recherches sur l'histoire spirituelle du XVIe siècle* (Paris, 1937).

Bedouelle, Guy, *The Reform of Catholicism, 1480–1620*, trans. James K. Farge (Toronto, 2008).

Bejczy, István, 'Tolerantia: A Medieval Concept', *Journal of the History of Ideas* 58 (1997): 365–84.

Bejczy, István and Cary J. Nederman (eds), *Princely Virtues in the Middle Ages, 1200–1500* (Turnhout, 2007).

Bell, Rudolph and Weinstein, Donald, *Saints and Society: The Two Worlds of Western Christianity, 1000–1700* (Chicago, 1982).

Bierlaire, Franz, 'Christoph Hegendorff', in Peter G. Bietenholz and Thomas B. Deutscher (eds), *Contemporaries of Erasmus*, vol. 2 (Toronto, 1986), pp. 171–2.

Bietenholz, Peter G. and Deutscher, Thomas B. (eds), *Contemporaries of Erasmus: A Biographical Register of the Renaissance and Reformation*, 3 vols (Toronto, 1985–7).

Biskup, Marian, 'Geneza i znaczenie hołdu pruskiego 1525', *Komunikaty Mazursko-Warmińskie* 4 (1975): 407–24.

Biskup, Marian, *'Wojna Pruska' czyli walka Polski z zakonem krzyżackim z lat 1519–21* (Olsztyn, 1991).

Biskup, Marian, *U schyłku średniowiecza i w początkach odrodzenia: (1454–1548)*, vol. II of *Historia Torunia*, part I (Toruń, 1992).

Biskup, Marian, *Wojny polski z zakonem krzyżackim, 1308–1521* (Gdańsk, 1993).

Biskup, Marian, 'Wawrzyniec Międzyleski, autor opisu hołdu pruskiego 1525', in Stanisław Bylina (ed.), *Kultura staropolska—kultura europejska: Prace ofiarowane Januszowi Tazbirowi* (Warsaw, 1997), pp. 211–20.

Blickle, Peter, *Die Revolution von 1525* (Munich, 1975); in translation *The Revolution of 1525: The German Peasants' War from a New Perspective* (Baltimore, 1981).

Bock, Vanessa, 'Die Anfänge des polnischen Buchdrucks in Königsberg. Mit einem Verzeichnis der polnischen Drucke von Hans Weinreich und Alexander Augezdecki', in Axel Walter (ed.), *Königsberger Buch- und Bibliotheksgeschichte* (Köln, 2004), pp. 127–55.

von Bockelmann, Berta, *Danzigs Politik in der Reformationszeit im Briefwechsel zwischen Johann von Werden und Herzog Albrecht* (Kiel, 1968).

Bogucka, Maria, 'Walki społeczne w Gdańsku w XVI wieku', in Gerard Labuda, *Szkice z dziejów Pomorza*, vol. I (Warsaw, 1958), pp. 369–448.

Bogucka, Maria, 'Reformation, Kirche und der Danziger Aufstand in den Jahren 1517–26', in Evamaria Engel et al. (eds), *Hansische Stadtgeschichte—Brandenburgische Landesgeschichte* (Weimar, 1989), pp. 217–24.

Bogucka, Maria, 'Die Wirkungen der Reformation in Danzig', *Zeitschrift für Ostforschung* 42 (1993): 195–206.

Bogucka, Maria, with Klaus Zernack, *Um die säkularisation des Deutschens Orderns in Preussen* (Hannover, 1996).

Bogucka, Maria, *Baltic Commerce and Urban Society, 1500–1700* (Aldershot, 2003).

Borawska, Teresa, *Tiedemann Giese (1480–1550): W życiu wewnętrznym Warmii i Prus Królewskich* (Olsztyn, 1984).

Borawska, Teresa, 'Alexander Svenichen: ein Preussischer Franziskaner in den Wirren des Reformationzeitalters', in Udo Arnold, Mario Glauert, and Jürgen Sarnowsky (eds), *Preussische Landesgeschichte: Festschrift für Bernhart Jähnig* (Marburg, 2001), pp. 175–86.

Borkowska, Urszula, *Dynastia Jagiellonów w Polsce* (Warsaw, 2013).

Bossy, John, 'Some Elementary Forms of Durkheim', *Past & Present* 95:1 (1982): 3–18.

Bossy, John, 'The Mass as a Social Institution: 1200–1700', *Past & Present* 100 (1983): 29–61.

Bossy, John, *Christianity in the West, 1400–1700* (Oxford, 1985).

Brady, Thomas A., 'The Reformation of the Common Man, 1521–4', in C. Scott Dixon (ed.), *The German Reformation: The Essential Readings* (Oxford, 1999), pp. 94–132.

Brecht, Martin, 'Das Wormser Edikt in Suddeutschland', in Fritz Reuter (ed.), *Der Reichstag zu Worms von 1521* (Worms, 1971), pp. 475–89.

Brendler, Gerhard, *Martin Luther: Theologie und Revolution: eine marxistische Darstellung* (Köln, 1983).

Brigden, Susan, *London and the Reformation* (Oxford, 1989).

Brückner, Aleksander, *Różnowiercy polscy: szkice obyczajowe i literackie* (Warsaw, 1905).

Budka, Włodzimierz, 'Przejawy reformacji w miastach mazowsza 1526–48', *OiRwP* 28 (1983): 185–94.

Bues, Almut, *Die Apologien Herzog Albrechts* (Wiesbaden, 2004; revised edition Wiesbaden, 2009).

Bukowski, Julian, *Dzieje Reformacyi w Polsce od wejścia jej do Polski aż do jej upadku*, vol. 1 (Kraków, 1883).

Bukowski, Waldemar, 'Salomonowie herbu Łabędź—ze studiów nad patrycjatem krakowskim wieków średnich', in *Cracovia-Polonia-Europa* (Kraków, 1995), pp. 113–45.

Bylina, Stanisław, 'Wizerunek heretyka w Polsce późnośredniowiecznej', *OiRwP* 30 (1985): 5–24.

Bynum, Caroline Walker, *Holy Feast and Holy Fast: The Religious Significance of Food to Medieval Women* (Berkeley, 1987).

Cameron, Euan, 'Italy', in Andrew Pettegree (ed.), *The Early Reformation in Europe* (Cambridge, 1992), pp. 188–214.

Cameron, Euan, *Waldenses: Rejections of Holy Church in Medieval Europe* (Oxford, 2000).

Cameron, Euan, *Enchanted Europe: Superstition, Reason, and Religion, 1250–1750* (Oxford, 2010).

Cameron, Euan, *The European Reformation*, 2nd edition (Oxford, 2012).

Caponetto, Salvatore, trans. Anne and John Tedeschi, *The Protestant Reformation in Sixteenth-Century Italy* (Kirksville, MO, 1999).

Cavill, P. R., 'Heresy and Forfeiture in Marian England', *Historical Journal* 56:9 (2013): 879–907.

Chisholm, M. A., 'The Religionspolitik of Emperor Ferdinand I (1521–1564): Tyrol and the Holy Roman Empire', *European History Quarterly* 38:4 (2008): 551–77.

Chmaj, Ludwik, *Bracia polscy: ludzie, idee, wpływy* (Warsaw, 1957).

Chmaj, Ludwik (ed.), *Studia nad arianizmem* (Warsaw, 1959).

Chmaj, Ludwik, *Faust Socyn (1539–1604)* (Warsaw, 1963).

Chodynicki, Kazimierz, *Reformacja w Polsce* (Warsaw, 1921).

Chrisman, Miriam Usher, *Conflicting Visions of Reform: German Lay Propaganda Pamphlets, 1519–30* (Atlantic Highlands, 1996).

Christman, Victoria, *Pragmatic Toleration: The Politics of Religious Heterodoxy in Early Reformation Antwerp, 1515–1550* (Rochester, 2015).

Christensen, Carl, 'John of Saxony's Diplomacy, 1529–30: Reformation or Realpolitik?', *Sixteenth Century Journal* 15:4 (1984): 419–30.

Christiansen, Eric, *The Northern Crusades*, 2nd edition (London, 1997).

Chrzanowski, Ignacy and Kot, Stanisław (eds), *Humanizm i Reformacja* (Kraków, 1927).

Cieślak, Tadeusz, 'Postulaty rewolty pospólstwa gdańskiego w r. 1525', *Czasopismo Prawno-Historyczne* VI (1954): 123–52.

Clark, Stuart, 'Inversion, Misrule and the Meaning of Witchcraft', *Past & Present* 87 (1980): 98–127.

Close, Christopher, *The Negotiated Reformation: Imperial Cities and the Politics of Urban Reform, 1525–1550* (Cambridge, 2009).

Congar, Yves, *L'Ecclésiologie du Haut Moyen Age: de Saint Grégoire le Grand á la disunion entre Byzance et Rome* (Paris, 1968).

Crossley, James G. and Karner, Christian (eds), *Writing History, Constructing Religion* (Aldershot, 2005).

Csepregi, Zoltán, 'The Evolution of the Language of the Reformation in Hungary (1525–6)', *Hungarian Historical Review* 2:1 (2013): 3–34.

Cynarski, Stanisław (ed.), *Raków: ognisko arianizmu* (Kraków, 1968).

Cytowska, Maria, 'Justus Ludovicus Decius', in Peter G. Bietenholz and Thomas B. Deutscher (eds), *Contemporaries of Erasmus: A Biographical Register of the Renaissance and Reformation*, vol. 1 (Toronto, 1985), pp. 380–82.

Czaski, Tadeusz, *Dzieła Tadeusza Czackiego*, vol. I (Poznań, 1843).

Czerniatowicz, Janina, 'Początki grecystyki i walka o język grecki w Polsce dobie odrodzenia', *Studia i materiały z dziejów nauki polskiej* A:5 (1959): 29–55.

Daniel, David P., 'Hungary', in Andrew Pettegree (ed.), *The Early Reformation in Europe* (Cambridge, 1992), pp. 49–69.

Danysz, Antoni, *O wychowaniu Zygmunta Augusta* (Kraków, 1915).

Davidson, N. S., 'Theology, Nature and the Law: Sexual Sin and Sexual Crime in Italy from the Fourteenth Century to the Seventeenth Century', in Trevor Dean and J. K. P. Lowe (eds), *Crime, Society and the Law in Renaissance Italy* (Cambridge, 1994), pp. 74–98.

Dixon, C. Scott, 'Introduction', in C. Scott Dixon (ed.), *The German Reformation: The Essential Readings* (Oxford, 1999), pp. 1–32.

Dolan, John, 'The Catholic Literary Opponents of Luther and the Reformation', in Erwin Iserloh, Joseph Glazik, and Hubert Jedin (eds), *Reformation and Counter Reformation*, vol. 5 of *History of the Church*, trans. Anselm Biggs and Peter W. Becker (London, 1980), pp. 191–207.

Dolezel, Stephan, *Das preussische-polnisch Lehnverhältnis unter Herzog Albrecht von Preussen (1525–68)* (Köln, 1967).

Domański, Juliusz, 'Der Einfluss der Erasmianismus und die Reformation in Polen', *Acta Poloniae Historica* 55 (1987): 41–56.

Duffy, Eamon, *The Stripping of the Altars: Traditional Religion in England, 1400–1580* (New Haven, 1992).

Duke, Alistair, *Reformation and Revolt in the Low Countries* (London, 1990; revised edition London, 2003).

Duke, Alistair, ed. Judith Pollmann and Andrew Spicer, *Dissident Identities in the Low Countries* (Farnham, 2009).

Dürr-Durski, Jan, *Arianie polscy w świetle własnej poezji* (Warsaw, 1948).

Dworzaczkowa, Jolanta, 'Kronika Pruska Szymona Grunaua jako źrodło historyczne', *Studia Zródłoznawcze* 2 (1958): 119–46.

Dworzaczkowa, Jolanta, 'O genezie i skutkach rewolty gdańskiej 1525/6', *Roczniki Historyczne* 28 (1962): 97–109.

Dworzaczkowa, Jolanta, *Reformacja i kontrreformacja w Wielkopolsce* (Poznań, 1995).

Dworzaczkowa, Jolanta, 'Jadwiga Jagiellonka (1513–1573)', in *PSB*, X (1996), pp. 293–303.

Dworzaczek, Włodzimierz, 'Andrzej Górka', in *PSB*, VIII (1959–60), pp. 401–5.

Dworzaczek, Włodzimierz, 'Łukasz Górka', in *PSB*, VIII (1959–60), pp. 409–12.

Eberhard, Winfried, 'Bohemia, Moravia and Austria', in Andrew Pettegree (ed.), *The Early Reformation in Europe* (Cambridge, 1992), pp. 23–48.

Edelheit, Amos, *Ficino, Pico and Savonarola: The Evolution of Humanist Theology, 1461/2–1498* (Leiden, 2008).

Effros, Bonny, *Creating Community with Food and Drink in Merovingian Gaul* (New York, 2002).

Eistreicher, Karol, *Bibliografia polska*, vol. 15 (Kraków, 1896).

Ekman, Ernst, 'Albrecht of Prussia and the Count's War, 1533–1536', *Archiv für Reformationsgeschichte* 51 (1960): 19–36.

Elliott, J. H., 'A Europe of Composite Monarchies', *Past & Present* 137:1 (1992): 48–71.

Elton, G. R., *Reformation Europe, 1517–1559* (London, 1963).

Elton, G. R., 'Government by Edict?', *Historical Journal* 8:2 (1965): 266–71.

van Engen, John H., 'Multiple Options: The World of the Fifteenth Century Church', *Church History* 77 (2008): 257–84.

van Engen, John H., *Sisters and Brothers of the Common Life: The Devotio Moderna and the World of the Later Middle Ages* (Philadelphia, 2008).

Farge, James K., *Orthodoxy and Reform in Early Reformation France: The Faculty of Theology of Paris, 1500–1543* (Leiden, 1985).

Febvre, Lucien, *Au coeur religieux du XVIe siecle* (Paris, 1968).

Fenster, Thelmer S. and Smail, Daniel Lord, *Fama: The Politics of Talk Reputation in Medieval Europe* (Ithaca, 2003).

Finkel, Ludwig, *Elekcya Zygmunta I* (Kraków, 1910).

Fischer, Georg, *Versuch einer Geschichte der Reformation in Polen*, 2 vols (Gratz, 1855–6).

Forrest, Ian, *The Detection of Heresy in Late Medieval England* (Oxford, 2005).

Fox, Paul, *The Reformation in Poland: Some Economic and Social Aspects* (Baltimore, 1924).

Fox, Paul, 'The Reformation in Poland', in W. F. Reddaway (ed.), *The Cambridge History of Poland*, vol. I (Cambridge, 1950), pp. 322–47.

Friedrich, Karin, *The Other Prussia: Royal Prussia, Poland and Liberty, 1559–1772* (Cambridge, 2000).

Friewald, Helmut, *Markgraf Albrecht von Ansbach-Kulmbach und seine landständische Politik als Deutschordens-Hochmeister und Herzog in Preussen während der Entscheidungsjahre 1521–1528* (Kulmbach, 1961).

Frost, Robert, 'Initium Calamitatis Regni? John Casimir and Monarchical Power in Poland-Lithuania 1648–1668', *European History Quarterly* 16 (1986): 181–207.

Frost, Robert, *The Oxford History of Poland-Lithuania*, vol. 1 (Oxford, 2015).

Fudge, Thomas A., 'Reform and the Lower Consistory in Prague, 1437–97', in Zdeněk David and David Holeton (eds), *The Bohemian Reformation and Religious Practice*, vol. 2 (Prague 1998), pp. 67–96.

Gabryel, Kazimierz, *Działalność kościelna Piotra Tomickiego 1464–1535* (Warsaw, 1972).

Glomski, Jacqueline, 'Erasmus and Cracow, 1510–30', *Erasmus of Rotterdam Society Yearbook* 17 (1997): 1–18.

Glomski, Jacqueline, *Patronage and Humanist Literature in the Age of the Jagellons: Court and Career in the Writings of Rudolf Agricola Junior, Valentin Eck and Leonard Cox* (Toronto, 2007).

Gogan, Brian, 'The Ecclesiology of Erasmus of Rotterdam: A Genetic Account', *The Heythrop Journal* 21 (1980): 393–410.

Górski, Karol, *Studia nad dziejami polskiej literatury antytrynitarskiej XVI w* (Kraków, 1949).

Górski, Karol, 'The Royal Prussian Estates in the Second Half of the Sixteenth Century and their Relations with the Crown of Poland', in *Acta Poloniae Historica* 10 (1964): 49–64.

Górski, Karol, *Zakon Krzyżacki a powstanie państwa pruskiego* (Wrocław, 1977).

Görtz, Hans-Jürgen, 'Eine "bewegte" Epoche: Zur Heterogenität reformatorische Bewegungen', *Zwingliana* 19:2 (1993): 103–25.

Grad, Stanisław, *Kościelna działalność arcybiskupa i prymasa Jana Łaskiego*, Studia z historii kościoła w Polsce 4 (Warsaw, 1979).

Greengrass, Mark, *Christendom Destroyed: Europe, 1517–1648* (London, 2014).

Gregory, Brad S., *The Unintended Reformation: How a Religious Revolution Secularized Society* (Cambridge MA, 2012).

Grell, Ole, 'Scandinavia', in Andrew Pettegree (ed.), *The Early Reformation in Europe* (Cambridge, 1992), pp. 94–119.

Grell, Ole, 'Introduction', in Ole Grell and Robert W. Scribner (eds), *Tolerance and Intolerance in the European Reformation* (Cambridge, 1996), pp. 1–12.

Grell, Ole and Robert W. Scribner (eds), *Tolerance and Intolerance in the European Reformation* (Cambridge, 1996).

Griffiths, Gordon, 'Francis I', in Peter G. Bietenholz and Thomas B. Deutscher (eds), *Contemporaries of Erasmus*, vol. 2 (Toronto, 1986), pp. 50–2.

Grulkowski, Marcin, Możejko, Beate, and Szybkowski, Sobiesław (eds), *Katalog dokumentów i listów królów polskich z Archiwum Państwowego w Gdańsku (do roku 1492)* (Danzig, 2015).

Guarino, Thomas G., *Vincent of Lérins and the Development of Christian Doctrine* (Grand Rapids, 2013).

Gundermann, Iselin, *Herzogin Dorothea von Preussen, 1504–47* (Köln, 1965).

Guy, J. A., *The Reign of Elizabeth I: Court and Culture in the Last Decade* (Cambridge, 1995).

Haberkern, Philip, 'The Lands of the Bohemian Crown: Conflict, Coexistence and the Quest for the True Church', in Howard Louthan and Graeme Murdock (eds), *A Companion to the Reformation in Central Europe* (Leiden, 2015), pp. 11–39.

Hajdukiewicz, Leszek, *Księgozbiór i zainteresowania bibliofilskie Piotra Tomickiego* (Wrocław, 1961).

Hajdukiewicz, Leszek, 'Erazm z Rotterdamu w opinii polskiej XVI–XVII wieku', *Zeszyty Naukowe Uniwersytetu Jagiellońskiego* 33 (1971): 55–67.

Hamilton, Alastair, *Heresy and Mysticism in Sixteenth-Century Spain: The Alumbrados* (Cambridge, 1992).

Hamilton, Bernard, *The Medieval Inquisition* (London, 1981).

Hamm, Berndt, 'What Was the Reformation Doctrine of Justification?', in C. Scott Dixon (ed.), *The German Reformation: The Essential Readings* (Oxford, 1999), pp. 53–90.

Hamm, Berndt, trans. John M. Frymire, 'Normative Centering in the Fifteenth and Sixteenth Centuries: Observations on Religiosity, Theology and Iconology', *Journal of Early Modern History* 3:4/4 (1999): 307–54.

Hatt, Celia A., *The English Works of John Fisher, Bishop of Rochester (1469–1535): Sermons and Other Writings, 1520–35* (Oxford, 2002).

Haude, Sigrun, *In the Shadow of 'Savage Wolves': Anabaptist Münster and the German Reformation during the 1530s* (Boston, 2000).

Head, Randolph C., 'Introduction: The Transformations of the Long Sixteenth Century', in John Christian Laursen and Carry J. Nederman (eds), *Beyond the Persecuting Society: Religious Toleration before the Enlightenment* (Philadelphia, 1998), pp. 95–106.

Heal, Brigit, *The Cult of the Virgin Mary in Early Modern Germany* (Cambridge, 2014).

Heinze, R. W., *The Proclamations of the Tudor Kings* (Cambridge, 1976).

Henderson, John, *Piety and Charity in Late Medieval Florence* (Oxford, 1994).

Henderson, John B., *The Construction of Orthodoxy and Heresy: Neo-Confucian, Islamic, Jewish and Early Christian Patterns* (Albany, 1998).

Hendrix, Scott H., 'In Quest of the Vera Ecclesia: The Crises of Late Medieval Ecclesiology', *Viator* 7 (1976): 347–78.

Hendrix, Scott H., *Recultivating the Vineyard: The Reformation Agenda of Christianization* (Louisville, 2004).

Henriet, Patrick, 'Sacrilege', in *Encylopedia of the Middle Ages*, vol. 2 (Rome, 2000), pp. 1273–4.

Hequet, Suzanne, *The 1541 Colloquy of Regensburg: In Pursuit of Church Unity* (Saarbrücken, 2009).

Hornbeck, J. Patrick II, *What Is a Lollard? Dissent and Belief in Late Medieval England* (Oxford, 2010).

Hubatsch, Walther, *Albrecht von Brandenburg-Ansbach, Deutschordens-Hochmeister und Herzog in Preussen 1490–1568* (Heidelberg, 1960).

Hubatsch, Walther, 'Albrecht of Brandenburg-Ansbach', in Henry J. Cohn (ed.), *Government in Reformation Europe, 1520–60* (London, 1971), pp. 169–202.

Hughes, Paul L. and Larkin, James F. (eds), *Tudor Royal Proclamations. Volume I: The Early Tudors (1485–1553)* (New Haven and London, 1964).

Hunter, Ian, Laursen, John Christian, and Nederman, Cary J. (eds), *Heresy in Transition: Transforming Ideas of Heresy in Medieval and Early Modern Europe* (Aldershot, 2005).

Innes, Joanna, '"Reform" in English Public Life: The Fortunes of a Word', in Joanna Innes and Arthur Burns (eds), *Rethinking the Age of Reform: Britain 1780–1850* (Cambridge, 2007), pp. 71–97.

Innes, Joanna and Phelp, Mark, *Re-imagining Democracy in the Age of Revolutions: America, France, Britain, Ireland, 1750–1850* (Oxford, 2013).

Jensen, De Lamar, *Confrontation at Worms: Martin Luther and the Diet of Worms* (Provo, UT, 1973).

Jobert, Ambroise, *De Luther á Mohila: la Pologne dans la crise de la chrétienté 1517–1648* (Paris, 1974).

Johnson, Anna Marie and Maxfield, John A. (eds), *The Reformation as Christianisation: Essays on Scott Hendrix's Christianisation Thesis* (Tübingen, 2012).

Kacprzak, Marta, 'Z problemów Reformacji XVI wieku. "Kryptoreformacja", Erazmianism, eklezjologia. Postulaty badawcze dla historii literatury i kultury polskiej', in Piotr Wilczek (ed.), *Reformacja w dawnej Rzeczpospolitej i jej Europejskie konteksty* (Warsaw, 2010), pp. 15–21.

Kaplan, Benjamin, *Divided by Faith: Religious Conflict and the Practice of Toleration in Early Modern Europe* (Cambridge, MA, 2007).

Kaplan, Benjamin, *Cunegonde's Kidnapping: A Story of Religious Conflict in the Age of Enlightenment* (New Haven, 2014).

Karant-Nunn, Susan, 'What Was Preached in the German Cities in the Early Years of the Reformation? *Wildwuchs* versus Lutheran Unity', in Philip N. Bebb and Sherrin Marshall (eds), *The Process of Change in Early Modern Europe* (Athens, OH, 1988), pp. 81–96.

Karant-Nunn, Susan, *The Reformation of Ritual: An Interpretation of Early Modern Germany* (London, 1997).

Karant-Nunn, Susan, *The Reformation of Feeling: Shaping the Religious Emotions in Early Modern Germany* (New York and Oxford, 2010).

Katalin, Peter, 'Tolerance and Intolerance in Sixteenth-Century Hungary', in Ole Grell and Robert W. Scribner (eds), *Tolerance and Intolerance in the European Reformation* (Cambridge, 1996), pp. 249–61.

Kempfi, Andrzej, 'O dwu edycjach "Anthelogikonu" Tidemana Giesego: z historii warmińskich polemik reformacyjnych w czasach Mikołaja Kopernika', *Komunikaty Mazursko-Warmińskie* 3 (1970): 455–64.

Kieckhefer, Richard, *The Repression of Heresy in Medieval Germany* (Liverpool, 1979).

Kienzle, Beverly Mayne, *Cistercians, Heresy and Crusade in Occitania, 1145–1229: Preaching in the Lord's Vineyard* (Woodbridge, 2001).

Kieszkowski, J., *Kanclerz Krzysztof Szydłowiecki: Z dziejów kultury i sztuki Zygmuntowskich czasów* (Poznań, 1912).

Kim, Lauren J., 'Censorship, Executions and Sacrilege: The First Twenty Years of Protestant History in France', *Trinity Torch Journal* 13:2 (2010): 152–72.

Klassen, Peter, *Mennonites in Early Modern Poland and Prussia* (Baltimore, 2009).

Kolankowski, Ludwig, 'Z archiwum królewieckiego, Polscy korespondenci Ks. Albrechta, 1525+', *Archeion* 6–7 (1930): 102–8.

Kolankowski, Ludwig, *Polska Jagiellonów: dzieje polityczne*, 3rd edition (Olsztyn, 1991).

Koniecki, Otto, *Geschichte der Reformation in Polen* (Breslau, 1872).

Koper, Feliks, 'Dary z Polski dla Erazma z Rotterdamu w historycznym museum Bazylejskiem', *Sprawozdania komisyi do badania Historyi sztuki w Polsce* 6 (1898): 110–38.

Kosman, Marceli, *Protestanci i kontrreformacja: z dziejów tolerancji w Rzeczpospolitej XVI– XVIII wieku* (Wrocław, 1973).

Kosman, Marceli, *Nowinki, spory i zbory—z dziejów polskiej reformacji* (Warsaw, 1981).

Kowalska, Halina, *Działalność reformatorska Jana Łaskiego w Polsce, 1556–60* (Wrocław, 1969).

Kras, Paweł, *Husyci w piętnastowiecznej polsce* (Lublin, 1989).

Kreem, Juhan, 'Der Deutsche Ordern und die Reformation in Livland', in Klaus Militzer, Johannes A. Mol, and Helen J. Nicholson (eds), *The Military Orders and the Reformation: Choices, State Building, and the Weight of Tradition* (Hilversum, 2006), pp. 43–57.

Kreigseisen, Wojciech, *Stosunki wyznaniowe w relacjach państwo-kościół między reformacją a oświeceniem* (Warsaw, 2010).

Krolzik, Udo, 'Joachim II Hector', in *Biographishe-bibliographisches Kirchenlexicon*, vol. III (Herzberg, 1992), pp. 110–15.

Kujawski, Wojciech, *Krzesław z Kurozwęk jako wielki kanclerz koronny i biskup włocławski*, Studia z Historii Kościoła w Polsce 8 (Warsaw, 1987).

Łabędzka-Topolska, Maria Danuta, 'Wpływy Reformacji w Poznaniu', in Jerzy Topolski (ed.), *Dzieje Poznania*, vol. 1 (Wrocław-Poznań, 1968), pp. 492–503.

Lalik, T., 'Kaplica królewska i publiczne praktyki religijne rodziny Kazimierza Jagiellończka', *Kwartalnik Historyczny* 88 (1981): 391–415.

Lang, Thomas, *Zwischen Reformation und Untergand Alt-Livlands: der Rigaer Erzbischof Wilhelm von Brandenburg im Beziehungsgeflecht der livlandischen Konfoderation und ihrer Nachbarlander*, 2 vols (Hamburg, 2014).

Lange, K. and Schwenke, P., *Die Silberbibilothek Herzog Albrechts* (Leipzig, 1894).

Lecler, Joseph, *Toleration and the Reformation*, trans. T. L. Westow, vol. 1 (New York, 1960).

León, Pablo Sánchez, 'Conceiving the Multitude: Eighteenth-Century Popular Riots and the Modern Language of Social Disorder', *International Review of Social History* 56 (2001): 511–33.

Leśnodorski, Bogusław, *Dominium Warmińskie, 1243–1569* (Poznań, 1949).

Levelt, W. J. M., *A History of Psycholinguistics: The Pre-Chomskyan Era* (Oxford, 2014).

Lindbeck, George, *The Nature of Doctrine: Religion and Theology in a Postliberal Age* (London, 1984).

Litak, Stanisław, *Od Reformacji do Oświecenia: kościół katolicki w Polsce nowożytnej* (Lublin, 1994).

Loetz, Francisca, *Dealings with God: From Blasphemers in Early Modern Zurich to a Cultural History of Religiousness*, trans. Rosemary Selle (Farnham, 2009).

Lorkiewicz, Antoni, *Bunt Gdańska 1525 r. Przyczynek do historyi Reformacyi w Polsce* (Lwów, 1881).

Louthan, Howard, *The Quest for Compromise: Peace Makers in Counter-Reformation Vienna* (Cambridge, 1997).

Louthan, Howard, *Converting Bohemia: Force and Persuasion in the Catholic Reformation* (Cambridge, 2009).

Louthan, Howard, 'Introduction', *Austrian History Yearbook*, 41 (2010): 13–24.

Louthan, Howard, 'A Model for Christendom? Erasmus, Poland and the Reformation', *Church History* 83:1 (2014): 18–37.

Louthan, Howard and Zachmann, Randall C., *Conciliation and Confession: The Struggle for Unity in the Age of Reform (1415–1648)* (Notre Dame, 2004).

Lubczyński, Mariusz and Pielas, Jacek, 'Krzysztof Szydłowiecki', in *PSB*, 49 (2014), pp. 551–6.

Lutton, Robert, *Lollardy and Orthodox Religion in Pre-Reformation England: Reconstructing Piety* (Woodbridge, 2006).

MacCulloch, Diarmaid, *Reformation: Europe's House Divided, 1490–1700* (London, 2003).

Maisel, Witold, *Sądownictwo miasta poznania do końca XVI wieku* (Poznań, 1961).

Małkus, Marta and Szymańska, Kamila (eds), *Reformacja i tolerancja: jedność w różnoródności? Współistnienie różnych wyznań na ziemi wschowskiej i pograniczu Wielkopolsko-Śląskim* (Wschowa, 2015).

Małłek, Janusz, 'Michał Meurer: reformator Mazur', *Komunikaty Mazursko-Warmińskie* 3 (1962): 561–8.

Małłek, Janusz, *Prusy Książęce a Prusy Królewskie w latach 1525–1548: studium z dziejów polskiej polityki księcia Albrechta Hohenzollerna* (Warsaw, 1976).

Małłek, Janusz, *Dwie części Prus: studia z dziejów Prus Książęcych i Prus Królewskich w XVI i XVII wieku* (Olsztyn, 1987).

Małłek, Janusz, 'Polska wobec luteranizacji Prus' *OiRwP* XLIX (2005): 7–16; in translation 'Poland in the Face of the Lutheranisation of Prussia', in Klaus Militzer, Johannes A. Mol, and Helen J. Nicholson (eds), *The Military Orders and the Reformation: Choices, State Building, and the Weight of Tradition* (Hilversum, 2006), pp. 31–42.

Marciniak, Ryszard, *Acta Tomiciana w kulturze politycznej Polski okresu odrodzenia* (Warsaw, 1983).

Margolis, Oren, *The Politics of Culture in Quattrocento Europe: René of Anjou in Italy* (Oxford, 2016).

Marshall, Peter, *The Oxford Very Short Introduction to the Reformation* (Oxford, 2009).

Mazurkiewicz, Karol, *Początki Akademji Lubrańskiego w Poznaniu (1519–1535)* (Poznań, 1921).

McConica, James, *English Humanists and Reformation Politics under Henry VIII and Edward VI* (Oxford, 1965).

McConica, James, 'Erasmus and the Grammar of Consent', in Joseph Coppens (ed.), *Scrinium Erasmianum*, vol. II (Leiden, 1969), pp. 77–99.

McGoldrick, J. E., *Luther's Scottish Connections* (Rutherford, NJ, 1989).

McGrath, Alister, *Luther's Theology of the Cross: Martin Luther's Theological Breakthrough* (Oxford, 1985; 2nd edition Oxford, 2011).

McGrath, Alister, *Iustitia Dei: A History of the Christian Doctrine of Justification* (Cambridge, 1986).

McGrath, Alister, *The Genesis of Doctrine: A Study in the Foundations of Doctrinal Criticism* (Oxford, 1990).

McGrath, Alister, *The Intellectual Origins of the European Reformation*, 2nd edition (Oxford, 2004).

Merczyng, Henryk, *Zbory i senatorowie protestanccy w dawnej Rzeczpospolicie* (Warsaw, 1904).

Militzer, Klaus, *Der Geschichte des Deutschen Ordens* (Stuttgard, 2005).

Militzer, Klaus, 'Introduction', in Klaus Militzer, Johannes A. Mol, and Helen J. Nicholson (eds), *The Military Orders and the Reformation: Choices, State-Building, and the Weight of Tradition* (Hilversum, 2006), pp. 5–9.

Miller, Clarence H., *Erasmus and Luther: The Battle over Free Will* (Indianapolis, 2012).

Miller, J., 'The Origins of Polish Arianism', *Sixteenth Century Journal* 16:2 (1985): 229–56.

Miodońska, Barbara, *Miniatury Stanisława Samostrzelnika* (Warsaw, 1983).

Misiurek, Jerzy, *Spory chrystologiczne w Polsce w drugiej połowie XVI wieku* (Lublin, 1984).

Moeller, Bernd, 'Was wurde in der Frühzeit der Reformation in deutschen Städten gepredigt?', *Archiv für Reformationsgeschichte* 75 (1984): 176–93.

Monter, William, *Frontiers of Heresy: The Spanish Inquisition from the Basque Lands to Sicily* (Cambridge, 1990).

Monter, William, 'Heresy Executions in Reformation Europe, 1520–65', in Ole Grell and Robert W. Scribner (eds), *Tolerance and Intolerance in the European Reformation* (Cambridge, 1996), pp. 48–64.

Monter, William, *Judging the French Reformation: Heresy Trials by Sixteenth-Century Parlements* (Cambridge, MA, 1999).

Moore, R. I., *The Formation of a Persecuting Society: Authority and Deviance in Western Europe, 950–1250*, 2nd edition (Oxford, 2007).

Mossakowski, Stanisław, *King Sigismund Chapel at Cracow Cathedral (1515–33)*, trans. Krystyna Malcharek (Kraków, 2012).

Możdżen, Julia, 'Miasto pod panowaniem diabelskim: Gdanski dominikanin w obliczu następstw rewolty społecznej z lat 1525–6', in Cezary Kardasz, Julia Możdżeń, and Magdalena Spychaj (eds), *Miasto jako fenomen społeczny i kulturowy* (Toruń, 2012), pp. 169–85.

Muller, Michael, 'Protestant Confessionalisation in the Towns of Royal Prussia and the Practice of Religious Toleration in Poland-Lithuania', in Ole Grell and Robert W. Scribner (eds), *Tolerance and Intolerance in the European Reformation* (Cambridge, 1996), pp. 262–81.

Muller, Michael, *Zweite Reformation und städtische Autonomie im Königlichen Preussen: Danzig, Elbing und Thorn in der Epoche der Konfessionalisierung (1557–1660)* (Berlin, 1997).

Müller, Ulrich, *Herzog Albrecht von Preussen und Livland: Regesten aus dem Herzoglichen Briefarchiv und den Ostpreussischen Folianten* (Köln, 1996).

Musteikis, Antanas, *The Reformation in Lithuania: Religious Fluctuations in the Sixteenth Century* (Boulder, 1988).

Newbigin, Nerida, *Feste d'Oltrano: Plays in Churches in Fifteenth-Century Florence* (Florence, 1996).

Nicholls, D. J., 'The Nature of Popular Heresy in France, 1520–42', *Historical Journal* 26 (1983): 261–75.

Nicholls, D. J., 'France', in Andrew Pettegree (ed.), *The Early Reformation in Europe* (Cambridge, 1992), pp. 120–41.

van Nieuwenhove, Rik, *An Introduction to Medieval Theology* (Cambridge, 2012).

Noga Zdzisław, *Krakowska rada miejska w XVI wieku: stadium o elicie władzy* (Kraków, 2003).

North, Michael, 'Danziger Münzen in Geldumlauf Königlich Preussens und des Herzogstums Preussen der Frühen Neuzeit', in B. Jähnig and P. Letkemann (eds), *Danzig in Acht Jahrhunderten* (Münster, 1985), pp. 241–50.

Novikoff, Alex J., *The Medieval Culture of Disputation: Pedagogy, Practice, and Performance* (Philadelphia, 2013).

Nowak, Zbigniew, 'Antryreformacyjna elegia Dantyszka o zagładzie Gdańska', *OiRwP* XVI (1971): 5–35.

Nowak, Zbigniew, 'Kultura, nauka i sztuka w Gdańsku na przełomie dwóch epok', in Edmund Cieślak (ed.) *Historia Gdańska*, vol. II (Danzig, 1982), pp. 352–402.

Nowak, Zbigniew and Urban, Janina, 'Pankracy Klemme: Gdański działacz reformacyjny i jego księgozbiór', *Rocznik Biblioteki Narodowej* IV (1968): 107–39.

Nowak-Dłużewski, Juliusz, *Okolicznościowa poezja polityczna w Polsce: czasy Zygmuntowskie* (Warsaw, 1966).

Nowakowska, Natalia, 'Poland and the Crusade in the Reign of King Jan Olbracht, 1492–1501', in Norman Housley (ed.), *Crusading in the Fifteenth Century: Message and Impact* (Basingstoke, 2004), pp. 128–47.

Nowakowska, Natalia, 'Jagiellonians and Habsburgs: The Polish Historiography of Charles V', in M. Fuchs and C. Scott Dixon (eds), *The Histories of Emperor Charles V (Nationale Perspecktiven von Personalichkeit und Herrschaft)* (Münster, 2005), pp. 249–73.

Nowakowska, Natalia, *Church, State and Dynasty in Renaissance Poland: The Career of Cardinal Fryderyk Jagiellon (1468–1503)* (Aldershot, 2007).

Nowakowska, Natalia, 'Diplomatic Relations between the Jagiellonian Courts of Poland-Lithuania and Papal Rome, 1492–1506', in Urszula Borkowska and Markus Hörsch (eds), *Hofkultur der Jagiellonendynastie und verwandter Fürstenhäuser* (Leipzig, 2010), pp. 119–25.

Nowakowska, Natalia, 'From Strassburg to Trent: Bishops, Printing and Liturgical Reform in the Fifteenth Century', *Past & Present* 213 (2011): 3–39.

Nowakowska, Natalia, 'Forgetting Lutheranism: Historians and the Early Reformation in Poland (1517–48)', *Church History and Religious Culture* 92 (2012): 281–303.

Nowakowska, Natalia, 'High Clergy and Printers: Anti-Reformation Polemic in the Kingdom of Poland, 1520–36', *Historical Research* 87 (2014): 43–64.

Nowakowska, Natalia, 'Lamenting the Church? Bishop Andrzej Krzycki and Early Reformation Polemic', in Almut Suerbaum, George Southcombe and Benjamin Thompson (eds), *Polemic: Language as Violence in Medieval and Early Modern Discourse* (Aldershot, 2015), pp. 223–36.

Odrzywolska-Kidawa, Anna, 'Stanowisko polskich dostojników kościelnych wobec idei reformacyjnych w latach 20 XVI wieku', in Urszula Cierniak and Jarosław Grabowski (eds), *Drogi i rozdroża kultury chrześcijańskiej Europy* (Częstochowa, 2003), pp. 237–46.

Odrzywolska-Kidawa, Anna, *Biskup Piotr Tomicki (1464–1535): kariera polityczna i kościelna* (Warsaw, 2004).

Odrzywolska-Kidawa, Anna, *Podkanclerzy Piotr Tomicki (1515–35): polityk i humanista* (Warsaw, 2005).

Onnekink, David and Rommelse, Gijs (eds), *Ideology and Foreign Policy in Early Modern Europe, 1650–1750* (Farnham, 2011).

Ososiński, Tomasz, 'Nieznane epigramy Dantyszka w liście tegoż do Albrechta I księcia Pruskiego', *OiRwP* 50 (2006): 245–55.

Ostling, Michael, *Between the Devil and the Host: Imagining Witchcraft in Early Modern Poland* (Oxford, 2011).

Ozment, Steven E., *The Reformation in the Cities: The Appeal of Protestantism to Sixteenth-Century Germany and Switzerland* (New Haven, 1975).

Pabel, Hilmar, 'The Peaceful People of Christ: The Irenic Ecclesiology of Erasmus of Rotterdam', in Hilmar Pabel (ed.), *Erasmus' Vision of the Church* (Kirksville, 1995), pp. 57–93.

Pagden, Anthony (ed.), *The Languages of Political Theory in Early Modern Europe* (Cambridge, 1987).

Pánek, Jaroslav, 'Bohemia and Moravia in the Age of Reformation', in Ole Grell and Robert W. Scribner (eds), *Tolerance and Intolerance in the European Reformation* (Cambridge, 1996), pp. 231–48.

Parsons, Gerald, *The Cult of Saint Catherine of Siena: A Study in Civic Religion* (Aldershot, 2008).

Patschovsky, Alexander, 'Heresy and Society: On the Political Functions of Heresy in the Medieval World', in Peter Biller and Caterina Bruschi (eds), *Texts and the Repression of Medieval Heresy* (Woodbridge, 2003), pp. 23–41.

Pawlak, Marian, *Reformacja i kontrreformacja w Elblągu w XVI i XVII wieku* (Bydgoszcz, 1994).

Pelikan, Jaroslav, *The Christian Tradition: A History of the Development of Doctrine*, vol. 4 (Chicago, 1984).

Peterson, Derek and Walhof, Darren, *The Invention of Religion: Rethinking Belief in Politics and History* (New Brunswick, 2002).

Pettegree, Andrew, 'The Early Reformation in Europe: A German affair or an International Movement?', in Andrew Pettegree (ed.), *The Early Reformation in Europe* (Cambridge, 1992), pp. 1–22.

Philpott, Daniel, *Revolutions in Sovereignty: How Ideas Shaped Modern International Relations* (Princeton, 2001).

Pociecha, Władysław, 'Walka sejmowa o przywileje kościoła w Polsce w latach 1520–1537', *Reformacja w Polsce* II:7 (1922): 161–84.

Pociecha, Władysław, *Geneza hołdu pruskiego 1467–1525* (Warsaw, 1937).

Pociecha, Władysław, 'Jan Chojeński', in *PSB* 3 (1937), pp. 396–9.

Pociecha, Władysław, 'Rzym wobec starań o sprowadzenie Melanchthona do Polski', *RwP* IX–X (1937–9): 418–22.

Pociecha, Władysław, 'Dantyszek (von Höfen, Flaschbinder)', in *PSB*, 4 (1938), pp. 424–30.

Pociecha, Władysław, 'Maciej Drzewicki', in *PSB*, 5 (1939), pp. 409–12.

Pociecha, Władysław, *Królowa Bona (1494–1557): ludzie i czasy Odrodzenia*, 4 vols (Poznań, 1949–58).

Pocock, J. G. A., 'The Concept of a Language and the *métier d'historien*: Some Considerations on a Practice', in Anthony Pagden (ed.), *The Languages of Political Theory in Early Modern Europe* (Cambridge, 1987), pp. 19–38.

Potter, D. L., 'Foreign Policy in the Age of the Reformation: French Involvement in the Schmalkaldic War, 1544–47', *Historical Journal* 20:3 (1977): 525–44.

Prügl, Thomas, 'Medieval Biblical "Principia" as Reflections on the Nature of Theology', in Mikołaj Olszewski (ed.), *What Is 'Theology' in the Middle Ages?* (Münster, 2007), pp. 253–75.

Ptaszyński, Maciej, 'The Polish-Lithaunian Commonwealth', in Howard Louthan and Graeme Murdock (eds), *A Companion to the Reformation in Central Europe* (Leiden, 2015), pp. 40–67.

Ptaśnik, Jan, 'Księgarze różnowiercy w Krakowie w XVI wieku', *RwP* I (1921): 43–50.

Radzimiński, A., 'Podziały kościelne', in Roman Czaja and Zbigniew H. Nowak (eds), *Państwo zakonu krzyżackiego w Prusach: Podziały administracyjne i kościelne w XIII–XVI wieku* (Toruń, 2000), pp. 67–80.

Reardon, Bernard, *Religious Thought in the Reformation* (Longman, 1981).

Rechowicz, Marian, *Dzieje teologii katolickiej w Polsce*, vol. II (Lublin, 1975).

Redondo, Augustin, 'Luther et l'Espagne en 1520 a 1536', *Mélanges de la Casa Velazquez* 1 (1965): 109–65.

Reid, Jonathan, *The King's Sister—Queen of Dissent: Marguerite of Navarre (1492–1549) and her Evangelical Network*, 2 vols (Leiden, 2009).

Reinhard, Wolfgang, 'Zwang zur Konfessionalisierung? Prologomena zu einer Theorie des konfessionellen Zweitalters', *Zeitschrift für Historische Forschung* 10 (1983): 257–77.

Rex, Richard, 'The English Campaign against Luther in the 1520s', *Transactions of the Royal Historical Society* 4th se. xxxix (1989): 85–106.

Rhode, Arthur, *Geschichte der evangelischen Kirche im Posener Lande* (Würzburg, 1956).

Robin, Régine, 'Le champ sémantique de 'feodalité' dans les cahiers de doléances généraux de 1789', *Bulletin du Centre d'Analyse du Discours* 2 (1975): 61–8.

Robinson, Adam Patrick, *The Career of Cardinal Giovanni Morone (1509–80): Between Council and Inquisition* (Farnham, 2012).

Root, Deborah, 'Speaking Christian: Orthodoxy and Difference in Sixteenth-Century Spain', *Representations* 23 (1988): 118–34.

Roper, Lyndal, *The Holy Household: Women and Morals in Reformation Augsburg* (Oxford, 1989).

Roper, Lyndal, 'Martin Luther's Body: The "Stout Doctor" and his Biographers', *American Historical Review* 115:2 (2010): 351–84.

Rosand, David, *Myths of Venice: The Figuration of a State* (Chapel Hill, 2001).

Rublack, Ulinka, *Reformation Europe* (Cambridge, 2005).

Russocki, Stanisław, 'Nieznany mandat księcia Janusza mazowieckiego w sprawie powstania chłopskiego w Prusach Książęcych w 1525 roku', *Przegląd Historyczny* 46 (1955): 608–9.

Saarinen, Risto, 'Lutheran Ecclesiology', in Gerard Mannion and Lewis S. Mudge (eds), *The Routledge Companion to the Christian Church* (Abingdon, 2008), pp. 170–86.

Sackville, L. E., *Heresy and Heretics in the Thirteenth Century: The Textual Representations* (York, 2011).

Samsonowicz, Henryk, 'Rola gdańska w życiu stanowym Prus Królewskich i w życiu politycznym Rzeczpospolitej', in Edmund Cieślak (ed.), *Historia Gdańska*, vol. II (Danzig, 1982), pp. 260–88.

Samsonowicz, Henryk and Tazbir, Janusz, *Tysiącletnie dzieje* (Wrocław, 2000).

Schaff, Philip (ed.), *The Creeds of Christendom*, 6th edition (Grand Rapids, 1983).

Schattenhofer, Michael, *Die Mariensäule in München* (Munich, 1971).

Schilling, Heinz, 'The Reformation in the Hanseatic Cities', *Sixteenth Century Journal* 14:4 (1983): 443–56.

Schilling, Heinz, 'Die Konfessionalisierung im Reich. Religiöser und gesellschaftlicher Wandel in Deutschland zwischen 1555 und 1620', *Historische Zeitschrift* 246 (1988): 1–45.

Schmidt, Christoph, *Auf Felsen gesät: die Reformation in Polen und Livland* (Göttingen, 2000).

Schöttler, Peter, 'Historians and Discourse Analysis', *History Workshop Journal* 27 (1989): 37–65.

Schramm, Gottfried, 'Danzig, Elbing und Thorn als Beispiele städtischer Reformation (1517–1558)', in Hans Fenske (ed.), *Historia Integra: Festschrift für Erich Hassinger* (Berlin, 1977), pp. 125–54.

Schreiner, Susan, *Are You Alone Wise? The Search for Certainty in the Early Modern Era* (Oxford and New York, 2011).

Scribner, Robert W., 'Images of the Peasant, 1514–25', *Journal of Peasant Studies* 3:1 (1975): 29–48.

Scribner, Robert W., 'Reformation, Carnival and the World Turned Upside Down', *Social History* 3:4 (1978): 303–39.

Scribner, Robert W., *For the Sake of the Simple Folk: Popular Propaganda for the German Reformation* (Cambridge, 1981).

Scribner, Robert W., *Popular Culture and Popular Movements in Reformation Germany* (London, 1987).

Scribner, Robert W., 'Preconditions of Tolerance and Intolerance in Early Modern Europe', in Ole Grell and Robert W. Scribner (eds), *Tolerance and Intolerance in the European Reformation* (Cambridge, 1996), pp. 32–47.

Simson, Paul, 'Wann hat der Danziger Priester Jakob Knothe geheiratet?', *Mitteilungen des Westpreussischen Geschichstvereins* 14 (1915): 2–3.

Simson, Paul, *Geschichte der Stadt Danzig*, vol. II (Danzig, 1918).

Skinner, Quentin, *Visions of Politics. Vol 1: Regarding Method* (Cambridge, 2002).

Smith, Jonathan, *Imagining Religion: From Babylon to Jonestown* (Chicago, 1982).

Sobel, Bogdan, 'O zaginionym druku mazowieckiego dekretu przeciwko luteranom 1525', *Przegląd Historyczny* 50 (1959): 81–5.

Spruyt, B. J., '"En bruit d'estre bonne luterienne": Mary of Hungary (1505–58) and Religious Reform', *English Historical Review* CIX:431 (1994): 275–307.

Steadman Jones, Gareth, *Languages of Class: Studies in English Working Class History, 1832–1982* (Cambridge, 1982).

Stöve, E., 'Zaccaria Ferreri', in *Dizionario biografico degli italiani*, 46 (Rome, 1996), pp. 808–11.

Stupperich, 'Vorgeschichte und Nachwirkungen des Wormser Edikt im deutschen Nordwesten', in Fritz Reuter (ed.), *Der Reichstag zu Worms von 1521* (Worms, 1971), pp. 459–74.

Stupperich, Martin, *Osiander in Preussen* (Berlin, 1973).

Sucheni-Grabowska, Anna, *Monarchia dwu ostatnich Jagiellonów a ruch egzekucyjny* (Wrocław, 1974).

Sucheni-Grabowska, Anna, *Zygmunt August: Król polski i wielki książę litewski, 1520–62* (Warsaw, 1996).

Sutherland, N. M., *The Huguenot Struggle for Recognition* (New Haven, 1980).

Szelińska, W., 'Wśród krakowskich przyjaciół książki erazmiańskiej w wieku Wielkiego Holandra', in *Erasmiana Cracoviensia*, Zeszyty Naukowe UJ, Prace Historyczne z 33 (Kraków, 1971), pp. 39–54.

Szorc, Alojzy, *Rywalizacja katolików z luteranami o kościół Św. Mikołaja w Elblągu, 1520–1621* (Olsztyn, 2002).

Szymaniak, Wiktor, *Organizacja dyplomacji Prus Książęcych na dworze Zygmunta Starego, 1525–48* (Bydgoszcz, 1992).

Szymaniak, Wiktor, *Rola dworu polskiego w polityce zagranicznej Prus Książęcych: studium z dziejów dyplomacji Prus Książęcych w Polsce w latach 1525–1548* (Bygdoszcz, 1993).

Tafiłowski, Piotr, *Jan Łaski (1456–1531), kanclerz koronny, prymas Polski* (Warsaw, 2007).

Targowski, Michał, *Na prawie polskim i niemieckim: kształtowanie się ziemskiej własności szlacheckiej na Pomorzu Gdańskim w XIII–XVI wieku* (Warsaw, 2014).

Tazbir, Janusz, *Państwo bez stosów: szkice z dziejów tolerancji w Polsce XVI i XVII wieku* (Warsaw, 1967); published in English as *A State without Stakes: Polish Religious Toleration in the Sixteenth and Seventeenth Centuries* (New York, 1973).

Tazbir, Janusz, *Dzieje polskiej tolerancji* (Warsaw, 1973).

Tazbir, Janusz, 'Społeczny i terytorialny zasięg polskiej Reformacji', *Kwartalnik Historyczny* 82 (1975): 723–35.

Tazbir, Janusz, 'Poland', in R. W. Scribner, Roy Porter, and Mikuláš Teich (eds), *The Reformation in National Context* (Cambridge, 1994), pp. 168–80.

Tazbir, Janusz, *Reformacja, Kontrreformacja, Tolerancja* (Wrocław, 1996).

Teter, Magda, *Jews and Heretics in Catholic Poland: A Beleaguered Church in the Post-Reformation Era* (Cambridge, 2006).

Teter, Magda, *Sinners on Trial: Sacrilege after the Reformation* (Cambridge, MA, 2011).

Thompson, John, *Popes and Princes 1417–1517: Politics and Polity in the Late Medieval Church* (London, 1980).

Topolski, Jerzy, 'Wielopolska na europejskich szlakach handlowych', in Jerzy Topolski (ed.), *Dzieje Wielkopolski do roku 1793* (Poznań, 1969), pp. 476–9.

Tracy, James D., 'Erasmus and the Arians: Remarks on the "Consensus Ecclesiae"', *The Catholic Historical Review* 67 (1981): 1–10.

Tracy, James D., 'Heresy Law and Centralization under Mary of Hungary: Conflict between the Council of Holland and Central Government over the Enforcement of Charles V's Placards', *Archiv für Reformationsgeschichte* 73 (1982): 284–308.

Trexler, Richard, 'Lorenzo de' Medici and Savonarola: Martyrs for Florence', *Renaissance Quarterly* 31:3 (1978): 293–308.

Turchetti, Marco, 'Religious Concord and Political Tolerance in Sixteenth- and Seventeeth-Century France', *Sixteenth Century Journal* 22 (1991): 15–25.

Tworek, Stanisław, *Działalność oświatowo kulturalna kalwinizmu małopolskiego (połowa XVI–połowa XVII w)* (Lublin, 1970).

Urban, Wacław, 'Reformacja mieszczańska na dawnym powiecie bieckim', *OiRWP* VI (1961): 139–74.

Urban, Wacław, *Epizod reformacyjny* (Kraków, 1988).

Urban, Wacław, 'Jakub z Iłży i jego uczniowie', *OiRwP* 36 (1991): 209–12.

Vetulani, Adam, *Lenno pruskie: od traktatu krakowskiego do śmierci księcia Albrechta, 1525–68: studium historyczno-prawne* (Kraków, 1930).

Wajsblum, Marek, 'Wyznaniowe oblicze protestantyzmu polskiego i jego podstawy społeczne', in *Pamiętnik zjazdu narodowego im. Jana Kochanowskiego* (Kraków, 1931), pp. 77–97.

Waldoch, Stanisław, 'Początki reformacji w Elblągu i jego regionie', *Rocznik Elbląski* IV (1969): 9–43.

Walsham, Alexandra, *Charitable Hatred: Tolerance and Intolerance in England, 1500–1700* (Manchester, 2006).

Walsham, Alexandra, *The Reformation of the Landscape: Religion, Identity and Memory in Early Modern Britain and Ireland* (Oxford, 2011).

Wandel, Lee Palmer, *Reformation: Towards a New History* (Cambridge, 2011).

Wanegffelen, Thierry, *Ni Rome, ni Genève: Des fidèles entre deux chaires en France au XVIe siècle* (Paris, 1997).

Warmiński, I., *Andrzej Samuel i Jan Seklucjan* (Poznań, 1906).

Watkins, John, 'Toward a New Diplomatic History of Medieval and Early Modern Europe', *Journal of Medieval and Early Modern Studies* 38:1 (2008): 1–14.

Watkins, John, 'Ambassadors, Factors, Translators, Spies: Agents of Transcultural Relations in the Early Modern World', *Clio* 38:3 (2009): 339–48.

Węcowski, Piotr, *Mazowsze w Koronie: Propaganda i legitymizacja władzy Kazimierza Jagiellończyka na Mazowszu* (Kraków, 2004).

Whaley, Joachim, *Germany and the Holy Roman Empire*, vol. I (Oxford, 2012).

Wicks, Jared, 'Roman Reactions to Luther: The First Year (1518)', *Catholic Historical Review* 69:4 (1983): 521–62.

Wijaczka, Jacek, 'Kanclerz wielki koronny Krzysztof Szydłowiecki a książę Albrecht pruski', in Zenon Guldon (ed.), *Hrabstwo szydłowieckie Radziwiłłów: Materiały sesji popularnon-aukowej 19 lutego 1994 r* (Szydłowiec, 1994), pp. 23–38.

Wijaczka, Jacek, *Stosunki dyplomatyczne Polski z Rzeszą Niemiecką (1519–1556)* (Kielce, 1998).

Williams, Rowan, 'Defining Heresy', in Alan Kreider (ed.), *The Origins of Christendom in the West* (Edinburgh, 2001), pp. 313–35.

Witkowska, Aleksandra, *Kulty pątnicze piętnastowiecznego Krakowa: z badań nad miejską kulturą religijną* (Lublin, 1984).

Wojciechowska, Maria, *Z dziejów książki w Poznaniu w XVI wieku* (Poznań, 1927).

Wojtkowski, A., 'Hołd pruski według relacji Maurycego Ferbera, biskupa warmińskiego', *Zapiski Towarzystwa Naukowego w Toruniu* XIII (1947): 95–9.

Wolgast, Eike, 'Die deutschen territorialfürste und die Frühe Reformation', in B. Moeller and Stephen Buckwalter (eds), *Die frühe Reformation in Deutschland als Umbruch* (Heidelberg, 1998), pp. 407–34.

Wooding, Lucy, *Rethinking Catholicism in Early Modern England* (Oxford, 1990).

Wotschke, Teodor, *Geschichte der Reformation in Polen* (Halle, 1911).

Wotschke, Teodor, *Die Reformation im Lande Posen* (Lissa, 1913).

Wotschke, Teodor, 'Polnische studenten in Wittenberg', *Jahrbücher für Kultur und Geschichte der Slaven* 2:2 (1926): 169–200.

Wünsch, Thomas, *Konziliarismus und Polen: Personen, Politik und Programme aus Polen zur Verfassungsfrage der Kirche in der Zeit der mittelalterlichen Reformkonzilien* (Padeborn, 1998).

Wyczański, Andrzej, *Zygmunt Stary* (Warsaw, 1985).

Wyczański, Andrzej, *Między kulturą a polityką: sekretarze królewscy Zygmunta Starego (1506–48)* (Warsaw, 1990).

Zabłocki, Stefan, 'Andrzej Krzycki', in *PSB*, 15 (1970), pp. 544–9.

Zagorin, Perez, *How the Idea of Religious Toleration Came to the West* (Princeton, 2003).

Zakrzewski, Wincenty, *Powstanie i wzrost Reformacyi w Polsce, 1520–1572* (Leipzig, 1870).

Zarębski, Ignacy, 'Hegendorfer, Krzysztof', in *PSB*, 9 (1960–1), pp. 337–9.

Żelewski, Roman, 'Dyplomacja polska w latach 1506–72', in Marian Biskup (ed.), *Historia Dyplomacji Polskiej*, vol. 1 (Warsaw, 1982), pp. 587–671.

Zins, Henryk, *Ród Ferberów i jego rola w dziejach Gdańska w XV i XVI wieku* (Lublin, 1951).

Zins, Henryk, *Powstanie chłopskie w Prusach Książęcych 1525 roku: walki społeczne w Prusach w początkach reformacji i ich geneza* (Warsaw, 1953).

Zins, Henryk, 'The Political and Social Background of the Early Reformation in Ermeland', *English Historical Review* 75 (1960): 589–600.

Zins, Henryk, 'Leonard Cox i erazmiańskie koła w Polsce i Anglii', *OiRwP* 17 (1972): 27–62.

Zonenberg, Sławomir, *Kronika Pruska Szymona Grunau* (Bydgoszcz, 2009).

Zonenberg, Sławomir, 'Wizerunek heretyka w Preussische Chronik', in Jacek Banaszkiewicz, Jacek Maciejewski, and Joanna Sobiesiak (eds), *Persona, gesta habitusque, insignium: Zachowania i atrybuty jako wyznaczniki tożsamości społecznej jednostki w średniowieczu* (Lublin, 2009), pp. 110–16.

Index

Rome 3, 13, 46, 49, 59, 63–4, 67, 89, 104–5,
110, 123, 127, 136, 144, 147–8, 152–4,
199–200, 202, 204–6, 211, 214, 233, 237
Rorario, Hieronymus 64, 153nn.12–13
Royal Prussia 7, 14, 17, 40, 43, 48n.6, 49–51,
54–9, 65–6, 69–71, 77–8, 81–6, 88–91,
93–6, 98–100, 102–5, 109, 129–31, 138,
144, 151, 155–6, 160, 164, 184–5,
208–9, 218, 234–6
royal register 66n.148, 105n.44, 121, 122n.23
Rubeanus, Jan 106
Rubens, Jeronimus 159, 226
Ruś 40–1
Russia 88
Russians 202
Ruthenia 41, 49, 119, 122
Rydziński, Piotr 24, 53, 155–6, 182, 185, 192,
205, 240–1
Rzeczyca, Stanisław 237, 239

Sabinus, Georg 140
sacraments 19, 22, 28, 30, 32, 90, 103–4, 117,
177, 192, 194, 198, 202, 207–8, 212
Sacranus, Jan 206
Elucidarius Errorum Ritus Rutenici 189n.117
sacrilege 15, 17n.62, 94, 111, 156, 176–7,
182–4, 188, 219
sacrilegium 183
Saint Appollonia 207
Saint Augustine (monastery) 107–8
Saint Barbara's church (Danzig) 50
Saint Brigit 19
Saint Dorothy 55, 200
Saint John 13
Saint Mary Magdalen church (Poznań) 61–3,
160
Saint Mary's church (Danzig) 51, 53, 58, 80,
83, 156, 163, 191, 217, 227–8
Saint Paul 13
Saint Peter's pence tax 59, 200
saints 19, 30, 32, 90, 93–4, 101, 156–7, 168,
177, 182, 187, 190–2, 198, 205, 207,
215, 221, 227, 229–30
Saint Sigismund 132
Saint Stanisław 43–4, 132, 191
Saint Stephen's church (Kraków) 228
Salomon, Andreas 61, 159, 229
salvation 13, 18, 27–32, 34, 36, 94, 109, 116,
191, 194–5, 204, 208–10, 214, 221
Sambia 56
Sambian Peasants' Revolt 80
Samostrzelnik, Stanisław 42–4
Samuel, Andrzej 62
Sancta Romana Ecclesia 199
Sandomierz 101, 108
Satan, *see* devils/demons/Satan
Savonarola, Girolamo 30
Savonarolans 20
Scandinavia 3, 40, 69, 138, 184, 214

Scharffenberg, Mark 240
schism 15, 144, 149, 176–7, 187, 189–90,
193–6, 205, 212–13, 216, 219, 226
Schleswig-Holstein 71
Schmalkaldic League 27, 60, 133, 138
Schnürlein, Christoff 103
Schwendi, Lazarus von 33
Scotland 17, 123
Scripture 19, 27, 32, 56, 115, 156–7, 185,
198, 200, 204, 208–9
sects 7, 15, 51, 60, 85, 90, 117n.116,
128, 136, 154–5, 159, 161–2, 168, 177,
179, 182, 186–7, 189–93, 214, 218,
225–9, 231
secularization 55, 63, 66, 107, 136
sedition 26, 80, 82, 91, 94, 130, 177, 187–8
sermons 11, 30, 49–50, 55–6, 59, 61, 69, 86,
156, 160, 163–4, 186, 193, 196, 207,
209, 227, 241
sexual crimes/relationships 59, 129, 161
Sichardt, Johannes 23, 157
Sigismund I, King 3–6, 10–16, 33, 35,
36, 40–1, 43–4, 46–8, 52–4, 56–7, 61,
63, 67–71, 73, 78–9, 81–92, 94–7,
99–103, 105–7, 109, 111–12, 114–18,
121, 127, 134, 136–43, 146–9, 151–3,
155–7, 162, 165, 167–8, 174–6, 178–97,
200–2, 204–9, 211–14, 216, 218–23,
233–40, 242
death 6–7, 66, 101, 119
funeral 77, 128
illness 65
march on Danzig 57, 77, 78, 80, 154, 178
piety 14, 126, 144–5
quarrel with Clement VII 64
Sigismund Augustus 5, 17, 64–6, 101, 106,
111, 140, 144, 153n.13, 220, 237
Silesia 41–2, 48n.6, 49, 52, 59, 61, 63, 122,
135, 140–2, 145–6, 155, 160, 163, 182,
200, 208, 237
Simon of Myathokowo 161
Slavonic surnames 72
Slovakia 61
Śmigiel 212
Snyder (tailor) 159, 167
Sobocki, Tomasz 64
Socinius, Faustus 71
Sokołowski, Jan 59
sola fide 28–32, 35, 62, 94, 156, 173, 176–7,
184–5, 188, 194–5, 209–10, 221
sola scriptura 176–7, 184–5
Sophia of Poland, Princess 49, 64, 97, 146
Spain 19, 52, 67–8, 124, 137, 212
Spanish Inquisition 52, 68, 141, 188, 193
Speratus, Paulus 56, 69, 104–5, 209
Speruli, Francesco 144
Speyer 27, 71, 127
spirituali 33
Środa 63

Printed and bound by CPI Group (UK) Ltd, Croydon, CR0 4YY